"THE VOICES OF REAL PEOPLE WHO SURVIVED A NIGHTMARE. THEIR IMPACT IS STUNNING!"
> —*Atlanta Journal-Constitution*

"TOUCHING, SHOCKING, AWE-INSPIRING READING!"
> —*Los Angeles Herald Examiner*

"A WORK OF EXTRAORDINARY SCOPE AND STARTLING INSIGHTS."
> —*Hadassah Magazine*

"GRIPPING, SHATTERING HUMAN STORIES . . . RECOMMENDED!"
> —*Library Journal*

"A DEEPLY MOVING WORK . . . A SIGNIFICANT DOCUMENT . . . THESE VOICES MUST BE LISTENED TO, THEY ARE THE EMBODIMENT OF A POWERFUL AND ANGUISHED CALL TO LIFE, TO FAITH, TO SALVATION."
> —*The Detroit Jewish News*

ABOUT THE EDITOR:

SYLVIA ROTHCHILD is a novelist, essayist, lecturer, and short-story writer. Her reviews, stories, and articles have appeared in *Commentary, Hadassah Magazine, Midstream, the Boston Globe,* and *Present Tense,* among others. For the last several years she has run workshops on Jewish identity under the auspices of The Council of Jewish Women and lectured widely on the experiences of survivors of the Holocaust. She is the author of one novel, *Sunshine and Salt,* and of the award-winning biography of I. L. Peretz, *Keys to a Magic Door.* Ms. Rothchild currently lives in Brookline, Massachusetts.

"The epidemic of evil that seized Europe in the 1930s and 1940s . . . was the most ferocious of its kind ever to appear on earth. Since this illness swept over the Western world in our lifetime, it is incumbent upon us to expose it in the most minute detail. Each of us who survived has the obligation to reveal what he came to know. Sometimes one moment, fully understood, can shed light on the whole."

Silvano Arieti, *The Parnas*

"To attain its heavenly Hell on earth the German dictatorship launched a war that engulfed the whole world. Over 35 million people were killed, more than half of them civilians. On the battlefields 1 out of every 22 Russians was killed, 1 out of every 25 Germans, 1 out of every 150 Italians and Englishmen and 1 out of every 200 Frenchmen. That war brought death to nearly 6 million Jews, to 2 out of every 3 European Jews . . ."

Lucy S. Dawidowicz, *The War Against the Jews*

VOICES FROM THE HOLOCAUST

════ Edited by ════

Sylvia Rothchild

and with a Foreword by
Elie Wiesel

A MERIDIAN BOOK
NEW AMERICAN LIBRARY
TIMES MIRROR
NEW YORK AND SCARBOROUGH, ONTARIO

NAL BOOKS ARE AVAILABLE AT QUANTITY DISCOUNTS
WHEN USED TO PROMOTE PRODUCTS OR SERVICES. FOR
INFORMATION PLEASE WRITE TO PREMIUM MARKETING
DIVISION, THE NEW AMERICAN LIBRARY, INC., 1633
BROADWAY, NEW YORK, NEW YORK 10019.

The hardcover edition of this book was published by The New American
Library, Inc., and simultaneously in Canada by The New American Library of
Canada Limited.

 MERIDIAN TRADEMARK REG. PAT. U.S. OFF. AND FOREIGN COUNTRIES
REGISTERED TRADEMARK—MARCA REGISTRADA
HECHO EN WESTFORD, MASS., U.S.A.

SIGNET, SIGNET CLASSICS, MENTOR, PLUME, MERIDIAN and NAL
BOOKS are published *in the United States* by The New American Library, Inc.,
1633 Broadway, New York, New York 10019, *in Canada* by The New American
Library of Canada Limited, 81 Mack Avenue, Scarborough, Ontario M1L 1M8

Library of Congress Cataloging in Publication Data
Main entry under title:

Voices from the Holocaust.

Transcript of tape recordings in the William E. Wiener Oral History Library
of the American Jewish Committee.
1. Holocaust, Jewish (1939-1945)—Personal narratives. 2. Jews—Europe—
Biography. 3. Holocaust survivors—United States—Biography. 4. Jews—
United States—Biography. 5. United Sates—Emigration and immigration—
Biography. I. Rothchild, Sylvia, 1923-   II. American

Library of Congress Cataloging in Publication Data
Jewish Committee. William E. Wiener Oral History Library.
D810.J4V63   1928   940.53'15'03924024 [B]   82-8289
ISBN 0-452-00603-1

First Meridian Printing, September, 1982

1 2 3 4 5 6 7 8 9

PRINTED IN THE UNITED STATES OF AMERICA

Contents

Life during the Holocaust   91

In memory of my parents
Bertha Neuberger Rosner and Samuel L. Rosner

Acknowledgments

I should like to acknowledge the help and encouragement of editors Barry Lippman, who introduced me to the Holocaust tapes; Ann Watson, who edited the early drafts of the book; and Bette Alexander, who oversaw the final production and publication of *Voices from the Holocaust*.

I am indebted to many writers whose books prepared me to take on the challenge of editing the tapes. In particular I'm grateful to Elie Wiesel and Lucy S. Dawidowicz for their share in my education.

My long immersion in the harsh world of survivor stories was immeasurably softened by Seymour Rothchild, my patient husband, and the many musical friends who were available for evenings of chamber music that mitigated some of the tensions that accumulated with each day's work.

I'm most grateful to the survivors who shared their lives and memories. Many spoke not only to me, but for me.

Foreword

by Elie Wiesel

These voices—I listen to them and they seem strangely familiar. They evoke an engulfed universe that was also mine.

The stories they tell—I know them. It's strange how similar they are. In those days all European Jews went through the same trials. Forced to enter the kingdom of night, they discovered the same truths.

Before, during, and after . . . A logical, simple, immutable structure. In adopting it, the editor demonstrates both intelligence and sensitivity: Sylvia Rothchild knows how to listen. She knows that survivors have their own way of talking, of remembering. Rather than evoke their sufferings during the torment, they prefer to describe what preceded it. To show what they have lost? No: in order to bring it back to life, in order to reattach it to the present that they bear within them: in order not to lose it a second time.

And so they tell their stories—stories about the serenity of the Sabbath, the preoccupations of their parents, the atmosphere at school, the darkening sky . . .

The names change, and the places too, but the story remains the same. In my little town, too, there were rabbis who opposed the Zionists; young people who tried to leave for Palestine illegally; assimilated Jews who came to the synagogue only once or twice a year; Hasidim and emancipated Jews . . . And all were to meet at the edge of the yawning abyss.

In our town, too, we should have taken steps. Rumors had reached us: the enemy was ruthless. We could have gone into hiding. We didn't. As elsewhere, the Jews in my town refused to believe that men—even Germans, even Nazis—could commit crimes so odious, so monstrous.

The consequence: we too were in the streets that spring of

1

1944 to see the Germans on their motorcycles. We too found them rather polite.

The trap, everywhere the same, was closing in on our illusions and smothering them.

Nevertheless, here and there, a few good people had warned us not to trust in appearances . . . Elizabeth Mermelstein of Viskovo recounts that in 1944 two German soldiers told her to flee because the concentration camps did indeed exist and Jews were being killed there. "And we thought," says Elizabeth Mermelstein, "It was not true. That couldn't be.'"

I myself remember a little shamòs (beadle) who had returned from Galicia in 1942, alone, without his family. He told stories that made us shudder: he had seen Jews forced by the Germans to dig their own graves; he had witnessed mass executions, massacres. . . . We thought: "It's not true. Such things can't be."

And I also remember a police inspector who just before we moved into the ghetto had promised by father: "If something happens, I'll warn you in time." One night we heard a knocking at the window. By the time we opened it, nobody was there. The liquidation of the ghetto began the next day.

It would therefore be wrong to generalize. In the other camp, that of the Gentiles, not all the people were good, and not all of them were bad. In Italy, In Belgium, in France, even in Poland and even in Germany, a man here and a woman there were determined to demonstrate human solidarity with the Jewish victims. Unfortunately—why not say so?—these were exceptions. In general, the Jews knew that they were alone. And abandoned.

In the following pages, many of the survivors evoke their feeling of isolation during that time. Consulates were refusing to issue visas; doors were closing. How many Jews might not have been saved with the help of a document, a rubber stamp, a scrap of paper!

Some—very few—were saved; others suffered through Sachsenhausen, Auschwitz, Buchenwald. In recalling this, the survivors employ the same tone—sober, restrained, almost curt in its precision. Sometimes a sentence stands out because of its passion (Hilda Branch: "I hated the French more than the Germans") or because of its restraint (Jack Goldman: "My father was shot in 1942"). Sometimes a word contains such anger, such anguish, that it explodes. The first doubts about the humanity of men, about divine justice; the lure of death, and the determina-

2

tion to survive in order to bear witness. To set it all down for history—that was our common obsession. To tell all, to relate everything. To fight against forgetting, because to forget is to make oneself an accomplice of the executioner. Only it wasn't easy. How could we speak of the unspeakable? How could we express the ineffable? The hunger of the old people, the death of children—that can't be recounted. And then there was also the fear of not being able to make oneself understood; what's the use of talking if it does no good? These inhibitions prevented the survivors from unburdening themselves. Some felt guilty because they remained silent; others because they did not.

But in this book—admirably edited, condensed and introduced by Sylvia Rothchild—they bear witness. Let us thank them as much for their courage as for their sincerity. Each in his and her own way contributes to keeping alive the tragedy of the Jewish people in the Thirties and Forties.

Thanks to them we learn that the blindness of the Jews was equaled only by the indifference of the Allied leaders to their plight. Because yes; on an individual level surely, on a collective level perhaps, the tragedy could have been avoided, or at least limited. If only Washington had been more understanding, if Switzerland had been more welcoming and London less hostile toward illegal refugees . . . And yet, with money, with a little luck, it was possible to cross into Switzerland, to hide in an Italian village, or to obtain false papers . . . If only one had known! But we didn't know. If the leaders of the Free World had taken the trouble to warn Hungarian Jews, to inform them, to advise them not to obey the evacuation orders, to flee the transports—how many might have managed to save themselves?

But we didn't know. Perhaps we didn't want to know. It was easier that way. For example, Marika Frank Abrams continued to live—to live?—in ignorance of the gas chambers even when she was already in Auschwitz! How then can we be surprised that Greek Jews changed drachmas for German marks in order to buy land in Poland? Or in order to pay for the trip?

This engrossing book must be read; these voices must be heard. You will find in it not only confirmation of things known but also new facts, undisclosed details. We knew, for example, that at Birkenau, before entering the gas chamber, an extremely beautiful woman had rushed at a member of the SS and killed him with his own revolver. But we didn't know that she came from Italy and that she was an actress.

3

We knew that the Jewish victims went to their death with courage and dignity, but now we learn that they were silent: listen to their silence; it is in this book.

On the other hand, here and there you will come up against some errors of fact or perception. For example: the revolt of the Birkenau *Sonderkommandos* seems to have been undertaken in cooperation with the Royal Air Force. That's what we read in this book. But, this doesn't agree with the findings of historians. It's depressing, but the facts must be faced: the Allies had decided not to bomb the death factories or even the rail lines leading to them. How can we explain that one of these survivors believes differently? Wishful thinking, perhaps. It doesn't matter: in this book historical facts are less important than the manner in which the witness remembers and communicates them. The errors themselves—of memory or of perception—deserve a place in the dossier. Besides, the error we have just mentioned is easily explained and can therefore be used to illustrate a point. The witness remembers a plan that involved the RAF because he undoubtedly heard rumors: every camp was an inexhaustible source of rumors. The Red Cross was going to take charge of us. The pope had intervened in our favor. Or Roosevelt . . .

It was not until the war was over that the survivors recognized their error: the world had known and had remained silent. How was one to re-enter that world? How was one to trust a humanity that was simultaneously betrayed and betraying? The pages that describe the *after* are as overwhelming as the others. How can we not admire all those orphans, those lonely women, those outcasts, those strays, who were able to overcome despair and hate and assert their right to life and even to happiness?

Let us listen to them. What they have to say about their past constitutes the basis of our future: fanaticism leads to racism, racism to hate, hate to murder, murder to the death of the species.

The danger lies in forgetting. Forgetting, however, will not affect only the dead. Should it triumph, the ashes of yesterday will cover our hopes for tomorrow.

The voices in this book must be listened to. They are the embodiment of a powerful and anguished call to life, to faith, to salvation.

(*translated from the French by Stanley Hochman*)

Preface

*"To our sons . . . May they never know the heartaches and ago-
nies their parents suffered during those years except by reading
this transcript or listening to the tapes. . . ."*

*". . . there is a fine line in cruelty that a person can commit
against another person—or a nation against another nation.
And once you cross that line, nobody will believe it was so. . . .
And I knew they really didn't want to know."*

*"It was the audience I dreamed about on my filthy, lousy mat-
tress when I was trying to give myself enough courage and hope
to believe I would survive."*

*"I tell you the only thing that kept me going is the burning
desire to tell, to bear witness. . . ."*

These are a few of the voices pleading to be heard among the
two hundred and fifty survivors of the Holocaust whose experiences, recollections and thoughts fill hundreds of recording
tapes. The memoirs transcribed from these tapes cover twenty-
five thousand pages. Together, they constitute the Holocaust
Oral History Project of the William E. Wiener Oral History Library of the American Jewish Committee—a major collection in a
treasure house of data about Jews in twentieth-century America.

The American Jewish Committee, recognizing the importance of collecting and recording such data, launched the Library
more than a decade ago as a unique memory bank for the use of
scholars now and in the future.

Today the Library's thousand completed memoirs reflect the
culture, ideas and issues of an era of social, scientific and historic
significance. On the one hand, impressive progress, with quan-
tum jumps in art and technology; on the other, unprecedented

5

social upheaval, with major migrations from the Old World to the New, with wars, revolution and wholesale destruction. And within this regressive aspect of the era squarely fall the lives and memories of the fifty thousand survivors of the Nazi Holocaust who found their way to this country as a tattered remnant of European Jewry when the war ended in 1945.

A quarter of a century later the William E. Wiener Oral History Library was one of the first American archival institutions to recognize the importance of recording, documenting and preserving the experiences of these traumatized survivors, both the ordeal they had undergone as Jews suffering Nazi persecution and the subsequent thirty years of their lives in the regenerating atmosphere of American democracy.

The Library's interviewers traveled to sixty-two cities in America, and met with survivors from twenty-four European countries. They came back with extensive recorded testimony, much of it heretofore untold—accounts of indescribable horror, spilling over into testimonies of resilience of spirit, and courage, and faith. These reactions were shared by the project's academic coadvisers. Professor Arthur Mann of the University of Chicago described the memoirs as "compelling human experiences," and Professor Sigmund Diamond of Columbia University observed, "There are certain kinds of events which occur in history which are so awesome that they are diminished by the attempt to provide an explanation. Over and above the explanation is the event itself—what it means in terms of human happiness and human suffering."

We of the William E. Wiener Oral History Library are grateful to the National Endowment for the Humanities for making these memoirs possible, and to the New American Library for the publication of *Voices from the Holocaust,* which brings this primary source material to the American reading public to help broaden understanding of the "human meaning of this awesome event." But above all, we are grateful for the opportunity this provides for the survivor-memoirists who participated in our project to "bear witness" once again to an audience that is ready to listen and does "want to know."

Milton E. Krents, Chairman,
The William E. Wiener Oral History Library
of the American Jewish Committee

Introduction

The Holocaust tapes came to me phonetically transcribed, neatly wrapped in individual folders. Stacked one above the other, they created a wall of words that reached to my shoulders. Months slipped by while I read through 650 hours of conversation, searching as I read for a form that would do justice to the stories and the storytellers.

Most of the material was unedited. There was poignancy in the errors that revealed the chasms separating the memoirists from the typists who recorded their words. "Holy cust" wrote one bewildered transcriber again and again. The survivor who described a *"pidyan haben,"* a special ceremony after the birth of a firstborn son, would have been astonished to find his words appear as "pig in a pen." Yiddish and Hebrew expressions were garbled beyond recognition. The voices, however, were clear, the cadences and accents intact. Strong feelings came through.

I gradually separated the essential stories from the interviewers' questions and the repetitions and digressions. The stories, laid bare, had a magnetic pull to them. They were full of answers to questions I hadn't thought to ask. They brought up questions I hadn't dared to ask. Expecting them to be sad, even morbid, I wasn't prepared for the flashes of exhilaration, for the strength and pride of life-obsessed people who had lived through the worst of times. I wasn't at all prepared for what they would teach me about myself.

I was in the generation that shared George Steiner's sense of himself as "a kind of survivor." Safe in America we felt scarred by dangers we had missed and mourned the losses of people we had never met. Though real survivors might see us as normal, complacent Americans, many of us were haunted by our connections to the people who were destroyed. I was born in Brooklyn but my parents came from Galicia before World War I; my mother from Lvov (now Lemberg) and my father from Yablonitz, a small village in the Carpathians. I knew nothing about those places except that I would not have escaped the Holocaust if they had not come to America in time.

It was not a pleasant thought. To avoid it I kept my distance from people, places and objects that would remind me. I did not want to visit Germany, Austria or Poland. I would not drive a Mercedes, set my table with Rosenthal china or Polish glass. My husband, knowing my prejudices, avoided bringing middle-aged German visitors home to dinner. I didn't apologize for my phobias, for I thought them an appropriate response to a loathsome time. I protected myself from feelings and fears I couldn't cope with, torn by the wish to know more about the Holocaust and the fear of knowing. Meanwhile I read and reviewed everything I could find on the subject, trying to come to terms with the literature without confronting it as a real event in my lifetime.

The Holocaust tapes made it possible to think of those years in a new way. Individual stories offered a human view of an inhuman time. Complicated truths emerged. Stereotypes dissolved. They told how Jews lived and worked before the war. They told of the early warnings of the disasters ahead, of the opportunities for escape and resistance, and of how men and women pushed to the edge of life felt about themselves, their fellow victims and their oppressors. They included a record of individual responses to danger, culture shock, severe loss and displacement, and told about human endurance and the capacity for recovery. The experiences in America during the last thirty years were as interesting as the recollections of life in Europe. Survivors had lessons to teach about the meaning of family, faith and freedom and the intricate web of givens and influences we call identity.

As the stories unfold, one senses how much the speakers are trying to reach out to fellow Americans. They know how their experiences have changed them and set them apart, but they also know how much they have in common with their neighbors.

The personalities revealed in the stories seem more like neighbors, relatives or friends than the near victims of the Nazi's, the real survivors of the real Holocaust. Human faces and individual lives were obliterated by German bureaucrats who spoke of their war against the Jews as "the final solution of the Jewish question." Jews struggling with the bitter consequences of that war called it the Holocaust. Both terms made it possible to refer to unspeakable events without thinking of living men and women. The tapes, however, bring both survivors and victims into focus as individual human beings, rather than statistics in a mass catastrophe.

Historians and literary people, trying to keep their distance even as they got close to what they felt was a dangerous subject, helped blur the genocidal aspect of the Holocaust by treating it as the Jewish component in a worldwide landscape of disaster that had no boundaries in time or space. It was fashionable to link Dresden with Auschwitz and to add Hiroshima, Bangladesh, Vietnam and Cambodia, as if all murderous places were interchangeable. In this perspective the concentration camp became a metaphor and Auschwitz a symbol of evil. It seemed less painful to speak of "Life's demonic undertow" (Terence Des Pres) or "hell made immanent" (A. Alvarez) than to examine deliberate actions of men and women.

The survivors of Hitler's "final solution," however, did not have the luxury of abstraction. For Elie Wiesel the Holocaust was "a sacred event to be kept from defilement." He compared its effect on the Jewish people to what happened at Sinai, sure that they would never be the same again. For ordinary survivors it was an unbelievable ordeal they happened to survive. Many were the only ones left of large families. They mourned the loss of parents and children, wives and lovers, the destruction of their homes and possessions and most of all of the culture in which they were prepared to live. It gave them no comfort to hear of the sufferings of the Gypsies or the tragedies of the Armenians. The statistics of the victims at Stalingrad did not help them forget their losses and sorrows. Their experiences with the realities behind the myths and symbols gave them a special perspective on life, but one not easily shared with those who had lived in safety.

Many survivors tried to tell what had happened to them when they were liberated and when they came to America, but they were rebuffed by people who didn't have the strength to listen. "I began to tell my family in Connecticut what happened," said one survivor, "but they didn't believe me. 'That can't be true,' they said. 'That never happened.' So I let them think it never happened and didn't bring the subject up again."

Survivors learned to be cautious about disturbing the equanimity of friends and relatives who were not prepared to cope with the harsh facts, whether they believed them or not. Writers

9

with great talent could risk unburdening themselves, but ordinary survivors were expected to keep their bad dreams to themselves.

Whether silent or outspoken, survivors were torn between remembering and forgetting, between shielding their children from their unhappy history and warning them that the world was a dangerous place. They urged each other to "forget the gruesome things . . . and look forward and see the good," but the speed with which the Holocaust was eased into ancient history frightened them.

Books that claimed the Holocaust never happened were an affront to the sanity of the people who experienced it. After thirty years in America the presence of men in Nazi uniform picketing their memorial meetings or parading in front of their homes still made some of them hysterical. They worried that their children would never understand them. They felt they had betrayed their dead relatives by their failure to explain what had happened to them. They knew that the Holocaust was not mentioned in most history books, not studied in America, Germany, Austria or the countries of Eastern Europe, which were still openly anti-Semitic. It was possible to look up World War II in the *Encyclopaedia Britannica* and find no mention of Hitler's war against the Jews.

Sometimes they found their story told, but in such a distorted way that it was unrecognizable. Robert Spitz in Dallas, Texas, followed what he calls "the literature of apologetics" in German, Hungarian, Czech, Polish, Russian, English and Hebrew. He found the Jewish victims of the Nazi occupation of Europe called Soviet citizens, Frenchmen and Austrian freedom fighters. The Warsaw ghetto uprising is described in the National Archive of Poland as "the resistance of the Polish people against the Nazis." Men and women who did not have the protection of citizenship when alive were usurped as pseudoheroes after their deaths. Robert Spitz, born in Budapest, deported to Bergen-Belsen in 1944, was concerned about "the whitewashing" of the Holocaust, which he saw as part of a process designed to make it all seem like an aberration that could be ignored and erased from history. Like most other survivors, he feared that history which is not faced is in danger of being repeated.

In the mid-1970s, when most survivors no longer expected any opportunity to speak about their experiences, there was a revival of interest in them, in their children, even in the culture that had been destroyed in Eastern Europe. Most of the five hundred thousand survivors of the Holocaust live in Israel. About fifty thousand came to the United States in the late 1940s and early 1950s. Their presence in cities and small towns throughout the country kept questions about the Hitler years alive. One can find men and women with foreign accents, with faded tattoos on their forearms and knowledge of distant places, in San Antonio, Texas; Albuquerque, New Mexico; Denver, Colorado; Canton, Ohio. Their neighbors, after thirty years, still sometimes call them "the refugees" and do not know whether they were snatched from the fire at the last moment or hidden in an Italian, French or Swiss village. But they are not invisible, and their children sometimes behave differently because they were brought up with values and expectations that their peers do not share.

Questions that survivors expected to hear thirty years ago finally began to be asked. Two hundred and fifty people living in sixty-two American cities were willing to have their recollections taped for the archives of the William E. Wiener Oral History Library. The stories that follow are told by survivors from France, Greece, Hungary, Denmark, Czechoslovakia, Poland, Holland, Rumania, Yugoslavia, Germany, Austria, Italy and Russia. Some had lived in Israel, Canada or South America before settling permanently in the United States. They had survived Hitler's occupation of Europe in beleaguered ghettos and concentration and slave-labor camps. A lucky few were sheltered by non-Jews. A handful who did not look Jewish lived through the war in quiet terror with false papers and assumed names. Some had converted to Christianity and were hidden in convents and monasteries. There were partisans who fought in the forests and Zionists who made the dangerous and illegal journey to Palestine. A privileged minority were smuggled to safety in Switzerland and Spain.

Until Hitler's occupation of Europe these people were separated by differences in language, education, faith and economic and social position. The Holocaust blew through their lives like a tornado, funneling them into a common abyss. When the war ended most of them were without family, home or country to return to. They became dependent upon the organizations that ran the displaced persons camps and refugee relief and came to America as refugees in search of health, safety and freedom.

Thirty or more years later they speak as Americans. They live in American communities and have American families. They tell stories of their early struggles, their adjustments and accomplishments. There are still, however, survivors who feel like pale ghosts from another world, who marvel that they are alive and wonder why they were chosen to be among the five hundred thousand rather than the six million.

Looking back, they find no blueprints for survival. Luck, they agree, was the most important thing. They nevertheless examine their early lives, their families, their communities and their own dispositions in search of qualities that might have given them an advantage. Every friend and stranger who came to their aid is remembered.

Though no generalizations can be made, the survivors in this collection found it helpful to have had a father rich enough to pay the smugglers who led the way over the mountains, the peasants who hid children, the officials who provided false papers, forged baptismal certificates and ration cards. It was better to be a doctor than a lawyer, an engineer than an accountant. Carpenters, electricians, auto mechanics, watchmakers and rifle experts had better chances than shopkeepers or teachers. It was better to be young and physically fit than middle-aged. Skiers, runners and soccer players had an edge over those who lacked stamina. Country people had survival skills that city dwellers missed. It was good to have a brother, sister or cousin to lean on while in the camps or on the forced marches.

When they pondered the mystery of their survival, the storytellers responded in terms of their private experiences. Some were convinced they would not have made it without faith in God. Others were sure they were sustained by Zionism. A sense of worth acquired in a secure and happy family was important in the years of harassment, but blond hair and blue eyes often seemed even more useful. It was hard to know because the requirements were not fixed. Qualities invaluable in one place could be worthless in another. In one situation it might be crucial to be able to climb a wall, leap from a moving train or cross a mountain in the dark. In another the challenge might be isolation, confinement in a small place for a long time.

Some survivors responded to questions as if they had been privately rehearsing the answers all the years they had been waiting to be asked. Others found their memories so painful that their speech became incoherent and disjointed. The past for some seemed distant, almost unreal. Others kept souvenirs, photographs and bits of torn clothing as evidence, and for them the past and present were equally close and problematical.

The pain stemmed from their need to speak for the relatives they lost as well as for themselves. Though they and the world at large were conscious of the division between victims and survivors, they spoke as witnesses for the multitude who couldn't speak for themselves. Their stories are also those of their closest relatives and friends who were deported or hiding with them, but who did not survive.

Choosing a necessarily limited number of stories for this volume was very difficult. A collection as compelling as this one could be created from the transcriptions that are not included. There were many variations on similar themes from which I chose the most candid and philosophical life stories, those most concerned with getting the facts straight.

Some of the transcripts offered rich life stories told by men and women who were convinced that they had survived in order to tell the truth as they saw it. Others offered only fragments, threads of memory, bits and pieces, shards of life along with explosions of feeling. Fantasies, dreams and imagined events slip in with the hard facts, just as they do for men and women who experience the normal pressures of life. Memory simplifies and softens. The many confirmations of particular details, however, make it hard to doubt the authenticity of most of the material. The longest transcripts were close to three hundred pages. The shortest were only ten or fifteen. Some were chosen because they described feelings, places or circumstances shared by many survivors in this collection. Others were chosen for their unique voice so that this volume would reflect the variety of individuals caught in the war against the Jews. Some survivors are represented by brief quotations, others by lengthy testimonies.

The decision to divide the book into three sections devoted to life before, during and after the Holocaust grew naturally from the form of the stories themselves. Survivors looked back on three separate lives with strikingly different demands and expectations. Arranging their stories in this fashion made it possible to include the fragments of experience as well as the more organized memoirs, and the introductions to each of the sections provided additional space in which to describe the insights of the survivors whose stories do not appear.

I kept two notebooks while reading the transcripts. In one I tried to pretend that I had no experience with the subject. I collected facts about growing up Jewish in European cities and towns, listed all the responses to Hitler's threats, noted the alternatives available, the risks that were taken, the consequences and the forms of resistance as they turned up in individual stories. I followed this pattern through liberation, during the years of waiting in displaced persons camps and of coming to America.

In the other notebook I gathered the details and observations that challenged the ideas and judgments about survivors and victims that I had acquired in a lifetime of reading fiction and nonfiction about the Holocaust. I became convinced that only survivors would be able to counter the stereotypes and misconceptions about the Holocaust that had burgeoned during their years of silence. As one survivor so movingly noted, "Each of us has a different story. All of them true. Believe them."

Life Before The Holocaust

Survivors begin their stories with memories of childhood. They describe parents, grandparents, even great-grandparents. Their lives and fates were determined by the social and religious status of their forebears. In America a person could have a fresh start unencumbered by the accomplishments or deprivations of the past, but it was not so in any of the countries of Europe in the early twentieth century.

In the excerpts that follow, survivors begin, "My family for a hundred and fifty years lived in Czechoslovakia, near Brno. My grandfather and great-grandfather were famous rabbis who published many books," or "My earliest relative in the Debrecin cemetery was born in 1776," or "I was born in Paris but my parents came from Poland and spoke only Yiddish"—all offering precise descriptions of their places in society.

Their stories of Jewish life in Europe before the coming of Hitler challenge the image of "the old country" as it was remembered by the immigrants who left Eastern Europe between 1880 and 1925. Those earlier arrivals in America made it clear that they had left their dark and muddy villages without regret. They had escaped from poverty, hunger, forced conscription and explosions of gratuitous violence, and brought their closest relatives with them.

To the children of Jewish immigrants in America who grew up before World War II, Eastern Europe was a mythical place populated by kerchiefed grandmothers and bearded grandfathers, a world of sad-eyed rabbis and boys with side-curls and funny clothes bent over thick Hebrew books. Pious and poor, innocent and unworldly, it was fixed in imagination like the faded photographs the immigrant generation brought with them. It was accepted that American Jews had moved on and up in the world and left all of that behind them. They did not understand that America was not the center of Jewish life; that before the Second World War two-thirds of the world's Jews lived in Europe, most of them in Eastern Europe; and that there had been many changes since the great immigrations.

Survivors tell another story. They grew up in families that chose to remain in Europe. There were religious people who would not risk transplanting their faith to America, and middle-class and affluent Jews who saw no reason to uproot themselves. In Kolo, Poland, Helene Frankle's father responded to the idea of emigrating with, "I have an America here. Why should I leave?".Even the Jews who would have come to America if its immigration policies had permitted had adjusted and made the most of the opportunities available to them. They thought of themselves as citizens of Germany, Austria, France, Italy and Hungary, just as their relatives on the other side of the Atlantic thought of themselves as Americans.

The stories of their early years in Europe reveal a broad range of religious and economic possibilities: all the stages of assimilation and related educational experiences. They offer clues to the differences between East and West, between urban and rural life, between French, German, Polish, Czech and Hungarian Jews. The age of the storyteller is an important factor, because Jewish opportunities in Europe shifted from periods of relative freedom to periods of repression and persecution, followed in turn by fresh promises and new hopes.

The energetic and flexible were constantly looking for the best places to live and work, moving their families to the cities where there were business opportunities, good schools and less virulent anti-Semitism.

It was an accomplishment for a Jewish family to have been able to live in the same place for a few generations. It was a measure of security and a sign of acceptance. There had been time to cultivate a farm, develop a business, acquire wealth and respect and "a good name," even a friendship with the mayor or the judge and influence with the police commissioner. When the time came for money to change hands to pay for protection, an old citizen would know where to go and how to make the arrangements. If he had served with honor in the army, that would give his children special privileges. They might be able to attend state-supported high schools that were not usually open to Jews. The cycles of acceptance and intolerance were accepted as facts of life. The objective was to survive in spite of the conditions.

One survivor came from a town so insignificant he didn't give its name, but he described it as one of the oldest in Poland where there had been "six hundred years of sizzling Jewish life." There had been pogroms, attacks and fires, but until the Hitler occupation the Jewish community had always risen "like a phoenix" and restored itself.

All but one of the survivors in this collection of stories said they came from middle-class families. What was meant by middle-class, however, changed from one survivor to the next. For Gastone Orefice from Livorno, Italy, it meant that his relatives were professionals rather than wealthy people. "Middle" might refer to a place in the religious as well as the economic spectrum. Abraham Morgenstern from Chortkov, Poland, claimed his family for the middle class because they were neither *Chasidim* nor assimilated Jews. Contrary to the old American perception of the Orthodox as pious and impoverished, there is no such correlation in the recollections of these survivors. They described Orthodox families that were rich and secular families that were poor. The young Jews who went to university were considered upper-class by their childhood friends who went to trade school or into apprenticeship at the age of thirteen, even though they described themselves as pariahs, lower than the lowest class of non-Jewish students. The "middle" was large enough to include the rich who were not very rich and the marginal who were little better off than their neighbors.

Some survivors concerned about describing their precise places in society in a world that has been destroyed express their sense of loss of identity, their nostalgia for a world in which a person was born into a place that was his for a lifetime. Others express their pleasure in being in America, free of the old restrictions. But other Americans, by confusing survivors with each other and with immigrants of earlier migrations, make them very determined to explain who they were and how they differ from each other and the people who came at the turn of the century.

They were especially fearful of being confused with earlier immigrants from Eastern Europe who had no opportunity for a secular education. Most of the survivors in this collection attended Jewish or state-sponsored elementary schools. Though usually excluded from the state-supported gymnasia by the small or nonexisting quota for Jewish students they were able to get a good classical education in the Jewish high schools to prepare them for the competition to get into a university. They studied science, Latin, mathematics and literature as well as Jewish history and religion. Religious instruction was part of education in the government schools and the Jewish schools. Engineers, doctors and lawyers could remember attending *cheder* at the age of three, just like the rest of the Jewish population. Assimilated Hungarian, Austrian and German Jews studied Hebrew and Jewish history in public school while the Catholic students studied their catechism and church history.

In America the objective of Jewish schools was (and is) to offer Jewish children a religious education not available in public school and to bolster their identity as a special group, separated from the mainstream. In Europe the Jewish private schools tried to help Jewish students out of the traditional religious training into the mainstream of Western life. The affluent Jews of Salonika, Greece, sent their children to a French-speaking school in the hope that they would go on to a French university. The Jews of Sarajevo, Yugoslavia, sent their best students to study in Vienna. Polish Jewish children studied German in their Jewish school. Young women in middle-class families went to university with their brothers. Even the daughters of Orthodox parents could be found in the universities before World War II began.

European Jews were caught up with ideas of each other as stereotypical as those Americans held of them. Though geographically close, they were separated by religious and class prejudices. Robert Spitz, growing up in an assimilated family in Budapest, described his childhood impression of the Danube as a line separating East and West. He thought that everyone west of the Danube spoke perfect German and was well-educated in German culture; in the East he expected no secular knowledge, no German-speaking Jews, only religious people involved in traditional Jewish study. He discovered later that there were Jews in Germany and France who spoke Yiddish rather than German and French. There were Polish Jews who spoke excellent German and no Yiddish. Some assimilated Hungarian Jews studied Yiddish as an exotic foreign language. There were Czech, Polish and Russian Jews untouched by Jewish culture or tradition. The myth of the Danube as the divider between East and West, however, was hard to shake. It survived the camps and the ghettos, where Western Jews thought themselves superior to Eastern Jews. It even crossed the ocean to America, where survivors discovered that Americans looked down on *all* newcomers who did not speak English or spoke with accents that exposed them as foreigners.

Vestiges and memories from all the Jewish worlds in prewar Europe turn up in the excerpts that follow. They are arranged according to country, though there was often as much diversity within a single city as there was between countries. There are glimpses into communities and families, into the conflicts between Jews of different generations, beliefs and political involvements. Individual stories offer some clues to the ways Jews lived until the last minute.

Joy Levi Alkalay was born in Vienna in 1923. Her parents were Sephardic Jews from Sarajevo, Yugoslavia. When Hitler occupied Austria they wore Yugoslav flags in their lapels to show they were not to be treated as Austrian Jews.

My father came from Sarajevo. He was sent to a boys' boarding school in Vienna to finish his education when he was fourteen or fifteen. Later on, when he was working for his father, he was sent back to Vienna to do the purchasing for his father's store. Then in World War I he served in the Austro-Hungarian army, but not as an active soldier because he had a heart murmur. He was attached to the censorship group, still in Vienna, for the four years of the war. And when the war was over he went back to Sarajevo, where the people had opted for Yugoslavian citizenship. This explains how we happened to be foreigners in Austria, even though I was born in Vienna.

My mother was born in Trieste, Italy. Her father came from Bosnia, which was then Austria-Hungary but is now part of Yugoslavia, and her mother came from Venice. They settled in Trieste and raised a family of four girls. My mother was the second child. When World War I began my grandparents took their children to Switzerland for safety. My mother was educated in Zurich. She came to Vienna to visit in 1922 and met my father. My

21

father represented various Italian factories that sold cotton and he covered all of Austria and the Balkans.

The majority of the Jews in Vienna were Ashkenazi but we belonged to the small Sephardic community, with our own *Talmud Torah* and worship services. I went to the Sephardic religious school and learned to pronounce Hebrew as it is spoken today in Israel. I enjoyed the classes very much and I was proud of being singled out as a good student.

In 1929 I began grade school. It was a very democratic public school. Everyone received free milk whether you could afford to pay or not. There was an effort to make no distinction between the poor children and those from well-to-do families. But I felt there was some resentment against me because I came from a well-to-do home. There was a little girl who would pour ink on my blouse and call me names. Her parents were the janitors in the apartment house in which we lived. She was the first one to call me "Jew." I used to come home crying and my parents used to explain what it meant to be a Jew, and they would tell me not to cry about it. They told me to ignore her and not get into a fight with her.

When it was time for high school my parents sent me to a private girls' school. They didn't approve of the public school because it was coeducational. I remember the first year there was a very large class, about forty-five girls, and each year the class was smaller. The last year there were only twelve of us left. The majority were Catholic. There were a few Protestants and even fewer Jews. The Protestants and the Jews banded together against the Catholic girls.

The Jewish girls were visibly intelligent and the most advanced in the class. The work seemed easy for them and some of the others were envious because they had trouble with their studies. There were some teachers who would say nasty things, just before Hitler. They tried to make everything difficult for the Jewish students and say, "Just wait and see what happens. A couple of months more and you won't be here." But otherwise it was all right.

There were signs of the growing anti-Semitism in everyday life. The day help left and never came back. They said they didn't want to work in a Jewish house. And then there were the remarks we heard when we went to the grocer or the dairy shop. Then Hitler occupied Austria in March 1938 and the Austrians were all wearing swastikas—they were just crazy about Hitler. Everyone who wasn't wearing a swastika was either a foreigner or Jewish. The English people began to wear a little British flag and we wore Yugoslav flags, and we always carried identification to prove we had the right to.

Edmund Engelman was born in Vienna in 1907. He studied engineering at the Vienna Technical Institute, and developed his talent for photography. He loved his city in spite of the anti-Semitism there.

Vienna was the cradle of anti-Semitism . . . the country where Nazism was born. It's where the biggest criminals, including Hitler and Eichmann, came from. When I was an engineering student at the Vienna Technical Institute there were times when the fraternities would beat Jews up and throw them off the school grounds. This was tolerated by the police because the academic ground was out of bounds for the police. I could come and go because I didn't look Jewish, but I didn't feel comfortable being among them.

I tell you this to explain that anti-Semitism in Austria was part of everyday life and you had to be defensive. Nevertheless, Vienna was a very interesting place. It had about two hundred thousand Jews and was a cultural center, the city of Max Reinhardt, Stefan Zweig, Sigmund Freud and many others. And it was really a fantastically interesting place for a young man, in spite of the feeling of uneasiness because of the anti-Semitism. It was also a beautiful city. It offered lovely surroundings, a good climate, beautiful theater, museums and libraries. It was an ideal place to grow up in.

You see, Vienna had a population of two million people; Austria had only six million. Vienna had been the capital of an empire of sixty million and now contained a third of the population of the country, and 10 percent of it was Jewish. The Jews were mostly poor and had little political influence, but they were productive and prominent in the arts.

We were actually sitting on a powder keg because Austria was a fascist country that held down the Socialist party and was struggling against the rising Nazi power. Though it was a hard place to leave I was thinking about emigrating. I was thinking of England, I was thinking of Palestine. But I had my parents and they had reached a certain economic level. They felt settled and secure and discouraged me from leaving.

Zionism fascinated me. After all, Vienna was also the cradle of Zionism; Herzl was a Viennese. I was strongly impressed by Zionism and I felt the need for this homeland, that the existence of this land was absolutely necessary to dispel the false images that the anti-Semites had given of the Jews. They called us swindlers, and physical and moral degenerates. They said we weren't creative and could only live off others, and so on. So I really did feel that having a country where the Jew's image would be projected in another light would help Jews everywhere. But at the time I decided not to go there because they needed agricultural workers and laborers and I was an engineer.

Another problem was that the government controlled the press in Austria and we were completely misinformed about what was going on. The press stressed the fact that the independence of Austria was guaranteed by the Allied powers and that Mussolini didn't want to have Germany as a neighbor and would defend the frontiers of Austria against Germany. And then, all of a sudden, Hitler came and everything collapsed.

Herman Herskovic was born in the small farming community of Benkovce, Czechoslovakia, in 1921. His parents and grandparents grew up in the same village. He spoke Hungarian and Yiddish at home, German and Hebrew in his cheder *and Slovak in public school. He planned to go to the university to study business administration, but Hitler came to power by the time he was twelve and his plans changed.*

My parents were farmers in a small town in the eastern part of Czechoslovakia. There were only three Jewish families in the village. It was a community of only forty-five homes. But my grandparents and parents were born there and had good lives. We had quite a bit of land and it was a privilege in those days to be a farmer. In many countries, including England, Jews were not allowed to own land, so my grandparents were happy to be making a living on their own land. They had five children. They sent one son to the University of Munich, where he earned his Ph.D. in philosophy and then went to rabbinical school in Bratislava, where he became a rabbi. All of my uncles were educated and my parents, even though they were farmers, were intelligent people. They made a good living and were contented. When I was six my parents brought a tutor into the house to teach me and my three brothers.

On holidays the Jews from six little towns in the area came together for services. They didn't need a rabbi because everyone had had a Jewish education and could lead the service. We took turns in leading the prayers and offering our homes. It was something we looked forward to. Most of the people worked hard to earn a living and the Sabbaths and holidays were very important. It was a happy community and there were not too many people who had an idea of leaving the good life in Czechoslovakia.

My parents worried, however, that the educational facilities in our town were too limited. The public school was also run by the church and we had to say the prayers with the priest every morning; we didn't want to abstain. They decided to leave Benkovce and open a grocery store in Humenne. It was a much larger community. I went to the public school and the *cheder*.

The educational system was good, especially for those who wanted to learn. On the Sabbath, after services and the Sabbath meal, it was the custom to go back to the *cheder* because the parents used to test the students to see what they had learned from the chapter of the week. We all knew each other and it was a terrible thing not to be able to answer the question asked by your neighbor. How could you face them afterward? So everybody tried hard to learn.

It was a good life in Humenne. The Jewish community had all the rights. We had no problems with our neighbors. We had non-Jewish friends at school but not at home. It was not possible to bring a non-Jewish friend into our home because of the fear that the friendship would lead to problems. In high school I had a friend that I did homework with but the time was limited and as soon as the studying was over I had to go home. I was planning then to study accounting and business administration.

Hitler, however, came to power in Germany in 1933, when I

was twelve. Three years later there was a new party in Slovakia that preached the idea that every business should be taken away from the Jews, that they should not serve as officers in the army, or be permitted in university. By 1939 it was dangerous to walk in the street.

> *Elizabeth Mermelstein was born in 1920 in*
> *Viskovo, a pleasant small town in Czechoslovakia,*
> *where her family enjoyed a relaxed and*
> *comfortable life before the war began. Even in the*
> *good times, however, all the young Jewish people*
> *belonged to Zionist groups—a sign that they were*
> *not sure of the future in Czechoslovakia.*

My father was always traveling. He was an apple dealer, and he would buy up orchards in the spring when the flowers were on the trees and then when the apples ripened he would have them picked and packed and people came from all over the country to buy his fruit. He also had a sort of general store in the town. Viskovo was a small town, about ten thousand people. But my sister and I had a nice life. We went to the beaches in the summer and sledding in the winter. And I was very active in Hashomer. Everybody belonged to some Zionist group. About half of the younger population were in the Betar and we had about sixty people in Hashomer.

We went camping and got together with other groups from other towns. I was the leader of the little ones and I learned some Hebrew. As a matter of fact, that's where I learned to read and write in Hebrew, because I had no other Hebrew education; the boys went to *cheder* but not the girls.

I was always an idealist and planned to go to Israel. But you know in Europe you don't just pick yourself up to go without your parents. You are more involved with your family. I tried to persuade my parents but of course they wouldn't leave their belongings, so we stayed.

My mother had her comfortable life. She cooked and canned

and embroidered and visited friends and relatives. We had a maid to do the things she didn't like to do. She didn't clean. She never made a bed. She never let me in the kitchen because I would make a mess, but I couldn't care less. When I got married I didn't know how to boil an egg.

I couldn't get into gymnasium because my father never obtained Czechoslovakian citizenship. He was born in Viskovo but at that time it was in Austria-Hungary. When it became Czechoslovakia he applied for citizenship but his birth certificate was lost in the city hall and they never found it. It was my whole ambition to go to the gymnasium but you had to have proof of citizenship. There was only grade school in our town. For three years I lived with my aunt and went to a high school in her town, but it was not the same as gymnasium. When I graduated I helped my father out in the store. But I was having a lot of fun. We went to the movies out of town and had a big social life. There was nothing else to do. By then they weren't hiring Jewish people anymore. There were no jobs for Jewish girls. My sister got married in 1934 and I stayed home with my parents until we were deported to Auschwitz.

Zdenka Weinberg was born in 1909 in Kolinec, Czechoslovakia. She grew up in a town of a thousand people in one of its six Jewish families. She remembers the Masaryk years as "the best of times." In the worst of times she was sent to Auschwitz and Theresienstadt.

I was born in a very small community where, many years before my time, there was a ghetto. The ghetto houses were no longer occupied by Jews in my grandfather's time, and he was born in 1827. The ghetto was just across from the count's estate on both sides of the city hall, on the three sides of a square with a large communal yard where there was a vegetable garden. There was a synagogue and a slaughterhouse and an ice barn.

Nobody knows when the Jews came to Kolinec but it looked like they were protected by the nobleman and they were probably craftsmen. My grandfather came to the town just after he was married and my father grew up and went to school there. His friends all his life were from the time of grammar school. There was a farmer, a miller, a count. My father was a gentleman farmer and he was also in the lumber and grain business. He used to buy whole standing forests and then employed the men who cut and processed the lumber. We grew wheat, barley, oats and potatoes and had horses to pull the logs to the railroad station.

It was a town of a thousand people with six Jewish families. The inhabitants were very nice people and it was in beautiful country, with gentle hills and streams and lakes and true tranquility. Most of our friends were gentiles. There were no *shtetls* in Czechoslovakia. There was no segregation, no quotas for university in Prague. Czech Jews had it much easier than Polish or Russian Jews. In the eighteenth century Maria Theresa drove the Jews out of Prague and they moved to little towns where they still lived. There was some anti-Semitism after World War I but it had disappeared until Hitler revived it.

I went to grammar school and high school, always the only Jewish student in the class. My sister went to gymnasium and then to the university to study law. She was absolutely not interested in any of the woman's work like cooking, cleaning and sewing. All my three siblings went to gymnasium. My mother did not want me to go. She sent me to business school where the practical subjects for life were taught. At that time I did not care one way or the other; I was sorry later. She promised I could go to art school in Prague but it never materialized. My father was seriously ill, and he lost much money. Staying close, I could help my parents. After my father died my mother was left with four children, three of them at school. I, at least, could get a job and support myself.

I should tell you that my sister's best friend was the policeman's daughter and he didn't have a speck of anti-Semitism in him. And I always had a bunch of friends on my side. I had a wonderful teacher in grammar school. Once some boy in the class called me a Jew and I told the teacher. He gave the class a long explanation condemning anti-Semitism and told me in front of the class to tell him again if anybody ever insulted me and he would punish the offender severely. It worked. No one ever dared. It was the best time of my life, the years I spent in Masaryk's times. All citizens were treated alike in the First Republic. It was a real democracy, with freedom and no anti-Semitism. Thomas Masaryk was revered in our family. My father read all his articles. The only books he read were by Masaryk.

My mother's father knew four languages. He was originally a teacher. When he acquired a large family he established a match factory. His original language was German because he came from Sudetenland. He spoke Czech perfectly but did not use the dialect of our region, which embarrassed us children in front of our friends. Our other grandfather spoke our dialect and sang revolutionary songs. It was not unusual for Jews to be Czech nationalists. When my sister and brother went to Prague they were active in the Social Democrats. I was not interested in politics at that time.

The best times were before 1927 when we lived in Kolinec, up on the hill where the farmers had their homes and barns. The fields and meadows surrounded the community . . . built in the old way for protection from invaders. In those days I used to visit my gentile friends who lived in the ghetto houses on the square. The ghetto houses were very narrow, with small entrances from the street, but they all had access to the big common yard which they surrounded. The windows were also narrow and it was dark inside. I spent many happy hours playing in that large yard with my friends, where the synagogue was. You see, my grandfather's house and store were just on the corner. Sometimes I would look up at the nobleman's estate across from the ghetto houses and wonder whether he was their protector . . . or whether they were his chattel. The synagogue was still in use then, but people in Kolinec didn't know what the ghetto was. They called the synagogue the "Jewish church." Chanukah was Jewish Christmas. Passover was Jewish Easter. The people were plain country folk who didn't know very much about their own town. But I have a cousin from Kolinec living in Boston now who still speaks of the synagogue as the "Jewish church."

After my father's death we had to leave Kolinec and move to Prague to stay with relatives. My mother sold our house and the barns and the fields and rented a small house and the rest of the fields to get a regular income. It was good that she sold most of it because everything was nationalized after the communists took over in 1948.

I was working in Prague, at first for an uncle who was a

lawyer and then for the Export Institute. That's where I was until 1939, the day after Hitler's troops arrived.

Rose Rosenthal was born in Paris in 1929. Her parents were Polish Jews who spoke Yiddish. They sent her and her sister out to a foster home in the country where she was brought up as a French girl. She wished she was Catholic and could be confirmed in a beautiful white dress.

My father was born in Russia, my mother in Poland. They were both on their way to America when the United States closed the immigration and they were stuck in Paris. They were traveling in different groups but there was something about their papers that was not in order, and there they were, young people speaking Yiddish. They didn't know any French. They met and married and opened a grocery store, the kind of store where both of them worked from early morning till late at night.

We lived above the store, a couple of floors up. It was in a poor Jewish neighborhood. The apartments were not comfortable. The streets were dirty and the air very polluted. My parents did what was common among Jews and other families with a bit of money who could not take care of their children. They sent me (at the age of six months) and my sister out to the country to a *pension.* The woman who ran the *pension* was our foster mother and her husband our foster father. She took in children to supplement her income. There were five or six of us, including maybe her grandchild, and when we were old enough we went to the school near her house. She was very good to us, just like a mother, and we called her mother. On Sundays our parents came to visit us so we knew that we had other parents. But this was how we lived until 1938, when my parents began to be afraid that something was going to happen to the Jews and that we should be together.

When I was six my mother took me to Poland to visit her family. God, I was scared stiff. It was a big house with a thatched roof and wooden floors. There were oil lamps and a big fireplace with a chimney. My grandmother had her head shaved and my grandfather had a long beard—observant Jews. The house was divided and I had an aunt with three or four children living on the other side, where there was a kind of dirt floor.

I was in tears the whole time I was there. The atmosphere was so strange. It was someplace out of this world, because I had been brought up in Paris or in the suburbs that were like Paris. But this was the way they lived in Poland. They were quite well-to-do, but everybody lived that way where they were.

When my parents left home they gave up that old life. They did not have a kosher house or go to synagogue. They were too busy to observe. My father went to the market at four in the morning, opened the store at seven and was there until ten at night. Sometimes they went to the synagogue on Rosh Hashanah and Yom Kippur and when we went back to Paris we went with them. We had no religious education whatsoever.

When I was nine we were back with our parents, and now we had a maid to take care of us because my mother was always in the store. The maid was very anxious to convert us but the priest told her she had to have our parents' consent. I really wanted that. You know, in Europe when a girl is twelve she is confirmed, and wears this beautiful white dress and looks like a bride . . . just gorgeous. The maid said that I could be dressed like that if I was Catholic, and I would have liked that very much, but we never even told my parents. You have to understand that children in Europe were not taken into their parents' confidence. They didn't talk to you and you couldn't talk to them. Children were children and that's it.

I remember that I liked the school in Paris. But our apartment was not so good. There was no bathroom, no running water. There was a toilet between two floors that both floors used and cold water in a room next to the john. If you wanted to take a bath you had to go across the street to the bathhouse. We lived there until the French government tore it down to put a street through, and then we moved to another neighborhood where we had a much nicer apartment, but it was too far from the store. We moved back to the old neighborhood in 1939 just before the war began. When I came back to school they gave each child a gas mask. The sirens would go off and we would have air raid drills. We would march out two by two and go into a cellar someplace. The teachers did not talk about Hitler or Germany. It was just the sirens and the drill.

*Ginette Yahiel was born in Strasbourg, France, in
1929. Her father was a Jewish engineer born in
Russia, her mother a Christian from Strasbourg.
Her paternal grandmother lived in Bialystok,
Poland.*

My father came from Russia. My mother was from Strasbourg.
My father was an engineer. He studied first in Russia, then in
Germany, and came to Strasbourg to work for an electrical
company.

I remember a fairly happy childhood. On my mother's side I
had a grandmother and great-grandmother who often took care of
me and my brother. My father's mother came to visit us from
Bialystok in Poland, but I do not remember her. Daily life was
what is usual in France—going to school, the strict discipline of
parents trying to have children make good grades. I belonged to
a scout movement with all kinds of activities. I did not belong to
any of the religious movements like other Jewish kids. My father
was not a religious man and my mother was Christian. I only
went to synagogue twice as a child. Until 1939 we had religious
classes in school and the rabbi would come two or three times a
week. It was a practice continued from the time that Strasbourg
was a German city.

Strasbourg had a large Jewish population with many religious
Jews. They were also known for their social commitments and I
would say that they were very similar to American Jews. Jews in
Paris were more assimilated, but in my town they were a community in themselves, a tightly knit group. We didn't belong to
it but knew many people through my father's contacts.

I remember leaving our apartment in June in 1939, just after
school ended. My mother sent me and my brother to my aunt's
place in the south of France. My aunt had a big place on the lake
in Grenoble and we usually went there in summer, so it didn't
seem unusual. We thought it was just another summer, and then
the war broke out.

It was the beginning of our hardships. First there was waiting for my parents with no news of what had become of them. Then they came by car with a few possessions. There was no panic. My father was drafted with a unit from his company and sent to electrify the Maginot Line. He was lucky that he was not there when the French army was overcome; the men who were, were taken prisoner. Meanwhile we were taken to a village in the center of France, because Grenoble was close to the Italian border and the Germans were coming. I remember everyone crying. My aunt from Grenoble came with us. My mother was driving the car . . . the car that was always packed and ready to go.

I was only ten. Parents then didn't talk too much to their children. They didn't explain like we do today. So it was exciting for us and we suffered no deprivation. Food was plentiful. I remember all the sausages hanging from the ceiling. There was no concern about money. Like every European, we all had some gold stashed someplace and there was always enough to live on. I remember my mother buying a fur coat when we were in Grenoble because it was cold in the mountains. I have a feeling that a lot of people were running around having a good time. It was a feeling of "let's live it up." My mother never worked. My father had a very good job. He was stationed somewhere where my mother could visit him and she was always going off. I think the company sent my father to the "free" part of France to electrify the buses. They thought he would be safer there, as a Jew. So we had nothing to worry about.

Hilda Branch was born in Essen, Germany, in 1910. Her grandparents in Frankfurt were observant Jews, but her father was a prosperous, assimilated, nationalistic German who had been an officer in the Prussian army. She graduated from the gymnasium in Cologne in 1931 and went to Munich to study political economy.

I was born in Essen but my parents moved to Cologne when I was six weeks old. My father was Maximilian Schurmann, the founder of a large furniture interior-decorating house. He left Essen with his younger brother to establish a branch of the business in Cologne. My mother was a Schiff; she was born in Metz when it was German. I have one sister, four years younger than I.

I went to school in Cologne, and transferred into the humanistic gymnasium from which I graduated in 1931. I went to Munich for a year to study political economy and then came back to Cologne for another year before Hitler came into power and I had to discontinue my studies. In Munich I saw one of my professors attacked by Nazis, and one day some friends took me to a beer cellar to hear Hitler speak. It was a frightening experience. He talked for two hours saying nothing. But his voice was very appealing to some people. They cheered and applauded and became very excited.

In January, when Hitler came to power, my mother and I were skiing in Austria and my father was on the Riviera. My sister was in boarding school. We all got together at the home of some friends in Stuttgart and my mother and I were ready at that moment to leave Germany. I was convinced that things would go from bad to worse and I did not want to be a second-class citizen. My father was more nationalistic than my mother or myself. He had been an officer in the Prussian army and really refused to believe that Hitler would come to power or keep power very long. My mother and I had both voted Social Democrat.

I knew some Italian and took lessons immediately in Business English and Business French. I quickly learned to take shorthand and bookkeeping in a school where it was still possible, and I found two possibilities for jobs in Verona, Italy. My father was very protective and possessive and wanted to arrange something for me in England or France, but nothing came of his efforts. My mother went with me to Italy, where I had no problem finding a room with a family.

It was still relatively quiet in Germany. When I came back to visit, the difference was only that you had to go to a synagogue to hear a concert or see a movie. Jews couldn't go to official events. My father was convinced it was just a passing phase.

You see, we were a very assimilated Jewish family, though my grandparents were still observing in the Reformed way. I have fond memories of the Passover *Seders* at my grandfather's house, but my father did not take such things seriously. I also had the usual religious instruction in school, which meant that I studied Hebrew, the Old Testament and the history of the Jews. But there was no strong feeling for it. The awareness of being Jewish came because the tennis club was restricted. I belonged to a Jewish club because there was no other way I could get to play.

During my four years in Italy I was mostly in contact with Italian families. The Jews in Italy were known to be very stingy and I avoided them. But there was no anti-Semitism. It was a little difficult, however, because Verona was an old-fashioned community. A woman who worked wasn't respected. I met a few refugees, but a girlfriend I made from Düsseldorf and I stayed mostly to ourselves.

Then an exboyfriend arrived from Cologne in 1937. He had left Germany with his parents; they were going to Brussels, where they worked with some Italians, running a factory. We met several times in Italy and eventually decided to get married in Brussels. I married him on condition that we would leave Europe. I saw the war coming and spreading and wanted to be as far away as possible. I had a visa for New Zealand and had already deposited a thousand pounds. I had done rather well at my job because I started out as a secretary and accountant and then my boss went to Africa on business and I was running the shipping company, hiring truck drivers, making arrangements at the ports. People were surprised to see how efficient I was. There were so many crooks in the shipping business; they were amazed to see how much I was on to their tricks.

In Brussels, the main problem was to persuade my husband to leave his mother. He was very attached to his family. I was also encouraging my parents to get out of Germany but my father thought he could only support himself in Germany and he had no money outside the country. His brothers who were in business with him had objected to him sending money out of Germany when it was possible, and by this time it was too late. It was not until my daughter was born in 1938 that my parents arranged to leave Germany, and this was just before the deportations began. They managed to get to Nice. We couldn't leave Brussels, however, because the French wouldn't let us through and we were afraid to cross the English Channel because of the torpedoes.

*Claude Cassirer was born in Berlin, Germany, in
1921, into an assimilated family. His grandfather
was a famous orchestral conductor; his father
worked for a democratic newspaper. The Cassirers
had been businessmen, doctors, publishers and art
importers. Claude Cassirer grew up without
knowing he was Jewish, though most of his friends
were Jews.*

My father was in the generation with great intellectual interests.
He was not one of the high intellectuals and suffered a little bit
from that fact. He was self-educated, a businessman, but very
well read. Though he had not gone to university his circle of
friends were artists and writers. He managed the advertising
department of a democratic newspaper in Berlin and was also
the advertising manager for Max Reinhardt.

My grandfather, who was also a Cassirer, was a famous conductor, the first to conduct an opera by Delius in Berlin. He
conducted the Comic Opera in Berlin and was a guest conductor
in London, a good friend of Sir Thomas Beecham, Delius, Otto
Klemperer and Arthur Rubinstein. Renoir, Degas, Cézanne,
Monet and Rodin were personal friends.

I was an only child. My mother died of the Asiatic flu when I
was three months old, so I never knew her. I lived with my
father and had a close relationship with my mother's mother,
who helped bring me up. There was always help in the house
and even though my father didn't remarry until I was thirteen
we managed quite well.

We lived in the suburbs; we had good schools, went on nice
vacations, had a rather intellectual life. German Jews at that time
wanted to get away from Jewishness, to forget their ancestors in
the ghettos of Eastern Europe. They wanted to be more German
than the Germans. I grew up without knowing I was Jewish,
with no Jewish religion, no Jewish instruction, no Jewish cultural interests. Many, if not most, of our friends were Jewish, but

the separations between people depended on economics rather than religion.

German Jews had prospered, and as in this country, they had been merchants and then industrialists. Their children, not needing to make money, went into the arts, the sciences, into literature and music. It was so for the Cassirer family. The name Cassirer means "cashier," and one of my forefathers was a cashier, a manager of the estate of some German nobleman. The family then got involved in the lumber and cellulose business, and in real estate and building. Other members of the family went into manufacturing of electric cables. Their children went into the professions. There is a famous philosopher by the name of Ernst Cassirer, and others became doctors, neurologists and publishers of scientific and art books. There were Cassirers involved in art who imported and promoted French Impressionism in Germany.

There was a certain amount of anti-Semitism; there were restrictions in universities and certain professions. Jews couldn't join the army or get any government jobs. They were not admitted to trade unions. But generally speaking, if you more or less minded your own business you could manage well and have a pleasant and agreeable life.

*Maurice Diamant was born in Heidelberg,
Germany, in 1922. His parents were Orthodox
Jews from Poland. In 1927 they moved to
Frankfurt, where they lived in a Jewish world and
had a strong sense of their identity.*

I spent the first five years of my life in Heidelberg, after which my parents moved to Frankfurt, where we lived until I was twelve. My father was a quilt-maker. He learned the trade in Budapest as a young man. My parents came from Poland and were fairly Orthodox; my mother was more so than my father. My father had a strong feeling of identity as far as

Jewishness was concerned but he was also a freethinker, a socialist politically.

Growing up in Frankfurt, if you were a Jew, you were bound to have strong feelings of identity, because your whole world was Jewish. Your friends, your teachers, everyone you associated with were Jews. You might have some real friendly neighbors who were not, but you were in a world within a world. I'm not talking about a ghetto. This was the Germany of the Weimar Republic and we were free to come and go before Hitler took over, but we definitely lived in a Jewish world and there was a strong sense of identity.

The schools were separated. I went to the Jewish school in Frankfurt and besides that had instruction in Hebrew, which I detested at the time. I had a beautiful soprano voice and was a member of the synagogue choir. It was a magnificent choir of baritones, tenors and sopranos. The services were Orthodox, not in the Eastern European sense, but in German style. But even then, whenever I had a chance, I escaped from the choir. My older brother who also sang kept an eye on me because I was constantly disappearing in the middle of the services. It was in 1932. I was ten. There were already signs of uneasiness that I couldn't understand. We would come out of school and there would be a whole bunch of kids waiting for us, throwing rocks. They would wait outside the synagogue and attack the older men . . . things like that.

Jack Goldman was born in Mannheim, Germany, in 1923. His parents were Orthodox, German-speaking Jews from Galicia. He went to the public grammar school in the morning and Jewish school in the afternoon. The family had plans to settle in Palestine, but their friends discouraged them.

My parents came from Galicia but my two sisters and I were born in Mannheim, where we also had uncles and cousins and a grandfather who lived with us. In fact my grandfather and I shared a room. My father was a traveling salesman. He worked with one of my uncles who had a wholesale dry-goods store in Wiesbaden. He traveled a lot but always came home at noon on Friday. he was never away for a holiday or *Shabbat*.

I was brought up Orthodox. It was something nice, something beautiful. It was not something I hated at the time. After dinner on Friday night the other uncles came to our apartment because grandfather was there, and the women sat on one side of the table and the men on the other side and all of us cousins were on the sofa in a dark corner listening in on the adults' talk. On *Shabbat* morning we went to services and then to a special class before lunch. We studied the weekly portion, the Torah reading, and then got into a completely unstructured discussion. It was very interesting. There was no preparation, no tests, just something we did for fun. In the afternoon the youth group met and we read stories about Palestine. We played games, sang Israeli songs and danced the *hora*. And then the afternoon service was given to the older members of the youth group and everything was led by them, and it was fun. When it started to get dark all the age groups would come together to sing and it was a very good feeling, something I liked very much. Our religious upbringing wasn't forced on us. Whatever our parents asked of us, they did too—not like today, when parents drop their children off at the synagogue and go off to play golf. We had a way of life and it was not that we didn't know any other way, but we felt comfortable. Even when we first started public school and had classes on Saturday morning, it was known that the Jewish kids didn't have to bring any pencils or books to class. We came but were excused from writing. The teachers knew it was our Sabbath and didn't ask us to do what was forbidden. We were absent on Jewish holidays and no questions were asked. There were no penalties.

There were two large places of worship in Mannheim. One was the Klaus synagogue, which was Orthodox. The other was the *Hauptsynagogue* and that was more liberal, like Conservative synagogues here. There was a community Hebrew school where all the Jewish children went to classes. We didn't have to go to the religious classes in public school because we were given credit for our afternoon classes, which went from Monday through Thursday. A religious education was mandatory in Germany. We paid church taxes and the Hebrew school system was supported by the government.

The youth groups, however, were sponsored by the synagogue. I first became involved when I was about eight. It was Zionist, of course, and my family wanted to go to Palestine. Whenever a family left Germany for Palestine we used to see them off at the railroad station and I would become so emotional, so happy for them that they were going and so frustrated because I couldn't go with them.

I was too young to go alone and in the early thirties people talked my parents out of going. "What are you going to do there?" they asked my father. "You're still making a living. This isn't going to last. Hitler will disappear. What will you do in Palestine? Work up in the Huleh swamps and get malaria? You have to think of your family." And so he was talked out of it. I remember he used to answer, "I'll be a truck driver. I'll do anything that might be needed," but we didn't go. After I was *Bar Mitzvah* and could go alone I applied to the Bezalel Art School in Jerusalem, but the stumbling block at that time was that you had to have foreign currency to be accepted and we didn't have it. Just about that time we all had to go to Jewish public school and the principal had a few student visas to permit students to go to the United States. He submitted my name but I didn't want to go. My goal and my idea always had been to go to Israel.

My parents had relatives in the United States who came there long before Hitler and my mother wrote letters to them but never got a reply. It was in the middle thirties and she wrote to them behind my father's back, hoping to get an affidavit so we could come to the United States. She was more of a realist than my father in this respect. We did get papers in 1938 but by that time my father and uncles were rounded up as Polish Jews. They came late at night. Nobody expected anything. They took them to a little village on the German-Polish border and kept them there for months. We couldn't get the visa to come to the United States because the papers were for the whole family and my father was not with us.

*Arthur Herz, son of a cattleman, was born in
Heilhaus-on-the-Rhine, Germany, in 1909. He was
sent to Westphalia to be apprenticed to a butcher
and was a soccer player on a championship team.*

My father was a cattle- and meat-man. We were middle-class
people in Germany and I went to public school and high school,
and then my father needed a butcher and said I had to become a
butcher. So he sent me away, as is usual in Germany, to Westphalia to become a kosher butcher.

We were simple Jewish people who observed the traditions
and went to synagogue. If a Jewish family in Germany was kosher it was strictly kosher, and it was only during the years when
food was scarce that we stopped being kosher, to survive.

We had Hebrew school in the public school. In Germany the
public school was run by the government and the rabbi was paid
just like the other teachers. We had Hebrew lessons every day
and got our *Bar Mitzvah* lessons in public school until the last
year, when we went for extra classes with a rabbi or cantor. We
were Jewish and German, so it was like here, where you're a Jew
obeying the flag of the United States.

I was apprenticed to a butcher in 1922 when I was fourteen;
I had a tough time but parents in Germany at that time were very
strict, and I had to stick it out for three and a half years without
any pay. And then I passed the test and got the papers. So I was
a butcher boy. Then I got paid maybe twenty marks a month for
two years. But I didn't go back to my father's business. That
didn't go so well and I became a union member in the meat
business. Then I had to go from city to city for a year as a "wan-
derer." You had to go to the town's *Obermeister,* the chief
butcher, and he gave you a job for a day or two for pay and the
butcher sent back a report to say, "This boy is good"; then you
go to the next city. You needed at least twenty-four stamps and
signatures from the head butcher of different cities showing what

you had learned and how much knowledge you had and then you could become a butcher. You received the master letter and took a test and then you were entitled to open your own butcher store. That's what I did.

There was something else I did as a young man. I was a soccer player—played professional for a little bit of money. I was quite a good player. I still have the papers. I was on a team that won the European championship nine times.

*Rene Molho was born in Salonika, Greece, in 1919.
He was educated in the French school and went to
the University of Athens. His father made and
exported wine, and the Molho family was part of
an affluent Jewish community until the Germans
came and the hunger began.*

My grandfather was a *shochet* and a teacher of *shochets*—very religious, very learned. My father made and exported wine and liquor. He had quite a successful business. I have a doctor's degree, a D.D.S. and an M.D.

I was brought up like all Jews in Salonika. We did feel we were Jews, because there was no real assimilation with the Greeks. You have to remember that the Greeks came to Salonika in 1912. My father was born a Turk and so was everybody of his generation. Jews also didn't have the same rights in the army, didn't have voting rights. We had only to choose a Jewish representative for the Chamber. We were a close-knit community, following the religious holidays. Everything closed on Yom Kippur, for instance, and nobody would think to go out to work because the other Jews would see them. The religion was really for my grandfather's generation. That's where it stopped. Observance for my parents was more for what people would say than belief.

Of course I was *Bar Mitzvah*, but everything was in Hebrew and I didn't understand very much. I wouldn't say I had a very good Jewish education. My friends were naturally all Jewish. I belonged to the Jewish Boy Scouts and the Jewish tennis club, and went to the French school with all the other rich Jewish kids. There were French, Italian, German and Greek private schools. The French was the best and the most expensive. It was a very good school because you could get the baccalaureate, the diploma that would open the door to any college you wanted anywhere in the world, without taking any examination. Ninety percent of the students were Jewish. We were all Francophiles. We were all crying when the Germans occupied Paris. We were sure the French would win. I think of French as my mother language and we had lived in Paris for a time before the war. My schooling, however, was in Athens. I went to the University of Athens and was comfortable there though my friends were all Jews. There were no restrictions but at the slightest argument with a Greek, the first words you would hear would be "dirty Jew." It was hard to be liked. I would have preferred to be a Greek than a Jew.

The Jews of Salonika were divided. There were many who were very rich, living in the best neighborhoods, and there were also the very poor, living in the ghettos subsidized by the Jewish community. The ghetto houses were practically rent-free but they were small and dingy, sometimes made of tin. They were actually the barracks left behind by the Allied troops in World War I. The Jewish community ran the orphanages and the Jewish hospital that was free for the poor. They fed the street kids and in general kept people alive . . . without being too generous. My father was very active in the Jewish community; I was not until the German occupation.

When I was growing up I wasn't sensitive to what was going on. I thought it was the natural way things were. Later when I talked with people who were not so wealthy I found out about the resentment, the real bitterness. As a student, I didn't understand. Most of us were liberal but we had to enroll in the student fascist organization to be able to take the examinations. Naturally they didn't want Jewish students, but I had a few friends and my father had enough influence to apply some pressure; we thought there should be an example of a Jew enrolling. It was 1938. Metaxes was the dictator and he had killed every leftist movement in Greece. What difference did it make? The Germans entered Greece in 1941. I remember 1942 as the year of hunger.

*Felix Magnus was born in 1900 in Holland. His
family lived in Emmen Drente, a village of about
ten to fifteen thousand people, among whom were
thirty Jewish families. His parents were Orthodox
Jews, owners of a clothing store. He was sent to
Berlin for his education. In 1932 he married the
young woman he met while going to school and
brought her back with him to his hometown.*

I grew up in a village with approximately ten to fifteen thousand
inhabitants. Nowadays it has grown into a town, but at that time
it was a village. There was a Jewish community of about thirty
families, and we had a *chazzen* and when I was a kid we had to
go to the synagogue on Friday night, on *Shabbat* morning and
when somebody wanted to make a *minyan* during the week.

We had *cheder* from four to six every day after grade school.
We did not learn too much because our teacher was lazy and not
much interested in teaching us. My parents were very Orthodox
and thought that going to synagogue, doing the prayers, putting
on the *tefillin* were very important. They put a lot of pressure on
me, which I didn't like too much.

After the time I was *Bar Mitzvah* they couldn't do very much
with me on the religious path anymore. I had a few friends and
usually we went to a café and played billiards instead of going to
the synagogue. When I was fifteen I entered the synagogue only
on Yom Kippur, to obey my mother whom I loved very much.
My father had died when I was young, maybe ten or twelve. I
don't remember the exact date. But he was not the driving
teacher in the house. The driving teacher was my mother, and
she had a tremendous job. Not only that she had a big family.
There was my oldest brother Noah, then my sister Sarah and my
brother Aaron, and then my sister Frouwein and my brother
Louis and my youngest brother Koos. Then there were my
mother's two brothers also living with us. The men went out

every weekday selling ready-to-wear things and she had to attend to the store too—and with no help whatsoever. She was always tremendously busy, and still managed to cook delicious meals every day and also help other people whenever there was an opportunity . . . a really great woman.

I was the only one of my brothers who got a better education. There was only a grade school in Emmen. To go to high school we had to take the railroad fifteen miles to Coevorden. I was the only one to do that. The others went into the store to sell things. After high school I worked for a time with my oldest brother in his store and then went to Berlin for more education. I lived with a Jewish family. There were two sons in the family and a daughter who later became my wife.

I came back from Berlin because one of my brothers died of the flu and then my brother Koos committed suicide. The number of brothers got smaller. Noah and Sarah married and moved away and I had to come home to help with the business. I was never a good businessman. It is my own fault. In my whole life I never knew what I wanted to do, but business is not what I can do. The idea of getting money which is in somebody else's pocket to put into your own pocket does not work for me. My brother Aaron and I tried to manage the two stores. I didn't do well. When I married and brought my wife to Holland she was more attentive to the new baby than to the customers, so she was no help. We decided to sell everything and move to Breda. It was 1936. We asked her parents to come stay with us because life for the Jewish people in Germany had already taken a very bad direction. They moved in with us and we formed one large family. Our house filled up with cousins and we had our own children, Ingrid, Helga and Anita. Everything went fine. We had a nice household and a big house. We loved each other and helped each other.

And then the Germans came . . .

Rachella Velt Meekcoms was born in 1928 in The Hague, the Netherlands. They were nonobservant Jews, and her first experience with traditional Judaism was in the Jewish orphanage to which she was sent after her mother died.

My father was born in Holland. His mother and father were born in Holland and his grandmother also. They go back so far they can't remember when anyone in the family was not Dutch. Probably they came from Spain in the 1490s, when Columbus went to America. I was Dutch. I never thought of myself as Jewish first.

My earliest recollection is of my mother dying. I was five. We had a cosmetic shop downtown near a big theater. All the artists came in to my papa's shop and I used to go backstage with them and all that. And I remember going to the hospital when my mother was dying. And then after she was gone we lived with an aunt for a year or so.

My father sold his business and went out as a traveling salesman on the road. When my aunt found it too difficult to raise two girls it was agreed that my sister and I would go to the Jewish orphanage until my father remarried. I remember going to the orphanage. I was eight. It was quite an experience. It was a very strict, very Orthodox home. My sister and I had had no Jewish training at all. I knew I was a Jewish girl but that was all I knew. We came from a very liberal family that was not at all observant and the orphanage was my first introduction to Orthodox Jewish life.

I loved it and so did my sister. We loved the warmth and the closeness of the people running the home. The director was a man with a long white beard and this fantastic warmth. We would have Hebrew class in his study every day and we really enjoyed it. And my father was very happy about it. He had had some Jewish upbringing. He had been *Bar Mitzvahed*, but he was the only boy in a large family of girls and his father died when he was young and he had all the responsibilities.

We were in the orphanage for four years. When my father remarried in 1939 we were upset about leaving the home. We had trouble leaving our friends in the Jewish home and went back nearly every week to visit. The director kissed us goodbye and told us to remember everything we had learned and to feel welcome to celebrate all the Jewish occasions with them.

There were not too many opportunities. The war broke out six months later. On my birthday, May 15, the Germans walked into Holland. They just walked in with their boots and their noise and we stood on the side of the street watching them come ... so many of them. I went home to my father and he looked pale and when he kissed me I felt his foreboding. He was really frightened and I could feel it. I was twelve that day. He had bought me a bicycle for my birthday. It was the first thing of my own in many years. In the orphanage everything was community property; you had a few little things of your own but everything had to be shared. That bicycle really meant so much to me.

After the Germans came there was the notice that all Jewish children had to give up their bicycles. It broke my heart to part with it.

Marika Frank Abrams was born in Debrecin, Hungary, in 1925. Her great-grandfather was one of three Jews given permission to live in Debrecin in 1860. Her father owned an elegant men's shop and was a prosperous, assimilated Jew—a Hungarian patriot who would have preferred not to be Jewish.

I was an only child. My parents were married thirteen years before I was born and I was the only girl grandchild, and was given the name of my grandmother who died when my mother was five. All this is significant because it will explain why I was spoiled so rotten. I was held very precious and surrounded by great love, care and affection, and throughout my life in my family I was made to feel that I was the most important thing in the world.

My father had a store, a very elegant men's furnishings store, and he was very proud of it. It was a very important part of his life. He and his brothers came to Debrecin when they were young men and apprentices in different artisanships. My father became a specialist in men's furnishings. His brothers were tailors. They opened shops and quickly became very prosperous. He was given my mother in marriage when he was only twenty-two. This was quite unusual because she came from another level of society. My father had not finished high school, something he felt very bad about all his life.

My mother's brothers had finished gymnasium and went to university. This made my father very uncomfortable even though he spoke Hungarian and German beautifully. He wrote poetry. He was really a very cultured man and most anxious to read and achieve. He was also the kind of man who would have preferred not to be Jewish. Jewishness was in his way. He was not observant and didn't care about the holidays. My mother, on the other hand, cared a great deal about being Jewish and wanted to keep the holidays. My grandfather, from what I hear, was a religious Jew and originally had a kosher household, but this had changed by the time I was born. They celebrated Christmas, for instance, and when I was growing up I always had a Christmas tree. This was very common; nobody questioned the custom. And two of my mother's sisters married non-Jews, and also one of her brothers and some cousins. My mother felt sad about it but it was accepted.

My mother's grandfather was one of the founders of the most beautiful synagogue in the city. Our family had many seats for life. My mother used to mention sadly that she and one of her aunts were the only two people from our family using the seats. The rest were rented. And downstairs among the men there were only my father and the aunt's husband. The rest were baptized or living out of Debrecin.

So you see we were a middle-class family, not exceptional in any way. Hungarian was the language we spoke at home. We also spoke German. When I was four or five a German girl came to the house to take care of us and to teach us German. I had four years of grade school and was able to finish eight years of gymnasium before things came to an end for us.

The grade school I went to was supported by the Jewish congregation. I had a good education with a very good teacher. She was a very intelligent woman and a hard-working teacher. She prepared me well to enter the Protestant gymnasium. It was also a teacher's school, where you could become a grade-school teacher. There were forty-five girls in my class, with five Jewish girls and two Catholics.

The Jewish girls had a religious class with a rabbi. We really treated this poor rabbi very badly. We refused to learn anything whatsoever. When I think back on it, it really breaks my heart. He was such a nice man and we made fun of him while he tried so hard to do something for us. He tried to teach us some Hebrew and something about our religion. He was a very learned man and well educated in Jewish matters. He tried to tell us that there was a language called Yiddish and a literature written in it, and we used to laugh. We couldn't believe it. We saw just a silly old man.

Yet when I went back to school after the first anti-Jewish laws were enacted in 1937, I looked around at the Jewish girls and the others and I realized we were much better educated than they were. The Jewish girls came from cultured homes with libraries. They had parents who read books and were interested in the arts and theater and the social issues of the time. The other girls came from very parochial, average middle-class Hungarian homes and had none of that cultural background. It became very obvious to me, and I decided that intellectually and emotionally I was a Jew and not like the others. I was apart. I belonged to the Jews.

I had a cloistered existence. Up to the time the Germans came into Hungary, our family lived very well, untouched by danger and the things going on around us. We were aware, but untouched. We were not political. I have a suspicion that my father was interested in politics when he was young but he became discouraged. He was completely thwarted in all his intellectual and social endeavors by the society in which he lived. He concentrated on his family and his business and nothing else. There was a Social Democratic party in Hungary and my parents always voted for the Social Democratic candidate.

My father felt himself to be a real Hungarian. When Hungary participated in the invasion of Czechoslovakia and recaptured the area that was once Hungary, my father cried for joy. There were tears of happiness that this part of Hungary, taken away in 1919, was coming back to us. So my life went on. I was a very spoiled and protected child up to the time of deportation.

Robert Spitz was born in Budapest, Hungary, in 1929. His parents were university-educated, assimilated Jews. His earliest ambition was to be a diplomat.

I was the only child in a totally assimilated family, and I could never understand why people would be against me just because I was Jewish.

My father was in the fruit export and import business and also imported coffee to Hungary from Colombia and citrus fruits to Hungary, Czechoslovakia and Austria. Consequently I spoke three languages interchangeably as a child. All of us did, because we were commuting between Prague, Vienna and Budapest.

My father had gone to two universities, to the Sorbonne in France and Bonn in Germany. My mother was also a college graduate. I went to first grade in the public school system, but a severe law was passed by the Parliament permitting only a very low percentage of the total attendance in the public school to the Jewish population. Only the Jewish kids whose father received a gold star or a Silver Cross in the First World War could go. There was some exemptions, but I was expelled.

All the Jewish teachers and professors, all the people working for the public school system lost their jobs. The Jewish community of Budapest was ordered to establish its own school system to create jobs for the educators out of work and educate the children who had no school. In the middle of the second grade I found myself in the crowded Jewish parochial school with sixty to seventy kids in a class and teachers with Ph.D.'s and master's degrees, who were totally in a strange land with elementary school kids, and we with them as well.

Going to this kind of school was an extremely harsh experience. First of all, competition was extremely tough. It was encouraged by teachers who were not trained to handle students of such a young age. One of the few incentives they had was the competition, and pushing everybody toward excellence. The requirements were quite unusual compared to American standards. For example, classes would start at eight o'clock in the morning, each class lasting fifty-five minutes. At twelve o'clock we would get ten minutes instead of five between classes so we could walk instead of run and during the ten-minute break we could eat a sandwich. There was no lunch period and classes would last until four. Those of us that wished to have a gym period, orchestra, acting or other activities did them after four on our own time. The persecution drove us to the philosophy that we had to outperform and outshine our contemporaries in the secular world. The majority of the kids knew that we had to be better or sharper to survive.

Other difficulties came from the fact that 91 percent of the Budapest Jewish community belonged to the Reform or liberal movement and 9 percent were Orthodox. The animosities between the two groups were indescribable. The liberal community held the Orthodox and Eastern Jews responsible for the majority of our problems. The Orthodox Jews insisted that our assimilation did not save us from persecution. So there was nobody who was right and nobody who was wrong. But I was raised in an environment where my friends and I wouldn't be seen with anybody who had a beard, sidelocks and the big *Chasidic* hat. My parents and their friends were prejudiced against those who refused to assimilate and held on to the traditions and influences of Eastern Europe. My mother would have nothing to do with traditional Judaism. So there were no religious affiliations in my family whatsoever. We knew we were Jewish because our ID cards had a section that said "Religion: Jewish," and we never denied that we were. But we didn't know what it meant nor did we care to know. We couldn't care less.

We were constantly accused by the more traditional members of the Budapest community of being assimilants, those that have forfeited their heritage to gain a more prominent position socially or financially. My father and his friends, however, insisted that the values of the assimilated Jewish society of the twentieth century were more enlightened and worthwhile than those of the fanatical *Chasidim* we battled with in Budapest.

In school, however, I learned Hebrew. Even today I'm strong in Hebrew, and by the time I was in the sixth grade I was very sympathetic to the Zionist cause. I honestly can tell you that Hitler made Jews out of us. Had it not been for Hitler I would have never become a Jew. You see, Zionist influence in my school became very, very strong. When you were treated like cattle and looking for a place where you hoped to be treated as a human being, Zionists had a strong hand. Of course the United States, England and all the Western democracies closed their doors to Jewish immigrants and the only land that beckoned, illegally I have to say, was Palestine. But I wasn't a real Zionist. At that time Zionism meant living in a kibbutz and that to me meant the annihilation of privacy and independent accomplishment, and I was not willing to give that up—I was glad to be recognized as an achiever in school. I wanted to be a diplomat, and I don't have to tell you what a dreamer I had to be, because nothing could be more remote than a Hungarian Jewish boy becoming a diplomat in 1939.

Eugene Weissbluth was born in Hungary in 1899 into a family of rabbis. His education began in the traditional cheder *at the age of three, but he went to secular schools as well and graduated from the University of Szeged and the graduate school at the University of Budapest before quotas excluded Jews. He became a history teacher and the principal of a high school in Miskolc. He was married at the age of thirty to a woman who was also well educated.*

My family came from Czechoslovakia one hundred and fifty years ago, from Moravia near Brno. My grandfather, my great-grandfather and my father were very educated, very famous rabbis. Among them they published maybe twenty books. It was a rich family. My father's brother owned big factories. My mother's father was a farmer owning four hundred acres. My mother had seven brothers and two sisters. Three went to Berlin to build big men's clothing factories. Another brother was in the First World War in Russia and emigrated to Brazil to work on a farm. My brother was in the coal business.

When I was three years old I went to *cheder*. Then there was elementary school with *Talmud Torah* in the afternoon. I had private lessons for high school and then went first to the University of Szeged and then to the University of Budapest. I studied literature and history and graduated in 1923. I had job offers to teach in high school, and after six, seven years I was the principal for the high school. This was a state high school in Miskolc—and I was also the secretary for the teachers' association. I published a couple of high-school textbooks and I had a very good name.

When I was thirty years old I married. My father-in-law was from Tokaj, a rich man who owned vineyards and was also in the wood business. I had a very nice wife, very highly educated in music and literature and we had five children, four boys and one girl.

I was very lucky. I was in univerity before the *numerus clausus* [quota]. I had no problems with professors. Maybe there were one, two bad people but I was always well prepared for examinations. Then when I was looking for a job there were not enough teachers for high school and the government needed Jewish people. There were only 4 percent Jews in university. Most Jews went to Italian universities to study. My certificates were excellent, maybe thanks to the yeshiva, where I trained my head. And, you know, I was interested in everything. I took lectures from Montessori in Italy. On vacation I made trips to Africa, to Egypt, to India. I was in Turkey and in Palestine.

Hungarian Jewish people were not Zionists, but I was a Zionist all the way back, years ago. I was a leader of the Zionist students, and also a soldier in the First World War. I was drafted when I was eighteen, and came out second lieutenant. I fought in Yugoslavia, Serbia and Bulgaria, against the French in Sarajevo, and I was in jail in Salonika for half a year; I had books and studied. When I came back home to Hungary there was already communism, and the bad life for the Jewish people was starting. I remember when I came to the Hungarian border the communist took off my uniform and said, "You crazy guy—you're no officer!" Officers were in trouble, so he saved me a few problems.

That was the end of the good years, I can tell you. Before the war there was a good life for the Jewish people in Hungary. They had high jobs. The attorney general was a Jewish man and his brother was in charge of the government railroads. There were Jewish colonels and generals in the army. It began in 1867 with the emancipation and the Jewish people coming out of the ghetto. But in the ghetto they had education. They had *Talmud Torah* and *yeshiva* and self-help, and when they came out they were ready to be presidents of the banks and factories. And then after all the good years it became very bad, very bad for the Jewish people.

Ora Kohn was born in 1921 in Turin, Italy, into an old Italian-Jewish family. Her relatives were intellectual, liberal, Zionist and anti-Fascist but she was obliged to join the Fascist youth association, in which membership was compulsory.

I grew up in a well-known and highly regarded Jewish family with a very deep Jewish background. They were not Orthodox but had this sense of values, a sense of tradition. My ancestors were freed from the ghetto in a town in central Italy in 1815, because of something they did for the church. I have the document hanging on the wall, if you would like to see it.

I went to school in Turin, the youngest of three children. My father, until the time of the depression, was in the leather import and export business. Later on he worked as an accountant.

I remember very little about my grandparents, but their house and household I do remember. They lived on the first floor of a very large apartment house and had a little garden. It was where they moved when they were married, where their seven children grew up. By the time I was growing up they were all getting older and some had married, but two aunts and an uncle who were single were very dear to me and had as much to do with shaping my values and personality as my direct immediate family did. The house of my grandparents was the kind of place where the doors were always open. If you happened into town and were hungry or didn't have a roof over your head you would come. If there were twelve at table there could also be enough for fifteen.

Grandchildren, cousins and aunts got together to socialize, to celebrate holidays, to discuss things that were important to them. In the days before the war when the German Jews were coming out of Germany there was constant coming and going. There was always room for more people, more ideas, and the only thing there wasn't room for was bigotry. It was a family that was extremely anti-Fascist, that was intellectual and politically very active. I had other cousins who were sent into *confine*. That is when you are sent to a small town and cannot leave the town limits. Carlo Levi, the writer, was a cousin of mine and he spent many years at the confine. All these worries and concerns were a part of my growing up, part of the shaping of my values, my outlook on life and politics and on the individual feelings of a person.

I had a really nice background and I'm sorry that my kids missed having such a family. Our sense of Jewish identity came from the family. It was not from observing holidays, because we weren't holiday-observing people. We didn't even bother with Christmas, like many Jews. We were not a celebrating family. There were no birthday parties.

The men went to services on Yom Kippur. The family got together for a family reunion on Passover. My mother went to services on Saturday and I went with her very often, but it was very boring because the women were behind a grate. My father and mother didn't work on the Sabbath but they didn't object to us kids working or riding the streetcar or going to school. I went to school on the Sabbath.

My father's family was intensely Zionist. I remember my mother being very opposed to it because she felt it was unpatriotic for an Italian, and I remember some very heated discussions. Needless to say, my mother changed her mind. The Zionism of the family was, however, strictly intellectual. There was no direct involvement with any group. I do remember seeing the little blue box for collecting coins for Palestine.

Most of my friends were not Jewish. They were the kids I went to school with, that I met at the seashore in the summertime. You became friends with whoever wanted to go hiking or swimming. Religion had nothing to do with making friends. Occasionally you might find someone who was anti-Semitic, who would act cool when they found out you were Jewish, but it was a big world. There were lots of other people.

I went to public school. In those days private schools were for the children who did not do well in public school. The big challenge was in public school. And then, of course, there were private language lessons and piano lessons. We had an English lady and a German lady. I went through five years of elementary school, five years of gymnasium and one year of high school in Turin. In 1938 we moved to Milan because my father had a chance to set up some small manufacturing outfit with someone in the family. In September of that year the government announced that no Jews could attend public school. So I had two years of high school to finish and I was kicked out. My brother, who already had his law degree and was an assistant on the law faculty at the University of Turin, was also kicked out. So that was the end of my formal education in Italy.

We had another kind of life in Milan. My mother's family there was entirely different from my father's family in Turin. They were more money-conscious, status-conscious, not intellectually and politically as active. They were more interested in making a lot of money than in defending human rights. They were manufacturing things made of by-products of cattle raising. Some were selling fertilizer. Others were in clothing manufacture and papermaking. The paper mill had been started by my maternal grandfather and his brothers. They were different from us, but very nice people.

In Milan I was mostly trying to get back into school. There was a movement to set up a Jewish school but it was not yet organized. The private schools didn't take Jews. Eventually one of my cousins who was friendly with the director of the British Institute in Milan arranged for me to go there. I remember Miss Isabel May saying she would take me in: "As long as the British flag is in this room, I will give you private lessons and you will get through school."

She did. I got through very fast. I did the five-year course in a year and a half and then went to Florence to get my Cambridge Certificate of Proficiency in English. Between that and my piano diploma from the Conservatory of Music of Turin I had some credentials. I never went to college, but the certificates I had were later accepted at Western Reserve as educational background.

Gastone Orefice was born in 1922 in Livorno, Italy. He thought of himself as a typical Livornois boy, even though he was the only Jew in his class at school.

I am Italian. I was born in Livorno. I am a Jew and my family are Jews. My mother's family is half Italian. The other part is English. My mother's mother was a granddaughter of a sister of Lord Beaconsfield, Benjamin Disraeli, Queen Victoria's prime minister. As with most Jews in Italy, the Italian part of my family comes from Spain and North Africa. They probably came at the end of the sixteenth century, when a law was passed welcoming Jews from Europe and North Africa. There are only thirty thousand Jews in all of Italy, a small minority in a population of 43 million.

The Jewish community was divided in three parts. There were a few very wealthy business people; and a larger middle-class group, well-educated, well-integrated in business or in the professions, doctors or lawyers. About three-quarters of the Jewish population was of a low class, less educated, doing small business in a shop or peddling in the original ghetto.

I was in the second class, the middle-class population. My grandfather on my mother's side was a pharmacist. My father's father had a big grain company and my father had a construction business. There were also doctors and lawyers in my family. I was a Livornois boy. It happened I was a Jew. It was just a coincidence. In every Italian community there were families that were kosher and went every Friday night to synagogue. That was not the case for me. I was quite assimilated. I used to go to synagogue for Yom Kippur, for Pesach, for Rosh Hashanah, but I was a Jew because of my family. Though we weren't strictly kosher we never cooked meat with butter and never ate pork. Maybe once or twice when I was outside and had some prosciutto I didn't feel guilty like somebody else would have. In my class I was alone as a Jew; in his class my brother was alone. Sometimes it was nice. In the hour for the religion lesson in school I was able to go out for a little walk. It was something different. I didn't know when I was young what it meant. I didn't know if I was proud or sorry.

My friends were mostly Catholic but I had the life of any boy of my age of the middle class in Livorno. My grandmother used to come down every morning at half-past seven saying her prayers. My grandfather didn't care very much and my father didn't care and my mother as well. But we were Jews. This was important to us. Our culture, our talking at home was Jewish.

Martin Berliner was born in Warsaw in 1906. He lived in the house his father had inherited from his grandfather, who had owned many estates. His father was an elected official in the Jewish community. A third of the population of Warsaw was Jewish but there were many problems with anti-Semitism. After graduating from the Jewish gymnasium, Martin Berliner went to France to study engineering.

We were living in a house in the outskirts of Warsaw, built by my grandfather. My father was born there and also his eight children. It was in the gentile neighborhood where grandfather had many estates. He owned a great deal of land and houses and my father, who was the oldest son, inherited the house where we were living. It was a one-story house with a big yard in which father had a factory producing Frambo, a carbonated soft drink like Coca-Cola. He had about a dozen people working for him. Most of the neighbors, gentiles and Jews, worked for father at one time or another. He had another place where he manufactured bricks, which did not prosper. The soft drink business was only good in summertime. He had trouble making a living in the winter.

Father was an elected official in the Jewish community. Jews brought their problems to him and he would go to the police and try to defend them or find some settlement for their problems. There were about a million and a half people in Warsaw and maybe a third of the population was Jewish. Most of the Jews were on the other side of town, the section which later became the ghetto. In spite of the large concentration of Jews there were anti-Semitic incidents in the street, usually hooligans attacking Hasidim. In the outskirts Jews used to fight back. I remember once a group of gentiles going into the Jewish section to have some fun. This meant—to beat up some Jews. The Jews, however, heard they were coming and let it be known in the market. In this market there were many workers who used to carry the meat and they were very strong. They left their work and came to the Jewish section where they gave the hooligans such a terrific beating that practically all of them had to be taken to the hospital. This stopped the fun for them and they didn't come back anymore.

It was not unusual for children to be beaten. I went to school in the center of Warsaw. It was a private, Jewish school, one of the best in the city, but I had to walk three kilometers to the tramway that went to the city. The three kilometers were through a gentile neighborhood and it was a rough trip; I was attacked every day. They knew when I was coming by and were always ready to fight. They called me and all other Jews "Beylis," for Mendel Beylis in Russia who was accused of killing gentile children to get their blood. They didn't know the meaning of it but they still called me "Beylis" and beat me as often as they could.

This didn't stop me from going to school, but I avoided telling my parents because I didn't want them to worry. They knew it wasn't easy for me from the bloodstains on my clothes when I came home. When the weather was nice I could ride a bicycle and that made it easier. In school we knew that if we wanted to go to the park to play ball we couldn't go alone. We went in a group and had a plan ready in case we were attacked. I must say we took care of ourselves very well.

In spite of all this, I, my brother, and even my parents had gentile friends and we went wherever we pleased. Warsaw at the time had very nice cabarets and my parents went to them. But anti-Semitism was part of Polish life, not only in Warsaw but in the small cities and villages. It was maybe less in the villages where the Jews could not succeed and improve themselves and they grew up with the gentiles. But the difference was always there. Most of the Jews were more educated than the gentiles, whether it was in the Polish language or in the Talmud and Jewish writings; in one way or another they got some education. In Warsaw there were many intellectuals and different clubs and organizations. There were also many groups of Zionists, including the followers of Jabotinsky.

When I finished the gymnasium I had to decide what to do next. It was hard for my parents to send me to another country but they decided that it was the only way I could get a higher education and they were ready for the sacrifice. I left for France with many other boys and decided to study engineering. The first year was in Nancy, where I had a lot of trouble with the climate and didn't know any French. Then I transferred to the engineering school in Grenoble and adjusted to it. In 1929 I got my degree in electrical engineering. I visited my parents in Poland and then found a job in the mines in northern France. I was the chief engineer for L'Entreprise de Bethune. I also became the intermediary between the Polish workers in the coal mines and their employers. There were about a hundred thousand Polish miners in France and many times when they were drunk and fighting there was a knife in someone's belly before the night was over. The judge would bring me in to translate for them so that he could handle the case.

My help with the workers turned out to be important for me. I was excused from military service for being a help to the Polish people in France and told it would be a waste for someone like me to spend time in the army.

In 1937, when the unpleasantness had started, I was doing very interesting work for the Brown Instrument Company and was even sent to Hamburg to do some special installation. The Germans wanted somebody to install the special equipment for a refinery and my French boss wanted to know what was going on there and though I didn't look forward to such a job, I was pressured into going. I was paid very well and stayed at the Kaiserhof Hotel in Hamburg. The food, wine and service were very good. I remember being annoyed because the restaurant was so fancy we had to dress in tuxedos sometimes. But it was very elegant—an agreeable way to spend four or five months.

I was picked up at five o'clock in the morning and taken on a little boat to this island where the refinery was constructed. It was one of the most important refineries in Europe, and very modern. It was my responsibility to take care of all the instruments because the refinery was going to be conducted from one tremendous room with hundreds of instruments that controlled all the valves and the whole automated process.

I did not tell the German authorities that I knew or understood German. I was strictly a Frenchman to them. On the second day I was called in by the main director of the refinery for a little talk. He spoke in French; I told him that I was Jewish, and that if there was any unpleasantness I would leave immediately. He assured me that there was no anti-Semitism, that everybody knew that I was French and if I had any problem to come to him. I don't know if I really believed him but the conversation gave me peace of mind. Meanwhile I was in a funny situation: I had a young engineer who knew French to translate for me from German and the others spoke in German, sure that I didn't understand a word, talking sometimes against me and sometimes for me. It was very amusing.

At work people were friendly and greeted each other by raising the arm in the Hitler sign. I wore my French beret so I didn't have to, but once in a while without thinking I picked up my hand also. But when I thought, I never did it.

One day an employee gave me a lift to the center of the city. We went into the brasserie for a glass of beer. He picked a place in a corner and filled his glass many times before he started to talk. He was German but he explained to me that Hitler was no good and talked against him very strongly. But he asked me that our conversation be strictly confidential. He was very scared. He talked about Hitler just as we talk about him now and I was very grateful that he explained it to me, even though later he avoided me, wanted no contact with me.

While I was in Paris a friend of mine, a chemical engineer, asked me to visit a very famous professor, Lederer, when I was in Germany. I called him and he asked me to come see him. I went to his office where the walls were lined with bookshelves, with many of the books written by him. He explained that he had been a professor in the university and had lost his job. He was a Jew who had converted but his wife was still Jewish and he had two kids who were suffering in school as Jews even though their father had changed his religion and brought them up as non-Jews. The Germans didn't want him and the Jewish organizations didn't care about him because he had converted. He was crying as he told me his story. He was sorry he had converted, sorry for himself and his children. I saw his conversion as a cowardly act but pitied him. He was intelligent, kind, good-looking, and he had made many discoveries in chemistry, especially in the field of petroleum, which was important for the Germans at the time. Regardless of his abilities, he was just kicked out of the university and didn't know what to do or how to act. He had no means to leave and they wouldn't let him leave.

At my job everything was normal. I didn't feel any special anti-Semitism against me. I could see that it was not going to be pleasant in the next few years with Hitler but I didn't feel that anybody was against me personally.

Betty Steinfeld Berry was born in 1917 in Sosnowiec, Poland. There were many synagogues in the city, but her parents belonged to the most Orthodox. Her grandfather was a rabbi as well as a businessman and a prominent leader in the community. He believed in secular education and permitted his granddaughter to attend the Jewish gymnasium. She was a good student and went on to the University of Krakow.

I came from a very religious, Orthodox family. My parents and grandparents were well known in the community. Though my grandfather was in business he was a rabbi, and known as a leader in the community. My father and mother were both in business and my sister too, when she finished her schooling. My father was a wholesaler dealing in food and salt. He also imported glass and crystal from Vienna.

I went to public school and then to the Jewish gymnasium for girls in Sosnowiec. I was very active as a Zionist in my growing-up years. It was very hard; the family was against it because we were religious, and the community was afraid because it was not permitted. We could not go to meetings in the open because we would have trouble with the government and they might close the school. We had to be very, very careful, but we did it. We organized a group and I was one of the leaders. On Saturdays we would organize the material. Everything had to be translated from German. We would meet secretly on Friday night to make the material ready for Saturday.

I had a hard time telling my family what I was doing. For a long time they didn't know. Then I had to explain that it was something I wanted to do and it was my desire and my life. My grandfather was very much against it, but in the discussions, in talking to him and explaining that we didn't do anything against the religion, he somehow gave in a little bit. Still I had to be at the table for *Kiddush* when the family came from *shul*. God forbid if I was not there on a Friday night on time!

My grandfather was very high on learning, my father too. That's why they let me go to the gymnasium even though it was not usual for Orthodox girls. It was pretty expensive, not like here. It was a private school founded by the parents of the children who went and also with the help of the Jewish community. My mother said, "If she wants to go, okay." I was a good student and that was important, especially later when I wanted to go to university.

It was a hard fight but they let me go to the University of Krakow. We had friends there and I lived with them. That was in 1934, and it was hard to get into the university. You had to have very good grades and then use a little influence, which my parents were willing to do for me. I wasn't alone. A lot of my friends, both girls and boys, were going. Some took mathematics. Some studied German. I was interested in Polish history. The troubles had already started and we had to stand in the back through all the lectures. The seats could all be empty but Jews had to stand in the last row.

Luckily I spoke good Polish. My friends and I spoke only Polish to each other, even though we spoke Yiddish at home with our families. And I didn't look Jewish so that made it a little easier. I even traveled at that time. One of our friends was studying in Vienna and my parents let me spend two weeks in Vienna in the middle thirties.

In all that time I kept my promise to my parents that I would not go to a show on Friday night, and when I was in Krakow I would take the trolley back to my parents' home every Friday, careful to get there before sundown.

*Sam Berry was born in Sendiszow, Poland, in
1910. It was a town with a hundred and seventy-
five Jewish families, and his father was "the so-
called well-off man in a town of poor people."*

I was born and raised in a small town called Sendiszow, where
there were around a hundred and fifty or a hundred and seventy-
five Jewish families. My father was the so-called well-off man in
a town of poor people. There were shoemakers, carpenters and
other working people and their kids, who helped their parents
because there were no jobs in factories, no other opportunities.

And the whole town was like one big family. We all knew
each other. It didn't matter if somebody was religious or not.
Most people were Orthodox. Some were not and the young generation was indifferent. But everyone knew the traditions. The
rabbi, his sons and his students were all friends. If someone was
not a religious believer he still went to *shul* every day, or at least
on Saturday.

My father had a wholesale liquor concession. That made him
a rich man in our poor town. Other families lived in one or two
rooms and we had five. We were five kids, three brothers, a sister
and one boy who died. We had a nice home, better furniture
than others, and the rabbi came to our house to teach the three
boys.

I also had to go to Polish school. As a matter of fact I was
better in Polish grammar than some Poles and some were very
jealous when the teacher said, "How come Sam speaks better
Polish than you?" I had a kind of gift for languages and I picked
up a few without going to school.

My father, you know, didn't wear a beard and the long coat.
He wore modern clothes. We were kosher at home and he went
to *shul* every Saturday and we went with him. He insisted that
we learn Hebrew but he wasn't religious. My mother was also
not Orthodox, but very Jewish, so something not kosher could
not be cooked or eaten in our house.

As a kid I was very close to my grandfather, and I think he liked me very much. I was interested in the stories of when he was young and he told me a lot about those years. I was very attached to him and I tried to please him any way I could, even when he was in the last years of his life. When I was a little boy I went with him to the fields in summer, harvesting and other things, and also later on, after my father died. My grandfather lived until ninety and died of old age. My father died of a stroke when he was fifty-four and I was seventeen.

My grandfather and great-grandfather grew up in Sendiszow. In my great-grandfather's time there was a reform made by the czar that gave everyone in the village twenty-four acres of land. There were only three or four families in the village then. My grandfather had this land at a time when it was very unusual for a Jew to be a landowner in our area.

I was fourteen when I finished the nine grades of school and began to help my father in his store. When he passed away the whole responsibility fell on me. My two older brothers were married and living in another town. My mother and I took over the business until she got sick and I was drafted into the Polish army. It was 1931 and I was away for two years. It was not easy to serve because you always felt you were a Jew. They let you know. The *goyim* were promoted even if they didn't know anything, and even though I could do better I never got beyond corporal. I had fights because I was a Jew. I wasn't afraid. I had the muscles to beat them up. I was a fighter.

When I came out of the army the rough time really began. The business was about gone. We were broke, bankrupt. People thought I still had money because my father was supposed to be a rich man but my brothers took and my sister took, and the rest went for taxes. There were no jobs in town.

I finally went to a friend of my father's who was in the lumber business and he took me on. I went to work for him in the forest. I would sleep in a barn and he would come once a week to pay me and the other workmen. It was my job to number all the trees, figure out how many cubic feet of lumber there were and then make out the payroll. He paid me piecework—so much a cubic foot.

When the season was over I had quite a bit of money saved. It was enough so I could rent a piece of land from an uncle of mine and set up my own lumberyard. It was only about five hundred square feet but I put a fence around it and made con-

nections with the lumber mills. There were already two lumber-
yards in the area but I was competitive, and I was able to make
a living.

It was a quiet life. There were no movies, no theater. The
only entertainments were from the Zionist organization. The Orthodox didn't like it because we went on Saturdays, Sundays and
all holidays. We sang and talked and discussed books. To go to
Palestine was a dream, only a dream.

My father went to Palestine in 1923 with the idea to buy
some land and eventually move there. But he came back, and I
remember as a young boy hearing him say to my mother, "Listen,
here I'm a businessman. You're a lady. Over there we're going
to have a piece of land and you're going to be a farmer and raise
chickens." He didn't think it was the right idea. My brother went
to Israel in 1919 when it was illegal. He was eighteen years old
and got a job as a coal stoker on a ship from Italy and then
remained in Israel for a few years. He was a follower of Jabotinsky. He became an engineer driving the train from Tel Aviv
to Haifa. From Israel he went to Australia. My mother was always complaining that she wouldn't see him again. So he came
back, got married and had two kids, and he was the first to be
destroyed.

*Stanley Bors was born in Sosnowiec, Poland, in
1912 and grew up in a secular family of Zionists
and socialists. He studied agriculture at the
University of Warsaw and hoped to settle in
Palestine.*

My father was not a religious man. He didn't go to synagogue,
didn't pray, didn't observe any holidays. He was a Zionist and a
socialist. I knew I was Jewish because I had an identity card
with my name, address and religion and when I came to grade
school I brought my birth certificate. The teacher let us know we
were Jewish.

Then there was my grandfather on my mother's side who was a religious man but not *Chasidic*. He observed the holidays and I went to the Passover *Seder* at his house, and I knew that he and my grandmother went to the synagogue. The things I found out about Judaism came from my grandparents.

Some relatives had converted and become Catholics but my friends were like me, Jews who had nothing to do with Judaism in everyday life. We knew we were Jewish, were part of the Jewish community, but if someone came to our house he would not see any signs of Jewishness.

The Jewish *Gemeinde* [community] was like the Jewish Federation in the United States. They had elected officers who were in charge of helping the poor and taking care of the cemetery and of Jewish education. My father-in-law was president of it for some time. He was a very ardent Jew, a socialist who worked for Jews, read Jewish newspapers, but had nothing to do with religion—or so it seemed to us as teenagers. We did not live in the Jewish neighborhood. Assimilated Jews and the more wealthy were mixed with gentiles in all parts of town. There was no restriction.

Free education was only in grade school. The poor people did not go to high school. We were poor but my parents made great sacrifices to send us. It cost $240 a term for the four children. My father was only a clerk in a store so he had little money for anything else but our education. In my family there was a tradition to go to college. All of my uncles went. One of my mother's sisters was a dentist and her brother was a lawyer. College was a necessity. You couldn't find a job when you graduated from high school and you didn't know what to do with yourself. You hoped the situation might change by the time you finished college and a degree would help you find a job.

One of the big differences between Jewish and gentile families was this pressure for higher education. Eighty percent of the Jews who went to high school went on to college, compared to 20 percent of the Poles. But the problem was to find a way out of Poland. There was no sense dreaming to go to the United States because it was too difficult. I remembered only one friend who left for America.

I decided to study agriculture with the idea of settling in Israel. Also I had an uncle who owned a lumber mill located on a large farm with horses and cows and vegetables growing; I would spend time there when I was a boy, and I really liked the farm life. I was able to get practical experience on a farm in southeastern Poland that belonged to the Jewish Agricultural Association. Non-Jews wouldn't hire a Jewish college boy.

I went to the University of Warsaw and lived in a home for Jewish students. There were many political parties but mainly two groups, the communists and the Zionists. The feeling was that either Poland would change or we would have to leave it. The Jewish men's dormitory was the center of political life. If I'm not mistaken, Menachem Begin was living there at one time and many other political figures from all over the world.

The campuses at that time were very difficult for Jews. The police kept order in the streets but the anti-Semites had a free hand within the university. The president of the college did not defend the Jewish students and there were too few to defend themselves. In 1938 when I was in the School of Agriculture there were only five of us in a student body of three hundred fifty.

Late in 1939 the Polish students decided to prevent Jews from coming to take the final exams. They waited for us at the entrance to the building and beat us up before we could get to the room where the examinations were given. My friend and I were trying every three months to get to the exam but the Polish students wouldn't let us in the building. Finally we smuggled ourselves in a few days before the exam and slept in the college, hidden in the basement, so we could get to the room before they saw us. It was not always so difficult, but this was 1939. Every few days they would declare "a day with Jews" and beat the few Jewish students up and throw them out of the college. In some universities the Jewish students organized self-defense groups, but we didn't have enough people. We couldn't carry guns without getting expelled. There was no sympathy from anyone. The gentile students had no contact with us. They didn't speak to us even to say, "What is the assignment for Monday?" If there were any liberal students they were too frightened to have any contact with Jews. In fact, I had second cousins who were born Catholics —their father had converted—and during all those years they pretended not to know me.

My wife, Irene, however, had another experience. Her father was an architect with his office in his apartment and gentiles came and went. Her grandmother owned a bookstore and the gentile girls working for her were her lifelong friends. Irene had gentile friends, went out with gentile boys. She went to a private college in Warsaw that was not under government control. There were Jewish teachers and many Jewish students and she felt that she was treated fairly, even by the professors who belonged to the anti-Jewish party. There were no Jew-beating days. Her earlier life in Lublin was also easier. She even went to a government school, which was very unusual for a Jewish girl. But the Polish people learned anti-Semitism early in life. They took it in with the first drop of mother's milk and afterward it was just taken for granted.

Helene Frankle was born in Kolo, Poland, in 1923. Her father owned the largest flour mill in the district, and she grew up as a protected "social butterfly."

Kolo was a small town in western Poland. My family had lived there for a very long time. My father was the owner of a very large flour mill and we were a very well-to-do family.

I had a sister who was five years older than I, and we had a governess who stayed with us for nine years. As you probably know, in Europe the classes were clearly delineated. There are those who have and those who have not, and we were of the ones who really had it made.

I went to school and had many friends, most of them Polish. The high school was privately owned, and there was a great emphasis on religion, which was Catholic. The Jews had their own religious classes but the teacher who held them was not the smartest man in town and he was terribly ridiculed. Looking back, I imagine that we didn't like those religious classes and behaved badly because we were forced to take them.

I was never in touch with a great number of kids. Elementary school was also private. A lady had a little group of kids from families with money. The Ministry of Education was in charge of all the schools and decided the curriculum, but all the high schools then were private, separating the kids who went from those who couldn't afford it.

My father came from a very religious home and was a religious man, but nobody was interested in teaching girls religion. I went to temple with my dad on some holidays but only because he didn't have a son. He was a very loving man and joked a lot about it, but it bothered him that there was no one to carry on his name and nobody to take over the business. My older sister married shortly before the war but her husband was an agricultural engineer and had no interest in running a flour mill.

My mother also came from a religious home. Her father was an Orthodox Jew who wore the long black coat and he too had a flour mill. He is the only grandfather I remember and I always felt that any positive qualities I have I probably got from him. He was a very loving man. He used to say that his grandchildren were the most beautiful and smartest in the world. He was also broad-minded; he did not force his values on us as far as I can remember.

My mother was a very interesting woman. She ran a kosher home but I was always getting two messages from her. One message was that it was very important and the other was that it was all right to look away if the maids cheat. There was a lot of cheating done with my mother's blessing—I guess she was a modern woman. The idea of "modern" in Europe had to do with not being as religious as one might have been.

She was a very beautiful woman, vain, energetic, concerned about keeping her figure. She took long walks and had a special diet. She was socially ambitious. She wanted the kind of house she felt she had a right to and also started a library in the club she belonged to. She loved to travel. My parents went to Italy, Norway, to Denmark and Austria many times. They skated and took skiing lessons. They would drop my sister and me and the governess off at a beautiful sea resort and go off for six or eight weeks at a time. Then mother would come back with pictures and stories. I think I inherited my love for traveling from her. I could pick myself up tomorrow morning and go—I would just love that. But I wonder, where did she get *her* ideas from, so many years ago? Where did it come from? Not from my grandfather. I didn't know my grandmother because she died before I was born, but it might have been her influence. I heard that she was a real lady, brought up in Switzerland, from a very fine family—a modern sort of a woman.

My mother was never sick but about three years before the war broke out she really received a terrible blow. You know, she was one of those people who would pooh-pooh any sickness, try to kid me and my sister out of our colds, because she was never sick. Then suddenly she came down with multiple sclerosis. I was ten. I can remember her telling a good friend of ours who was a physician that she had this lack of feeling in her left leg and he took a pin and pricked the sole of her foot. After that she traveled only to see doctors. There was no more walking and skiing. She played cards a lot. The ladies would come in the afternoon to play poker and bridge with her.

I was going to school, where I had my problems—mostly caused by my sister. She was very pretty and also the brilliant one in the family. In the graduation tests, which only seven out of twenty students passed, she came through with flying colors and got all the prizes. So she was the good student, and I couldn't care less. I was a social butterfly and school meant nothing to me. I was just pushed from class to class by my parents and the teachers. The problem was that there was only one high school and all the teachers remembered my sister, and every day I had to hear, "Why can't you do as well? You could if you wanted to." And of course I didn't want to, so I didn't. But I managed somehow. I did graduate when I was sixteen. My sister went to the university in Poznan, where she was very popular and had a million friends and many boyfriends. She wanted to go to medical school and my father pulled all the strings. He knew many people in high places, but it was totally impossible. She finally went to study languages and this pleased my mother, who thought a nice girl from a nice home should know languages.

In 1939 my sister left the university and got married. I was sixteen. The war broke out. I didn't go to university.

Dr. William Glicksman was born in 1905 in Czestochowa, Poland. After a traditional Jewish education he went to a gymnasium and the university. He became a history teacher in the Jewish school.

I was from a middle-class Jewish family. I call it "higher middle-class" because I divide middle-class in three parts: into low-middle, middle-middle and higher-middle. My father was a businessman, a dealer in scrap iron and metal. My mother was at home. My two sisters and my brother and I had the usual routine of life for Jewish Poland between the two world wars.

I began my education in the tradition. With *cheder*, then the modern *cheder*. After that I went to gymnasium and then to university. The Jewish schools were not for special religious education as you understand it here. The minute you were born you were in a hundred-percent Jewish atmosphere. You didn't need any school to educate you religiously. The home, the street, the social and cultural life told us who we were.

Contact between the Jewish community and the non-Jewish was mainly economic. Culturally, religiously, in language we were two different groups. Jewish children were not admitted to the Polish public schools. There was a *numerus clausus* [quota] for the university, later a *numerus nullus*. And then, as in any society, there were exceptions. You could find in my hometown Jews who were culturally assimilated. It was an assimilation which stemmed from knowledge, not like here—here when one is assimilated he doesn't know anything. I'm speaking by and large. Please don't misunderstand. We had, for example, the Polish Socialist party, the Second International. There were some Jews in the party, maybe three or four in my town. Jews were more likely to join the Bund, the Yiddish Socialist party. The Bundists and the Polish Socialists were ideologically close and worked together against discrimination. Jews could also be accepted in the Communist party but that was illegal. There was no other place for a Jew in Polish political life.

I was not a Bundist. I had respect for them as a cultural factor but politically I was opposed. I was a Zionist. I belonged to Hashomer Hatzair and believed in the kibbutz movement in Israel. That was my life while I was getting an education. You must understand, I got a good general education: I studied Latin and mathematics and history in the Jewish gymnasium. We also had about twelve hours of Hebrew a week and Bible and authors like Bialik and Ahad Ha-am and many others.

I became a teacher, teaching mathematics and history in the Jewish public school. I married. I had a child.

When the war broke out I was thirty-four years old. The schools were closed. My father's business was taken over by a Pole. It was on September 3. Warsaw fell. The Polish government broke down. The Germans occupied the city and our suffering began.

*Sally Grubman was born in 1919 in Lodz, Poland
—a city of seven hundred and fifty thousand
people, a third of whom were Jews. Her father
worked in the textile industry. Her parents were
Bundists. She and her sister were sent to a fine
Jewish school.*

I come from very good, very decent people, what you call the salt of the earth. They never had much money and had little formal education but they were intelligent and broad-minded, and my parents were determined to give me and my sister the best education available.

My mother came from a small town in Lithuania, from Mariampol. She grew up in a very Orthodox family but she herself was not Orthodox. My father was also a Bundist, not Orthodox. Religion for him was a way of life, an approved way of doing certain things . . . going to synagogue sometimes.

My father came from the town of Grodno, which once belonged to Russia. Some of his earnings went back to help his family there ever since he began to work when he was thirteen. In Lodz he was involved in textiles, like most of the men. He was successful for a time but when the economic conditions became bad he had losses. We lived from day to day. Jews did not have state jobs or city jobs. They were never on a payroll.

My sister and I were sent to an excellent Jewish private school for girls even though my parents had to sacrifice a lot to send us. The language was Polish but we also studied history and Hebrew. I had one of the best teachers. There were many Jewish schools. Some were Hebrew-speaking. Some, like mine, had Polish for the language but also taught about the Jewish heritage. Many of the schools were on a much higher level than the Polish schools.

There was a rich, full, Jewish life in Lodz. There were Jewish newspapers, two beautiful Jewish theaters where the best actors came. It was a city of three-quarters of a million people, and a third of them were Jews. There was much more Jewish culture and Jewish learning in Lodz than I have here in Canton, Ohio.

I belonged to a Zionist organization. At one point I had a boyfriend who was going to Palestine and I wanted to go with him, but my parents wouldn't hear of it. They didn't want me to go off to a strange country without them. Many of their relatives were poor and went to the United States in the early immigrations, but a kind of inertia kept my father in Poland. The family wrote and begged him to come. They sent him all kinds of papers but he kept finding excuses. At one time it was that the children were too young and then it was that the children were in school and they didn't want to interrupt our education. And then it was that maybe he's too old to change. By the time he made up his mind, it was too late. He was the only brother who did not come to the United States.

So I grew up in Lodz with parents who spoke Russian and Yiddish. I spoke Polish and felt part of Polish culture. I thought they were not sophisticated enough because they couldn't handle the Polish language, just as my children when they were younger felt about me because I didn't speak English as well as they.

We lived as a minority in a Catholic country. I was born in the same apartment house that I was forced to leave when the war broke out. I never even knew another neighborhood. It was one of those integrated areas where Jews clung together and had nothing to do with the gentiles. We never visited our gentile neighbors and they didn't visit us. The children didn't play together. I remember once there was some Easter celebration and the girl next door wanted to show me the beautiful table. She sneaked me in for a moment when no one was looking—just to look—and then I left.

I didn't play with non-Jewish children. I was afraid of them. They were so sure of themselves and always had the upper hand. They had dogs. We didn't. They trained their dogs to run after us. "Go get the Jew," they said, always scaring us.

I was not allowed to come home after dark. My parents would wait up for me, waiting to see me home safe. And I grew up with the thought that wherever we lived it would not be good.

*Simon Grubman was born in Lodz, Poland, in
1919. When he was young he thought he was a
Pole. When he learned that Jews could not be Poles
he dreamed of going to Australia, a far-off place
where he could become a textile engineer.*

I guess you'd describe my parents as traditional rather than Orthodox Jews. We went to the synagogue only on holidays. My
father worked all his adult life as a broker in the textile industry.
Lodz, as you know, was called the Polish Manchester. Buyers
came from Warsaw to buy textiles in Lodz and my father was the
one who took them to the different outlets. It was a kind of feast-
or-famine type of occupation. But without professional background or education the opportunities for Jews were limited. It
was a way to support a family.

As a youngster in Poland I thought, "I'm a Pole." I went to a
Polish school, grew up on Polish literature, and until I was able
to think for myself it didn't dawn on me that I lived in a highly
anti-Semitic country which didn't want to have Jews among
them and would do everything to make their lives difficult.

In the thirties, as I was growing older, I realized more and
more what kind of surroundings I lived in. I would ask my parents, "Why do we have to live in Poland? We're not wanted here.
We're not needed here. We're hated and oppressed." The standard reply was, "Where would we go? Nobody wants Jews anywhere." It was a very difficult thing to adjust to, but life had to
go on. When you're young you feel that life is ahead of you and
you go along and you hope that something will happen that will
enable you to break away.

I went to school mostly among Jews. It was a ghetto life
without the security of a ghetto. We lived in a mixed neighborhood on a remote street, far from the main arteries. Coming home
late at night was a pretty tricky business for a Jewish boy. You
could wind up in a dark alley with a knife in your back and the

next morning there would be a small notice on the back page of a newspaper, and the police wouldn't exert themselves too much to find the guilty party. Every day you had to outwit the non-Jewish neighbors in the apartment building where you lived. You had to know their timetable and go home on a different side of the street at a different time. At Easter time Jewish boys were not supposed to be on the street. The problem was that the anti-Semitism was not only not checked but encouraged by the government. And the biggest culprits, actually, were the priests, who inflamed the people from the pulpit on Sunday.

I had friends in Betar and they got me into it but it didn't last long. I thought getting out of Poland was the solution, but I was very naive. I didn't realize that there was hardly any country in Europe that would open its doors to Jews, or for that matter any other continent. I had a dream of going to Australia. I thought it was far, far away, far enough from Europe to make me secure. I liked the idea of a new continent, just developing, and that it was a land of sheep and wool, which would tie in with my background in textiles.

I had finished my education early. I was blessed with a good head, as they say, and skipped classes and got my degree in textile engineering just about a year or two before the war broke out. I immediately got a job with a Jewish firm in Lodz and for the moment my prospects were excellent.

If you're stuck in a place where you have no prospect of getting out, it's self-preservation to disbelieve that anything bad is going to happen to you. Otherwise how can you live? And my parents were not receptive to any suggestions about leaving the country. They said they were too old to learn new customs and languages. Bad as life was in Poland, it was a life they knew and through adversity had learned to cope with.

*Abe Morgenstern was born in Chortkov, Poland, in
1923. His father, a manager in a grain mill, was
considered a modern man because he didn't wear
a beard and a long black coat. He sent his son to
the public school run by the state and then to a
private business school, where the languages were
Ukrainian and Polish.*

Chortkov was in eastern Poland, part of the Ukraine. It was a city
of forty thousand people, maybe 25 percent Jews. My father and
mother stopped there to rest on their way from Russia to America. It was just at the time when America passed the quota system, so they got stuck there, and that's where I was born.

My grandfather was already in America. I was told that he
had been a leading citizen in the Russian town he left, a righ-
teous man who lived by the precepts and he was well off, whatever that meant in those days. I remember when he died and
was buried on Staten Island. My father said *Kaddish*.

My father was the only one of his family to stay in Europe.
He had acquaintances in Chortkov and got a job as a manager in
a grain mill and settled down. Later on in the 1930s we had a
chance to emigrate to Turkey. An uncle in California sent us
papers and money to go to Istanbul and my mother was just
raring to go. My father, however, was reluctant. He went to the
Turkish consul in Warsaw, traveling a day and night to get there,
but he came back with the word that he couldn't get the visas.
Later we found out he didn't try hard enough. He took the first
excuse because he didn't want to go. My mother and I were very
disappointed. We were looking forward to Istanbul. I was excited by the idea of living in a big city.

My mother was more open-minded and adventurous than my
father. Her father had been a big lawyer in Kiev and you had to
have a modern education for that. Her family lived in a big house
that they owned, but the house was shelled in World War I and

her parents were killed. My mother didn't know Yiddish; Russian was her language. My father, of course, knew Yiddish very well and was also learned in the Scriptures. He sometimes led the congregation in the prayers.

We were a traditional family. My father made sure to be home on time on Friday. Every Sabbath and holiday was observed. We were kosher, like 98 percent of the Jews around us. Everybody was Orthodox. Some were more modern, some less, but assimilated Jews were very rare in Chortkov. My father was considered modern because he didn't wear a beard and the big hat and the long black coat and he sent me to public school. I went to *cheder* for a couple of years, learned Yiddish and then my father took me to a modern teacher with whom I studied until I was thirteen.

We lived near the rabbi's palace in Chortkov. He was a very famous rabbi and on a Saturday you'd see the old-timers going to the *shul*. He had followers from Rumania and Hungary as well as Poland. On Rosh Hashanah and Purim people came from everywhere to the palace and the beautiful synagogue that was part of it. They were built by Italian architects two or three hundred years ago. I still remember the gold and black mahogany ceilings. The palace was destroyed but the *shul* still stands in Chortkov. The Germans used it as a stable for their horses and today it is used as a grain warehouse.

When I was a boy the Jewish population would double when the rabbi's followers came. They would stay for two or three weeks and a lot of people made a living charging them for lodging and meals, and even the gentile carriage drivers were involved, transporting the visitors from the railroad to the city.

We had an apartment at the edge of the town. My mother liked the open spaces and didn't want to live in the Jewish section. There was a little garden where she grew her flowers. We could see the river and an open field from our window. It was a mixed neighborhood. The language was Polish. I didn't run around with the kids who spoke Yiddish. I went to the public school run by the state.

I remember being happy as a child. I had a lot of friends who were not Jewish and I went to their houses and they came to mine. There was no distinction in the early grades. The separation was in the fifth, sixth, or seventh grades. I happened to keep a few friends after that but of course when the Germans came they looked the other way if they saw me.

I finished public school in 1936. It was also the year of my *Bar Mitzvah*. I was called up to the Torah at *shul* in the morning and in the afternoon the rabbi who taught me came to the house. There was no one else. That was all there was to it. My father gave the *Kiddush*, the usual schnaps and fish and herring. There were no gifts. My father gave me a pair of *tefiliin* and I was so happy with them that I kept them until the very end of my wanderings. All that I had saved was a little sack of pictures and the *tefiliin*. Two weeks before liberation they were stolen. I took such care of that sack people thought there were valuable things in it. It was valuable to me—all my memories: my pictures, my mother's, my father's, from their house and their childhood, and the grandparents. I really felt bad losing them.

I should mention that I went to a private business school after finishing public school. We wore uniforms and had the little shield on the left arm with the number of our school. The language in school was Ukrainian and also Polish. We also had German as a language to study and I learned to write and speak it quite well. But all the Jews had an accent when they spoke Polish. If you closed your eyes and listened to the best kid with the most learning in the school, you could pick him out as a Jew by his voice. The minute he opened his mouth you could tell from his pronunciation that he wasn't a Pole. Even the Jewish kids who went to gymnasium and to university would have a few words, or the letter *r* that gave them away. It was a real problem for kids who tried to take a chance and go over to the Aryan side.

Even if we wanted to be Poles, we were Jews. Those who converted and considered themselves Poles and were completely assimilated still were not accepted. We grew up knowing we had no country and wondering why everybody else has a country and we have no country. When we started to be indoctrinated with the Zionist idea we felt better. We could at least strive for something. We could hope that after some years there would be a state in Israel. Everybody's dreams were for that. People who were emigrating to Israel were so envied.

I joined the Shomer Hatzair when I was twelve. They came into the neighborhood and opened a club with games, Ping-Pong and chess. They had a good library. On weekends we went on hiking trips in the country, and they taught discipline and self-defense. When we passed the little villages the gentile kids used to throw stones at us and we learned to throw them back. I'll tell you the truth, I'm not a big fighter, but the Shomer taught me about the countryside and that came in handy, and also to look ahead and anticipate, to know when to fight and when to be passive. It was a leftist organization but when I joined I had no idea about what's left or right. I joined for the Ping-Pong and the social life. I stayed with them until they moved out of the neighborhood in 1935.

When I was in business school I joined Betar, this time out of conviction. Jabotinsky had come to our city and attracted thousands of people. He came to warn us to leave. I was too young to go to the rally but when I was old enough I knew what he advocated. He was the only one to believe in armed resistance, the only one who believed that we would have to take Palestine by force of arms—because they would never give it to us. Betar was also a social club as well as a political group. It had the nicest library and they let us play cards and meet our friends. Other organizations looked down at cardplaying but they didn't mind. They were also the only Jewish organization that took part in the parades on Polish national holidays, carrying arms. We had uniforms with nice caps and guns they borrowed somewhere for the parade. It looked impressive to see Jewish soldiers marching.

Then in 1939 the Russians came and no Zionist organizations were permitted. Betar was considered a right-wing group and if they found out that someone was a leader, they sent him to Siberia. The Russians made a pact with Hitler but outlawed Betar as a fascist organization.

I was sixteen. It was on a Friday. My mother had the big meal ready. She always made *challa* and *gefilte* fish, the chicken and the soup. It was just like every other Friday, except that the streets were full of people. There was a general mobilization, and at this time I was concerned as a Pole, a member of a Polish state.

Stephan Ross was born in Lodz in 1931. His parents were poor, religious people, fearful of rebellion and resistance.

I was born in Lodz, Poland, September 20, 1931. This was not the original date. I chose it when I was liberated from Dachau in

1945. I never knew when I was born but I did know that I was six years old in 1939 when the war broke out.

My father and my mother couldn't read and couldn't write; they didn't know when they were born and it was kind of difficult to determine when I was born. They were very religious. My father had a little butcher store but we were very poor. We had a little to eat but no money. We were eight children living in two rooms with a kitchen, and I was the youngest.

My father was a good person, concerned for his children. His major wish was to provide for his family in a very difficult time. He was a loving man. He could hug us, kiss us even though he was a European father, a bit of a tyrant, strict, rigid, traditional. When I was a little boy my mother used to say, "Don't fight. Don't shed blood. You musn't speak bad language!" Because of that teaching I became bitter—whatever happened to us was because we were taught to be this type of being. I was from the younger element that talked about rebelling and fighting back.

I used to go to Hebrew school when I was little but I didn't learn much because I was hungry most of the time. I don't know any Hebrew today. I can't even read the script. I started public school just before the war broke out. Immediately after that there was no school so I didn't learn how to read or write. It was a hectic time and when the Germans came into Lodz I really learned what it meant to be a Jew. There had been pogroms and persecutions before. There had been plenty of anti-Semitism before the war. But after the "master race" occupied us, we became subject to any abuse. It was a time when the Jews used to say that the Messiah is coming, but the Messiah didn't come.

*Dr. Emanuel Stein was born in Krakow, Poland, in
1905. His father was a Chasid, but he went to the
University of Krakow and became an assistant
professor in internal medicine. His wife, Rose
Stein, came from a wealthy, Orthodox family. She
had studied languages and music, and graduated
from the University of Krakow with a degree in
law. They were interviewed together at their
apartment in New York City. The voice in the
following excerpt is that of Dr. Stein. Some of his
wife's comments have been incorporated in this
text as well.*

I was reared and educated in Krakow, except for the three years
during the First World War when I went to school in Vienna. I
went to the gymnasium and then studied philosophy at the university. I got a Ph.D. in philosophy when I was twenty-three and
right after vacation went to medical school, which I finished in
1934. I've been practicing medicine for about forty years.

My father was a merchant who devoted most of his time to
Jewish study. He was a follower of the Belser Chasidic Court.
My mother came from an enlightened family, also Orthodox but
educated in the Polish schools. My brother and I went to the
gymnasium in spite of my father's protests, but then he died
when I was fourteen and we had to fight to survive.

We survived. My brother became a lawyer and a city council-
lor, well known and respected in Krakow. We were not Orthodox. We were both Zionists and played a role in the Zionist
movement. I met my wife because she worked as a lawyer for
my brother. We were married in 1938 just as Hitler was about to
burst upon Europe. We went to France and Corsica for our hon-
eymoon and stopped in Vienna on the way back to Poland. There
was already an atmosphere that gave me the feeling that destruction of the Jewish people was on the way. I had read Hitler's
Mein Kampf and I believed every word of it.

Some people thought the men would be leaving and property would be taken, but I knew what was in store and tried hard to get my mother to leave before it was too late. I told her I didn't want to be destroyed because of her. I was a mountain climber. I felt confident I could get away if I didn't have to worry about her and my wife. My brother was at that time at a Zionist Congress in Switzerland so he was no help to me.

Finally I convinced her, and my wife took her on the train to Lublin, where my wife's parents lived. And while they were in the railroad station the first bomb exploded. My wife's parents, her sixteen-year-old sister, a twenty-month-old niece and a governess had already gone to the estate of a friend of theirs. It was in the village of Siedliska, totally cut off from the real world. My father-in-law had packed over a hundred Persian rugs into a truck and taken them there for safekeeping. The arrival of the family at the Eichenbaum estate was described in the novel, *An Estate of Memory,* by Ilona Karmel. It was a very beautiful place but there was no radio, no television, no way of knowing what was happening outside.

I remained in Krakow. I had a good practice and I was working in a big hospital with about twelve hundred beds, and we began evacuating patients to make room for the war victims. I slept at the hospital rather than in the empty house, and I remember going out on the terrace between the two internal medicine wings. It was about four in the morning and I saw the first low-flying airplanes and bum, bum, bum, the first bombs started to fall. I thought it was a Polish plane on maneuvers or something, but when they began to bring in the wounded we knew the war had begun.

Bernard Brown was born in Viseul de Sus, Rumania, in 1918. His father dealt in lumber and owned a sawmill and a candle factory.

When I was three I started going to *cheder.* I don't remember it actually, but I was told. Before I was six I started public school.

At that time I used to get up around six in the morning to go to *cheder* and then home for breakfast at eight, and then to public school until twelve and then home for lunch and back to *cheder* till six. We used to break for a snack at six and then keep studying till nine o'clock in the evening.

Our family was very religious. When I got sick from all the work the doctor said they should take me out of school for six months. School for my parents meant public school. So I had a rest from that but kept on the schedule for *cheder*. I went back later. I went even to the gymnasium, even though my father had a lot of opposition. The city was very religious and my father's friends felt it was wrong for me to go to secular school, especially since I had to go on Saturday. I did it all, getting sick all the time. I was excused from gym and music on Saturday so that was a little help.

On Saturday mornings we Jewish kids had our *minyan* until around eight. Then we went to school and came back in time to be with our families when they came back from the synagogue and had the Sabbath meal with them. I had a brother and three sisters.

When I was fifteen I went away to a yeshiva for four years. When I came back at nineteen my father gave me a retail lumberyard to manage in the city of Timisoara. My father had a lot of property. He owned a candle factory, a big sawmill and was in the lumber business.

In 1939, two years after I took over the lumberyard, I went into the army. But in Rumania you could arrange everything, so I arranged to do my service in the city of Timisoara. After the six weeks of training I could go home, sleep and eat at home and even attend to my business while doing my hitch in the army.

By the end of 1939, however, the political situation was already very anti-Semitic. They sent me with the other Jews to a labor detachment in civilian clothes. The Germans had a settlement to give part of Rumania back to Hungary. The part where my parents lived was now Hungary and I was still in Rumania. I liquidated my business and got out of the labor detachment. In February 1940 I decided to go home to my family. I didn't have the papers so I had to go over the border at night. I went right to the sawmill to help my older brother and my brother-in-law with the business. This went on until 1941.

Then I got my conscription papers for labor in the Hungarian army. Somebody told me that the letter was in the post office so

I just ran away. My parents had already left Visuel de Su because the governor was interning all the Jews who owned businesses. My father went to a different state where the governor was a good guy. He rented a sawmill to a gentile company and conducted the business under their name. Officially he was just working there; actually he was the manager. But he could never show himself. He had a trimmed beard and the situation was very, very anti-Semitic.

A week after I ran away I got a message from my father, who said I had better come home or they would intern the whole family. So I went home and they sent me to Russia. We were in civilian clothes with a yellow arm band that showed we were Jews and we were for labor.

Lydia Brown was born in Viseul de Sus, Rumania, in 1926. Her father, an ordained rabbi, owned the local hotel and restaurant and managed the bus depot.

I was born in a province called Transylvania in a beautiful valley in the Carpathian Mountains. It was a community of about seven thousand Jews, an almost equal number of peasants and Germans. They spoke a funny twisted German, but that's how it was.

I was one of four children in an Orthodox family and we also had a grandmother living with us. My parents had a hotel, a restaurant and a bus depot to manage. My father was a leader in the community, especially in the field of education. I should mention that Jews were mostly poor in our area. There were a few families that had businesses but the rest were shoemakers and dressmakers, tailors and roofers and the main industry was lumber. The Jewish people worked mostly in the sawmills.

Ours was a very religious community. I don't think there were two families that didn't keep kosher. When the Sabbath came it was like a beautiful curtain of peace coming down upon the community. My husband likes to tell about the *mikvah*, which had a whistle. On Friday morning they blew the whistle to announce that the steam bath was ready for the men. In the evening it blew one time for the closing of the stores and the second time to say it was time to put the *cholent* in the oven and the third time to let the women know it was candle-lighting time. After that there was not an open store or tavern. Everything was at peace, and you could see the streets filling up with people going to the synagogue, and the beautifully lit homes, and you could smell the freshly cooked food, and the shoe polish, because everyone polished their shoes for *Shabbat*. Most people had only one pair of shoes.

I had seven years of grade school. As a Jewish girl I couldn't go to high school. When I was fourteen, that was in 1940, the Hungarians occupied our country. I took private lessons to learn Hungarian and also other subjects. At that time we felt that we were lucky to have the Hungarians. The Rumanian anti-Semitism was so bad we thought we would have to leave our homes and our beautiful town. There was a law that Jews were not to be allowed to live in small communities anymore.

For about a year after the Hungarians came in Jews really thought they had it a little better. Although it was already 1940 and Jews in Czechoslovakia and Poland were in concentration camps, we were not yet threatened. We ran our hotel until 1941. That was the year they took our license away. The hotel was closed for two months. The Hungarian military took it for clothing storage, leaving us about ten rooms. Then they let us take a few guests because they needed a place for people coming to the city and it had a reputation of being clean and beautiful. The buses still came to the depot. We kept the restaurant going until 1944 and accommodated as many people as we could.

At that time we were not allowed to have any non-Jewish help so my father called the family together and we agreed to organize ourselves to maintain our livelihood. Everyone took a different job. I myself loved to clean so I took over keeping everything clean. I was just about fifteen years old. My sister was in the restaurant with my mother. My grandmother was sort of the overall housekeeper and father carried the wood for the fire and the water from the well.

Those were very hard years because the anti-Semitism became more and more harsh. My father was a very religious man. He was an ordained rabbi as well as a businessman. He also spoke and read Hungarian, Rumanian, German, Yiddish and Hebrew—a learned and an interesting man. He had a beard that he never cut and on the days when he had to go out on the street to the synagogue he came running home many times with Germans chasing him. They were beating up men with beards on the street. Then we had lots of military people, officers, who slept in the hotel and many times at night when he was taking them to a room to see if it was all right they used to ask him what the price was and when he told them they would punch him with a fist instead of giving him the money. After a while he took to wearing a bandage as if he had a toothache. It hid his beard and he was less exposed to their slaps.

My sister, who was four years older, and I were threatened many times. We had an attic where we had two mattresses and blankets. Many times my father would take us up there and pull the ladder up so no one could get in to harm us. The life we had was so hard; we were always afraid. It was a very hard childhood, even in the Rumanian times. I never remember easy times.

Angela Yaron was born in 1927 in Dorohoi, Rumania, where her father was an attorney and a leader in the Jewish community.

I was born in a small town in the northern part of Rumania, close to the Russian border. There were about five thousand people in Dorohoi, and maybe ten thousand if you included the surrounding villages. The geographic location and the size had a lot to do with its fate during the war. There were also five hundred Jews in Dorohoi.

My father and mother were both born in Dorohoi; their parents had been raised there as well. My father was an attorney. He was a very prominent man in the community. He and his brother were on the board of Jewish persons conducting the affairs of the Jewish community. Uncle lived with us and was part of our family. My grandmother lived with my aunt in another town but she came to stay with us for Passover, and also my father's oldest brother who lived some distance away. The family was close.

My mother was an unbelievably kind woman. She was not educated; all she had was high school. But she had this warmth. If we passed each other on the steps or some place she would hug me, kiss me and say, "You are the most fantastic girl, Angela. There are not two like you in the whole world." And she would cover me with her wet kisses and hug me, and I could see that she really believed I was somebody very special.

My dad is a very rational and just person and very caring about his family. I won't say that he's a warm person but he was extremely concerned about our growing up as persons, not necessarily as Jews. He was not at all limited in what he would allow me and my brother to do because of his biases. Even when we were five years old he would have these discussions with us and we could see how interested he was in us as individuals. He is still like that today.

I remember our lunch discussions to this day. In Rumania it was the main meal and this was a celebration. We didn't have to wait for the holidays or Yom Kippur. Friday night dinner was no special occasion because we celebrated family life every day we could. And we could not miss the lunch together. My father would not stand for that. Every day my mother set the table in the main living room and always with the good dishes and the flowers and the best cooking. At that time, dad would drop absolutely everything he was involved in to talk with us. He did this without having to transfer from his concerns to ours. He just involved us in conversation and shared his concerns as an adult with us, on an equal level. I never felt left out because "this is not for children."

He and my uncle were very verbal and they taught us to discuss things in a civilized way without having to hit each other or without having to reject each other because we disagreed. The only time he ever gave us a beating was when we had a case where some Gypsies stole a child. It was not unusual for Gypsies to steal a child and blind him to make a beggar of him. They came to my dad to defend them in court and he took the case. I don't remember now whether it was for the parents or the Gypsies—he would have taken either one. But the Gypsies and the child were parked in front of our house, and my brother and I stuck our noses in the Gypsies' covered wagon to see what was there. Dad was so terrified that he pulled us out by the hair and beat us up. It was the only time I remember my dad giving us a spanking.

My parents grew up in the Jewish sector of town. I was born there as well. When I was two my dad became more known and had more money so he bought a big house in the non-Jewish sector. It was a very big house with maybe ten bedrooms, in the area where the affluent professional people lived. There was no imposed ghetto in the town but most Jews chose to live close together. There were only five hundred Jews in Dorohoi.

I went to the secular grade school just as my parents had gone. I did not go to any religious school. My brother had a tutor to prepare him for his *Bar Mitzvah* and I just fooled around him and his teacher. Hebrew learning in Rumania then was just prayerbook Hebrew, not the spoken language. There were no youth groups.

The Jewish community was not centered around the synagogue, as it is in America. The synagogue was just one of many institutions, something for the Jews who wanted to pray. Being Jewish in Rumania was like being Jewish in Israel. Whether you were a religious person or not was a private matter, a matter between you and your conscience. You did not throw a big show by going to the synagogue. The synagogue, however, was a community responsibility, maintained by the community board, who were in charge of the rabbi, the *shochet* who killed the animals, the cemetery and so on. The Jewish community board, where my dad was president for years, was the representative body speaking for the community in relations with the state, non-Jews or whatever. Jews paid dues to the board and it was responsible for the administration of the community as well as paying the employees.

My father, as one of the pillars of the community, had his seat by the eastern wall and we kids roamed around and played in the synagogue. We were raised to feel Jewish but never told to be good because God will punish you if you do this or that.

In our small community everybody knew who was Jewish but you didn't go around proud of it. You didn't advertise it. The feeling that we had was that if you are a Jew, you are and that's it. If you had a chance to pass, to merge with the larger population you definitely preferred that. Because the moment you tell a friend in school that you're Jewish, you are going to be mistrusted. By the time I was ten or eleven I had acquired the feeling that I would be rejected if I said I was Jewish. I did not want to be outstanding; I wanted to be accepted and to merge with the others. In the family, however, I had no identity crisis. It was a structured family. Everybody had a role to play. At home we knew what we were and who we were.

Life During The Holocaust

In places where there had always been discrimination against Jews it was hard to tell exactly when the bad times began. Hostility and violence escalated gradually. Anti-Semitic laws were passed, but not rigorously enforced at first. Orthodox Jews saw only a modern variation of older persecutions. They knew they were outsiders in the gentile world and hoped only for economic security and peaceful coexistence. Affluent, assimilated Jews in Germany and Hungary learned to live with official and social anti-Semitism while denying the realty of it. They felt themselves to be Germans and Hungarians rather than Jews and chose to believe that anti-Semitism was directed against Orthodox Jews, especially those who had come from the East and were visibly different in language and appearance.

Middle-class Jews in the process of assimilating in all the countries that Hitler occupied were caught between two worlds. Their attachment to traditional Judaism had weakened, and many imagined themselves to be secure and integrated in their communities. The terror came upon them overnight. They felt it like a bolt of lightning. Every survivor vividly remembers the private moment of awakening to the magnitude of the danger, the awareness that ordinary life in a predictable world was over.

Officially, anti-Jewish legislation began in Germany in July 1933. The mass killings in death camps were halted in April 1945. In the years between, the war against the Jews spread into every country occupied by Hitler. Harassment and expropriations became legal in Austria and Hungary in 1938, in Czechoslovakia and Poland in 1939, in The Netherlands, France and Rumania in 1940 and in Italy and Greece in 1943.

Thousands of Jews in Germany lost their jobs the day that Hitler came to power. Survivors remember when their driver's licenses were confiscated, when they were pulled off a trolley by young hoodlums while the police watched. They remember the day the Gestapo took their factories and businesses. The women who had never cooked or cleaned remember being deserted by their servants, who were forbidden to work in Jewish households. They were shocked by once-polite shopkeepers who became surly and insulting and drove them out of their stores. Ugly posters appeared overnight, caricaturing Jews as monsters who must be removed from society. The survivors who were in school during the Hitler years remember the humiliation of being expelled from school for being Jewish. Very young children knew that the word "Jew" was an insult usually followed by a blow. They expected to be attacked on the way to their classes or to the soccer field and came prepared to do battle with their gentile schoolmates, but they did not expect to be harassed and humiliated by their teachers.

The first act of resistance was flight. German Jews fled to The Netherlands, Poland, Hungary, France, Italy and Greece. Some went to England and America. About 150,000 left between January 1933 and November 1938. Another 150,000 left after *Kristallnacht*, the Gestapo-managed pogrom on November 10, 1938. They were taken in by relatives and supported by refugee relief committees organized in every Jewish community. They were the first to bring the news no one wanted to hear.

Polish, Hungarian and Czechoslovakian Jews were disoriented by their respect and affection for German culture. Their good experiences with German soldiers during World War I made it hard for them to believe the stories the German refugees told them. Jews in Italy and France took in refugees and gave them food and shelter but resented them as Germans. The politically sophisticated understood that all of Europe was vulnerable, but most people helped refugees without feeling personally threatened by what was happening in Germany.

Young Zionists and communists in Poland were better prepared than their apolitical elders. Zionist groups had for some years been training for communal life in Palestine and they increased their efforts to leave Europe. Jewish businessmen who were attached to their homes and work thought the dangers were exaggerated. They looked for non-Jewish partners to save their businesses from confiscation. The wish to believe that the horror stories about concentration camps were not true was so strong that one survivor in a labor battalion in Hungary watched the long trains carrying people off to Auschwitz without believing such a place could exist. By the time the danger was realized, it was too late to escape. "Anyone could harm us," said Zdenka Weinberg, who was trapped in Prague with her sister in 1939. "There was no place to go for justice." All decent people were on the blacklist and put themselves in danger if they tried to help Jews. In 1942 Hungarian Jews found they could no longer "arrange something." It was not possible to make a deal or pay a bribe. Doctors, professors and factory owners were sent off to slave labor camps like the rest of the Jewish population.

In the worst of times there were some good people who risked their lives to help Jews. Survivors remember even those who offered the smallest encouragement. They were always searching for the "decent human being" who would restore their lost confidence in the world at large. Every gesture of help and sympathy was hoarded like a precious souvenir. The Dutch stranger who waved to a young Jewish girl with a star on her arm band and said, "We're with you! Be brave!" is remembered forty years later. One survivor, Peter Bloch, never forgot the teacher who stopped him in the street after he had been expelled from school in Frankfurt. "I want you to know that I know how many good people there are among Jews," was what he remembered from his childhood.

Some describe the strangers and relatives who saved their lives. A city hall clerk fired with a mission to outsmart the Germans occupying the town of Breda in The Netherlands saved the Magnus family from deportation by arranging new identification cards with non-Jewish names and a hiding place for them. A priest in Krakow, Poland, urged his Jewish neighbor to hide while he looked after his family. The family was caught and destroyed, but Fred Veston hid in the mountains for six years and survived. A few survivors from Berlin were married to Christians who hid them and cared for them. Temporary safety was more often purchased with gold, silver and jewelry. A pair of diamond earrings bought tickets for a family escaping on the Trans-Siberian Express. Vodka, cigarettes or a few jars of preserves were sometimes enough to persuade a guard at the border to look away while the refugees passed over.

In the ghettos of Lodz, Warsaw, Vilna and Sosnowiec, people had few chances to escape and few offers of help from strangers. Most of their possessions were confiscated and they were controlled by food deprivation and fear. All their strength went into efforts to maintain some semblance of normal life until the siege was over. The efforts to care for the old and the young, the struggle to maintain schools and community services, the marriages and births, were acts of defiance. The passion to go on living under the most miserable of circumstances was their resistance to the programs of destruction.

While some survivors were confined in ghettos and camps others were taken from one end of Europe to the other. There were thirteen main camps and hundreds of annexes throughout Nazi-occupied Europe. Many survivors could compare the internment camps in Italy, France and Greece to those in Germany, Austria and Poland. Slave laborers were taken from Telefunken to Phillips, to I. G. Farben and other great German corporations. Simon Grubman was in five different camps. Stephan Ross spent time in eleven, including Auschwitz.

Survivors describe the years of conditioning and the physical, economic and political persecution that left them so vulnerable. They describe the Jewish leaders in the ghettos during the early stages when respected members of the communities held positions of responsibility and in the later years when the decent men had been deported or killed and replaced by marginal or criminal figures. Some were decent but passive people, civil servants concerned with law enforcement who could not comprehend that obeying the law would lead their constituents to their deaths. Survivors who worked for the Germans believe there was nothing else they could do and are convinced that they tried to help as many people as they could. Others are proud of their refusal to be in the Jewish police or leaders in the labor groups. They remember the difficulties coping with the German idea of collective responsibility. If one German was killed a hundred people might be killed to avenge him. A whole village might be wiped out. After an act of sabotage in a plant, every tenth person was killed.

Survivors are often hard on themselves but slow to judge each other. They know how difficult it is, even with hindsight, to say what actions were proper or improper, what decisions would save lives or destroy them. They are sometimes surprisingly tolerant of the errors and miscalculations of the Jewish councils. Along with the bitter comments about them, there are indulgent recollections of even the most odious of the ghetto leaders. Moses Merin, the hated leader of the Sosnowiec ghetto, is described as "a kind of playboy," the unreliable son of a good family who was incapable of managing the responsibilities he accepted—responsibilities that no experienced decent person would take on. Chaim Rumkowski, the strutting dictator of the Lodz ghetto, was remembered by Sally Grubman as the ineffectual failure he was before the German occupation: "A laughing-stock, really. A ridiculous man who took care of the orphanage and sold a little insurance to people who bought from him only because they felt sorry for him." Even though many of the ghetto leaders were killed by Jews after liberation, as collaborators, they are remembered with pity as well as disgust. No one envied them their responsibilities and pressures.

There are few accusations in the stories that follow but much agonizing about the prevailing images of millions of Jews going passively to their deaths. Survivors know of the efforts to resist in every place and they also know how difficult it was to jeopardize the lives of parents and children even if one were willing to sacrifice oneself in an act of defiance. Simon Grubman was convinced that those who could resist did, and those who couldn't, didn't. He, like other survivors, felt that those who did not go through the ordeal had no right to make accusations about Jewish behavior. The survivors think it futile to speak of "Jewish behavior" when there were so many different responses to the disintegration of normal life and such a variety of circumstances that only individual stories can suggest the range of choices and possibilities.

Survivors do not speak of resistance as something apart from survival. To be alive was to have resisted. The price of resistance was high, and the punishment different in each circumstance. Mental and physical strength for resistance was closely linked to the possibility of getting help from sympathetic people. Marta Feuchtwanger, the wife of a world-famous writer, escaped from Auschwitz in 1940. She dug her way under the barbed wire, crept on her belly through the high grass till she came out on a road, and then went looking for help for herself and her husband who was in another camp. She happened to be one of the best women athletes in Germany and had no trouble creeping across a field or climbing a mountain. Her most important asset, however, was that she had powerful friends who were concerned about her and her husband. They included President Roosevelt, the American consul, Reverend Sharp from Boston and many writers and editors. She remembers going by the long line of desperate people waiting in front of the American consulate in Marseilles. She said, "Only those who were known were saved.

97

Millions of people had to die in the gas ovens because nobody knew them and nobody cared to save them."

The survivors who managed without the help of people in high places were grateful for every crumb and gesture that helped them believe that the world had not come to an end. They remembered the gift of a needle, a shoelace, a bit of sausage. A half-starved laborer paving a street in Vienna thought his life was saved by an apple and a sandwich that fell to him from a window opened above his head. Former servants who came to the ghettos with gifts of food, friends who offered hiding places and strangers who closed their eyes to save a life are remembered as saviors.

In and out of the ghettos the first act of resistance was to refuse to obey the order to register which preceded the notices to report for deportation. The problem with not registering was that food was sold only to people with ration cards and ration cards went only to those who registered. In the large cities it was easy to hide, but difficult to find food without a ration card. In the rural areas food was plentiful but each person was known, and visible. Survivors live with the knowledge that their brothers and sisters were taken in their place when they didn't come to register.

Orthodox Jews had additional problems. They suffered the pain of breaking the laws that had structured their lives as well as the harassment and deprivations they shared with the rest of the Jews. They forced themselves to eat forbidden food, to be seen naked, to work when work was forbidden. They resisted by snatching every opportunity to follow the traditions that gave meaning to their life. To refuse bread on Passover and to fast on Yom Kippur were gestures of self-assertion, evidence that the essential human being was still there.

Though the stories told by survivors from Sobibor are not included in this collection, they must be mentioned because they described another kind of resistance. Two hundred and fifty thousand people were taken to Sobibor with all their possessions, expecting resettlement. Sobibor, however, had no industrial purpose. No records were kept. People came, undressed and were gassed. The revolt at Sobibor was organized by a former officer in the Soviet army. There were plans to cut telephone wires, to lure the German guards out and kill them. A stepladder was raised over the barbed wire and about four hundred Jews broke out, only to fall to the land mines and the bullets from the watch tower. Ten Germans and thirty-eight Ukrainians were killed and sixty Jews were left alive to tell what had happened. They remembered an orgy of violence, panic and wild stabbing as emotional young people sought revenge for all the deaths they had witnessed. They also remembered how the young people paired off. Everyone tried to find a friend or a partner to comfort them.

Survivors reveal themselves and those who were overwhelmed in the places they escaped as life-obsessed people even while they were in an environment geared for death. Their extraordinary problems were superimposed on the ordinary challenges of life. They describe their struggles with identity and maturity, the conflicts between parents and children, the loss of faith. There were battles with parents who tried to keep their families together when it would have been better to separate. Children were often angry with parents who sent them away even though their lives were saved by the separation. Mothers who brought crying children to non-Jewish families to raise, telling them, "I'm not your mother. You are not a Jew. Your name is not Yossele. This is your mother . . ." never recovered from the pain.

Histories of the Holocaust dwell on the "machinery of destruction," on the "bureaucratization of murder" and the "technological aspects of genocide." The survivors have nothing to say about the machinery of destruction. They express only astonishment at the immorality and cruelty of men and women. They keep speaking of humanity and morality as if the old order was eclipsed but not destroyed. Their wish to be good citizens in a "normal" society attests to their refusal to see the world as nothing but a slaughterhouse. They tell of "the will to survive" and their certainty that the future of the world depended upon their ability to tell what happened so it would never happen again.

Believing that liberation *would* come was a prerequisite for survival. Those who lost hope rarely lived to see it. Survivors describe their struggles to believe from the moment of deportation until their rescuers arrived. Atheists prayed for the intervention of men and the religious prayed for God's help. A survivor described finding some Russian soldiers after his escape from the Vilna ghetto: "It was like finding God or Moses. We thought they were our saviors."

In the last days of the war the passion to hold out till the end was overwhelming. To resist death was to have resisted the Germans. Every blast of Allied gunfire was a sign of hope and vindication. Meanwhile liberation came differently to each survivor. Sometimes it was preceded by false starts. "It was April 27," said one survivor. "There were about five thousand of us packed into a freight train and suddenly they say we are liberated." The Germans jumped off first and then the prisoners began pushing their way off the train and running into the fields. But suddenly there were machine guns firing at them and many were killed. It was a mistake. They were not yet liberated after all.

Those who were confined in ghettos or concentration camps remember liberation as the opening of the gates and the arrival of American or Russian soldiers. There were other images for survivors who were put on trains to unknown destinations. Prepared for the worst by past experience, some came out to emotional welcomes in Copenhagen. Sally Grubman said, "The whole population was there to see us with children on their shoulders and throwing flowers and the rabbi was singing *El Mohleh Rachamim* (God of Mercy)." Many survivors remember liberation only as the time the guards disappeared, leaving them too weak to move, without food or clothes, not even knowing what city they were in.

Liberation began as a brief explosion of joy and hope, immediately followed by a time of reckoning and rehabilitation. One by one, survivors had to pay attention to the ravages of the war years. Hospitals and displaced persons' camps were overflowing with patients suffering from wounds, severe malnutrition, tuberculosis and typhus. Those who were not hospitalized were set free in war-torn Europe, some to cope for the first time with the totality of the devastation.

Survivors holding on to life before liberation imagined they would go home and be reunited with their loved ones and return to what they remembered as normal life. When they made their way back to their villages and cities after liberation they usually found themselves to be the sole survivors of their families. Entire families were gone. Whole villages were destroyed. Where homes were left standing, they were occupied by strangers, hostile to those who returned to claim their property and possessions. Where the population believed that all Jews had been killed, the rare survivors were thought to be ghosts, spirits, not real people. "My neighbors crossed themselves when they saw me," said one survivor. "They told me they were sure I was dead."

In the displaced persons camps, survivors were sorted out according to nationality. The people from France had their French flag to reassure them. The Czechs, Spaniards and Italians displayed their flags. The cabin set aside for Jews did not fly a flag. They could not return to their old homes and had no place that would weclome them. Those who came from Poland heard conflicting messages. Representatives from the Polish government came to the rehabilitation camps to urge Jews to return to Poland. They promised an end to anti-Semitism, a hero's welcome and the best jobs, especially for those who had the technical training the country so desperately needed after the war. The men who came from the Polish consulate to visit survivors recuperating in Swedish hospitals brought other messages. They saw only Polish citizens. They would have nothing to do with Polish Jews.

Stanley Bors, who had graduated from the University of Warsaw in 1939, went back to Sosnowiec to see if it was possible to remain in Poland. He immediately found a job in the Agriculture Department and was given an apartment and a car. He and his wife were sent to Katowice in Silesia, where they lived peacefully until members of the Polish underground began killing the handful of Jews who had survived the Holocaust. As soon as the shooting began, he and wife fled to Berlin for safety.

Most survivors did not try to return to their old homes. One eighteen-year-old who went back to her village in Rumania found only two hundred people left of the town of seven thousand. There were only two older people among them; the rest were under twenty-five.

Liberation, at best, was a time of transition, a break between the heartless years and the new life that had to be created. At worst, it was the last stage of the war against the Jews. Men and women who had survived the stresses of the concentration and slave-labor camps were broken by the loss of hope that came with liberation. When they tried to explain what they had been through, they discovered that people didn't believe them. In spite of official pronouncements to the contrary, they were constantly made aware that they were unwanted people.

Ben Gurion traveled from camp to camp urging survivors to come to Palestine to fight for a country of their own. Young Zionists went to Palestine. Most survivors, however, had no strength for new dangers. They were trying to locate friends and relatives in Europe and America and wanted only to repair their personal lives.

Decisions about the future had to be made before the survivors were ready to make them. They had to choose between the Russian and American zones, and some families were divided even before they were united. Some survivors couldn't decide whether to continue as Jews if their appearance allowed them to assimilate. They found it dangerous, however, to be Jews if they were in the Russian zone. But if they claimed to be Polish and refused to go back to Poland, the Russians assumed they were fascists, afraid to return.

The years of propaganda against Jews produced ugly images that did not disappear when the war ended, even though laws were changed. In Rumania Jewish children were permitted back in the public schools on a quota system. Angela Yaron, an excellent student, described the two worst years of her life in a school where neither teachers nor students would have anything to do with her. "No one would talk to me," she said. "The teachers were afraid to relate to a Jew. The image of the Jew as a beast was too strong."

The postliberation malaise touched those who had lived with false papers in Bucharest, Limoges or Aix-les-Bains as well as those who had been in the camps and ghettos. A delayed experience with the ugliness and hatred came to Limoges after the Germans left and the dancing in the streets was over. The shooting of collaborators, the passion for vengeance instead of peace, left a strong impression on Ginette Yahiel, who had lived through the war years comfortably with her Christian mother. She was among the young survivors who had not suffered deeply during the war years and yet felt depressed and lost afterward.

Many went to Israel in the hope they might find a new life in a country where they would not feel themselves to be outcasts. In Rumania Angela Yaron found she was not given a chance to belong no matter how hard she tried. In Israel, for the first time in her life she felt it was all right to be Jewish.

To be in Israel in the early days of the state was an expression of resistance. An American woman describing her husband, who was a survivor she met in Israel, said, "Jacob's attitude was, 'The world doesn't care about Jews anymore, but I care.' It was the idea that 'I'm a Jew and I'm going to do my darnedest to be, and I don't care what you say.' You see, it was, 'I'm going to exist. We're going to exist. We won't die out to please the world.'"

A survivor from the Lodz ghetto came to Palestine in May 1946 to fight with the Seventh Brigade. He was full of determination to "show the world that we can do everything and show those who hated us that they're a bunch of liars." Behind the bravado, however, was a deep longing to find relationship, kinships. Nathan Sobel, one of forty-three orphans who came to Palestine with Youth Aliyah in 1945, said, "I was like a finger, a sole finger on two hands. I had nothing and nobody, only this drive to go to Palestine."

Many survivors tried to live in Israel and left because of health problems or because they needed more peace and security than Israel could offer after the ordeals of the war years. There were also survivors who knew they wouldn't be able to adjust to life in Israel, and they waited as long as three or four years for the chance to come to the United States.

The American Jewish Joint Distribution Committee, an international agency created by the American Jewish community to deal with refugee problems, supplied food, shelter, transportation and life-saving support for destitute survivors all over Europe. The Joint had been the most visible Jewish refugee relief organization during World War I, when millions of Eastern European Jews were caught between the invading and retreating armies on the eastern front. At that time Eastern Jews living in Germany without naturalization papers were expelled as enemy aliens and forced to make their way home without help or transportation. During World War II Joint again responded to the needs of survivors and refugees in every city where there were homeless men and women trying to find a place for themselves. It was especially helpful in verifying documents, diplomas and passports for people who had lost their papers during the years in which they had had false identity cards. In 1939 its officials in London and Paris were petitioning the governments of England, France and Belgium to admit groups of refugees who had been turned back from Cuba, and they even provided financial guarantees that the people would not become public charges. After the war most Jewish survivors who came to the United States were indebted to Joint. Other sources of help included the United Nations Relief and Rehabilitation Administration (UNRRA), the B'nai Brith Hillel's Foreign Student Service, the Workmen's Circle in Paris and London and the Scholarship Funds of the Council of Jewish Women. Many survivors found jobs in the hospital and rehabilitation centers and they describe the process of giving as well as receiving help.

Survivors had their first experiences with America through

their contacts with American government offices in Europe. They were often bitter about the treatment they received at the American consulates before the Displaced Persons Act was passed. American officials were still using the old quota system and openly displaying their lack of enthusiasm for Jewish immigration. Precious quota numbers expired unused while people languished in displaced persons camps. Families were needlessly separated while a business-as-usual attitude prevailed.

The survivors' experiences with the Russians in Europe, however, made them aware that they would be better off in America. The Russians interfered with aid to survivors while the Americans offered support. American army trucks transported people from the concentration camps to the displaced persons camps. Ordinary American soldiers and officers were remembered with great affection. "To see them," said one surivivor, "told me something about America and the American people."

The Holocaust years brought a great longing for safety and freedom to the men and women who had lived through ordeals they couldn't explain and couldn't bear to think about. Orthodox Jews longed for the right to be themselves without harassment. Assimilated and untraditional Jews looked for a place where they could think, speak and believe what they pleased. After the camps, the ghettos and the hiding, to be free meant to be free of German decrees, Russian humiliation, Polish, Hungarian and Ukrainian harassment. Freedom for survivors meant freedom from hunger, disease, violence and the physical misery and mental anguish with which they had learned to live.

Joy Levi Alkalay and her Yugoslav family fled from Vienna to Zagreb in their native land, then to Sarajevo, Split, and the island of Korčula. They eventually reached Bari, Italy, and after liberation worked helping refugees in Milan.

Austrian Jews had to wear the Star of David and that was very uncomfortable. We didn't live in the second district, which was

considered the Jewish neighborhood; we were in the fourth district. But we saw people being taken away and dragged outside
to scrub the sidewalks and all that. We didn't like to use the
trolleys because you never knew when they would round up a
street car. If we had to go someplace we just walked very
quickly. And we were always afraid they would come into our
apartment. The Yugoslav embassy gave us a certificate that was
sealed on the door to say that the apartment was under the protection of the embassy. That helped us a little but one day somebody was showing the Nazis where Jews lived and pointed us
out. They came barging in one day and went looking through our
books to see if they could find anything subversive. I was terrified.

We didn't have to leave right away because we had the Yugoslav passport. My parents were very anxious for me to complete school, which was a big mistake. I was so uncomfortable in
school that it made me dislike going to classes ever after. At the
end of the term, however, we got our things together and prepared to go back to Yugoslavia.

I still remember the pleasure of seeing the Yugoslav police at
the border. They were very nice to us and said, "Aren't you
happy to be back?" and all that. But it was all new for me. I had
never been to Yugoslavia and didn't even speak the language. I
had spoken German and Italian at home with my parents and
Ladino and Spanish with my grandmother who lived with us.

We went to Zagreb to join the family. My father still had his
business connections in Italy and it was easy for him to make the
adjustment. I immediately got a tutor to teach me the language
and then I went to high school after passing the entrance exam.
We settled into normal living until 1941, when the government
of Yugoslavia made a pact with Germany.

There were lots of Yugoslavs of German descent and there
were Croatians out of sympathy with the government in Belgrade who were pro-Hitler, so it was easy for the Germans to
come in. My father thought it would be safer in Sarajevo, where
many of our relatives lived. There was a real Jewish community
there and we had lots of aunts and cousins to be with. My aunt
had a ladies' store there that sold dresses and underwear and I
used to like to go to the store with her to play saleslady.

We had some problems getting on the train because lots of
people were leaving Zagreb and they were moving troops. It was
a very exciting time. People in Yugoslavia were very optimistic

about fighting the Germans. The troops were singing on the train. They were sure they would defeat them in a day or two and I was feeling as patriotic as all the others.

We came to Sarajevo in time for Passover and stayed at my aunt's house. On the sixth of April the Germans bombed Belgrade. Sarajevo was bombed on the twelfth. We had Passover in half darkness because of the blackout and spent half the night in the basement. Most of the people in the apartment house were Jewish. When we came out in the morning we found that many people had perished in the ruins and many had lost their homes even though they escaped unharmed. People moved in together to help each other; there were people sleeping on the living-room floor in my aunt's apartment. Everyone did the best they could.

On the thirteenth the Germans came in on their motorcycles. They stopped in front of our house. They had little Turkish boys with them. There were three religions in Yugoslavia, you know: the Catholics, the Serbo-Orthodox and the Muslims. There was a large Muslim population from the time that Sarajevo was under Turkish rule, and though the Muslims and Jews had gotten on well in my grandfather's time the Muslims were quite anti-Semitic in the Hitler time. And the Turkish boys took the Germans around and showed them where the Jews lived.

The German officer came into our apartment, counted the rooms and requisitioned one. The German officer who moved in with us was polite. He shared our bathroom and his batman came every morning to clean his shoes and get his clothes in order. Since I spoke German I used to chat with the batman. I found out he was a baker in peacetime. He was just an ordinary soldier. He wasn't too crazy about the war. He would rather have been home in his bakery. He was really afraid of being ambushed in Yugoslavia. We sensed the fear the Germans had of being in a strange place where they weren't welcome. They drove all their tanks into the cathedral in Sarajevo. They opened the big doors and just drove in and we thought it was because they believed that no one would bomb the cathedral.

They immediately began with a curfew and rationing, and then they closed the Jewish stores or put non-Jewish managers in to run them. At the beginning it wasn't so bad for my uncle. One of his employees became the manager and he continued working in his textile store but after a while they began taking men away to work. My father and uncle were brought to a mill to carry flour sacks and then to clean the barracks and latrines for German soldiers. And then my father began to worry that they would take me too.

Jews were not permitted in the railroad station so leaving was a real problem. But we succeeded in getting travel permits because my father convinced them that we were not residents of Sarajevo and that we had just come to visit the family for the holiday. His plan was to take us to Split, which was near the coast; from there we could get to Italy.

It was a very strange trip. There were lots of Jewish boys we knew on the train being taken for a work detail, and they pretended not to know us because they were afraid we might be harmed. And there was fighting between the partisans and the regular army and bullets flew over the train. When we got to the coast in the morning we found there was no boat to Split. We also heard that Italy was divided between the Germans and the Italians, and we were anxious to get to where the Italians were in charge. We finally got on an old-fashioned wood-burning bus that bumped over the rugged roads for about eight hours until we reached Split.

We went to the Jewish community center as soon as we got there and we found out where to rent a flat. I remember we had an absolutely empty flat with just some mattresses on the floor, and I spent a lot of time on the beach. There was a special section set apart for Jews. We went to the police station to get identification cards and we had to say where we came from and why we were there. We told them we were not from Split but they didn't send us away. They gave us ration cards and they were satisfied to know that we were Jews and they could find us if they wanted us.

After a few months the police came to tell us that anyone who was not a resident before a certain date had to go back where they came from. Jews were to be interned. They wanted to send us to Albania but we begged them to let us stay in Italy. A lot of Yugoslav Jews were sent to Ferramonte in southern Italy. The trouble was that Italy had a large population of refugees from Austria and Germany. They had come in 1936 and 1937 when we were living normally in Yugoslavia.

The Italian camps were humane places. The people who were interned in them were given five or ten lira a day for food and not harmed in any way. Even when Mussolini was printing anti-Jewish slogans and caricatures and plastering them up on the walls everywhere, the Italians were still letting the Jews live. After a while the police offered to send us to some primitive island if we could show we wouldn't be a burden on the population. As soon as we showed that we could take care of ourselves we were put on the boat to Korčula.

Korčula was a beautiful island, but totally unprepared for visitors. We stayed at the hotel for a week and then rented rooms in a house that was owned by a woman who was half Italian and half Yugoslav. Little by little we met many of our friends in the market where we went to buy fish. There wasn't very much to eat on the island. After the local people had bought whatever they needed the Jews and foreigners could buy whatever was left. If the fish was gone we would pick up some spinach or beans.

We were very fortunate to be there. There were about three hundred of us. We never knew from day to day what would happen to us but we actually had a very peaceful time. The island was like a fortress, with very narrow streets. It had canals like Venice and we walked on little bridges from one street to another. Of course we couldn't leave unless there was an emergency to see the doctor on the mainland. But actually there were doctors on the island to take care of us.

I was particularly lucky because I met my husband in Korčula. His parents were in Belgrade and he had come to the island with his uncle. We were married on the island in November of 1942. An official from the Jewish community in Split came to make it official, not only for us but for several other couples on the other side of the island, where there was another group of Jewish refugees. Then my grandmother's brother married us in the Jewish rite. We had a *chuppa* and the men wore *talleism*, the prayer shawls, and the whole village came to watch. My parents still have our *ketuba*. All the guests contributed some sweets and brought me a little present, and then my husband moved in with us.

My grandmother lived with us in Korčula. She was most affected by the fact that while we were living peacefully on that sunny island terrible things were happening in other places. She was always brooding over the fate of our relatives. We got many postcards that said, "They are coming for us and this is the last time I can write to you." And then for a while letters and cards came from the concentration camps, after which there was silence. My grandmother brooded over the silence. She was a very religious woman and said her morning and evening prayers, but when she became depressed she wouldn't leave her room and didn't participate in anything.

Meanwhile we were hearing rumors that the British were coming, and then that the Germans were coming. We didn't know what to believe.

One quiet summer night a man from the village came by and said, "Don't you know the Italians are leaving and the whole community is trying to get away?" We hadn't heard anything and since there was a curfew we couldn't leave the house. But we went down to the pier and there were all the Italians with their luggage waiting for the troop ship that would take them off the island. And lots of our people were trying to get away with them because of the Germans coming, but they wouldn't take us.

When we got up the next morning the island was deserted. We found a few friends and decided to go up in the mountains to hide and see what was going to happen. We stayed all day, ate the food we brought, watched for boats but saw nothing. When we came down we passed the police station and they were burning documents and preparing to leave. The small police force was getting off the island and we begged them to take us, but they said no Jews could leave. And then we realized that there were people left on the island, because we saw partisans getting ready with their rifles. We were afraid that the partisans would think we were traitors if we stayed so we just kept begging the police to take us with them. Finally we just got on the boat and they wanted to throw us off but the army officer said he was in charge and we could stay. So there we were, twenty or thirty people leaving Korčula and my parents were not with us and I didn't know what would happen to them.

We left at night and we could see the lights on shore and hear some shooting and we just sailed around until they came to shore on a promontory north of Foggia. It was a very lonesome, primitive place, nothing but a beach, a small city hall and a few houses. When we arrived the beach was full of Italian soldiers throwing their uniforms away, trying to get into civilian clothes before the Germans came.

We stayed on that beach for several days and our only problem was that there was no food to be had, even for money. There was a young woman with a little baby who was naturally worried about what to give the little one and I went with her to see the mayor because I could speak Italian and I could ask if she could just have some food for the baby. He said, "How many people are you there?" and I told him and he just gave us ration cards. Then we could go to the store and buy rice. Rice and pasta were all they had to sell.

We took our rice to the field kitchen where the soldiers were and offered to share it if they would let us cook it. And that's how we managed, sharing with the soldiers. When the Germans came through we hid in the bushes near the beach. We stayed through the night watching the planes strafe the beach and they didn't bother us. They were more concerned with themselves and had no interest in civilians.

The next morning a fishing boat arrived offering to take passengers who could pay with gold. We didn't have any money at all so we watched the people get on the boat; even some who we thought were our friends just dropped us when we needed their help. But there was an Italian man who remembered us from Korčula and offered to smuggle us on and he did, and that's how we got to Bari. We had no papers and no money but the day after we arrived the British occupied the island and came to our rescue. They opened a transit camp on the site of a former prisoner-of-war camp, and they took us in and gave us food and a temporary shelter. The Red Cross brought clothes and shoes and I agreed to remain in the camp for a while and help them out. Lots of people were arriving from all directions and they needed someone who could speak Italian and German and a little English.

All this time my parents were looking for us. They went first to Split to find a doctor because my grandmother was sick, and then back to Korčula to look for me and Joe. But all they found in Korčula were the partisans, and the partisans moved them to Valle Grande and from there to Ancona. The partisans then wanted to take them to Egypt, where there was a large community of Yugoslav refugees who had been evacuated from islands where the fighting was going on. And just then they found some soldiers from the Jewish Brigade, soldiers from Palestine wearing the Star of David. These were the soldiers who brought my parents to Bari, looking for me, so they didn't have to go to Egypt with the non-Jewish Yugoslavs.

I was working in the hospital and my husband was an interpreter for one of the British companies. It was naturally great to have the family together again and we all remained together in Bari until Milan was liberated and my parents went there to see who was left alive in my mother's family. There had been deportations to a camp near Trieste. The camp was in an abandoned salt mine and few of the older people survived.

After a few months we too went to Milan. I immediately got a job with the Joint Distribution Committee and my husband was put in charge of the warehouse that was supplying the camps and the refugee boats. There were three or four refugee camps in Milan and lots of training places for people waiting to go to Palestine. The JDC was very busy with the survivors coming out of Auschwitz, Bergen-Belsen and the other camps. Some came in by themselves via Munich and Austria. Others came in on the JDC trucks. They were picked up and taken over the borders illegally and brought into camps in Italy as refugees. The Italians didn't ask how they came, they just made camps available, and later on the JDC rented villas and large estates in the countryside. They organized them as kibbutzim or training camps for Palestine, and the rehabilitation began. Schools were set up for the children, hospitals and recuperative centers for people suffering from tuberculosis and malnutrition. They did everything they could to help the refugees recover and whenever a boat was ready they took those who wanted to go to Palestine. My husband always knew when a boat was leaving because he was in charge of providing the blankets and the food.

The Italian police were cooperative. I wouldn't say there was bribery, but arrangements were made and there were money transactions, and it was all very hush-hush. But money was given to the Jewish Agency to get people out of Austria into Italy, and so one day a camp might be empty and then suddenly it would be full, with people coming from Austria and Germany. Those who didn't want to go to Palestine were sent to a special immigration department where they tried to find relatives in the United States or get information about going to Australia.

The JDC took care of the Jewish refugees; UNRRA was in charge of the others. For the Jews of Poland, the Joint was a magic word. They knew it from before the war. And it was very important for us as well. We liked working for the people involved in it and when the time came to leave Italy it seemed natural to come to the United States. We didn't at that time think we were ready to adjust to Israel. We knew only prayer-book Hebrew and the idea of learning another language was too much. We couldn't stay in Italy. We weren't citizens and any day they might tell us we had to go back to Yugoslavia. Actually lots of people did stay and became Italian citizens, but we were grateful when the JDC immigration department got us the visas. We applied in 1949 and came to New York on the fifth of July in 1950.

Edmund Engelman escaped the stormtroopers on Kristallnacht *in Vienna. He had a visa for Bolivia and spent his last days in Vienna making a photographic record of Freud's apartment, in spite of the Gestapo guards in the street.*

Until the takeover of Austria, Jews could live relatively securely within their own culture. They were excluded from teaching but they could travel abroad. The Jewish situation in Vienna, however, changed overnight. Austria had a very strong Nazi underground, and when they found themselves in power as part of Nazi Germany they went berserk in their cruelty. They went through the streets smearing "Jew" on every enterprise, smashing windows, beating people up, arresting them, subjecting them to all kinds of indignities. They looted apartments and the police stood by and didn't do anything. Every bank account was closed. People couldn't leave the country, even with a valid passport.

We felt we had to prepare immediately for emigration, but when we went for visas they stamped every Jewish passport with a *J*, indicating that it was not valid for a return trip. All the embassies refused visas to holders of passports with the *J*. At about this time the so-called civilized nations had a meeting in Evian-les-Bains to decide how many people every country would accept, and they finally decided that nobody would take any Jewish refugees. The borders were sealed and you could not get out.

This was in 1938. Then on November 10 a desperate young Pole in France whose parents had been deported entered the German embassy and killed a minor official. His name was Greenspan. After this there was the biggest pogrom in the history of central Europe. It was the night of the flying glass, the smashed windows and the burning synagogues. I called home and my parents said the stormtroopers were already at the house looking for me.

I took a taxi to a Nazi lawyer who was specializing in such problems. His waiting room was crowded and I felt safer surrounded by so many people. Then I took a taxi to a friend who had an antique store in the inner city with an apartment on the top floor. It was not a residential section and I thought nobody would go looking for me there. The next day I went into the hospital for a hernia operation. So I had two weeks of safety in the hospital. Later on they came into the hospitals to look for people.

After that I was mostly looking for a way to get a visa. I bought one for Bolivia. Actually I bought a ticket on a boat leaving from Marseilles and this gave me the right to a transit visa through France. Actually, I didn't plan to go to Bolivia. I just wanted to get together with my fiancée who came from Lodz in Poland. Poland was still free so she could travel.

Before I left Vienna, however, I had promised to make a photographic record of Freud's apartment and offices for a museum in later years. It was a very foolish and dangerous thing to do because the apartment was under Gestapo surveillance, but I took the pictures as promised. I didn't use any flash or floodlights in order not to attract attention, so it was all done by natural light. It took four or five days and then I developed the film at night. I took over a hundred pictures and left the negatives with one of Freud's coworkers. Then I left for France.

The French were very unkind to foreigners and had absolutely no feeling for what the Jews were going through. According to French law every political refugee had the right of asylum, but when Austrian and German Jews climbed over the mountains the police would intercept them and send them back, because in order to be a political refugee, you have to be at the *commissariat spécial* and declare yourself a political refugee. So they would use this technicality to send people back.

Later on I was involved in helping people get smuggled into France. Boats would carry them at night to the shore of Nice and then they would come out at the right time and declare themselves as political refugees. I would pick people up and take them to my apartment until the office opened. Everything that was done for refugees in France was done by French Jews. The government did not move a finger.

Meanwhile I would go to the American consulate to ask about my quota number, but the quotas were all filled. By then I was married. But I found that the consul would not take a wife on the quota of her husband. So she came as a student and I had to hide the fact that we were married.

We had tickets for an Italian liner going to the United States, but the ship was converted for troops at the last minute and did not sail. Then we had tickets on the *Normandie* but that didn't come back from New York; then for the *Athenia*, which didn't have room for us, which was lucky because it was sunk. I would go from ship to ship asking if somebody would take us, but they were taking only American citizens. Meanwhile the war had broken out. Everything was blacked out and we saw a big poster at the hotel saying that everybody from Germany has to check in at the internment center. There was this tremendous fear of spies and this idea that Jews were spies.

We were saved by our American *carte d'identité* that was part of my visa. I screamed and yelled and bluffed until they let us go and so it went on and on until we took the *Conte di Savoya* which left from Genoa. My parents escaped through Russia and Japan and came out on the last ship before Pearl Harbor. My wife's parents and sister and brother-in-law all perished. The parents died in Lodz; the sister and brother-in-law died in Auschwitz.

Herman Herskovic left his family in Humenne, Czechoslovakia, in 1939. He was one of five hundred teenagers who tried to escape to Palestine on a leaky riverboat.

The Jews in Humenne felt comfortable with their non-Jewish neighbors. We were not separated by language. In my own home we spoke Hungarian because my parents had gone to Hungarian schools. We also spoke Slovak because that was the language of the public school. We studied German in Hebrew school, and naturally all the Jewish people spoke Yiddish as well. We had family living in Poland, Russia and Germany as well as Hungary and it was easy to speak all the languages, without any accent to show where you came from.

Humenne was a town of eight thousand people with five hundred Jewish families. The Jews were Orthodox and closed their stores on Saturday and went to services. You did what was expected. It was not like a large city where some people took liberties. If you did not follow the Orthodox way your kids became outcasts.

The Jews were tailors, shoemakers, small shopkeepers and also wholesalers in groceries and textiles, visible as business people in a small way in the small town. In 1939, when the bad times began, we were asked how Jews who spent so much time in synagogue and refused to work on the Sabbath could make so much money unless they were stealing. My friends sitting next to me in school said we robbed their parents. There was a depression at that time and the average people blamed the Jews for their troubles. Suddenly they noticed that Jewish kids had Sabbath suits and good shoes and they were getting a better education and becoming professionals. When Hitler marched into the Sudetenland we realized that something bad would happen to us.

From the time I was fourteen I had been attracted to a revisionist Zionist group under Jabotinsky's leadership. The rabbis, of course, were against Betar and they would go to the parents and tell them if they caught any kids going to the Betar meetings. But the young people like me realized we had no future in Czechoslovakia and we were enthusiastic about leaving for Palestine. This was not something you discussed with your parents. If you were going against your parents and the rabbis you had to do it in secret.

In 1939, in Slovakia, a group of about five hundred were getting organized to go to Palestine. By this time my father had lost his business. But even worse was that Jews couldn't walk in the street at night without getting beaten. It was all done by the youth, with the police watching and not stopping them. So it was at this time, when I was eighteen years old, that I decided to join the five hundred who were leaving. I came home and told my parents. "This is what I intend to do," I said, expecting them to argue with me. The rabbis were still trying to stop people from going. My parents, however, surprised me. "If you have the guts to go," they said, "if you really want to do this you will have our support." It was the biggest thing for me that they were willing to let me go and were even willing to pay for my passage. My brothers were both Talmudists studying in the rabbinical academy in Bratislava, so I was the only one to even think of getting away.

Five of us left from Humenne on May 15, 1940. There were twelve hours on the train to Bratislava where we would take the boat with the others. We had one-way passports, which meant we could not come back to Slovakia.

I was anxious to get to Bratislava and see the ship that was to take us to Sulina, where we were to get the big liner that would go the rest of the journey. I had envisioned a real ship and I was not prepared to find that we were going on a riverboat, a boat that carried chickens from Yugoslavia. There were no beds, only shelves, there was just enough food for five days, and naturally it smelled like a chicken boat. But it was full of enthusiastic young people from all over Slovakia and the feelings of comradeship were strong. Right away we were singing Hebrew songs and in a very good mood. Our parents had filled our rucksacks with hard cookies. We did not carry more than the basic clothes because we knew we were coming illegally and we would probably have to swim to shore at the end. We weren't expecting a welcome with a brass band.

The captain of the ship was a Russian guy. His wife was a nurse. He was a very nice guy, over six feet tall, and the crew was mostly Greek. We left Bratislava and got to Budapest, where the Hungarian immigration authorities decided they didn't like the idea of a group like ours traveling on the Danube. We showed our passports. They searched the ship for contraband. We begged and pleaded and cried for permission to continue on to Yugoslavia and, to make a long story short, they kept us in Budapest for three weeks.

We sat on the boat in a secluded place in the port. There was no electricity. The food and oil gave out. The ship was so fragile and the balance so terrible that the ship tilted if five extra people went to one side. Of course we were young and eager and saw it all as an adventure, and the Jews in Budapest were wonderful. They brought us food and oil. They sent medicine because we had some sick kids. Most important, they convinced the authorities to let us continue on to Yugoslavia.

It didn't take us long to get to the Yugoslav border once we got started, but we had the same trouble there in Dobra, a harbor town on the border, that we had in Budapest. This time we knew what to do. We contacted the Jewish community in Belgrade and they sent supplies, because there too we were kept for three weeks, and they also persuaded the authorities to let us continue. Persuasion involved money as well as words. But they finally let us continue to Rumania.

The big problem, however, was that we had been on the boat so long. We didn't have enough soap and hot water. We were washing in salt water and we were having our struggles with lice and cockroaches. And even though we were young and strong, six weeks on the smelly boat were hard to take. Just after we left Hungary we all shaved our heads; even the pretty girls couldn't stand the lice. And we were not the only ones suffering. We felt sorry for the crew because they were working for nothing. They couldn't go back either. The Jewish community in Belgrade made it possible for us to continue on the Danube to Rumania. But just as we were coming in over the Rumanian border the Rumanian coast guard stopped us on one side and the Bulgarians came to the other side to tell us they wouldn't let us through.

So there we were in a no-man's-land in the middle of the Danube. After a few days the food and oil ran out again and the captain put up a hunger flag. I've forgotten what the flag looked like, but it sent out the right message. The bishop of Varna sent us food and it was the first time I realized there were people who were not so bad as we feared. And after a while the Rumanian Jews intervened again and we were permitted to continue toward Sulina. Of course by then the ocean liner had left without us a long time ago and there was no other ship available to take us.

We had no way to go forward, no place to go back to, and the Rumanians said we absolutely couldn't stay in Rumania. We had a meeting and decided to try to get to Palestine in the chicken boat. I can show you a picture of the ship and you will see what it means to be young. No one with common sense would have agreed to go on the Black Sea in that broken-down riverboat. That we got to Constantinople was absolutely a miracle. We were shaking in a storm. Everyone was seasick. We were dirty, hungry and thirsty and looking forward to getting help from the Jews of Turkey. I remember seeing the city of Constantinople. It was a beautiful sight from the ship. The lights, the mosques, the traffic moving . . . it was very inviting, except that the Turkish coast guard wouldn't let us into the harbor.

So there we were, disappointed again. We were lucky that

our captain was a very fine navigator and knew the area very well. He remembered a Greek island called Mytilene and took the ship there. All the inhabitants came to see us. They were very poor people but they were throwing apples and pears to us. It was the first time I saw Muslim women with covered faces, but they were beautiful people and helped us immensely. The way we were treated in Constantinople had made us feel terrible. At least on the island of Mytilene we were still considered human beings.

The Jewish community of Athens brought us food and enough oil to get us to Piraeus. We couldn't get off the boat but we had water, food and light, and they gave us enough to last the three days' journey to Israel. We spent Rosh Hashanah in Piraeus and were really praying that we would be in Jerusalem by Yom Kippur.

We left Piraeus at around eleven o'clock at night. At two in the morning the captain was at our door. He said, "Young men, our boat is sinking. I want no panic. If anybody panics I will shoot him. So please be calm. As soon as the young ladies above jump into the ocean you will come up and follow them. When I say jump, you will jump." There were no life jackets, no lifeboats. We had no radio. At first we thought he was joking, but soon we could feel that something was very wrong with the boat, and before we knew it we were in the water—brother hollering for brother, sister hollering for sister, with only heaven above us and water beneath.

The captain told us to swim north, where he remembered an island, and we did the best we could to stay afloat and help each other. There was no panic because there was no time for panic. That captain was a tremendous person. He knew the ocean like the palm of his hand and all but sixty of us reached the island. There was nothing on it but stones. We tried to catch fish with our hands without much luck. When Yom Kippur came there was no problem with fasting. There was nothing to eat. And there we were, practically naked, having a Yom Kippur service. There was a young man from Bratislava who led the prayers and all the hungry boys and girls following. If ever prayers came from the heart it was those prayers from that naked, hopeless congregation.

The next day we were seen by Italian planes flying over us. An Italian submarine came to rescue us. I can still remember us hollering "Viva Italia" when we heard the voice from the submarine. They couldn't come close to the island but they picked us up in little boats. They took the girls first and then the boys who were in bad shape. When we were all on the submarine they brought us to an internment camp on the island of Rhodes. We slept on the bare ground and had only oranges, onions, tea and a slice of bread every day. But we were thankful we were alive. To this day I go back to Italy and feel a special closeness to the Italians. If not for them I would not be here today. They shared what they had and guarded us against the Germans when they came to Rhodes. We spent a year on the island. I learned to speak Italian like a native during that time and even to read some poems and history in the language. Our guards were our teachers. They found us good students.

We might have remained on Rhodes until the end of the war but the father of one of our boys was a schoolmate of the bishop from Slovakia. That father went to the bishop, who was his old friend, to see what could be done for us. The bishop begged the Pope to intervene on our behalf and the Pope arranged for the Red Cross to help us out. So one day the buses came and brought us to the port, where a Red Cross ship was waiting. There were now only 410 of us left. It was on that Red Cross ship that we had our first hot meal in years. We had a bed to sleep on and a blanket to cover ourselves with. They took us to Ferramonte, a camp with over three thousand people of every nationality and also Italians who were political prisoners.

We kept right on studying Italian. When the lieutenant felt we were too advanced for his help he found us a more sophisticated teacher. They were just tickled pink that we wanted to learn their language. There was only one problem we couldn't handle. They sent in priests to convert us. They promised us better food and clothing. They offered us allowances. But with all their offers and promises, there were no takers. We had come so far as Jews we were not about to change. Meanwhile we knew the Allies had already landed in Sicily. This was already 1943. We heard the shooting, closer and closer, and one day the commander of the camp told us that the Germans were retreating and coming toward the camp. He felt that our lives were in danger and his solution to the problem was to open the gates of the camp and tell us to run for safety into the mountains until the Germans had passed the area.

We ran to the mountains, to the small villages without roads, and the farmers were very good to us. They took us into their homes for a few days until the Germans passed through. And then we went back to the camp to wait for the American and British soldiers. They came and with them was a delegation from the Czechoslovak army in England. The majority of the young men in our group were anxious to get into the fight and those who were physically able were given uniforms and sent to England to be trained. The girls were also transferred to England and from England to Palestine. We went quite suddenly from the feeling of being fifth-grade human beings to the pride of being soldiers in uniform, from the misery of prisoners locked into a camp to the excitement of doing something to help the cause. The time of leaving with a one-way passport from Czechoslovakia was over. We were Czech citizens with Czech passports in the Czech Free Army.

We got our training in a factory town in Scotland. I was very lucky, and the luckiest bit of all was that I was transferred out of the tank corps into the intelligence service. It was my job to interrogate German prisoners. And that's what I did until the war ended and the Czech army came back and got a hero's welcome in Pilsen, and we marched in front of President Beneš in Prague with all our equipment.

This was in 1945. We had lots of opportunities for the best jobs. I went back to my hometown, hitchhiking most of the way. I found that my parents and brother had been taken away with the rest of the population. A gentile family lived in my house. I had no claim on anything. I couldn't bear to stay in Slovakia. I couldn't stomach the people and the hatred. I went to Prague to the ministry for a paper to show that I had been a soldier and was entitled to some privileges. Then I began traveling around trying to decide what to do with myself. I had just barely finished school when I left. But my last responsibility in the army was as a quartermaster, and with this experience I was able to get a job as the manager of one of the co-op stores. And then I found my brother and my sister-in-law. I was able to get a house because I was a veteran, and we all lived together.

Once we got a roof over our heads and a paycheck coming we began looking for Jewish people, and before long we found enough to establish a synagogue. But I just wasn't happy in Czechoslovakia anymore. I went to the American embassy in Prague and was told that according to the Czech quota I would have to wait fourteen years. I just wasn't prepared to hang on the yo-yo for all that time once I'd made up my mind, so I began corresponding with a friend I had made when I was in the intelligence corps, an American in Houston, Texas. He wrote and said that the only possibility for me was to come as a student. Since I had experience at a yeshiva I wrote to the Teishe Yeshiva and it wasn't long before they sent me papers inviting me to come to the Telshe rabbinical college in Cleveland.

Elizabeth Mermelstein from Viskovo was nineteen when Hitler invaded Czechoslovakia. Her father was deported, her town was turned into a ghetto, and she was sent to Auschwitz and then to Theresienstadt.

I was nineteen when Czechoslovakia fell to the Nazis. All the men were taken to the army or to labor camps. The time of steady fear began. We had never heard of concentration camps, but we heard that people were taken to Poland and never returned.

Hungary took over Czechoslovakia. Some borders were closed, others opened. We could never travel beyond the border because of the citizenship problem. But then I went to Budapest, to Rumania and part of Transylvania . . . just traveling around.

Then there was the Pesach in 1944 when the Nazis came to our town. We were holding the *Seder* and two of them came into the house and sat down at our table. We were scared to death. They just sat and watched us and then left. The next day I was walking down the street with my cousin on the way to my aunt's house and two German soldiers came toward us and began talking to us. We were too frightened to answer them, just afraid they would want us to go with them and we wouldn't be able to say no. But they went all the way to our aunt's house, and were telling us about concentration camps. They were suggesting that we escape because there was really such a thing as a concentration camp and they were actually killing the Jewish people. And we thought, "It's not true. That can't be true."

That same day they called three distinguished Jews to the police station. One was my father, the other two were my uncles.

They gave them the news that we had three days to pack and get ready for deportation. We were to take all our valuables to the neighborhood school for sakekeeping. We could take 250 kilos of belongings with us per person.

My mother filled a big laundry basket with the silver candelabras. She took off her rings and collected all her jewelry and my dad carried it all to the school and got a receipt, everything itemized neatly. He came home crying. After all, he and his father were both born in Viskovo and suddenly he didn't know where he was going or what would happen to him.

We sat around for a few days while they made plans for the so-called ghetto. My mother was busy cooking and baking the food to take with us. And then we were fortunate. The neighborhood schools were turned into the ghetto and also a few large Jewish houses, and an uncle lived in one of those houses. He was the director of a bank. Eight of us were taken into that house. We youngsters slept on the floor, but we were much more comfortable than the people in the schoolhouse. My sister was with us with her two children. We spent four weeks in that house before they gathered us all in the school. They brought more and more people into the school, making life more miserable and crowded, and people died from contagious diseases. It was a big mess.

Then one morning they gave us five minutes to dress and line up in fives in the yard. They let us take only what we could carry and took us to the station. They stripped us of everything we had and hustled us into the boxcars. I was still with my mother and sister and her two children. My father didn't make it into our car and was in the next group.

I don't know how many days we traveled. We saw we were in Poland. We saw Krakow but we didn't know where we were or where we were going. Any time they stopped the train the Germans came on to look us over. We were all wearing yellow stars, even some who wore the religious medal to show they were Catholic. If they had a Jewish grandmother they were sent along with us.

And so we ended up in Auschwitz. They unloaded us and there was the famous Dr. Mengele saying, "Left, right, left, right." And there were lots of Jewish people advising what to do. But we were totally bewildered. Mothers ran after children. Children ran after parents. I was running after my parents and Mengele said, in German, "You there, fatty—you can go to work.

You're young enough." I'll never forget that. Three times I ran to be with my parents and three times he threw me back. My sister was with me. They took her children.

I don't want to go through the details of what we had to go through . . . how they cut our hair and stripped us and what have you. We slept a great deal. We couldn't move much. There was dope in the water and the food, dope in everything.

The people from Prague were in the barrack next to ours. There were lots of children and older people and we hoped our parents and children were with them and that they were being taken care of. We didn't believe that that whole camp full of people would be exterminated after a few days. The *kapo* over us was a mean, mean woman. She would point to the cremato-rium and say, "See, that's where your parents are burning. That's where your kids are burning," and we just thought she was mean. She was Jewish but she had been there for five years and had become inhuman. The *kapos* were Slovak girls and they were put in a position of power over a thousand people, a thou-sand suffering, miserable people. Looking back, I don't know whether to condemn them or just feel sympathy for them, locked into that hell for so long.

We were just packed into the bunks over a dirt floor with the rain leaking from the roof and wired in with electric wires. All we could do was hope—hope the war is over tomorrow, hope the parachuters will come and rescue us. It was just an unex-plainable situation . . . how to survive and not run to the wire and finish it all. Nobody ran.

I was six months in Auschwitz. I escaped the gas chamber three times. They picked me and my sister after about a week or so. They told us we were going to peel potatoes in another camp and lined us up—two hundred women. But it was my luck that I understood Slovak because I heard one of the *kapos* say that there was a little girl only sixteen with us and why do they take her, and when I heard that I knew they were taking us to the end.

A group of girls passed us on the way to the kitchen and I just slipped in among them. The German was there but he didn't see. Once you got into a group nobody could tell one of us from another. We all looked hideous and the same. Heads shaved, if you were short you got a long dress, if you were tall you got a mini—you know, just to look ridiculous. Anyway, I saved myself. That was the first time. My sister also got away.

One day they picked my sister to take away and I went to the woman in charge and cried and cried and she sort of had sympathy and let my sister go. The third time my sister didn't make it. They came and picked certain people out for work. Again it was "Right, left, right, left," and I was picked for work, but not my sister. They didn't speak of gas chambers. When I was crying because my sister was not coming with me they only said she was not as strong as I was and she was going to another camp. So this was it.

Another time I was the first in line. We were just out of the shower and it was very cold, and the way we used to warm each other was to stay very close, body to body out there in the cold. I was shivering on the outside and asked if I could go between the line to warm myself and just then the leader grabbed the girl who took my place in front. They needed one more to make the six hundred for the transport to the gas chamber. It was fate. A few minutes before it would have been me.

I was sent to a camp where there was a bomb factory. It was nothing like Auschwitz. There were heated barracks with single beds. They took us into a dining room and gave us a hot meal with regular bread instead of the black piece of mud we had been getting. We had hot potatoes and a bowl and a spoon. We were treated like *menshen*.

We were given new old clothes and shoes—real shoes, not the wooden slippers from Holland—and underwear. You can't know what it meant. And I had always been chubby and now I was quite slim, and I even refused a job in the kitchen because I was afraid of getting fat again. My hair grew in pretty blonde as it once was.

Everybody in the factory was Czech and they were so good to us. They just couldn't get over how we got there. The only bad thing was they shaved a crisscross on your heads so we wouldn't be confused with the regular workers. But still, the workers were always bringing us clothes and food. They would put the stuff under a crate and tell us where to find it. It was incredible after Auschwitz, where people were fighting over a piece of bread.

We were at this place for six months, but there wasn't enough work. One day they had us move a whole lumberyard from one place to another just to keep us busy, heavy trunks of trees and things like that. And then they cut down on our food because they didn't have it to give. The two girls in the room with me were real intellectuals. They could both speak eight languages. I knew six, but they talked English and French. They were Hebrew gymnasium graduates, which I had wanted to be but couldn't. And they decided they wanted to learn Italian, and an Italian prisoner gave them dictionaries and grammar books. When they caught that poor boy they punished him severely. They put him in prison till the end of the war for talking to us and helping us.

The bombing had begun by then and there was sabotage on the night shift. Someone had left a time bomb, but unfortunately the whole shift was kept ten minutes later than usual and seventy-five people exploded with the factory.

Just before the war ended they transferred us to Theresienstadt. They behaved real nice—gave us each a loaf of bread and a whole stick of salami and a pound of butter because they didn't know how long we would be on the train. And some of the Nazi women tried to help us. They had to watch out for their superiors, but they did what they could. When I told this to the people in Theresienstadt they found it unbelievable. They didn't believe we had come from a camp with hot showers and decent food. In Theresienstadt there were so many people and just barely enough to eat.

Theresienstadt had a gate like a train ramp painted red, white and blue, the Czech colors. It was like coming home again. There was a Czech policeman in Czech uniform. It was a city for prisoners and you could walk freely wearing a Jewish star. It was heaven. Mothers found their daughters and husbands found their wives. I saw my uncle but he unfortunately died two days later. And we had nothing to do but walk around the city and see the sights. Nobody cared anymore. We were sort of free, but kept in quarantine because there were so many diseases around. The days till the end of the war were counted.

We went to Prague in an open truck after liberation. I found a cousin who had been in the Czech army; he had some clothes that belonged to the girl he was engaged to and he gave me a blue dress with a white collar and white shoes. I looked so good some people didn't think I was Jewish, what with my blonde hair and all.

Then I went to Budapest to pick up the things I had left with a neighbor. There were gold rings and diamonds, my mother's necklace and bracelet. I met another cousin who was a lawyer at the Russian embassy and he warned me that the border would be closed on September 4 and not even a bird would be able to fly over it. So I packed and took the embroidered tablecloth and some material my mother had saved for me and went back to Prague.

But then we heard again that the Russians were coming, and we fled to Germany. All of us, the whole family—brother-in-law, cousins, and all—came to the displaced persons camp in Bamberg . . . to start life all over again in a barrack with paper walls. This time I got myself a job as a street-sweeper.

Meanwhile I came to love my brother-in-law. After a year and a half we knew my sister was gone, and we were slow about making the decision because I was so worried he'd see my sister in me. But we were married in Furth, Germany, on February 11, 1947 and we registered to go to America and Israel with the idea we would go to the first place that would take us. Relatives in Detroit sent us the papers and three years later we came to this golden land.

> *Dina Leiser was born in 1927 in Paris. Her parents*
> *had come from Warsaw in 1926. Yiddish was her*
> *first language, but she wanted most of all to be*
> *accepted as a true Frenchwoman. She remembers*
> *the Germans coming in to Paris and fleeing to a*
> *village to hide.*

I was born in France but always felt like a foreigner. We never went to synagogue, never observed religious holidays, but we were Jewish. Now anyone born in France is a French citizen, but my brother and I were not citizens until my parents naturalized us in 1937.

My parents came to Paris from Warsaw in 1926, poor Jews. My father was a presser. My mother also worked in the tailor shop. We lived in one room in a residential hotel in the twentieth *arrondissement,* where there were lots of immigrants from Poland. There was a kosher butcher and a Jewish baker and they all spoke Yiddish. I did not learn to speak French until I went to school. And the French teachers are very chauvinistic and always reminded us that we were foreigners, outsiders, marginal Frenchmen.

I was very nationalistic anyway. I was very proud of Napoleon and Joan of Arc. I wanted so much to be accepted as a true Frenchman. I remember one year in school one of the teachers asked, "Who was born in Paris?" So naturally I raised my hand along with so many other children. Then she said, "How many of you have parents who were born in France?" I wasn't one of them anymore. You know?

I was called "dirty Jew" many times when I was a child, not by my own personal friends but by other children, and I felt terrible. I was in tears each time because I considered myself French. And yet at the same time I knew I was Jewish, that my parents and grandparents and all my ancestors were Jewish and I didn't want to be any different than they were. I knew that my parents had left Poland because there was a lot of anti-Semitism, and there was also a lot of anti-Semitism in France. It just was not as brutal and violent as it had been in Poland.

In 1936 when I was nine I met a young German boy. My brother and I taught him many French words. His family fled Berlin because of the German persecution. It was the first I heard of it. I remember feeling very safe and secure in France because I never thought such things could happen to us. I felt very sorry for the people who had to leave Germany and those who were still there; I hated the Germans as a Frenchman, not as a Jew. The teachers in school spoke against the Germans but never said bad things about Jews.

In 1940 my father enlisted in the French army. France didn't draft foreigners. I was feeling very bad because as soon as the war began in 1939 the teachers would ask whose father was in the army, and when I couldn't raise my hand I felt terrible. I was saying to myself, "Why in the world isn't he in the army like everybody else?" But he joined in April and by June the army fell apart and we didn't know where he was. There was no mail in those days. He came back after the fall of France, put on civilian clothes and said he was off to Brussels where he thought he could get a job. He wanted me to come with him and I wanted so much to go but my mother wouldn't hear of it. So he went by himself and it was the last time I saw him. Later we found out that he was deported in October of 1942. A friend gave us the convoy number. He was shipped to an unknown destination.

We didn't know where to go. Paris was deserted in June of 1940. School was out. Everything was closed. We had the gas masks they gave us when we were still in school. There were a few alerts and German bombers came over Paris and we ran to the shelters in the middle of the night. But no bombs fell . . . only refugees coming from the north and Parisians making their bundles and going on the road. My mother didn't want to do that. We lived in an apartment building six stories high. We were the only family left in the building. Everyone else was gone. There had been a kind of panic to leave, but my mother didn't have the initiative to say, "Let's go" without knowing where she would go.

I remember the Germans coming in. It was a beautiful day, very warm and sunny, and you could hear the roar of the motorcycles everywhere. They looked so formidable to me. They looked like they were going to conquer the world. I was standing in line in front of a store—there were only a few open and we had to wait for hours to get any kind of food—and they came roaring by.

Then the people who fled came back and school started. The only difference was that food was scarce and we had to stand on line for hours. In the spring of 1941 they took the Jewish men away and we had to register our radios, and then we couldn't go to the movies anymore, and there were the posters in the subways with people with big hooked noses, saying all kinds of violent anti-Semitic slogans.

When things got bad for the Jews I remember getting a lot of sympathy from the teachers, and all the Jewish school children had to write to Marshal Pétain to intercede on behalf of the Jews. I never felt any anti-Semitism in my class, even when we started to wear the star in May of 1942.

We had to buy three yellow stars with the word "*Juif*" in black letters to sew on our clothes. We got them at the police station. Then we had to use only the last car in the metro, and go shopping only at certain times of day, when there was nothing left anymore. My mother sent my younger brother away to the little village where we used to spend our vacations. I went to school until the day a German soldier came up to me and asked for my papers. I didn't have any papers, I was too young. But I had heard by then about concentration camps and I began to cry and Frenchmen, just passersby, formed a circle around me and one of my teachers came out and explained to the soldier that I was too young to have papers and he let me go. But I came home crying and I said to my mother, "I'm not wearing the star anymore. I'm not going back to school. And that's that!" My mother had no choice. She couldn't keep me at home alone so I took off the star and went off to join my brother in the village.

My mother didn't think of going. They had only taken men so far and we were still thinking that nothing is going to happen to women and children. It was still unbelievable to us that women and children could be put in concentration camps. We felt some sympathy from people. I remember one instance when I went out one Sunday with a Christian friend. I was wearing my star and I had another Jewish girlfriend who was wearing the star, and my Christian friend felt brave. She got between the two of us and walked with us arm in arm. It was during daylight and she felt she was defying the Germans. She thought she was accomplishing something.

It was a hard time. A lot of Frenchmen were sent to labor camps and many were prisoners of war. There were attempts on German soldiers in Paris in those days and the Germans used to take hostages left and right and kill them. Food was only obtainable on the black market. You could get anything if you had the money. We had ration cards for bread and meat because the Germans were carting everything away to Germany.

Then Gabriel Caquineau, the son of the farmer my brother and I stayed with, came to warn my mother that the Germans were rounding up all the Jews on July 16. He worked for the French police and knew what would happen. She hid with some friends the night they came and they sealed the door so she couldn't get back in the apartment. Then she had no choice. She changed her name and bought false papers on the black market. She took off the yellow star and took the train out of Paris to join me and my brother in the little village.

We stayed in the village with the Caquineau family for two years. We paid them a nominal amount and then more later after the war. I did not go to school. I used to guard the cows and knit. We had a radio and we used to listen to the BBC every night. That's where I started to read the Old Testament on my own and learned what it means to be a Jew. My mother helped Madame Caquineau. We all helped a little on the small farm. There were four cows, chickens, rabbits and a pig. We ate together like a family. We called Madame Caquineau *"grandmère"*; she and her husband were the only grandparents we knew. My mother's parents and my father's all died in the Warsaw ghetto. And we were protected by good Catholic grandparents, peasant people without education. They knew we were Jews and let it go at that. They never questioned us about what we did or didn't do. It didn't make any difference. They loved us as if we were their own grandchildren.

We were the only refugees in the village of two or three hundred people. Everybody knew we were there and there was no question that anyone would go to the police or Gestapo to denounce us.

Rose Rosenthal was eleven years old when her father was smuggled across the border to Vichy France. Later the family followed, joining him in Aix-les-Bains, where a small colony of Jews were hiding. Some were caught and sent to Auschwitz. The Rosenthals were more fortunate and received their affidavit from relatives in New York just in time.

When the war broke out we heard that the Germans were coming through Belgium, and we heard about Dunkirk. The French were saying, "Look how cowardly the British are; they're deserting us. The British don't know how to fight." As we heard they were coming closer, my parents closed the store and took as many belongings as they could in the car and we left Paris to go southwest. There were thousands of people on the road, some with horses and some with carts. There were cars and people walking, and while we were in the car there were planes strafing everybody. And I remember sleeping in the fields at night, and finally coming to a beach resort on the Atlantic at Pouligain. And when we got there the Germans were there before us.

It was a nice little town, a beach resort, and so my parents thought that since the Germans were already there and the store was closed, we might as well take a vacation. Paris had been taken. Everything was taken. So we stayed for about a month and went swimming and fishing with the soldiers all around us with their tents and their trucks and their motorcycles. And we kids knew that you don't go near them. You just stay out of their way. We were just kids and didn't realize the impact of what was going on. Most of our friends were there with us. Our parents didn't talk politics to us. What went on in Germany went on in Germany and you didn't hear about it in France. As for Poland, we had lost all contact with the family in Poland.

When the vacation was over we drove back to Paris. There was no problem going back. Every once in a while you had to stop by the side of the road to make way for Germans coming down the road, but the refugees were all gone.

We went back to our apartment and reopened the store. Everything was rationed very tightly, but they managed. I went back to school in October and found that in history we were forbidden to study past the beginning of World War I. In fact, we studied only up to 1870, because France went to war with Germany in 1870, or something like that. And we also had to stop learning English.

The Germans were everywhere, but there were no more air raids and no more gas masks. It took about six or eight months after they occupied Paris before they got rough on the Jews. Jewish businesses were taken over and then they stamped "Jew" on the identity cards and put yellow flags with the Star of David on the windows of businesses owned by Jews. My uncle was taken away with a lot of other people and then a German and a French inspector came into our store and asked for my father. My mother said he was at the market and they said they would come back the next day and the next day he was still at the market and my mother asked the French inspector how long she could stall and he whispered that he would see what he could do. But the German explained that they were going to take over the grocery store, and that my parents could work for them if they wanted to, but the store would no longer be theirs.

A Jewish customer told my mother about a group of people leaving that night for unoccupied France. She knew about a man who was paid to smuggle people over the border and she said, "If I were you I would get my husband out of here."

This was in July 1940 and when my father came back from the market he didn't want to go. He didn't know his brother had already been taken away and he was sure nothing would happen to him. We didn't have a phone. The brothers lived some distance from each other; they didn't see each other too often. So that was no help. But my mother convinced him anyway and he left the very next morning.

It cost $200 a person to get across the border. The man was a farmer who lived near the border and he knew when the guards changed and he smuggled people over in between the changing of the guards. My father told me they walked fifteen or twenty miles that night and went through a river and across fields and streams, and when they finally got into unoccupied France they were so moved that they went to the church and kissed the church because even though it was not a synagogue it was a place of God and they were all so grateful to be safe.

My parents had friends from Poland living in a little town in the Alps. It was a beautiful little town with hot baths like Baden-Baden called Aix-les-Bains. My father went to see them and stayed with them and then he met the smuggler, who told him that whenever he wanted to send for his family he could find him at a café in Lyon. He came there every Thursday at noon to make arrangements.

All this, of course, I heard later on. At the time we were just asking, "Where did Daddy go?" and my mother said only, "Daddy went away for a while. He had to go somewhere." And we didn't question it because in Europe you don't tell children things, especially important things. And then one day we left. "Where are we going?" we asked and she said, "We're going to see Daddy." And that's it.

We didn't know that my uncle was taken away and that my mother was very scared because the Germans kept coming to ask about my father. Later she told me that she called my aunt and said, "I'm leaving. Here are the keys to the apartment and the store. After I leave take anything you need." We didn't see the man who came to tell her that my father had paid him to take us over. But I do remember the night before we left, because my mother was up all night sewing money inside the lining of our clothes. And I knew without being told that something important was about to happen.

The next day my mother took a little bag, almost like a picnic basket, and there was a man who said he was going to pretend to be our father, even though he looked too old—maybe about sixty, and my mother was about forty. And we took a train, the four of us. My sister was seven. I was eleven. We didn't have any idea where we were going.

We slept on the train and the next morning a man came to explain that we were going to go up a hill and through a vineyard and if we were questioned we were to say we were the owners of the vineyard and he was the tenant farmer showing us around our property. He took his bicycle and put my sister on the little seat in the back. She rode while we walked. Then he parked his bike and we started going up the hill and he told us to be casual and not talk loud because a German might come by. I recall that I was very frightened and he kept saying, "Once we are on the other side of the hill everything will be all right."

Nothing happened. No Germans came. We went to a farm house where they gave us something to eat, and it was like a feeling of relief. And shortly after we took the train to Aix-les-Bains to join my father. You can imagine how good it was to be together again and to be among friends. You see, Aix-les-Bains was not a strange place for us. My mother, sister and I visited there every other summer, and my parents' friends had lived there for years and years. They had a store that sold woolens, sweaters and ski clothes and they knew everybody in the town and were very well liked. The woman, whose name was Ginette, was one of those people who can always manage to get what they need and she was able to get us papers and ration cards.

So we rented an apartment and my sister and I began to go to school. Ginette had two daughters. One was a little younger than my sister and there was Fanny, who was my age, and we all became best of friends. It was very joyful. Fanny and I were in the same grade and did our homework together. She was taking piano lessons just as I had when we were in Paris. Except for the fact that my father wasn't working we had a normal life, and there was enough money sewn into the clothes to keep us going for a long time.

There were other Jewish families in Aix-les-Bains, a colony that had escaped from Paris and helped each other out. They all had enough money, but money was not the only thing. They got ration coupons for each other and told each other how to get food and papers. Newcomers were bringing news from Paris and telling how it was getting worse and worse. Nobody knew about concentration camps but we knew people who escaped from the work camps, and they told that very few came back.

My mother had lived through World War I as a little girl and she was very determined to get us to freedom before it was too late. She is a very forceful woman and my father goes along with her in times of stress. It was her idea to write to her sister in New York for papers to come to the United States. So they sent my aunt a telegram saying we would never live out the war if we did not get away.

You see, the Vichy government began to complain that there were too many people in Aix-les-Bains that didn't belong there. They sent people to the small towns in the area but my mother couldn't bear to live in those places. "If we have to live here I'll die," she said. "I know that we're going to die if we have to live here." We had a notice that visas were coming, but the police wanted all the Jews out of town that didn't live there before the war. My mother kept going from office to office begging for a little more time. And it was very hard for her, because she had these bad legs with varicose veins and the steps were too many for her.

We left just in time. Our friends took a room outside of Aix-les-Bains where they would go at night and kept their apartment in the town so they could keep the business going and send the children to school. One night somebody tattled to the police and the Gestapo and they came and took everybody to the jail in Aix-les-Bains. Just by luck my friend Fanny was sleeping at a friend's house—you know how kids sleep over at each other's houses, and she had many non-Jewish friends to visit.

They had many friends in the town who were working to get them out of jail, but it so happened that the Gestapo was due to send a shipment of Jews out and they took Fanny's father. The next day they were going to separate Fanny's little sister from her mother and Ginette became hysterical, so they shot the kid in front of her eyes and then shot her.

When Fanny came home the next morning the concierge told her to get away as fast as possible. She got on her bike and went into the mountains to hide in one of the farm houses. Later she came back to Aix-les-Bains. The principal at the school hid her for the rest of the war. She just put her in as one of the children in the school and saved her.

*Ginette Yahiel lived "normally" in Limoges during
the Hitler occupation of France. Her father was
hidden in Grenoble for three years. Her aunt and
uncle were caught and deported to Auschwitz.*

My father was working in Limoges when the Germans occupied
the totality of France in 1942. I was out in the street and saw
them come in with tanks and motorcycles. There was no resistance. They just took over.

At this point we started to be frightened. We knew already
about the Jewish plight. We were always listening to the British
radio and we heard the reports from London. We didn't want to
accept it and we didn't want to believe it. We didn't want to
know what was going on but we knew.

A law came out that every child born of a mixed marriage
who had a baptism certificate before the law was promulgated
was considered non-Jewish. So we found an old priest to give us
a certificate with a date before the law. My mother was a Catholic, but not a practicing one. My father started to take out false
identity papers with French Christian names and my mother was
also considering taking out divorce papers, like many non-
Jewish women were doing at that time. It was a very difficult
situation. There was very little one could do short of leaving the
country, but a lot of people tried and didn't make it.

My father worked for a time and then went into hiding. We
stayed in Limoges. He went to hide in my aunt's place in Grenoble. His brother was with him, and his sister-in-law. There
was also my cousin who had been sent to private school but was
too lonesome and came back to Grenoble to be with her parents.
There was also a brother, but he was with a woman in Valence,
luckily not with the family.

They were confined in the house for three years. My father
was forty years old. He spent the time reading, learning English
and listening to the radio. At night he would walk in the garden

to get some fresh air. My uncle was a little younger. He too spent most of his time reading. My aunt couldn't take being locked in the house so long. She just couldn't cope with it and was determined to find a way to leave.

At first my aunt wanted to go to Switzerland. A cousin of hers left with his wife. Actually their group was caught, but they talked their way out because they were both very blond and didn't look at all Jewish. He told the Germans he was just taking a vacation in the little border town and did not plan on leaving the country. He and his wife were the only ones in the group to escape deportation.

This narrow escape discouraged my aunt from going to Switzerland, but then she became determined to go to Israel. My aunt's parents and brother had been going back and forth from Europe to Israel since 1925. Her brother left Paris for good in 1939 and had settled in Israel. In 1943 he secured a Palestine visa for his sister and her family. It was part of some deal made between the Germans and the Palestinian government, where captured German officers were to be exchanged for European Jews.

My mother took them to the station. Somehow she felt right away that something was wrong. My aunt told her to go home and not to worry because she felt so sure that her papers were in order. By the time my mother got home she received a telephone call from my uncle that the family was caught and that was that.

We went to a lawyer to see what we could do and he said that nothing could be done. The German government was giving cash bonuses for every Jew captured and the Gestapo didn't care about papers. Every Jew was worth something to them. So they took my aunt, uncle and cousin away and we never heard from them again. The only one to escape was the boy cousin staying with old friends of the family in Valence. The woman in Valence was Jewish but she was married to a Frenchman and nobody bothered her.

My father remained hidden in Grenoble. My mother went back and forth from Limoges. My brother, mother and I had an apartment in a two-story house with a couple of retired people living downstairs. I was thirteen and going to school. The big events were going to see my father and coming back to go to classes. We were far from any action. Life almost seemed normal. And yet the town was occupied by Germans. Once in a while men from the French underground came to town. There were many young Jews in the underground. I had a Jewish friend whose grandfather was a rabbi and she told me things I didn't hear at home. She knew about the town of Oradour, where the Germans killed all the men and put the women and children in a church and burned it down.

On the one hand the routines of life went on as usual. On the other the war took over our lives. The Germans had checkpoints all over town and we had to go through these checkpoints on the way to school. I even knew a girl who was in the French Nazi party. She wore the uniform and everything. With this girl I never talked politics because I thought it could be dangerous and she might turn me in. I remember thinking I had no personal life because of the war and wondering when it would be over and what we would do then.

We were accustomed to the fear and the excitement. We never knew what would happen. I remember once standing in line to get potatoes and there was a German officer in front of me. He took the bag and threw it at the salesgirl because he was not pleased with the way she helped him and everybody in line was frozen with fear.

In 1945 there was the landing in Normandy and when it occurred it was the big event in our life. It was the biggest excitement. We were really the children of war.

We never saw anything, actually. We couldn't even listen to the radio. My father had a map on the wall with all kinds of little flags, and every day he would move them.

And then we were liberated. The *milice* [troops] left and the Germans left and the underground took over. I remember the dancing in the street. And then the ugly things began. People who had collaborated were shot on the spot, even the girls who went out with the SS. All the anger came pouring out.

I had this friend whose grandfather was a rabbi and her father was a lawyer, a Jewish lawyer. She told me her father was fighting for legal justice and that it was wrong to repay violence with more violence, but that was not the mood of the time. But the ugly time didn't last very long. Everything returned to normal in a month. My father came back from Grenoble. He had to walk a lot of the way because the railroad tracks were blown up. And then we all went to Paris.

I was fifteen and had three more years of high school. But there were no privations for us in Paris. My mother was very clever at managing. We had no ration cards. We never stood in line. I can't remember not having a beautiful meal on the table. My mother was and is a superb cook. And I finished high school and went to the Sorbonne. I was interested in philology, the study of languages—but I didn't know what I wanted to do. I remember feeling sort of low and uncertain, depressed. I had all these choices but didn't know what to do with myself.

I had friends, both boys and girls, but no dating permission. To be involved with a boy emotionally was maybe to sit and look at him on a bus or follow him to the movies and sit five seats away from him, hoping to be noticed. In every way my life had no direction.

Then I got the idea to go to Israel and live on a kibbutz and maybe there find a solution for my life. I had cousins there so that I didn't think of it as a strange place. And I did go. I met another girl on my kibbutz who had been to the Sorbonne with me and an Australian girl who was just divorced and trying to find herself. After four weeks on the kibbutz the three of us left and went traveling all around Israel. I had a marvelous time but I was still out on a limb. When I went back to Paris my father was very angry at me because he thought I was not serious enough and just out to have fun. He wasn't any more pleased with me when I told him I was thinking of going to the United States to visit a friend of mine who had married and moved to San Antonio, Texas. She had given my name to a young man from Salonika who had also come to San Antonio and he had been writing me letters. There was something about William's letters that appealed to me very much. He had very deep thoughts and an analytical mind and that pleased me. I could see from the letters that he was a very tender man and alone in the world.

I came to the United States looking for a commitment. I suppose I had gone to Israel for the same reason but there I had just continued my life as before—having a good time, not finding out what was going on. In the three months I was there I couldn't decide to work on anything. I was just drifting along.

I thought I would go to San Antonio and then to California. I came at the end of June in 1956. San Antonio was very hot. I could understand English but I couldn't speak very well. I met William. In less than three weeks we were married. He was thirty-five. He had been in Auschwitz. All of his immediate family had been wiped out.

*Hilda Branch from Essen, Germany, fled to
Verona, Italy, and then to Brussels. From Brussels
she, her husband and baby made their way to
southern France, where they were interned by the
French. She and her family escaped to Brussels,
where her German appearance made it possible
for her to get a job until she was able to leave
Europe.*

On May 10, 1940 we were awakened at five in the morning by
sirens and planes, and in a few hours we were rounded up by
the Belgians. We had permits to live in Belgium but they interned us all anyway—my twenty-two-month-old daughter and
my husband's aunt, who was over ninety. They kept the men
between sixteen and sixty and let the rest of us go after a day. I
was ready to immediately put on a rucksack, take the baby and
try to get a train to southern France. My in-laws hesitated and I
was the only who could drive. I finally fled by car to the coast
near the French border. Later my parents-in-law and a cousin
and her son caught up with us and we started driving toward
France. We were stopped at the border because we were, after
all, Germans. So there we were, and we saw the searchlights and
the planes and we watched the French army marching north
with their World War I equipment.

In the morning after we came to the border they confiscated
all our possessions, including the car, and put us on a rickety old
bus. They took us to an internment camp on the coast, somewhere between Boulogne and Calais. Of the hundreds of people
there, there may have been about ten real Germans. The rest
were refugees, being held as enemy aliens.

The men and women were separated but they let my mother-
in-law bring her husband his insulin. He was a diabetic and she
brought him some bread and the injection. She had been hoard-
ing insulin for a long time for such an emergency and she also

carried enough barbiturates to kill the whole family. My father-in-law was on the blacklist because he had refused to turn over his patents for making rubber to the Germans and his life had been in danger for some time.

The night before the French set us walking to Calais, my parents-in-law took a large dose of barbiturates. My mother-in-law offered some to me but I refused. I had my daughter and I thought I would try somehow to get out of the mess. My in-laws told me to tell their sons that they had had a good life and were not sorry to end together that way.

The next morning we were "liberated" by the German army. I left my parents-in-law unconscious but still alive. I remember putting some jewelry in their pockets just in case they made it, so they'd have something. And I had to run through the city of Calais, carrying my daughter, with the bullets flying over our heads. After that we began walking toward Brussels. There were two Austrian women, a seventeen-year-old girl, my cousin and her eight-year-old and my daughter and I. We slept in stables and begged food from the peasants. We sometimes got food from the German army who came through on modern tanks. They thought we were Belgian refugees. I remember at the end of May I found an old-fashioned baby carriage from about 1890; I could put my daughter in the carriage with some cans of food we had acquired and keep on walking. We found a farm that had been taken over by refugees where we got some food, and stopped at every Red Cross station we could find. We even got a ride in a car that belonged to a German colonel. We could see the collapse of the French and Belgian forces. And though I was always expecting to be caught and put on a cattle car to Poland whenever I met a German officer, and though I kept trying to think who I would contact, what I could manage in such an emergency, it was not in their minds at the time. The army people were too busy to bother with catching Jews.

I bought a seat on a truck going to Brussels with some jewelry and finally got back to the city. There were no streetcars. The telephone lines had been cut by the English before they left. The German occupation had begun. My cousin's mother and mother-in-law had tried to get away. When they were stopped at the border, they bought a bottle of wine with their last bit of money and cut their wrists. The mother-in-law survived and told us the whole story.

I set up housekeeping in my parents-in-law's apartment and

my cousin was in the one next to it. The Italian maid, who had left, came back and helped and I went looking for work because all the accounts were closed and we had no money.

I found a job with a German company. I had very good credentials and I was intelligent and spoke Italian, German, French and English. When the man was ready to hire me I told him I was Jewish and he said, "I didn't hear you." I was later betrayed by a Belgian woman who had been my father-in-law's secretary. She had stolen some equipment from the factory and was working for the Germans, and she told the commandant. My employer, who had taken the risk of hiring me, had to get rid of me.

I still had advantages because I didn't look Jewish and nobody ever questioned me. When I heard that my husband had escaped from the internment camp and was in unoccupied France I had the nerve to go to the adjutant of the commander of Belgium to ask for permission to go through to unoccupied France. As it turned out, I used to go horseback riding with this man's son in Cologne and he gave me the permission. I got my daughter and my possessions on the train from Brussels to Paris in August 1940. But by the time I got to Nice, France had fallen and my husband was no longer there. He had gotten some false papers and was working. My brother-in-law was already in the United States and was trying to get us out of France. And we were constantly at the American consulate trying to get an emergency visa.

We had all kinds of passports. Fortunately my father had been honorary consul of Turkey and he had a better passport than most Jews had at that time. My father, however, didn't want to leave at all. He preferred to stay in France. He had rented his house in Cologne to the French consul and this gave him enough money to stay in Nice.

I hated the French more than the Germans. They began to denounce the Jews in Nice. The French were cooperating with the Gestapo and breaking the windows of Jewish shops. We heard Maurice Chevalier make pro-German remarks during a performance. The Germans, after all, had never promised us anything, but the French had promised a haven to the refugees. It was the country of *liberté, fraternité, egalité,* so it was worse for them to behave so badly.

*Claude Cassirer fled from Berlin to Prague, then
to England, to Paris, to Vichy France, to
Casablanca, and finally took a boat to New York
City.*

People have asked me why the Jews of Germany, having read
Mein Kampf, were so foolish as to stay on. Why didn't they all
just leave? I tell them that if you were to tell an American Jew in
Cleveland, New York or Chicago that something might happen,
very few would sell their businesses, very few would be willing
to leave their homes and friends to move even to California,
which is in the same country with the same laws and language.
They would be very unwilling to move to a different country
where they would not be able to practice their professions,
where they could not speak the language or make a living.

My father, however, was in a special position, which turned
out to be a blessing for us. You see, when Hitler came into power
in 1933 the first thing he would not tolerate was a free press. The
newspaper my father was connected with was closed the day
that Hitler took over. My father was politically more astute than
most people. He knew that Hitler got in because of the severe
depression, the political unrest and the bad economic situation.
Even before Hitler came to power he announced that he would
create a boycott against all Jewish businesses. My father decided
at that time that this would not be a good time to be in Germany
and decided that we should go for a little vacation to Switzerland. When we got to the border, however, the stormtroopers
were already in charge. They looked at our passports and said
that Jews had to leave the train and were not permitted to cross
the border. They took our passports away and brought us to the
Brown House, the Nazi headquarters, where we were detained
for a while. They did not mistreat us physically because this was
in the earliest days of Hitler, but we found the experience very
frightening and it helped my father decide to leave. There was

142

then no *J* for Jew marked on our passports. They pulled us out because of our names and faces, put us into open trucks and drove us into a city, I think it was Nuremberg, where we were surrounded by Nazis with guns giving the Hitler salute.

We went back to Berlin and my father decided to move to Czechoslovakia. It was close by, it was a democracy and, unlike many other countries, it did permit Jews to come in. My father was able to take 90 percent of his fortune with him, and he was confident about making the move. He is and was a very energetic person, a doer, a man who could make quick decisions. He wanted to put out a German-speaking, anti-Hitler newspaper in Prague. He was determined to fight Hitler but he hurried so quickly into this venture that he didn't realize that most of the German-speaking people in Prague were Nazis. The only other ones who spoke German were Jews and they were a small minority. From an economic point of view the newspaper had no chance for success, and even from a political point of view it had little hope. The Czechs did not like German-speaking people, including the German-speaking Jews in Czechoslovakia. The German-speaking Jews were afraid to buy the paper or read it in public. The newspaper had to sell advertising to sustain itself and the circulation was too small to make it interesting for advertisers. It was a dismal financial failure. It also did not succeed as a political venture. It came out before Munich, and the world was still saying that Hitler wasn't so bad and that everything will be all right as long as he stays in Germany. And Hitler was saying, "Just give me this and that and I will be a good boy."

We came to Prague in the fall of 1933. I was twelve. I did not speak Czech. I had to choose between a German-speaking school and an English-speaking school, and I decided on the Prague English Grammar School. My English was pretty good but they required that I learn Czech within a year. It was the law that you could not be promoted to the next grade unless you mastered basic Czech. I had a terrible time and just made it by the skin of my teeth. Even harder than the language was the fact that I was confronted with anti-Semitism for the first time. The principal, the teachers and the students considered me a Jew and a foreigner who was not welcome. If I spoke German on the street, for example, Czech people might come up and give me a little shove and say, "Why don't you go back to Germany where you belong?" It was a very unhappy time for me.

My father kept to his business people and others in Prague

from Germany because of the language barrier, but I did learn to speak Czech. I eventually made friends in the school who were not anti-Semitic but I never got over the feeling that I was a stranger.

In 1935 I went to summer camp in England and liked it so much that I begged my father for permission to stay in England. Fortunately my grandparents, who were still in Germany, were permitted to send money out of Germany for educational purposes and they agreed to pay for my schooling in England. I was there from 1936 to 1939 and passed the exams that qualified me to go to Oxford, Cambridge or London University.

I had no problems with being Jewish. I was considered a novelty, a strange novelty, and I made some very good friends that I still have. I was what they called "a bloody foreigner." The school was for the children of intellectuals, for example the son of Julian Huxley was there, but the English didn't travel much in those days. They were not aware of what was going on on the Continent. They were fascinated by Hitler's screaming speeches. They felt the excitement but had no political opinions. I would translate the speeches for them and try to explain why I was so disturbed by what was going on.

I remained in close contact with my family. During the long holidays I would go home, traveling in a roundabout way from London to Czechoslovakia through Austria, which was then still an independent country. My father did not think it was safe for me to travel through Germany, not only because he was Jewish but because he was politically fighting Hitler. On the way to Prague I would stop in Salzburg. My grandparents lived in Munich and we would meet on a little bridge that had barbed wire across it. My grandparents could stand on the German side of the barbed wire and I on the Austrian side and we would visit together. We did this until the Naži frontier guards became suspicious and accused my grandparents of handing me money through the wire. It was not true, but we had to give up these visits because they were afraid of getting into trouble.

A couple of days before Hitler marched into Czechoslovakia my father received a telephone call from a stranger who told him that Hitler was about to march in and my father's name was on the blacklist and his life was in danger. My father and the woman he had recently married left all their belongings and went to Paris, where his wife had relatives. He had their papers in order and ready for such an emergency. France permitted people to come as visitors. The only problem was that they did not permit visitors to work.

My father found a way to support himself in spite of the restrictions. When he was thirteen he began collecting minerals and crystals. Over the years he built up a fine collection and had contacts with dealers, collectors and museums all over the world. He began building up his business in minerals in Prague when he lost all his money on his newspaper. Though he had to leave all his specimens behind when he came to France he had enough contacts to continue collecting and selling, from a new address.

During that time in England they were giving out gas masks in school and we were digging trenches. At the end of the term I found myself very short of money. I wanted to work but England did not give foreigners work permits, and I needed a place to live as well. I put an ad in the London *Times* saying, "Young refugee boy looking for family to live in as paying boarder, must be reasonable." One of the answers I received was from "the Honorable Terence O'Neal." His place was on a very fancy square. He offered me a beautiful room that had belonged to his sister who had just married, and there was also a woman who came to clean and cook and I was invited to partake of the meals. When I told him I couldn't possibly afford it, he said I could because it was for free. He said he was well aware of the plight of German Jews and wanted to do something to help somebody. He saw my ad in the paper and picked me.

When I called my father to tell him my good luck, he thought there was something fishy about it. He was afraid of a homosexual trap to catch a nice Jewish boy and insisted I ask for references before I move in. Can you imagine the *chutzpa?* But I couldn't go against my father, so I did ask, expecting O'Neal to throw me out on my ear. But he was very understanding. He gave me a list of six people high in British society, and they all vouched for the fact that he was a very nice young man and it was safe to move in. It certainly was. I had a very pleasant time in his house. He showed me where he played as a child when his mother was lady-in-waiting to the queen, and told me a lot about British society. He even visited my father when he was in Paris, and my father was very impressed with him. I, unfortunately, had to leave because I couldn't find any work and felt I was wasting my time.

I went off to a camp in the Pyrenees to study French—I knew

a little but not enough. A day or two after I arrived in the camp Hitler invaded Poland, England and France declared war on Germany, and I became an enemy alien with a German passport. In spite of the years I had spent studying in England, and despite the pressure of my headmaster and the Hon. Terence O'Neal, I could not return to England. They did not differentiate between Jews and non-Jews; anyone with a German passport was German.

I joined my parents in Paris where foreigners also had to register. We were all sent to detention camps. Fortunately my father had some friends high up in the French army and they got us released. We were not permitted to return to Paris but we could go to Vichy. In Vichy I was able to support myself by giving English lessons. There were many Germans waiting for affidavits to come to America and they all needed to learn English. And then in 1940 Hitler began his blitzkrieg and we were all interned again.

We were in a camp with about sixty German Jews and half a dozen guards. We were very frightened, not of the French but of the Germans, who were coming closer and closer. They were coming by motorized tanks and parachutes and we had no idea when they would be on top of us. But we were sure they'd kill us if they found us. We pleaded with the French guards to let us go. We begged them to understand that we were friends of France, not Hitler. The French commander said, "I have orders to keep you here and this is where you will stay." The guards, however, seemed to have a better grasp of the situation. One day when the commander was on leave the guards turned their backs on us and we left. When he came back he rounded us up and locked us up again. It was only when he realized that his life was in danger as well as ours that he let us go. By then there were no buses, no trains, no transportation of any kind.

The big predicament was that everybody in France had to have an identification card. All I had was a German passport with a swastika on the outside and a J for Jew on the first page. I knew that I would be shot as a German if I was picked up by the French police and shot as a Jew if I were picked up by the German police. The important thing was not to be picked up by anybody. I more or less lived in a park, sleeping on benches and trying to get along on as little food as possible. This was in the fall of 1940. I hid out this way for a few confusing days. Nobody knew what was going to happen. I was separated from my family and had no idea where they were.

When I left the camp, which was in the south of France, I figured that Hitler had to be coming from the north and the safest thing was to head south. So I walked about a hundred miles, always expecting the Nazis to catch up with me. In a couple of cities in my path I contacted the French Jewish community and they were very decent about feeding me. I would ask where a synagogue was and go there and tell them my predicament, and they would always contact some Jewish family that would give me a meal and put me up for a night. I was not in a group. We all went in separate directions after we left the camp. But I was reunited with my family in Nice. We both kept in touch with a family in England so we could find each other once it was possible to send telegrams.

At this time all our thoughts were directed to getting to the United States. The Vichy government in France made it very clear that Jews were not welcome. They learned from the Gestapo very quickly. We were forced to register and could not leave certain areas without police permission. My father was not allowed to work but had to prove he had money. The Jews pooled their money in a bank account. Every six months we had to go to the police and say how much money we had in the account. After we went we would give someone else the money to put in his account.

There was other harassment that was much worse. They would arrest us when we had a visa to leave, an American visa and a boat reservation, and purposely detain us until the boat left and the visa expired. Then they would say, "We told you to leave." And we would say, "You detained us. You prevented us from leaving." They didn't at that time go in for physical torture, but they were experts at petty harassment that made it impossible to stay and very, very difficult to leave.

To get a visa we had to spend days waiting in Marseilles at the consulate. Luckily we had the affidavits my father applied for as soon as things got bad. He had this sense of impending disaster that saved us, and we had friends in America who helped us and sent us money as well. But there was an endless business with correspondence and telegrams and waiting at consulates and embassies. And then to get transportation at a time when boats were being confiscated for war was a very uncertain affair. I left France in the summer of 1941 on a boat that was supposed to go from Marseilles to Martinique. It was a boat full of refugees. My parents were not on it; their visas had not yet arrived. Anyway, we went through the Straits of Gibraltar, and just after we got through the captain of the ship received a message that the boat could not go any further because General Charles de Gaulle in London was confiscating any French ships he could lay his hands on. So we were taken to the harbor at Casablanca, where they didn't know what to do with a boat full of Jews. They took us off the ship after a few days and brought us to a deserted French Foreign Legion camp in Quedzem near the Sahara desert. So there we were with our visas and affidavits and passage paid for. The French lieutenant at the camp greeted us by telling us, "Now I'm going to make you people work, not the way you're used to, but with your hands," with the anti-Semitic implication that Jews only use money and never get their hands dirty. But we had already elected spokesmen for the group and we made it very clear that we would not work, not with our hands or heads, not for love or money. We had not asked to come to that camp. He was welcome to throw us all into jail.

We stayed three or four weeks under miserable conditions. I got very sick and decided I had malaria, without the benefit of a doctor's diagnosis. But malaria or not, I went to Casablanca and got on the boat, and this time we were really on the way.

Maurice Diamant grew up in Frankfurt, Germany, in a completely Jewish world. He was ten in 1932 when he was frightened by a Nazi parade. Two years later his family moved to Milan. They spent the war years as alien Jews in Italy, relatively safe until the Germans arrived in 1943.

I remember a particularly frightening experience that left a deep impression on me. It was of a whole troop of brownshirts marching down the street, singing a song about Jews howling: "Heads will roll and Jews will howl." I was ten or eleven. I couldn't get it out of my mind.

I also have a positive memory of a neighbor who was in the stormtroopers. My mother went down to the basement to get some potatoes we stored there in the winter. She was carrying a heavy sack up the steps and our neighbor in his Nazi uniform with the swastika and everything came running to help her. "I won't let you carry this," he said. "It's much too heavy for you."

Soon after, my father left to go to Israel, with the plan that we would join him. He went as far as Trieste when his partner was arrested. They held the man hostage until my father came back. They insisted there was a sinister deal to take money out of the country. As soon as my father returned he was put in jail. At that time they were trying to give some semblance of legality to their procedures. But they could find nothing illegal and told him to sell his belongings and leave the country. At the time it seemed like a disaster to part with everything and sell the business for a ridiculously small of amount of money but it was, of course, the best thing that could have happened to us.

The problem was that we didn't know where to go. The plan to go to Israel fell through because of the British restrictions. We didn't have the papers to go to the United States or any other country. The only place open was Italy. It was Fascist, but Mussolini was not yet involved with the Nazis and they had opened their doors to Jews. We knew of people who had settled in northern Italy and were quite happy.

It was 1934. I was twelve. We sold our things and went to Milan. It was sad for my parents but for us children it was a marvelous adventure. When I parted with my teacher he seemed jealous because I was going to "the land of the sun where the oranges and lemons grow." We were happy on the train to Milan. My brother and I were singing all the way. There were two German clergymen traveling in our compartment and they were delighted with the German songs we sang.

In Milan we went immediately to the Jewish Italian community, and they helped us find a place to live. We arrived during the summer vacation and I could go out in the street and play with the Italian children. By the time school opened I could converse pretty well, and some of the kids in the street had even learned some German words, not always the best kind.

My father had a harder time. He didn't know the language and had to find a way to earn a living for his family. Fortunately he was both an outgoing and a very determined man. He adjusted and started speaking Italian long before he knew how— he massacred the language but made himself understood. He found another immigrant with a little money and opened a little quilt-manufacturing place in Milan. He struggled and worked very hard and didn't do too badly. We were not wealthy or even well-to-do, but we managed. By the time we left Milan he had five or six people working for him.

My father was anxious for me to attend a Jewish school be- cause Catholic teaching was part of Italian education. He found a good, relatively small school that taught all the usual subjects along with Hebrew. It was an experience for me to be with Jews who didn't know a word of Yiddish and had no experience with the world of the ghetto in Poland and Russia. My parents joined a small, new Ashkenazi congregation but my school was Se- phardic and most of my friends were assimilated Sephardic Jews. They had their temple and observed the holidays but they also observed Italian customs and traditions. For example, if there was a funeral we wore uniforms with capes and fancy hats with the school's insignia and walked behind the hearse to the temple for a service before going to the cemetery.

I remember when Mussolini began to introduce the so-called racial laws in Italy, and the Italians were laughing and making jokes about it. They were very sophisticated and very much aware that they had been occupied by so many invaders that talk of racial purity was ridiculous. There was no anti-Semitism. Milan had about ten thousand Jews in a population of over a million. They lived scattered throughout the city and there was no discrimination. The Italian Jews didn't think of leaving. They felt some financial pressures, Italian Jewish officers in the army were dismissed, but they felt it was a passing thing. They were so enmeshed in Italian life that they were sure that the unfortu- nate things would blow over.

We, however, were alien Jews. Just before the war began we were told we would have to leave the country. My father gave up his business and we began looking again for means to emi- grate. I was eighteen or nineteen, and I wrote a letter to Australia offering to volunteer in their navy. They answered that I had to have financial backing to come to the country. The Italians had their orders from Rome but the orders filtered down slowly to the local police department. We knew several of the officers. We knew they obeyed the orders without any hatred. They would warn us in advance of things so we could get away. They came and told us we had to leave by February and then in January came again to say they'd give us another three months.

When the war began, however, alien Jews were arrested. They took the heads of families first. My father was sent to a concentration camp in southern Italy. My brother was taken five months later. A few months later they came for the whole family. They brought us to Ferramonte in Calabria. It was a camp with thousands of Jews. The barrack I was in with my two brothers was composed mostly of young Polish medical students who had gone to Italian universities, graduated and been caught by the war.

Our guards wore black shirts. They were not soldiers but Italian Fascists, and quite different from German Nazis. They treated us humanely, and there were even letters sent to Rome complaining that we were being treated too gently. We didn't have enough to eat but that was because the Italians were being rationed and didn't have very much for themselves. The farmers in the area, however, would come to the barbed wire around the camp and sell us fruit and other things we needed. The guards would chase them but a few lire would change hands and then a watermelon could be smuggled through. Some people had money, others had things to trade.

One day they decided to do things in the German style and put an end to the trading through the barbed wire. They put the man they caught in the sun and tied his hands to a pole. After three hours in the Calabrian sun he fainted. The camp doctor came and they cut him down and put him in the infirmary. Then the director called a general assembly of the prisoners. He was crying as he begged us, "Please don't make me do this again." He said, "Remember that things will not always be as they are now. Don't forget that I'm not inhuman. I'm not a barbarian."

The camp was not an inhuman place. We could get together with members of our family. The only jobs we were given to do were the maintenance chores for the camp. We peeled potatoes and split wood. There was no work outside the camp while I was there.

When the camp grew too big they adopted the *confine* system: families were taken to a small village where they could live peacefully under police surveillance. Our family was sent to the town of Arsiero at the foot of the Apennines in northern Italy. There were ten other Jewish families, from Poland, Germany and Yugoslavia. We were given a small allowance by the government and had to report to the local police every day. That was our home for a year and a half.

My father, as I said before, was an enterprising individual. And with Italians rules can be bent to fit the circumstances. One of my brothers had learned something about the fur business before being interned. My father arranged to have a couple of fur machines shipped to our town and we began to make fur plates. This was done by sewing together scraps of fur into a kind of mosaic that furriers could turn into coats. We all learned how to do it and we all worked so that we could buy enough food to live on. If you had a little money you could go to a farmer and get some food.

We were treated very well. In fact, I almost brought disaster on my family by getting involved with the mayor's daughter. We met in the tiny library, where they had a handful of books. I was interested in D'Annunzio and Pascoli, and she had a collection of books of their poems. So she invited me to her house and I went. She was my first big flame. I was about nineteen and became very much involved. I was careless enough to write her letters that her mother found, and eventually the mayor called my father to tell him that we would all have to go back to the concentration camp unless I stopped seeing his daughter. It had little to do with the fact that we were Jews, but we were the enemy aliens he was supposed to be guarding and we had to behave. I was heartbroken. She was sent to another town about thirty miles away. I once drove out to see her without permission. A friend lent me his bicycle for the journey. We saw each other and talked and hoped things might be different after the war.

Otherwise things went smoothly in the little town. We got together with the other Jewish families to celebrate holidays together. There was an older Orthodox family that needed our support. My father was not Orthodox but he kept the holidays and had strong feelings about Passover. Even though he didn't believe in supernatural things, he could pray and read Hebrew and participated with great feeling with the older man, who needed the observances more than he did.

I, myself, was not a very practicing Jew. Until I was *Bar Mitzvahed* my mother kept a kosher home. My father, however, ate anything outside the home, which troubled her. So we had these divisions, and naturally my father was my model. Even as a small child I had rebelled against the restrictions of Orthodoxy. My older and younger brothers, however, went along with the observances.

Before we left Germany I had been involved with Zionist groups. I have nice memories of the long hikes in the mountains and the Hebrew singing. I was really interested in the idea of being a pioneer. But when we came to Italy there wasn't too much going on, and I was turned off by the militarism of the Revisonists. I assumed that I would stay in Italy when the war ended.

At the end of 1943 Germany occupied Italy and our nightmares started again. The Germans came marching through, rounding people up, sending us off to hide in the mountains. My father had the nerve to do extraordinary things at that time. He'd walk into the places where German soldiers were drinking wine and talk to them in German. He was a tall, blond, blue-eyed guy and he would say that he was of German ancestry and try to find out what they were doing in the area—and they would tell him. One day he brought two German officers home and my mother nearly fainted. He wanted to find out as much as he could from them.

Then the Italian army disintegrated and the countryside was full of young men throwing their uniforms away, and the Germans began stopping everyone to ask for papers. Once I was walking down the street and saw two German soldiers coming toward me in an armored vehicle. I didn't know what to do. If I turned and ran that would probably have been the end, so I just kept walking and looked in their faces with indifference. It was one of those moments I'll never forget. They didn't stop me, but I felt as if I had aged twenty years. After that I begged the mayor for papers with an Italian name and he got them for all of us. It was touchy for my parents because their Italian wasn't that good. People in the town kept assuring us that they wouldn't betray us to the Germans but we began making contact with the underground to see if we could get smuggled out of Italy into Switzerland. We were terrified of being taken to a German camp. We knew very well what went on there.

Every night at a certain hour we would lock the doors and barricade the windows and go down to the basement to listen to the BBC. There was a death penalty for that but we needed the information. We begged the other people in town to leave with us but they said that the police chief assured them that they were safe, and the secretary of the Fascist party promised to protect them, but all the people who remained were deported and never heard of again.

We took the train to Milan where an old friend promised us a place to stay until we could leave for Switzerland. It was a terrifying journey, with the Gestapo patrolling the corridors, asking for papers. I was stopped and interrogated. I stuck to Italian and didn't let them trap me with German, and eventually they let me go. We stayed in Milan for a month and then the police began searching there. The policeman knew there was a family hiding in the apartment and came to the concierge to tell her that they would be back the next morning to arrest anyone they found hiding in the apartment. Actually what he was doing was telling her to warn us to get the hell out. I'm sure that Italians did cruel and inhuman things but I never experienced any personally.

There was an Italian attorney who had a small house on Lake Como not far from the Swiss border. We went there by train and he hid us in his house until he could contact the people who would smuggle us across the mountains. The whole family was there except for my sister who had gotten married and was in the concentration camp in Ferramonte with her husband. They remained there until they were liberated by the American troops.

We were not the only ones hidden in the attorney's house. There were people coming and going all the time. It was the headquarters of a patrol that was organizing sabotage against the Germans.

We left in a boat that went across the lake. It was a very tense crossing, especially for the young people—they were constantly looking for young Italians who had left the army. We managed to get across, went through the town and reached the people waiting for us. It was the winter of 1943. I never thought my mother would make it across the mountains but the people who led were very fine. They were just incredible people.

We gave them some money. They made their living by smuggling objects from Italy to Switzerland and vice versa in times of peace. During the war they became involved with the underground and smuggled people with or without money. They brought lots of Jews to safety. The journey took about ten or twelve hours. The area was patrolled by Germans with police dogs. Never could we have made it ourselves. Our guides knew all the back roads. One led the way, another was in the middle and the one in the rear erased all the traces with a willow broom that covered our footsteps in the snow.

The barbed wire was electrified along the border, but they knew where the ground was soft and they dug under the post so we could slip through. It was the place where they normally smuggled cigarettes. We had a cigarette together and they went back. They told us to find some Swiss patrol guards and ask them to get in touch with the Swiss authorities. We walked for about five hours before we found anyone. God, it was cold, it was bitter cold.

We weren't prepared for them to want to send us back. The guy in charge of the post said he couldn't accept us unless we could prove that our lives were in danger. What a letdown that was. He wanted to send us back to the border and I was so mad. "We'll never make it back," I said. "My parents can't go any further. Why don't you just shoot us right here?" He threatened to turn us over to the German guards if I said another word. So there we were, my parents, my two brothers and I, and fortunately also the daughter of an Italian former general who crossed with us. She wanted to call Bern where she had some connections. She made the call and got permission for all of us. It was an incredible piece of luck.

They took us to camps where we were subsidized. Various governments paid so much per refugee, depending on the nationality. My brother and I were sent into the mountains to split wood and build small mountain roads. It was a semimilitary kind of life. We were not at liberty to go off because the Swiss did not want to be overrun by refugees. But it was a healthy life and we were safe. We were a very lucky family.

Jack Goldman, though born in Mannheim, Germany, was jailed with his father as a Polish Jew. He was in Auschwitz during the uprising of September 1944.

My father's first problem was that he had to give up his driver's license, and he couldn't travel as a salesman without a car. I, of course, couldn't go to public school anymore. Everywhere we went there were the signs *"Juden verboten"* [Jews forbidden], in the stores and the cinemas, all along the Rhine River and at all the parks and beaches.

The signs bothered me, but I learned to live with them. You

can walk around a sign. I had a friend in the Hitler Youth who would come by and say, "Jack, let's go swimming." He went in his uniform and took me along. But those were rare occasions. I was afraid to get myself and him in trouble.

When the war broke out we were living with my uncle, who owned a bakery. We had given up our apartment and sold our furniture while we waited for the affidavits for United States to come. The police came in the meantime, however, and arrested us all. They took my father, my uncle, a cousin six weeks older than I, and me. The police set me free because I was not yet sixteen, but the others were put in prison.

My mother got busy trying to smuggle me to Belgium but that was not so easy. As soon as I had my birthday the police came looking for me and arrested me for the second time. They didn't send me to the same prison as the others but kept me in a cell in the city jail. I was all by myself with nothing to do and nothing to read but the newspaper that was cut up into toilet paper. I spent my time putting the pieces together to try to have a page to read. I kept nagging them to send me to the jail where my father was and one day they took me there, and I shared the same cell with him and my uncle.

The Germans kept all the Polish citizens confined until the war with Poland was over. The Poles who were not Jewish were then sent home. The Jews were kept in jail until they were sent to camps. My uncle was on the first transport to Buchenwald. The rest of us were sent to Sachsenhausen, near Berlin. We were kept in a Jewish barrack and not permitted to mingle with other prisoners. We were not the first Jews to arrive. Some had been in the camp for years, but the life in the camp changed radically at this time. Before our arrival Jews worked in their own trade. They were carpenters, mechanics, orderlies in hospitals, depending on the training they had received before their arrest. But when we came Jews were treated as entirely different beings. We were put in quarantine and expected to sit on a hard floor in a specific position, and the only people who came into our barrack were the SS. They would beat a few people, give us a little fresh air and exercise and chase us around the barracks, whipping and beating us as we ran.

In our barrack we put the oldest and weakest men in the center and the youngest and strongest guys in the first row, which was only a step from the door. When an SS man came in he was likely to slap the first guy in his way, so we changed the first guy so that the same one wouldn't get slapped all the time. Then we practiced the domino theory of falling—that means the guy that gets hit falls at the first blow and pulls the others down with him. This made the SS very happy. As soon as they saw somebody falling down they had accomplished what they wanted. Very often two guys came in, SS men with white gloves on, and they would pick two of us youngsters and ask us to fight each other. We didn't want to hurt each other so we practiced how to make a little bit of blood flow from the nose or a scratched cheek, because as soon as they saw blood they walked out.

After a few months they gave us shovels and took us out to work. We would carry sand from one place to another and then back again for no purpose. That went on for months and months until they picked a few of us to learn bricklaying. This too was frustrating because we would build a wall and take it down and build it again. The only thing good about it was that we were given an extra slice of bread at the end of the day.

When we became expert at laying bricks the camp commander had us build a pigpen with tiled stalls. It was his own animal farm with a kitchen where they prepared the food for the animals. We could see that the animals had much better food and shelter than we did. We would steal the animal food when nobody was looking and bring back our slice of bread to someone in the barracks who was hungry.

I would give my bread to my father. We were consciously trying to keep ourselves mentally and physically alive. We didn't waste our time in the barrack. Before going to sleep there were discussions and entertainments. We had a man who was a professor of music in the Berlin Conservatory and a cantor from Krakow, and there was a journalist. The professional people undertood the responsibility of keeping us mentally alert. I heard my first operatic aria in the barrack. Two guards were watching for the SS and we were listening to *Aida*.

We were very fortunate to have a nice man in charge of our barracks. He wasn't Jewish but he was also a prisoner and had been there since 1933. On Yom Kippur he kept ten men back on the pretense of cleaning the barrack. We had these straw sacks to sleep on and during the day they had to be stacked up against the back wall. So what he did was to leave a couple of feet between the wall and the straw sacks and the ten men stood back there and prayed. The cantor from Krakow led them as best he could from memory.

The Germans were always cooperative on a fast day. They didn't give us any food for those twenty-four hours.

After a few months I began to ask "Where is God? How could He let this happen?" I was seeing people get killed every day— they were jumping into the electric wire—and I began to ask the whys and wherefores. I began getting into hot discussions with my father, who still wanted me to recite some of the prayers but I said, "I can't. I don't want to." I hurt him quite a bit. I'm only just admitting it because I regret having hurt him. At the same time I felt stronger in my Jewishness.

I was not alone. I had many discussions with other youngsters in the camp. Some had been members of Hashomer Hatzair and had a leftist viewpoint. Almost everyone had been a Zionist. We observed Herzl's birthday in camp. One of the boys wrote a poem—I still have it—about all the obstacles we had to overcome, and it ended with our determination to make it to Palestine in spite of all the difficulties.

It was a shock, coming from an observant, Orthodox home, to eat nonkosher food, to work on Sabbaths and holidays. We had talked about it in religious class with the rabbi before our arrest. The rabbis said, "You eat whatever you get. You don't ask whether it is meat, or where the meat comes from. Your job is to remain alive."

We all had to learn to live with other prisoners and to change our colors to survive. I learned to talk like a communist with communists and to talk like a pimp with the pimps. I was sixteen. I could pretend to be whatever would get me preferential treatment at the moment. I knew what people wanted to hear and I responded to their wishes, to get their help. Not all the prisoners needed that kind of treatment. There were some very fine individuals at Sachsenhausen with whom no pretense was necessary. I especially think of Ludwig Hoppe, a non-Jewish political prisoner who would come late at night with a bucket of soup. It wasn't enough for everybody but it kept us young guys a little bit satisfied. He was a good man.

Russian POWs began to arrive. They were kept in separate camps in unheated barracks and with no clothes to keep them warm. So many of them died that we had to build a crematorium. There were no gas chambers at that time. The Russians were taken into a room for a physical exam. They were told to stand against the wall to be measured and shot in the neck while they stretched to their full height. Those were the first mass murders

I heard of. Jewish prisoners were murdered individually. They would be beaten to death or the guards would take a guy they didn't like and put his head into a bucket of water until he died. That went on every day but the systematic mass killing started when the first Russian POWs arrived. When we were working a guard would take somebody's cap and throw it over the line we were not allowed to cross. "Go get your hat," they would say. If you didn't get it they might shoot you for disobeying an order; if you did they would shoot you for trying to escape. But with the Russians there was no teasing. They just killed them, without any ceremony.

In 1942 my father was shot. It was in the spring when the governor in Czechoslovakia was assassinated. That same evening the Jews had to remain in formation after the others left. At random they picked a hundred Jews to retaliate for that killing. My father wasn't with me. He had hurt his knee and was in the camp dispensary. My cousin was standing next to me and the SS pulled him out. When they started to march away I pulled him back. He would never have had the guts to do it himself. They went off without him and for the moment I thought I had saved him. He died a little later of tuberculosis. My father, however, was taken with all the patients in the hospital and shot the next morning.

I still had one uncle left alive. He had been a jeweler and watch repairman. He remained in Sachsenhausen in a camp within the camp where they repaired the watches and jewels that had been taken from people. He was the only one of my relatives to survive.

One fine day in 1942 they took the Jews in Sachsenhausen to the far end of the parade ground. We had to stand far enough apart from each other so we couldn't touch each other. After a while they began taking small groups away and they didn't come back. We had heard by then about gas chambers and Auschwitz and we were wondering what was going on. When they finally took us to the bathhouse one of our young guys, one of the group that had been together from the beginning, said, "Hey, I forgot my toothbrush." The SS man just said, "Never mind, you won't need it." So we really didn't expect to come out of the shower alive.

We went through, came out clean and were given some clean clothes but without a belt or socks, just patched old clothes and wooden shoes. Our group huddled in a corner and made up our minds that we would try to take some of them along if they tried to kill us. We weren't going to give up without a struggle. We decided that we would jump out of our barrack windows just before evening formation, run barefoot to the parade ground and just jump on the SS, just tackle them and grab them any way we could. There were sixteen of us. The oldest were in their early twenties. We didn't dare spread the word further than our group but we hoped others would follow and that by the time the SS woke up to what was happening some of us would get out.

We jumped out as we planned and tackled the SS. Fortunately for us the camp commandant gave orders not to shoot. If they began to shoot from the towers his men would be in danger and he would have to report the incident to headquarters, which would be bad for his record. So we fought with the SS until they subdued us, and we were lying on our stomachs with our faces to the ground and the rest of the camp stood around absolutely silent, waiting for the worst.

The commandant came over and said, "Boys, what were you trying to do? Do you want to get yourselves killed?" He was talking so nice and sweet to us, as if he were our schoolmaster. It was unbelievable. "Get up," he says to us. "Don't be there on the ground. Stand up!" So we stood. He wanted to know who the ringleader was and he finally made us talk. We told him that we thought for sure we were going to be killed and we wanted to take some SS with us. He listened sympathetically, told us we were silly and there was nothing to be afraid of. He gave orders to get us socks and hats and belts for our pants. He even arranged some hot soup for us and that same night put us on the train to Auschwitz.

I don't know whether to speak of luck or the hand of God but we were not sent to the gas chambers. We were assigned to barracks and sent out to work details. The majority of the prisoners were Polish Jews who were arrested when Hitler invaded Poland. We were tattooed and given prison numbers and taken to a labor camp to build a small railroad. I didn't know where it led to or where it came from. I had the feeling it led to a mine. One of my very close friends was with me. He was about a year older, a tall, blond, blue-eyed fellow who had been a cantorial student in Frankfurt. We became known as brothers; a lot of people didn't know that we were not brothers.

When the ground froze too hard to lay the tracks we were sent to work in a factory that made windows and doors. My friend was sent to work with the group called "Canada." It was their job to sort out the clothes, food and jewelry confiscated from the transports. Then one nice lucky day for me a German prisoner passing where I was working heard me speak German. I did not have an accent like the other Jewish prisoners and he could tell that I had been brought up in Germany. He offered me a job as cleaning boy. The work was easy but it put me in contact with the SS all day long.

I had to clean the office of the man in charge of the factory and I usually made a point of being out of his office by the time he arrived. The rest of the day I ran errands for him in the factory. One day the prisoner who got me the job said, "This guy has thousands of cigarettes that he was supposed to distribute among prisoners, and he keeps them all for himself. Why don't you bring me a pack of cigarettes?" I told him to go to hell and steal his own cigarettes—why should I risk my neck for him? And he told me he could find someone else to do my easy job.

So one morning, sweating blood, I stole a package of cigarettes, and figured out I could just as well steal two. I didn't smoke but it was to trade with. Once I began it was hard to stop. I made special containers with small pockets to carry the cigarettes that wouldn't be noticed if I was searched. I had pockets in my socks and along my shin. It was part of our smuggling system. We made containers with false bottoms. For instance, there were tar buckets that looked as if they were full but only three or four inches at the top were tar. The bottom was hollow, a good place for a salami, a piece of bread or a stick of margarine. We hollowed out a place for a bottle of vodka in a large plank. We were always looking for a new way because the SS eventually got on to our tactics.

There was a psychology to bringing things into the camp. For instance, we are in a column coming back from work to the camp. I have a bottle of vodka strapped to my arm. If you have the nerve you are the first in line because they will think the first man will be too frightened and give it to someone in the rear. Then for extra security you make an innocent guy look as if he's bulging somewhere so he is the decoy. The way the system worked was that I could trade cigarettes for vodka. The vodka could be traded for a jacket or a pair of pants or shoes.

One day it became clear that the pile of cigarettes was shrinking. The SS officers also used them for black-market deals. One morning while I was cleaning the officer came in and opened the door of the beautiful cabinet where the cigarettes were kept.

161

"I knew it," he said. "Somebody has been stealing my cigarettes. If I ever catch you taking anything . . . ," he said. But I assured him I didn't smoke. I even had the nerve to say that everybody kn.ew what was in the cabinet and the office was open so anybody could take them. So he and I made a hiding place for the key. I was the thief and I knew where the key was. So I kept on stealing, and when a man came to take my job while I was pretending to be sick in the hospital I told him that he would have to keep stealing so that I wouldn't be suspected.

We took risks because we lived just for the day and nothing else. Under those circumstances we tried to live as well as possible. We had the hope of getting out and yet didn't believe we ever would. Meanwhile the transports kept coming. I never had the job of meeting the trains but I knew people who did. They would give the warnings: "Do something! Fight! The prisoners who are here are too weak. Fight back while you have the strength."

We talked about the actress from Italy. She was also an opera singer. The SS tried to molest her and she let them make advances until she was undressed and then at the last moment pulled the soldier's pistol from his shoulder holster and shot him. She lost her life but killed him too.

We had not heard of the Warsaw ghetto uprising in Auschwitz. We knew something had happened but didn't know what. Our own efforts were small and ineffectual by comparison, but efforts were made. In September 1944 there was a plan to blow up the gas chambers and that was to be a signal for the camp to break out. The British air force was to bomb the area and set us free. We communicated with the British by an underground radio. We worked in cells, three or four guys who were in touch with three or four other guys. Nobody knew who the leader was. But the SS men were in the habit of killing the prisoners who worked in the gas chambers about every six months and the men had to jump the gun. Also there was a foreman who was a traitor, even though he was Jewish. Jews are human, and you have rotten apples everywhere. He told the SS that something was going to happen. There was a small Krupp factory nearby where male and female prisoners were working. They smuggled explosives, powder and small arms over the wall. When the men working in the gas chamber saw they had to leave they started to blow up the gas chambers. We were all at our work stations. A fight erupted between the few Jews around and the SS. All they had were a few small pistols and handguns. The mutiny sirens were sounded and we were brought back to the main camp where they had machine guns in every corner and it would be suicide to try to get away. The British bombed at night, according to the plan. Our wonderful Russian friends were only about fifty kilometers away in Krakow. They could have come to help, but we didn't expect them.

There were great problems to planning an escape. The partisans who came to the aid of Polish prisoners usually refused to help Jews. If you think of an uprising you have to consider where the borders are, whether the civilian population will help or hinder. You have to ask yourself where you will go, who will help you, who you can trust. It was a different story for a non-Jew than for a Jew. Nobody, absolutely nobody, helped the Jews.

My friend Chaim was killed in an effort to get away. In the first camp whenever anyone tried to escape the whole camp had to stand for three days and nights while they searched the barracks and the surrounding area with bloodhounds. If the guy really got away we would feel it was worthwhile but if they brought him back after three days it was very painful.

Staying alive from day to day was our resistance. When I could, I would *nudzh* the SS. I would innocently ask about Birkenau: "What's going on there? What are those flames?" The SS man would say he had no idea and never gave it a thought. "So you leave the thinking for those with bigger heads," I would say, digging, digging, trying to undermine his morale, trying to see if there was any bit of humanity left in him.

But there were no more killings after the uprising in Auschwitz in September 1944. Two gas chambers were destroyed. And one day we had a call for volunteers to come and tear down the gas chambers. They got lots of volunteers. We marched to Birkenau singing Hebrew songs. I'll never forget the sight of the gas chambers and the grapple hooks and ropes connected to the chimney. We danced the *hora* around the buildings. We sang Hatikvah at Birkenau.

When the Russians began to come close to Auschwitz the Germans began marching all the prisoners who could walk right into Germany. It was January 1945 and we walked through the night in the cold and snow. We slept as we walked. We were five in a row and the man in the middle slept; then we would rotate and give someone else a chance to be carried. Then they put us in open freight cars and took us to a transit camp. The group I was with ended up in Dachau.

I was in the main camp in a barrack no bigger than a doll's house. Ten to fifteen men slept in it. During the day we worked. The Americans were coming closer and closer and the bombs were falling all around us. I contracted typhoid fever, didn't know what was going on—I was delirious. I remember one time they wanted us to march again and I couldn't move and I told the German army guy, "Shoot me. Do what you want. I can't go another step." He hit me with his rifle butt and told me to get up. "Go," he said. "The Americans are here. Go." So he saved my life. The others who couldn't move were shot.

When the Americans came I didn't have a stitch of clothing on. All I had was a dirty blanket to cover myself with. I knew English but when I tried to talk to them I couldn't say a word. It simply didn't come out. A Jewish Hungarian girl took off her slip and sewed me a pair of underpants—my first clothes. The Americans brought us some food they had captured from the warehouses and they made us go through an army shower to get rid of the lice. Then they gave us German army uniforms. We refused to put on the black uniforms. So they got us green uniforms and that was better. (Black meant the SS.) And then the different countries came to reclaim their citizens, Jews and non-Jews. The French came and the Belgians. A few went back to Hungary and Rumania, but no one wanted to go back to Eastern Europe. And I didn't know what would become of me. There was no German government to reclaim me and I was afraid to follow any German order. Meanwhile there was no transportation for civilians anywhere.

After a while we were taken on a truck to Stuttgart, and from there we went to Heidelberg. We were brought to a very nice house and had beds and food. We had to get used to the idea that we could walk in the street and go anywhere we wanted. And we looked around our shoulders to see who's behind us. We wouldn't dare to go alone. We were shorn and wearing those German uniforms. We devised a patch that we sewed on our jacket so we wouldn't be mistaken for German soldiers; we thought of that as the worst thing that could happen to us. I wanted to go back to Mannheim but was afraid of what I would find.

Three Jewish American doctors met us and took us into the medical company as civilian workers to clean up the dining room. Their main thing was to watch us eat. So we were the first ones on the chow line, with every GI making room for us. And when it came to seconds it was, "You guys, come on, seconds. In there first before it's gone." We couldn't believe it. Afterward they'd make us rest. And what did we do? We couldn't eat it all so we found an upright piano and hid the food in it in case it might disappear again. It went on for days until we realized that there would always be something else for the next meal. But you see we couldn't talk to anybody; we didn't trust anybody. I would be walking in the street among people and suddenly feel scared—where the hell am I? It was a tremendous shock to be free.

I got a job working for the military government. I met a man who worked for UNRRA who promised to try to find my sisters in the Bronx. I had the names of some relatives they were with, but no address. He put an ad in all the New York dailies saying I was alive and looking for them and actually got a letter from them for me. Meanwhile I began to get my papers in order. My relatives had already paid for my passage in New York. I had the affidavits from before the war. I went to the Joint Distribution Committee to see what they could do for me.

I hung around with the American GIs, practicing my English. They seemed to me like a bunch of kids. Who would think of grown-up people playing ball in the middle of the street? You played on a soccer field or a handball court, but not out in the street. They seemed utterly naive in their belief that the people around them weren't Nazis or sympathizers.

In May I was able to get on the *Marine Flasher*, a troop ship that had been used in the Pacific, on its maiden voyage in the Atlantic. I got on at Bremen. And there I was with an American Jewish chaplain learning to sing "The Star Spangled Banner," and the ship going so fast we got across in eight days. We had to stay in the harbor overnight and there were fireworks and fire-boats spraying water, and we could see the lights and the traffic on the shore. It was a marvelous sight. We came to the pier in New York and Mrs. Roosevelt, Eleanor herself, was there to greet us. And I remember that my older sister broke through the lines to run to meet me and my relatives were all there. And I had the feeling that it was up to me to take care of them. I was the oldest. It was not only that I needed to be with them but I felt responsible for them. I wanted to look after them and settle where they were.

Rene Molho, the wine-dealer's son from Salonika,
helped set up the public kitchens to feed the poor
there until he and his family were deported to
Auschwitz.

There was no food to be had. The rich paid high prices in the black market. The poor were dying like flies. My father was active in the Jewish community, trying to help the German Jews who had come to Salonika. He was trying to help them get to South America or wherever they wanted to go. I was trying to collect food and money from the rich Jews to give to the poor. We had to force them to give money.

We knew then that the Jews in Germany had lost their jobs and money, but we didn't know they were actually killing them. We didn't hear about concentration camps.

I was involved in setting up public kitchens to feed the poor, and was active with the International Red Cross in Greece. They gave us some free food and stuff.

In 1942 the Germans began carrying out their program against the Jews. They wanted all seventy thousand Jews in Salonika to register. Dr. Koretz, the chief rabbi in Salonika, came from Germany and he encouraged us to do what was asked. The president of the community was also a German Jew, and he also reassured us that there was nothing to fear. I don't think they knew themselves what was in store. It wasn't by meanness, only by ignorance, that they lead us astray.

After the Germans had the lists they called all the Jews for forced labor. They first had to pass a medical examination by three Greek doctors and one German doctor, and that gave me my first bad taste of anti-Semitism. I was the secretary of the board appointed by the Jewish community to record the farce they called a medical exam. There was a specific case with somebody who had a very bad case of tuberculosis. I went to the Greek doctors and told them not to send him because he was just

166

not well enough to work. They said that could only be arranged if I gave them some money. I came to the Jewish community with the request for money. After all, I didn't want the guy to die; I knew his sister, I knew the whole family. The next thing that happened was the Greek doctors wrote to the German doctors, and a copy of the letter fell into my hands. The letter said that the Jews, with habitual cunning, were trying to buy their way out of the forced labor.

The doctors started doing things that were more and more un-doctorlike. Jews were sent to labor camps in very swampy places. They claimed that they were sending them to drain the areas, but they were actually trying to kill them. They didn't get enough food and it was very hot. Thousands came back with malaria and we didn't have any quinine to give them, and they just died. The Jewish community representatives went to Dr. Martin, who was the head of the Gestapo in Salonika, and asked him to stop the forced labor because it was taking such a heavy toll, and he said he would stop it if we gave him a large amount of money, an astronomical amount.

My father was on the Jewish community board and I was present at the meeting as well. We immediately started to figure out how to raise the money and we forced the rich Jews in Salonika to give large sums of money so we could have the amount the Germans demanded.

We raised the money and he stopped the forced labor. A month later Dr. Martin started forming ghettos. He started with seven ghettos in Salonika. The wealthy Jews were forced out of their homes and had to move to the ghettos in the poor district. We left our home and went to live with an aunt who already lived in the ghetto area. They also organized the Baron Hirsh district, the poorest neighborhood near the railroad, and began loading Jews into cattle cars to send to Auschwitz (except of course we didn't know then where they were sending them).

There was a Jewish police with the Gestapo above them and we had our Jewish traitors, Jews who hit other Jews and stole their belongings. I was still involved in the administration of the Jewish community and still in contact with the International Red Cross because I was trying to get food into the Baron Hirsh ghetto, the worst of all of them. I even had a pass from the Germans that made it possible for me to go out of the ghetto to try to get not only food but maybe some insulin for a diabetic or a substitute for quinine for people who had malaria. I would go from ghetto to ghetto to see what I could do. Every now and then the Germans would get angry and take my pass away but after a lot of phone calls and pressure they would let me go again.

At this time I was engaged to a girl in Athens and she sent my family a truck with Italian soldiers to take us south. You see, Greece was divided. Northern Greece was occupied by Germany and southern Greece was occupied by Italy, and the Italians were not mean; they didn't have anti-Semitic laws at the time. I was naturally very anxious to go to Athens but my father felt he had to stay with the Jews of Salonika and where they would go, he would go.

I was twenty-four years old but it was unthinkable that I would go without my father and mother or that I would do anything different from what they did. It was understood that I would work with my father and support him if necessary.

The next thing we knew we were changing Greek money for Polish zlotys and getting ready to work in a labor camp in Poland. We went in the crowded cattle cars. My father and mother, my younger brother and his wife and I were together. It took about ten days to get to Auschwitz. There was no water on the train. People got crazy on that train. They lost their minds. They couldn't believe what was happening to them. Many died on the way.

When we got there the infamous Dr. Mengele made his selection—what for, I didn't know. I was glad when my father and mother were put on the truck so they wouldn't have to walk. I thought it was good that they didn't have to go for forced labor. I remember the big sign that said *"Arbeit Macht Frei,"* which means "Work makes you free." And there was an orchestra playing Bach when we went to the barrack where they shaved our heads and took our clothes. I had some doctor's tools—I thought I could practice medicine—but everything was taken. They tattooed my forearm and made us take a cold shower and gave us the striped clothing and wooden shoes.

Suddenly everything was different. We went to the barrack. It was very cold. There was a smell of burning flesh and somebody said, "That's people they're burning." I was ready to slap him. "Let's not crack up," I said. I thought he was crazy. We saw the flames, we smelled the flesh burning, but our minds couldn't realize anything that awful.

We were kept in quarantine in a barrack. Next to us was a big stack of bodies. We thought that they were burning the bodies of people who died of sickness and malnutrition. My brother and I used to wave across the barbed wire at some people we thought were our father and mother. That went on for a month at least. My brother and a cousin were with me, and we bundled up together at night. It was freezing with one blanket but with the three of us close to each other and three blankets we could stay warm.

Because I could speak German I got a job as night watchman. When everybody was asleep I had to stay up. There was a big barrel where people relieved themselves and I had to watch until it was full and get a couple of guys to empty it. I would shout at the guard and he would get the *Scheissekommando* [shit squad]. In the morning when everybody was gone I had to clean the place and go to sleep. I was very lucky to have that job. The men came back from work with broken jaws and broken feet. They were half-dead from exhaustion; they were covered with dirt and had no way to clean themselves. A lot of people killed themselves on the wire the first month. Some tried to escape, but no one made it. And they made us stand for hours while they searched. Five, six, even ten hours we had to stand in the cold. They hung the men they caught and we all had to watch. It was very easy to get completely depressed, to let yourself die . . . or to get so mad that you were kept alive by your anger.

My brother was taken for experiments with the genitals. That's how he died. It's hard for me to speak of this time in a chronological way. I just have recollections, not in any order. . . . I was in the camp from April 1943 to April 1945, working most of the time, getting weaker and weaker. When they didn't have enough people to fill the gas chamber we had to go and assemble people. One cold day the Germans put me in icy water and left me to dry outside without clothes. I was like a dummy; I didn't know what was happening around me.

Then I had a lucky break. I had told them I was a doctor. I was only a medical student, but I heard that it was never a good idea to say you were a student. My big chance was that they were looking for a doctor to work in the Canada barrack. That was the best place; it was where they collected the clothes and the shoes and the food from the transports. The transports were coming like mad. Five hundred thousand Hungarians came in a month. The crematoriums were working night and day. And that was the first time I had enough to eat, the first time I got some strength back. I would go out where the people were coming off the trains to tell them what was going to happen and to tell them to start something, but nobody believed me. I couldn't make them believe it, just like the others couldn't make me believe it when I came.

When the Russians came close the Germans put us in cattle cars again and shipped us to Germany. There was no food or water. When they let us out we tried to eat grass. A lot of people drank their urine. And then when we came to Oranienburg, near Berlin, they opened the doors and about thirty or forty German Red Cross girls had coffee and food for whatever was left of us. Who could explain how they did things? There was no rhyme or reason.

We were brought to Oranienburg to work in an aircraft factory, but every night the Americans came and bombed it. After a few weeks they took us to Dachau. It was very crowded. There was no kitchen and not enough to eat. People were dying of hunger. We built barracks and when they were finished they put us to work building underground tunnels of cement. Carrying the heavy sacks of cement up and down was another killer for lots of people. And then suddenly we began to receive Red Cross packages from America.

There was lots of talk in the camp about the Germans losing the war. The communists in the camp thought the Germans would kill us and so they tried to escape. One day the guards lined us up and we began marching. They took a bunch of Russian prisoners from another camp along with us and machine-gunned them. In the confusion some of my friends and I escaped. We made it to an abandoned German military camp and hid in one of the kitchen cupboards. I don't know how long I was there—days, maybe. I was too weak to move; I didn't even have the strength to be hungry. When the Americans came I tried to stand up and fell down. And that's how I was liberated.

*Tillie Molho from Salonika was fourteen when the
Germans occupied Greece. Her father refused to
register and took his family to Athens where the
Italians were in control. She was hidden by Greek
friends until liberation.*

I had two brothers, a mother and father, a grandfather on my
father's side, and a grandmother on my mother's side. My father
made wine. My grandfather was very religious. He prayed every
morning and on Friday night at the table. But we didn't keep a
kosher house. I didn't go to religious school. My father and
mother went to temple only on the High Holidays.

I was fourteen when the war broke out in Greece. I went to a
private school. The school closed and when it reopened they
started with the Jews. That's when we moved to Athens. My
father and my husband's father were business partners. When
they started concentrating the Jews in ghettos my father refused
to register. He was always expecting something bad. He was
afraid that we would not come back if we went to register.

The Italians were in Athens. For a while we could live there
in a normal way. When the Germans came in we had to hide. We
left the house with all our belongings. We took a little suitcase
and moved to a Greek friend's house. We stayed for a couple of
weeks and then split up, each of us in another house. Even our
Jewish maid went into hiding. My father called his partner and
said to send Rene and his brothers to Athens, but his partner
said, "You don't know what you're talking about. Why do you
think you're so smart and know it all? Whatever we do, we will
do together."

I was so scared. In the house where I was staying I wasn't
allowed to go to the window. I wasn't allowed to go out. The
only time I could open the window and look was when it was
dark. When friends or neighbors came in I had to hide in my
room. I couldn't go out, even if I had to go, excuse me, to the
bathroom.

The family had two boys and a girl and they all knew about me. I could move freely around the house except when I heard the doorbell. Nobody in the neighborhood knew I was there—*nobody*. The family would have been in danger if anybody saw me. They were a very good family. The man was a Mason and my father was a Mason; they knew each other from the lodge. The man said, "I'll take the little girl. Don't worry. I'll say she's mine. If something happens I'll say she's my niece or something."

So he took me into his house as if I were his daughter. They shared their food with me. Food was scarce. You had to have an ID card and be registered and then stand in big lines and get so much per person. I didn't have anything, no ID, no registration. So they were really very nice to me.

I had only one bad experience. One day I didn't know what to do with myself so I opened the dictionary and started writing down the Jewish alphabet. I couldn't go to school; it was just something to do. That night some Germans came to search the house. They opened the door at two o'clock in the morning: "Open up! Open up! We want to search if you have any guns." So they opened. I was in bed. They took us out of bed and wanted to see the IDs. I had a fake ID to show I was the niece. But then they found the paper with the Jewish alphabet and said, "What's that?" And I said, "It's mine. It's Phoenician writing." And they didn't say anything else and left. Oh, what a sweat! That night my mother, hiding in another house, had a terrible dream about me. She thought I was dead. The next morning there was a knock at the door. It was my mother. She wore sunglasses and had a black scarf around her face, and she looked like an old lady. "Where's Tillie?" she said. "Where's Tillie?" She came into my room and started hugging and kissing me. And she told me about the bad dream she had at two o'clock at night.

I stayed in that house until after the liberation. I hadn't been out once in two years. When I came out people stared at me. "My God," they said, "look how white she is." I was white . . . white . . . white.

*Rachella Velt Meekcoms was twelve years old
when the Germans came into the Netherlands. She
and her sister were hidden by their neighbors, but
they were caught and taken first to Westerbork
and then to Auschwitz.*

The bombs were dropping all over the place all night long. We crept into bed with my mother and father and were terribly frightened. The next morning when we went to school the school was full of refugees from Rotterdam. My father tried to get a train to Rotterdam—it was his day to see his clients there—and the train actually went right up to Rotterdam, up to the blockade just before the city. There was nothing left of Rotterdam. The city was bombed flat. I remember my father coming home, crying.

After five days the Germans walked in. Wherever you went you saw German soldiers. But life went back to normal. I went to school as usual. It was a long day, from eight to four, but we got a lot more learning done in the six years of grammar school than they do in schools in America. My father went to business every day, traveling as he used to. My sister and I enjoyed our beautiful home after the years in the orphanage.

They didn't start with the Jews until 1942. My eighty-year-old grandmother lived in the old downtown Jewish neighborhood and she couldn't understand what was happening. Kids from Nazi families were throwing rocks at her windows and into the Jewish stores, and she worried that they were brought up so badly. She couldn't believe it was because she was Jewish.

Then the orange star came out. I was very conscious of it on my coat. It was a stigma. I had always felt terrific being a Jewish girl, it was something special, but with the star I felt everybody was looking at me. And a German officer would come to school to check to see if the Jewish kids wore the star.

In the beginning people stopped me on the street and said, "We're proud of you. Wear it with pride." There were some non-

Jews who sewed stars on their clothes. People were hurt that we had to do it, but they were also afraid. They were arrested for speaking up for us and interrogated. Right away there was a Dutch underground movement. There was a good feeling that everybody was behind me. I never heard a nasty remark and on the way to school when people would pass on their bicycles they would see my star and wave. They would say, "Good luck! Bear with it! We're with you."

But the bad things were happening. There were signs saying that no Jews were allowed in the park and we couldn't ride the tram, and one by one Jewish businesses were taken over by non-Jewish people. My father kept on working because he had so many friends in different cities but it was getting hard, even though he didn't complain.

The next thing was the letter that came for my sister. It was an order to come to the station with a suitcase with her favorite clothes, books and personal things. All Jewish sixteen-year-olds were being sent to a camp for special training. This was 1943 and she had just turned sixteen. It was an order saying that you had to be there or the whole family would suffer. I went hysterical when that letter came. Flora and I were very close and I didn't want her to go. We had no idea about concentration camps. It was something we couldn't imagine. We were Dutch. They couldn't do that to Dutch people. But I had this feeling that something terrible would happen if she went and I cried and cried all night.

That night the doorbell rang and a man we had never seen came in. He said he was from the Dutch underground. "I know you have a young girl in your house," he said. "Give us your child and we will hide her. We cannot let the Germans have this young blood. We don't know what they are going to do, but we hear terrible things. Do not give your child to them."

We were terribly confused. The Dutch were very pro-Jewish and very good people as a whole, but there were among them also some who would give Jews to the Germans and we didn't know who this man was. He said he would be back in a week and we promised to make up our minds. My sister had two weeks to get ready.

We didn't sleep that night. Flora and I crept into bed together and just trembled with fear. People came to the door for a whole week asking if they could help us. Meanwhile we prepared the suitcase for Flora in case anyone came to check. There was a list of things like sheets, blankets, boots and pants to get ready. We let the neighbors see we were getting it all ready. Then my sister disappeared one day while I was at school. My father said he couldn't tell me where she was but she had not gone to the station.

At that time all the Jewish children were expelled from school. I had to go to another school where there were only Jewish children and Jewish teachers. There was a tremendous bond in that school. The teachers were very fine and they had all lost their jobs in the regular schools. The classes were very crowded in the beginning but every week there were less students. The Germans had begun coming in the middle of the night to pull people out of their homes. Many families had gone into hiding. There were very well-to-do families who could afford to pay to hide and many who could not afford it. There were also families who were afraid to go into hiding.

I came home from school one day and found my father had been taken away to a work camp. He received a letter that said they would take his wife and child if he didn't come. So he went. He and my uncles had discussed it a lot and they were sure nothing bad would happen. The camp was in Holland. They expected to come back for vacation. He was in the camp for about six months. He sent us a letter once a week, and I wrote to him every day. He said the work was hard but they had enough to eat and he was among friends and relatives, and that we should be brave and not worry.

My stepmother took in some boarders to help pay for the house. They were Jewish people and we lived as a family, eating together. Then one day a German soldier came into our class in school and picked up some children and after that I was too afraid to go to school anymore. I went just one more day and when I came home nobody was there. The boarders were gone, my stepmother was gone, and I sat in the living room and wondered what had happened to all of them. There was no note or anything. Finally my aunt showed up and said the doctor had taken my mother to the hospital because they were picking people up from their homes and she was no longer safe in the house. The doctors were putting Jews into hospitals all over the place because they hadn't yet thought of raiding hospitals. She told me to get a nightgown and clean clothes and to put them in my school bag and to wait until somebody came for me. She assured me that she would be in touch with me and I would find out where everyone was. She kissed me goodbye and I sat and waited to see what would happen.

When it got dark a man came. I knew him; he had a grocery store in the neighborhood. "Hello, Chella," he said. "You are coming with me and you are going to be happy because I have a surprise for you." We walked together for about twenty minutes and came to his store. We went into the back room and I saw my sister. He was the one who had hidden my sister all this time. I felt safe. I felt good. I didn't know where my stepmother and father were but I was sure they were all right. Actually my father had had an accident and broken his leg and hip, and he was in a cast up to his neck in a hospital near the camp, but I didn't know that. He stayed in the hospital until the doctor heard the Germans were coming to the hospitals to take the Jewish patients.

We were all in hiding. My sister passed for a cousin in the family and helped in the house. I had to stay out of sight. My father joined us. It was fantastic to see him but he had changed greatly. He was a cripple and very thin and had a look on his face like he'd seen things and been somewhere. But at least he was alive and it was so wonderful to see him again. My stepmother had been at a different house but she joined us as well. So the grocer had the four of us, which was really too much.

The Germans were doing house-to-house searches and we had to get into a closet in the back of the bedroom. My father couldn't walk very fast. We helped him up once just in time. The four of us climbed behind the clothes closet and we heard the heavy boots come up the stairs, and we were standing a few feet away, not breathing. A sneeze or a cough would have destroyed us. When they left we were all shaking like leaves and my father was white as a sheet. But he was absolutely determined that we avoid getting caught. "We will stick it out," he said. "We will stay in the smallest attic room if we have to and we will not complain."

We separated. I went to stay with a family of five children. They were working people and they took me into their home as one of their own and I never felt more loved or wanted in my life. They were marvelous people. The kids ranged in age from nine to sixteen and they brought their books home to me so I could continue studying. They taught me to play the piano and the guitar. I did everything with them. When the children were in school I cleaned the house and did the laundry with the mother. If anyone came to the door I went into the back bedroom until they left. The children treated me like another sister. It was a happy time in an unhappy time.

My sister in the meantime was with a family in Rotterdam. She passed as their nursemaid. She was the live-in maid and she took care of the children, cleaned the house and went to church with them. Our grocer friend had moved to the inner city and opened another store. My father and stepmother were with them. They had an attic room just large enough for two beds. My stepmother passed for a member of the grocer's family and helped his wife in the house, but never in the store. My father never left the room.

I stayed with the family of five children until the Germans came one day. I hid in the water closet in the hall that time but the Germans seemed to have some idea that something was wrong so I went to stay with a young couple. They were not good people and were only doing it for the money. They had a run-down place and a little child they left me with all day and all night. It was very depressing. Mice were running around and the lights were out because they had no money to put in the meter. I didn't want to complain but I often thought it might be better to get caught than to stay there and go insane.

I got this idea of going to see my father. I had been hiding for nearly two years. Sometimes on a dark night I would go out for a walk just to get a breath of fresh air. But now I decided to take off my star and take the tram at night. It was a foolish thing to do but I had false identity papers and I had dyed my hair red and I was determined to take the risk. I remember standing on the tram so conscious of myself. It was very crowded and nobody noticed me. It was also dark because of the blackout. My sister Flora did the same and we both got there safely and went upstairs to see Papa. It was his birthday. When the shop was closed he came down and we had dinner together with the family. People also came from the underground to see us. We were always in touch with them because they brought us food stamps, and also information about other people in hiding and about who had been picked up. Bit by bit our friends were being caught, and Flora and I were scolded for taking unnecessary risks. They wanted us to go right back and stay where we were safe.

We didn't listen. We stayed with my father for a few days— all of us together in that little room. My father spent all his time reading and we talked a lot about what we would do after the war. He had great plans for me. He wanted me to finish my education and then he was going to open a business for us. He was a wonderful human being. We spent marvelous hours together. I got a lot of strength that helped me later on in the camp. Here he was crippled, in constant pain—never complaining. You could see in his face that he was in pain but he never let on. He had a tremendous wish to survive.

Then one morning while we were all together a dream that I had had so many times came true. In the dream I would wake up in a cold sweat but this time I couldn't wake up. I heard those heavy footsteps on the stairs and the German voices saying, "Where is the family Velt? We've come for them." At first I thought, "I'm dreaming and it's not true," but then I heard my father say, "God be with us." Within a second there were two men with guns in the attic. They knew who we were and they waited outside while we got dressed. It was hard for my father to walk so they took us on the tram to a huge villa. They took us one by one for interrogation and to fill out forms and then took us to the federal penitentiary, the biggest jail in Holland. There had been a tremendous roundup and every room was full of people. Many of our friends were there and people from the underground.

They separated the men from the women and I didn't know if I would see my father again. My sister was crying and they made us stand with our faces to a brick wall. People had been there for hours. The cells were full. When the policeman came to take me to a cell he inadvertently gave me my last message from my father. He said he had transported a crippled man on the trolley and the man had said to him, "You see the cables on the street where the trams go? My life hangs on that cable and it can snap any time. But as long as the tram holds onto that cable, I will fight to hold on and I hope my family will do the same." When I told him that it was my father he said he was a wonderful man and a good example and he apologized for taking me to the cell. He was a Dutch policeman, and ashamed of his job.

They put me in a cell with my sister and stepmother and two other women. It was about six feet by six feet and there was straw on the floor and a pail in the corner. The other women were not Jewish; they were from the underground, and had already spent several months in jail. They played cards and read books and kept their sanity. We stayed in that cell for the six longest weeks of my life. At night there was a girl with a beautiful voice who sang Dutch freedom songs. She was a fantastic girl and her spirit was an example for all of us. And most of the time I was reading. We had a good selection of books, and that saved me.

After the six weeks we were all sent to Westerbork. My father was put in the hospital. My sister, stepmother and I were in a barrack but were not part of the labor force. We knew many people there and found the brother of a cousin who was involved in the administration of the camp. He told us that he could arrange for us to be among the people working in the factories. If we stayed we would surely be deported to Poland. I went to see my father in the hospital and said goodbye. He urged me to do anything that would keep me in Holland and to stay healthy and eat whatever they gave me and I promised to find him after the war. I had no idea that he would be sent to Auschwitz and right to the gas chamber. The next morning my sister and I went by train to Vught where we worked in a factory that made electrical equipment for radios and airplanes. It was the Phillips factory. We had to wear the striped prison clothes but we had enough to eat. All the workers were prisoners, even the managers.

Just after my sixteenth birthday we were sent off on another transport. We went through the mountains and came to places with Polish names. It was very dark when we came out of the train and when I looked up I saw a red sky with flames shooting up and the air was smoky. I heard the Germans say, "This is the Phillips group," and they marched us five by five through a huge gate. I was the youngest. They brought us into a sauna and then we stood naked for hours and waited for our names to be called. "Your name is now Sarah," they said, and tattooed a number on my arm. It stung but I was so full of anxiety and pain on the inside that I didn't feel pain on the outside. They kept us standing all through the night. They shaved us and gave us a gray prison dress to wear.

We were in barracks with a lot of nationalities, Gypsies and many vicious criminals. There were three levels of bunk beds and the Dutch girls huddled together and tried to give each other strength. The sleeping situation was awful. There were five people in each bunk and when one turned everybody had to turn. The bathroom was very far away and the path was muddy so we slipped and fell and there was no water to wash. When it rained we would catch the drippings from the gutter and wash our hands and face.

Every day was terrifying. I lost about twenty pounds the first two weeks. We were all sick but afraid to go to the hospital barrack because they made selections there. My number was 81793 and my sister's was 81792. We tried always to be called up together because we held each other up. When we were working together on the bricks I would get so weak from carrying the heavy bricks that I would just cry, "Dear God, where the hell are you?" And when I was ready to drop Flora would come and carry the bricks for me. She was always stronger and she would take four and I would take two. One day the overseer beat her for helping me. She kept telling her I was her sister and I was sick but there was no pity there, no pity at all.

A few weeks there seemed like years. There was never enough food and we were all exhausted and depressed. Just to survive each day seemed like a miracle. We were going insane with the agony around us.

Then one day a man came and asked for the Phillips group. He was the manager of the Telefunken factory, and he interviewed us and marched us out of the gate of Auschwitz. As I walked out I said the *Shma* with all my heart, and I said, "God, if you are there please listen, and keep us safe and save all these people in hell." I prayed very hard. I had cursed God a week before. I couldn't believe there was a God. I was really sick in my mind.

They put us on a train and gave us some food. And we went to work in the factory. A lot of people there came from Berlin. It was the same kind of work we did for Phillips and we were treated as workers during the day. We worked eight hours at a shift but there were breaks for meals and then they would march us back to the camp. I remember the little children on the side of the road spitting at us when we went by. Five-year-olds were already taught to hate Jews.

At the factory we were still prisoners. The Germans were always trying to get us to increase production and we tried to work as slowly as possible. One night a Dutch girl dropped a whole night's production. She had done it on purpose, and they beat her and we could hear her screams. They shaved her head and those of all the others who worked with her, including my sister. They had them parade in front of the rest of us just in case we had any plans for sabotage.

We were there for several months and the Russian front was getting closer. We could hear the cannons and the planes. The Germans were scared to death, but we just thought it was terrific.

We really wanted everything destroyed for them. We saw German people marching on the road with their wagons and belongings. They were marching on the icy roads just like us. When the Russian front came too close they marched us for four days and four nights over the Carpathian Mountains. Sometimes we slept for a while on the side of the road. There was lots of snow and no food. My sister had a touch of pneumonia. In the last camp she was in the hospital barrack. I was so worried about that. The Germans came every now and then and took the sick people away. I told her she had to get up and get out of there, but she kept saying she was too sick. She had no willpower left. I took her out anyway and brought her back to the barrack and she went to work the next day. But when it was time to walk she really couldn't. All of a sudden she ran out of the line and went up to the German soldier and said, "Shoot me, shoot me please, I want to be out of this life," and I was frightened to death he would do it.

I ran after her and he laughed, "Look at this one with the bald head, she wants me to shoot her. Shall I shoot her?" And I told him she was a little sick in the mind and I pulled her back in the line. I slapped her face to wake her up and promised to carry her if she would just not give up. I don't know where I got the strength from, but she leaned on me and the girl on the other side of her and we pulled her along with us. And the Dutch girls began singing to show them. Sick and downtrodden as we were, we were singing Dutch national songs.

The only thing was that my feet hurt so. The sole of my boot had worn through and I had a blister on the bottom of my foot a couple of inches thick. I showed my sister my foot and she went up to a girl who carried an extra pair of boots on her belt and took them from her. They had a terrible fight over those boots but Flora held on to them. So at least I wasn't walking barefoot over the mountains.

We came to a camp with a small barrack and hundreds of people. It was very confusing. They didn't seem to know what to do with us, but I was convinced we had escaped Auschwitz and could live through anything else that happened because nothing could be as bad as that. They dragged us around on the cattle wagons with Gypsies, Poles, Russians, Czechs and Germans— all prisoners. We spent our time taking the lice off each other. But mostly we had to secure a place to stand in those terrible wagons where eighty people were crowded into a space for thirty or forty. And my sister got sicker and sicker. I put my arms around her and found her a little place to sit and anyone who came close to her I would put my elbow in their face and I would stand up with all my five feet to make sure nobody came near her. I would have killed someone for her at that time. But our minds were only on our own survival. We were six or seven Dutch girls and we would share a drop of water with each other, but we didn't care about the others.

We wound up in a camp where we went to work in a salt mine. It was in Wiesbaden in West Germany. Then after a few weeks we were moved again. By this time nearly everyone in our Dutch group was ill and suffering from malnutrition, but we felt some change in attitude among the German people guarding us. They would crack a smile and say hello. We heard rumors that the war was coming to an end. We were praying to God the war should finish because we didn't know how long we could last. There were some mean people in charge who still did beatings, and we were really sick.

Then one day early in May we got called to attention in the yard and were told we were going on transport. German soldiers came and took us on a train. And then the train was stopped and we were left out on a big field. We were stuck there for a day and a night. We had already been on the train for a day and a night without anything to eat or drink. We were crazy from hunger and thirst and the lice eating us. We didn't know what was ahead of us.

When we went back on the train there were German soldiers all around us. They were not SS, just ordinary, friendly soldiers. They said the war was ending and they didn't want to be in it. They wanted to go home to their families. They also didn't know if they had relatives alive and if their cities were in one piece. So we were together in a way and not fighting each other. And then we saw we were coming to a border and we thought now they would surely do away with us because we were really ballast for them. They didn't know where to put us. So the pessimists among us kept saying that this was the end and I thought, no, I wouldn't give in to that. And then I saw the names changing outside and we came into a Danish station. And the German Wehrmacht left the train and Danish Red Cross people jumped on the wagons in their blue uniforms. "You are in Denmark," they said in German. "You are free."

And we said, "Are you sure? Are you really sure? It's not

true . . . It can't be true." And we touched them as if they were not real. They kept repeating that it was true, and they took us to a camp where we could have baths and good food. And we were free and the war was over.

I remember sitting in a corner, huddled, crying and crying, saying, "Thank you, God, that you helped us. You did help us. Oh thank you, God, thank you." I kept saying it over and over, and we kissed and hugged each other and told each other over and over again that we were free and not going to another camp.

Later we found that we were among the prisoners exchanged for German war prisoners by Count Bernadotte and the Red Cross. At the time we knew only that Hitler was dead and the war over. When we arrived in Copenhagen there was a man at the station who kept shaking our hands and congratulating us. "You are beautiful people," he kept saying to each one. "Ladies and gentlemen," he said, "welcome to Denmark." And one of the women said, "Lady? I'm not a lady," and he answered, "To me you are very much a lady." And she said, "Look at me!" And he said, "You are very beautiful." He just kept on talking and when he left us we found out he was the king of Denmark.

They gave us a beautiful welcome. The trains were turned into hospitals and half of the people were put in beds. Everybody was X-rayed. I remember a big barrel of hot-cross rolls and everybody got a plateful. It was so good, and we were so sick afterward because it was too rich. After a few days the Swedish Red Cross took us on a train and a boat to Malmö. I'll never forget walking from the train to the boat. People lined the streets and they were crying so much. I kept asking my sister why they were crying so hard. We were used to the way we looked. Such a sight we were! When we saw pictures of ourselves in the newspaper it looked like a bunch of dead people walking in the street. We were so worn and filthy and bad-looking, and the people kept calling out their congratulations. "Freedom," they kept shouting to us, and we were smiling and happy, waving and throwing kisses to them. We were so happy and they were so touched to see us, such a terrible sight we made.

There were dear, kind people on the boat, lots of women from the Red Cross, and they asked us questions and talked to us. We told them our stories and they couldn't believe the atrocities we had seen. They were crying all the time. We really opened out hearts to them.

When we came to the dock in Malmö the Dutch consul was

there with the whole Dutch legation and there were musicians playing the Dutch national anthem and everyone was singing. That's when I started to cry and didn't stop for hours; many people couldn't. I cried and cried. The tears just kept on flowing and I couldn't stop them. It was a week before my seventeenth birthday. I had a birthday party of sandwiches and hot chocolate in quarantine in Sweden. By then I had had many baths and scrubbings. We were so dirty from all the months without a bath, it took a lot of soap and water to scrub us clean.

They gave us clothes, good meals, a spoonful of cod liver oil and a spoonful of sugar every day. My sister was sent to the sanitarium because she had tuberculosis. I was very ill with ty-phus. The nurse told me that when I was delirious I kept saying, "I'm not going to die now. I'm going to live." They didn't know if I'd pull through. I weighed about seventy pounds. My sister was much taller and she weighed seventy-five. We were just bones.

In January of 1946 the doctors said we could go back to Holland if we wanted to. Our stepmother, however, was in England and wanted us to come to her. We went to London and she was waiting at the airport for us with her sisters. The son of one of her sisters was Daniel Meekcoms. He was in the Royal Air Force and had come home on leave. He was twenty-one, and I was seventeen. We fell in love. He wanted to get married immedi-ately, but I wanted to go back to Holland and work for a while. I had had a full life and was ready to settle down, but I had this need to walk the streets I grew up in and see who was left of my old life. My father had a large family. I needed to know what had happened to them.

We came to Holland in May 1946. The Germans had taken our house and everything in it. Another family lived in it. We had left that house, stepped out of it as if we were going down-town for an hour. It was very weird to come to the door and think of what had happened since I left. We were so grateful to be alive, but the pain of all the losses was very great.

I still wanted to find a job and settle a while to see if it was possible. I found one aunt who had been hiding and her two daughters and a fifty-year-old cousin who was very ill. Other than that the whole family was wiped out. And my sister and I looked at each other and thought, why us, of all those people, why are we left? We were no better than any of the others. We looked and tried to see what saved us. The Phillips factories were a tremendous factor in our still being alive, and the fact that we came in a group. I couldn't have lasted much longer in Auschwitz. My will to live was very strong, but my body couldn't take it. And then it was also because we were caught at a late date in the war. We were in camp in 1944 and 1945. I don't think I could have made it from 1942. So we were grateful for the years in hiding, and the Dutch people who risked their lives for us.

The first people I came to see in Holland were the family I stayed with. It was fantastic seeing them again. I am still in contact with all. They are even planning to visit me. Marvelous people! A terrific family! And the other family, who betrayed us to the police, were interrogated and one was put in prison. There were so many collaborators that the prisons weren't big enough after the war. Many people right after the war took the law into their own hands and there were a few killings, but there were too many to cope with.

I lived in Holland for a year before I went back to England to get married. My husband-to-be during that time was working for British intelligence hunting for Nazi criminals. He had very strong feelings about what I had told him.

We were married in June 1947. My sister remained in Holland. We lived with an aunt and uncle in England. It was impossible then to find a place to live on your own. They were loving people and like parents to me. My two sons were born in their house. My sister came to visit when my oldest arrived and she said she had a chance to go to America. She found it too painful to stay in Holland, but she was afraid to go so far from me because we wouldn't see each other again. So I made her a promise —I promised that if she went to America and married there I would come with my son and my husband. I was nursing the baby and I said, "I promise you by this baby." She said then that she would go, and a week later she was on her way to New York. She had a visa for six months, but then she met her husband. He came from Portland, Oregon, and was in New York for a visit.

A new era had begun. I lived in a suburb in England, isolated from the world, even from any Jewish identification. I had my husband, my two little boys and Grandma and Grandpa. I concentrated on the babies and the house. A new life opened up for me. I wanted to wipe the old one out of my mind. I had many nightmares. Many, many nights Dan woke me because I was crying or screaming in my sleep. He would take me in his arms and give such comfort and love that I got through the hard times.

Then my sister called from America to say she had gotten married to a Dutchman who came to America before the war and he was in business in Portland. She said, "Chella, you promised you would come when I was settled. Are you ready to leave England?" And I said, "Of course I'm ready."

Marika Frank Abrams, in her own words, "a very spoiled and protected child up to the time of deportation," was sent with her family to the ghetto in Debrecin and then, at the age of nineteen, to Auschwitz and Bergen-Belsen.

We were at a summer resort near Budapest in September 1939 when the war broke out. It did not break out in Hungary until June 17, 1941. In those two years my personal life hardly changed. My parents were so Hungarian that they couldn't believe they would be harmed by Hungarians. There was a large segment of the population which was violently anti-Semitic and the general population was mildly anti-Semitic. There were also people who were friendly, and my family knew only those who were friendly to Jews. How many personal acquaintances can you have? They recognized the dangers but couldn't really accept them. It was not foresighted and not intelligent but that was the way it was.

There were two issues that caused us anxiety. First was the deportation of the Jews who came to Hungary after World War I. They were not considered Hungarian citizens. We didn't know they were sent to Poland and killed, but the idea of sending them away was troubling. The other problem was with the army. After 1941 Jewish Hungarian boys were not given uniforms and were put only into work battalions. When they went into Russia with the Hungarian army they were used for the most dangerous services, like clearing mine fields, and were so badly mistreated that hardly any of them came back.

There was also the question about the Jews who had become

Christian. There were many who had married non-Jews and been baptized long before the anti-Jewish laws. It was a shock to find that the army treated the baptized Jews just like the others. The only difference was that the baptized Jewish boys were put in a separate battalion and wore white armbands instead of yellow ones.

And then the Germans came into Hungary on March 19, 1944, and this was the end of everything for us. All the Jews in Debrecin had to leave their homes and move into a certain part of the city they called the ghetto. This was a great circus. You can imagine: all the people living there who were not Jewish had to move out and all the Jews had to move in. It was actually accomplished by the end of May.

My father was full of life and hope, very positive in his thinking. We had a number of air raids and he volunteered to help clean up the rubble. This was in May and June of 1944 when the Russian army was in the Carpathian Mountains, about four hours away by car, and the American army was in France. So we thought we were just waiting the war out, and adjusted to the situation. We were in a house with our Christian aunt, her son, two of my girlfriends and their families. We got our food together and distributed the work and everybody was willing to do their share.

We also had non-Jewish support. There was a nineteen-year-old boy who had worked in my father's store who came to the ghetto door every day to bring us food and things we needed. The other was a woman who had been my mother's maid and married out of our house. We were very close and addressed each other in the familiar way, and she too came regularly to bring us things. And then there was a non-Jewish woman who was engaged to my uncle. They couldn't marry because of the anti-Jewish laws, but she was accepted as a member of our family and she was the one who saved all the members of my family who survived, except for me. She was very brave. She hid them and arranged false documents. When my father arranged for my sixteen-year-old cousin to leave the ghetto, she was the one who got the papers and took him to a summer resort to stay with a gentile family. It was possible for him because he was a golden blonde with blue eyes.

We had other gentile contacts. All our jewelry was saved by a Protestant judge who was a friend of my father's. Our aunt who was gentile kept our silver and china in a huge footlocker in her basement. We left money with different people, but there was such fantastic inflation after the war it wasn't worth anything.

When we were in the ghetto my mother was the only one who knew what was going to happen. She had always had great strength and spirit, but it was gone. She participated in the cleaning and cooking with the rest of us, but it was as if she were frozen.

About four weeks after we came to the ghetto the whole population was taken to the brick factory and deported in three transports. The first included the political people—the Zionists, the socialists—and also people with large families. There were many children in that group. The second transport included the hospital, with all the doctors and nurses. We were in the third transport. Each had about five thousand people.

The first transport was very lucky. The tracks to Auschwitz had been bombed and they were sent to Vienna instead. My girlfriend was on that one and she said they were treated as prisoners of war, housed in school buildings and assigned jobs in the city. The second transport with the hospital went straight to Vienna. All the people on it came back to Hungary unharmed. The third transport went straight to Auschwitz. The tracks, by then, had been repaired.

When we arrived we were asked to come out of the boxcars and the men and women were immediately separated. This is a scene as clear in my brain as if it happened today. I wish I could describe it but I really can't. . . . My father said goodbye to us in a very positive way. I was in a row with my mother. She was fifty-two years old. I'm almost that old now. She looked seventy-five. And there was my beautiful aunt, who must have been about thirty-eight, and her son, who was eight years old. I was holding the little boy's hand and my arm was in the arm of my mother. We had to form rows of five. That was the rule. And as we were walking by the selection officer, he asked me how old I was and I said nineteen. He put his hand on my shoulder and pushed me off to the left. I looked back and couldn't see the others anymore. And that was that.

I was in Auschwitz a very short time and my survival there is truly miraculous. We came on July 1, 1944. Not very long ago I read a book (*The Theory and Practice of Hell* by Kogon) that had the numbers of Hungarian Jews killed in Auschwitz. Between May 1 and July 31, 1944, 140,000 were gassed in Auschwitz immediately upon arrival. I, however, was sent to Birkenau, which was a section of Auschwitz, not yet finished. I was in a barrack with about five hundred other women. There were just empty rooms, no bunks, just the floor to sleep on. And we could not lie down until we lined up in a Z on the floor, one woman next to the other, very, very close. No latrines, only a few buckets between the barracks. I'm sure it has been described many times how we were taken into a room in which we undressed and left our clothes. Our heads were shaved. After the showers we were given a piece of rag to cover ourselves with. This was all we had. This first time we were allowed to keep our shoes, which was a blessing, because the camp roads were covered with sharp pebbles. There was of course no running water, no water to drink and no water to wash with. The only drink we had was some so-called coffee in the morning.

In the beginning I couldn't eat the food. Six months later I would eat anything. All they gave us was a thin slice of bread and a thin slice of sausage. Everybody started losing weight and because of the poor sanitary conditions we began to get typhoid fever, diphtheria, scarlet fever and dysentery. Many women began to have very swollen legs. One of the blessed things that happened was that all the women lost their period. Word went around that the Germans put something in our food that caused it, but that was absolute nonsense. It was caused by shock. It was lucky because we had nothing, not a rag, except for what we were wearing.

I came down with scarlet fever but just three days before they had set up a barrack for people with contagious diseases. They put me in there and I survived the scarlet fever. While I was in the hospital barrack everyone from my city was taken to West Germany. I had a very high fever but they let me alone. I made friends with a young girl from Budapest and I met Polish Jews for the first time; there were two lovely young girls from the Lodz ghetto and they spoke German.

Polish Jews made a big impression on me. When I was out of the hospital barrack I saw a transport of Polish Jews arrive. What I remember is the perfect silence with which these people descended from the boxcars and the quiet dignity with which they gathered in the lines of five. I suspect they knew what was awaiting them and they were moving to their fate with extraordinary dignity. Usually there was a mad jumble and screaming. When I was lying in the hospital I used to hear heartrending screams and wails all through the night. I heard later that it was the

Gypsies being taken away. Those screams have been with me all my life. Also the silence and composure of the Polish Jews—that also stayed with me.

I was taken from Auschwitz to Bergen-Belsen. This trip across Germany in a boxcar was nightmarish. We were given some food and water and locked in for three days. There were tiny windows and I looked out at this beautiful landscape. There were hills with little houses and forests and all the beautiful colors. In Auschwitz everything was gray; it was nothing but clay and gray barracks and gray sky and the devastating mass of miserable women. And all of a sudden I looked out and I saw there was the world. That was life. It was touching and disturbing. It filled me with great pain and longing. How nice it would be to be in one of those little shacks with my mother.

Then when we arrived we were put onto trucks and taken to the edge of a beautiful forest. We marched through the forest in absolute silence, sure that they were going to shoot us. But we really were in Bergen-Belsen, a very large camp with huge tents, army tents used to store equipment. And there was straw in neat rows to lie on and we were each given two blankets and a dish. There was running water and latrines. We were given food that was edible and didn't have to stand for hours to be counted. The conditions were so superior to Auschwitz we felt we were practically in a sanatarium. The camp was run by a member of the Wehrmacht, an older man very different from the Auschwitz personnel.

I was separated from my girlfriend when she was sent to the punishment barrack—they were always making up reasons to punish people—but I became friends with a younger girl. She was only fifteen and her aunt was also taken for punishment, so I took care of her. I was in a very large tent. Anne Frank was there at the time. There were six or seven hundred women, so I didn't know her. But there was a storm in November in which the tent blew away and it is described in the account of her last days, so I recognized my tent.

Let me explain that even though I had been in Auschwitz I did not know about the gas chambers. Can you imagine that? We thought, when we were there, that our parents and the children were taken to camps which were much better. We assumed that they couldn't live through the camp we were in. It was not until a large contingent from Auschwitz came to Bergen-Belsen that I had to give up that idea that they were safe. I met two women in their thirties who spoke Hungarian and they asked if it was true that the Hungarian transports were so severely selected—people to the camps and the others to be gassed. I said, "What are you saying?" And they looked at me as if I were foolish, but they didn't want to destroy my hope and so didn't try to explain.

I ran back to the tent and collapsed. I think I cried for weeks. I finally realized that everybody was killed. And this little girl with me couldn't believe it either. But I knew it was true and I really didn't want to live then anymore. It's very easy not to live, you know, in a camp, very easy to lose that bit of thing in you that makes you want to go on.

After the tent collapsed we were moved into permanent barracks and miraculously I found myself next to a woman from our city, a woman my mother's age who knew my family and who talked to me at great length about my mother and her childhood. And all this was very, very soothing. It built me up emotionally to go on living. Then I met another older Hungarian woman who had been deported from Paris. She told me about her life in France. She was a painter and also a designer of clothes.

I didn't mention when I talked about my childhood that I painted when I was growing up. Art education in the Hungarian schools was very bad, but I was painting and drawing nonetheless. The only one who appreciated my efforts was my father. He kept my sketch books and was proud of my work. Everybody else ignored it and there was no thought that I should have an art education. But at that time in Bergen-Belsen I realized that I would like to draw and paint and this helped me to go on living.

Early in December I was taken out of Bergen-Belsen with my girlfriend and my adopted aunt. We were sent to a camp in Magdeburg where there were Jewish and gentile prisoners. It was fortunate that we were housed separately. The Jewish prisoners were people of all kinds. Some of us were very good, some were very bad, and most were average, ordinary people. The gentile prisoners were a mixture of criminals, prostitutes and political people from many different countries. Some were also very anti-Semitic. It was fortunate that the Jews were together.

There were many factories in Magdeburg and about a hundred thousand POWs working in the area. I was in a barrack with three hundred Jewish women. We went on foot to the factory every morning. I leave to your imagination how we looked. We were starved, we had no hair and hardly any clothes and we marched in rows of five with the German citizens watching us, as many as twelve hundred coming together from different barracks.

If the German people say they didn't know about the camps, don't believe them. They would have had to have been blind and deaf. The camps were right in the midst of their lives. We worked alongside Germans in the factory. They saw us. They were even good enough to bring us needles, which were very valuable in the camp; a needle was worth a few rations of bread. Sometimes they gave me a pencil and I could get a piece of paper and draw. When the women discovered I could draw they would come and describe the clothes they used to have and I would draw figures with different dresses they wished to see.

There was not too much time. We worked twelve hours a day at the factory. They manufactured shells for bombs, and I measured the circumference of the shells, which had to fit a special pattern if they were to work. There were two girls and a man at each machine and our small contribution was that we sometimes let the machine run for a long time after we knew the shells were faulty.

We preferred the factory to the barracks. In the barracks there were lice and there was no water, no way of keeping clean, no way to wash clothes. We would steal the rags they gave us to wipe the machines and make things out of them.

And this is how we lived and worked while we waited for the Russians and the Americans to meet on the Elbe River. In March there were lots of bombardments and I could see the Germans were scared. I was not a bit scared. I felt that if I had to die it was a good time because I had had such a marvelous life before. I had been so happy and had lived with marvelous people. We had had a beautiful life together and it was all over. It was all gone. So I wasn't afraid of dying and I was very happy when the planes came. It meant that justice would be done.

And then one day we weren't taken to the factory. The doors were opened and the sun was shining. It was April 11, 1945. We went out and saw the SS insignia on the ground and the SS was gone. And there we were, in complete confusion. We began wandering around but we were in our prisoner clothes. We didn't know anything about the city we were in. The first thing we went looking for was food, and we found some potatoes and jars of jam. We just stayed there, hoping one of the liberating armies would come, but they didn't come. Six days later some Germans in uniform came to get us. They put us in rows and started marching us out of the city. We stopped to rest for a while in a large soccer field and suddenly the guns bombarding Magdeburg were turned on this field, and a lot of us died there. I flung myself on the ground as soon as the shooting started. A number of us crawled out of the field and reached the Elbe River. We walked all the way to a village where peasants opened a large barn for us to sleep in. And by that time we were together with lots of others prisoners coming out of the camps. My friend and I were very frightened, but when we got up in the barn in the morning all the guards had left. And we were just there in the village, not knowing what to do.

We set out on the road, not knowing where to. In the evening we came to another village where there were farmers looking for workers to help them gather in the crops. I was billeted on one of the farms with two friends, to work in the fields. There were two Polish men and two Ukrainian women taken from Poland and the Ukraine as slave laborers. The owner of the farm was a German woman who had lost her husband and family in the war. Meeting these Ukrainian women was a very significant experience for me. I was very sympathetic to them—they were so obviously miserable—and I asked them how they got to the farm. One of the women said she was just picked up off the street of her city, loaded onto a truck and brought to Germany to work. I said, "How tragic, how awful," and asked if the Germans killed many people. And knowing who I was and where I had come from, she looked at me with terrible hatred and defiance and said, "Only Jews were killed, not Ukrainians." She taught me a lesson I never forgot. There we were in that horror and misery together, and all she could think of was hating Jews.

There were also French prisoners in the area, and I had a lot of respect and admiration for them. We talked to each other but they would not even look at the Germans around them. They would come in to eat in silence and not recognize the people serving them. They lived by themselves and held themselves separate and proud. As soon as there was news that the Americans were in a nearby city they marched to see them and we went along.

I met my first Americans in Zerbst, and I'll never forget the sight of them coming together with the Russians. In every culture people grow up with different facial expressions and body movements. We don't notice it when we live in a homogeneous society, because we're so used to each other. But it was very dramatic to see young Americans who played baseball when they were kids, who had this loose-jointed way of moving their arms and legs, and the Russians who were tall, straight, very stiff. They were shaking hands and examining each other's guns and equipment, and it was very pleasurable to see such different kinds of people together.

The American Army wasn't interested in us, however. They completely ignored us except for two young Jewish soldiers from New York. They searched us out and knew who we were and what had happened to us. One of them spoke Yiddish and was very disappointed because we didn't. But we communicated and they would have given us their hearts. They brought blankets and clothes and food, and tried to help us in every way. We took their names and promised to write to them but lost the piece of paper and never did.

There were six of us women left and we found a baby buggy into which we put the clothes and blankets we acquired. We pushed it along the railroad tracks when we went from one place to another. I remember stopping in a house that was occupied by Italians, former prisoners of war. One or two spoke French, so we could communicate. They were young men of all kinds of backgrounds, most of them very simple fellows. But they were very enterprising and had a tremendous store of food. And they just took us over out of the goodness of their hearts. They really took care of us. And I have the warmest feeling about Italians in general from that experience.

And so little by little we made our way back to Hungary. A number of my relatives had survived, and they told me about the deaths of others. I found two of the cousins I grew up with and they were very nice and willing to take me in and look after me. They had survived the war in Hungary, hiding. Life had been a continuous thing for them in spite of the hardships. But for me, life was over and I had to start fresh. They thought they would be able to rebuild their lives as before, in spite of the Russians. I saw no future for myself in Hungary. The loss of my parents and my favorite aunts became harder to bear every day that I remained in Budapest. My cousin Vera had the same feeling, only a hundred times stronger. She decided to go back to the American zone in Austria and try to leave Europe.

When I heard from her after she reached Vienna I was determined to join her. I had met a young Russian officer who was Jewish. He came to visit in the spring of 1946 and told us he was going to Vienna and I begged him to take me along. The next day I packed up and left with him. I crossed the Hungarian border under his coat: I cuddled up in a corner of the train and he threw his big army coat over me and smuggled me across the Austrian border.

My aunt, the non-Jewish woman who saved much of my family, had an uncle in Vienna, and I went to stay with him until I could contact my cousin in the American zone. This uncle took me to the people who arranged illegal Jewish immigration. I went to the Rothschild Hospital in Vienna. It was the reception center for displaced persons, and made it possible for me to get over into the American zone. This all happened in early 1946. I found my cousin in Linz, working for the American Joint Distribution Committee as a receptionist. Since I spoke a little English they hired me too. They also gave me an application for a scholarship for foreign students arranged by the Hillel Foundation in America, and I filled it out with no hope that anything would come of it. All of us who applied, however, were accepted. My cousin Vera and I were accepted together because the Hillel Foundation realized from our resumés that we were the only survivors of our immediate families and should not be separated.

It took a year and a half of waiting before we could leave. American authorities in Europe were not enthusiastic about Jewish immigration, even on student visas. They were still using the quota system and they even let precious quota numbers expire unused while people remained in the displaced persons camps. The consuls were just very Anglo-Saxon and didn't want immigrants. So it took a long time to figure out what to do with us, the stateless students. The decision was to give us a stateless person's passport with permission to return to Germany after our studies in the United States. We finally got the visas, and we left in December from Bremenhaven to come to New York.

Robert Spitz and his father were picked up by the the SS in Budapest in March 1944 and taken to Bergen-Belsen.

My first girlfriend was the daughter of a Hungarian Jew who had settled in Czechoslovakia after World War I. She was the first displaced casualty of World War I that I was close to. Her family was permitted to leave German-occupied Bohemia because they were Hungarian citizens, even though they were Jewish. They made me aware of events that were not seen on the newsreels. I believed their stories of shootings and massacres that most people dismissed as propaganda.

By the time I was ten I was already interested and knowledgeable about political developments. My friends and I studied the appeasement at Munich and discussed everything we read in newspapers and magazines. We were naturally influenced by our parents' discussions around the dinner table, but we went out of our way to learn as much as possible.

The pressure came from the restrictions imposed on Hungarian Jews. First my father had to fire a great number of Jewish employees and replace them with non-Jewish workers, whether they were competent or not. The people he let go had shared in the company and been with him for many years; the new workers had the upper hand and were abusive, which was hard to tolerate.

My father was drafted into a forced-labor battalion several times in 1941, 1942 and 1943. He would go off for six months to build railroads and would come back suntanned, looking healthy from the outdoor activity, which he had never had before. But he complained bitterly of the abuse he and his comrades suffered from anti-Semitic commanding officers. Fortunately he was too old to be sent to the Russian front—only 15 percent of those who went returned. My uncle was one of those who came back, with terrible stories of abuse, hunger, cold, lice, typhus and shooting by members of the Hungarian army. He told of the thousands of Hungarian Jewish labor battalion workers who contracted typhus and were herded into barns on the Russian front. Hungarian soldiers poured gasoline on the barns and set them on fire, destroying the men and the typhus together.

Then one day in March of 1944 my father and I were walking down the street together and we were picked up by Hungarian police and SS troopers. It was the day that Germany invaded Hungary. We were marched to the railroad station, packed into cars with others Jews and taken to Bergen-Belsen. It was the camp that became famous for manufacturing lampshades from human skin.

We came out of the cattle cars. Those that looked as if they could perform physical labor were directed one way and those who looked too weak or ill to work were sent in another direction. My father and I were sent with those who were able to work. We spent two months together before the guards found out that we were related. Then I remained and he was sent to Mauthausen.

I worked on a stretch of railroad tracks that were bombed by British and American planes as fast as we put them together. It was a spur that led to the main railroad connections. Keeping this section out of order made it impossible for German munition cars to keep moving. We were given six hundred calories a day and didn't have warm clothing to protect us from the cold German winter. Punishments for breaking any rules were severe and public to discourage future offenders. Our biggest problem was the hunger that made men take risks that cost them their lives.

We had no communication with the outside world. We didn't know about the Allied landing in Normandy. We didn't hear about the pastings the Germans were taking on the Russian front. We didn't know what was happening in Czechoslovakia. In October 1944 we found a couple of Dutch Jewish engineers who had put together a radio from the tubes they stole while working for a German aircraft factory. Then all the prisoners knew about the Battle of the Bulge. Unfortunately the engineers were caught and executed, and we had to march around their bodies for three or four hours taking in the sign that said, "This is what happens to those who violate the orders of the camp."

Three hundred thousand prisoners came to Bergen-Belsen in six weeks toward the end of 1944. Many were Polish Jews who had been through the ghettos and other camps for four or five years. The experiences they described to us were unbelievable, but the way they looked made us believe. The women with shaven heads did not look at all like women. The men were like skeletons.

In February of 1945 a German medic came to my compound and announced that anyone who wanted to take a shower could do so. I hadn't had a shower between March of 1944 and February of 1945—a long time between showers. I went into the shower. The water was ice-cold, there were no towels and no soap, but it was delightful. What I didn't know then was that there were other showers in the same building where gas came out instead of water.

Meanwhile conditions kept deteriorating. The pile of the dead in front of the barracks got higher and higher. The guards blamed the lack of food on the bombing of the tracks; later British troops found tons of sugar, bread, jam, butter and ham that could have kept the starving alive. People were falling like flies from hunger and typhoid.

At the beginning of April, when the British army was eight miles from our camp, 4,800 of us were marched to the railroad station to be taken to Theresienstadt in a suburb of Prague. Several days later we encountered a train heading westward, and for the first time I saw hundreds of German soldiers covered with bloody bandages, torn, tattered, filthy and thoroughly disgusted with war. They were antiaircraft artillerymen, and they confronted our SS escort and insisted on looking into the sealed railroad cars where we were confined. The SS were outnumbered ten to one and were forced to show them their cargo of starved, filthy, lousy Jews. The artillerymen insisted that they leave the doors open and brought us food and water.

The days that followed were complete chaos. We went a few miles forward and then a few miles back. The Free French were within a few miles of us, and then we ran into British patrols. The sky was full of planes and bombs. When we looked up we could see hundreds or thousands of tiny glittery bodies in the sky. This went on until Friday, the thirteenth of April, when we ran into the Ninth American Army. By then the artillerymen had deserted and the SS had padlocked us back into the cars. The Americans shot off the padlocks and when the doors opened they were overwhelmed by the dead bodies that fell out on them. They had their fingers on the triggers of their submachine guns and at first they reacted by shooting. But by the time they came to my car they knew what to expect when they opened the door, and there was no more shooting. The mess officer organized a team of American tanks and went to the neighboring German villages. At gunpoint they ordered every *Burgermeister* [mayor] to start cooking and bring food from every household to feed the liberated prisoners. The food, of course, made us all very sick. But he meant well. When I weighed in at the army field hospital I was all of sixty-four pounds, including the lice.

I was taken by Americans to an army field hospital and deloused with American DDT. After three months of excellent care and fantastic food I weighed a hundred and thirty pounds and was ready to get to work. The United States Army Occupation Forces treated the displaced persons very kindly but I had had enough of camps. I went to the employment office of the United

States Army and applied for a job as a linguist. I passed the entrance exam and was shipped to England with 380 other DPs [displaced persons]. We were sent to the United States Army General War College Institute of Advanced Linguistics at the College of St. Mary in Oxford.

I had by this time added the Polish and Russian I had picked up in the camp to my knowledge of Hungarian, Czech and German. I had studied English and Hebrew in school, and also Latin and ancient Greek, which I never spoke. So at the age of sixteen I was fluent in seven languages. To pass the examinations you had to translate conversationally at 140 words per minute from one language into another. I was certified in six languages. Memory retention was part of the training. You had to play chess against eleven fellows at the same time, with one minute in which to make up your mind to move, and do exercises that involved looking at digits on a screen, starting with ten that you learned in two seconds, after three months working up to thirty digits that had to be rearranged in a particular way.

Then I was assigned to a counterintelligence corps with the United States Army and traveled with a team over western and northern Europe and in French North Africa. I was mostly assigned to small war-crime cases and Nazi party abuses. The most interesting assignment I had was the evacuation of the Russian military commission out of Frankfurt. In western Germany we found lots of liberated Russian prisoners who did not want to return to Russia. In a way they helped me decide not to return to Hungary. My reasoning was that these people were refusing to go back to their victorious country, so something must be wrong with the system. What chance would I have in the Jewish minority in a losing country? I was right to wonder.

The officers of the Russian military mission in the American and British zones were pressuring the liberated Russians to return home, and General Clay was insisting that people had to be free to do as they wished. He was also against the Jewish Agency pressuring the youth in the camps to go to Palestine to fight. The Jewish youths who refused to go were ostracized by the Jewish DP community. I was not pressured because I had a big job with the U.S. government, but I was aware of what was happening and also aware that the American occupation forces were against pressuring people to go where they do not want to go.

The unfortunate Russians who were persuaded to be repatriated were later described by Solzhenitsyn in his *Gulag Archi-*

pelago, but at the time we didn't know what would happen to them. The diplomatic battle went on for weeks. Finally we were ordered to discontinue electricity, gas and telephone connections to the magnificent villa the Russians occupied in a suburb of Frankfurt. They were desperate. They cut up the furniture for fuel and blocked the entrances with their trucks. But eventually they ran out of food and water and surrendered. I was the interpreter that escorted them, with dozens of American MPs, to the border between the Russian and American zones.

Vera Steiner was born in 1925 in Rakamaz, Hungary, the oldest of four children. Her father had a general store, but he was a country man and looked like a peasant. When the Hungarian fascists began shooting Jews, he got false papers for his family and took them to Budapest. He passed as the German porter in the Jewish center while they waited for the Russians to come and liberate them. Vera Steiner married at eighteen and came back to Rakamaz to have her first baby. The welcome she received in her hometown convinced her to leave for a displaced persons camp in Germany.

I was born in Rakamaz, in the neighborhood of Tokay, the famous wine country. My father had a general store and we lived like average Jews in the country. I had two sisters and a brother. I was the oldest. I'm the only one left in the whole family.

We were not a very religious family but in the country in Hungary everybody belonged to the temple. There was no such thing as somebody not kosher. My father talked about politics a lot. All the newspapers were about Hitler and what he did here and there and what would happen to us in Hungary. My father was a big Hungarian. He loved his country. Both of my grandfathers died in the first world war. My grandmothers were widows. My father had a decoration from the war and he was very proud of it.

When I was about twelve I began to feel what was coming, but we didn't accept it—we felt it would never touch us. But we knew there were riots in the university and that they were hitting the yeshiva boys. It wasn't from the government, though, it was just small groups. Then on March 15, when they have a big national holiday in Hungary, I was picked to recite one of the patriotic poems. It was a privilege for the good students and I had good grades. But one of my teachers said, "No, you cannot do it." I asked, "Why not?" I was crying. It was like shame in front of the class. She told me to ask my father if I didn't understand: "What do you want? You are a Jew and you cannot go and say you are Hungarian and how you love your country." And the children were cruel and made fun of me.

Then there were laws that Jewish stores couldn't have a license to sell liquor and sugar and other ordinary things. In 1938 Jews were drafted and had the yellow star instead of a uniform. The army was going toward Russia and the Jewish units went ahead picking up the mines in the field and digging trenches. My father was called up and we didn't hear from him for three years.

My mother and my little brother tried to squeeze a living out of the store in Rakamaz. My sisters and I went to Budapest to learn a trade. I studied dressmaking. I had to work for two years without pay as an apprentice. Then I took the test and got a license so I could work for a firm. Meanwhile I was hoping to hear from our relatives in America. We had turned in our papers but never got a passport or a visa.

In the spring of 1944 we woke up one morning and they were shouting that Jews shouldn't go into the street. They were picking people up. The next day we all had to wear the yellow star. We could only go out between eleven and one to do shopping. Then they picked the ghettos and had houses with a big Jewish star on the front. We had to leave the apartments and furniture and move into the Jewish houses where they packed four or five families in the space where one had lived.

It was worse in the villages. They knew exactly who was a Jew and picked them up and took them to the ghetto in the nearest town. They took my mother and brother that way and then sent them to Auschwitz. My mother was forty-one. My brother was ten years old. Usually when people went with a youngster they didn't come back.

There were a few people who spoke up against what was happening, but the large majority was happy to see the Jews disappear. All the Jewish apartments were right away occupied. The beautiful homes and furniture were taken. In the beginning Jews gave things to gentiles to save but most of them never gave the things back. Even when somebody came home from the concentration camp and asked for their things, they would say, "Nobody came back and *he* had to come back." In 1945, after liberation, I went back to my village to try to get some of my parents' belongings; we had nothing. And we went to the house next door and I saw an embroidered tablecloth I had made on the table. It was a horrible feeling. It was not the value but the feeling that you had been taken apart and nothing was left. I asked if I could have it and the neighbor said, "Well, I bought it from a Gypsy woman. I don't know what I gave her for it. Maybe she stole it from your parents." I recognized the stove my mother had for twenty years. I grew up with that stove. It was my mother's pride to keep the chrome shining.

People prospered off Jewish misery. They robbed the houses and made a county fair and sold the things. The bedding, the dishes, the silverware were all auctioned off, for practically nothing. People got cows and horses.

I came back with my husband. We were married when I was eighteen, just before he left for the army. There were rumors that Jewish girls were being picked up and taken to the army for the German soldiers and he thought I would be safe as an army wife married to a Hungarian soldier. We were married on April 16, 1944. At the time it was so dangerous to go out on the street that we paid two people to come to city hall to be our witnesses.

I was working, helping a relative of my cousin who had just had a baby. The husband was away and there was an old mother and father, so I helped with the baby and the housework. It was a family that had been very wealthy before the war and had had maids and cooks, so they didn't know how to do anything.

My father had come back to Budapest by then and he took a job as the superintendent in a Jewish building. It was a kind of Jewish center with a synagogue and social hall, and they gave him the job because he was very handy. He made the steam heat and shoveled the coal and worked as a porter. He was a country man with a big moustache and wore boots. He looked like a handsome peasant, really. When Szalasi took over the government from Horthy my father took the star off his clothes and got false papers, and we started to hide. The Hungarian fascists were picking Jews up and shooting them. They wanted to show the

Germans how they could do it, and all hell broke loose around us.

My father passed as the German porter in the building. He had a little room in the basement and we moved in, my husband and I. My husband left the army when his unit was deported. The Russians, meanwhile, were very close. We could hear the shooting a hundred kilometers away. Then the building we were in was converted into a hospital under the protection of the Red Cross. There were doctors and nurses and sick people, and then others looking for safety. They would come with a little suitcase and a piece of bread to wait for the Russians, who they expected to see very soon. They came by the hundreds to sleep on the basement floor and stayed from one week to the next and then the next, from October to January. They set up a soup kitchen because there was nothing for them to eat. There were no sanitary facilities and no water. The water froze in the pipes and no one came to repair them. A woman gave birth and the baby was wrapped in newspaper and died.

And they hated us because they thought we were gentile. They didn't know that my father risked his life every time he went to find food; he had these junky papers that anyone could see were false. But all these Jewish people sleeping on the floor didn't know we were one of them.

The Russians came in on January 25. Everybody went looking for family and there was no transportation. We walked miles and miles. And it was a time without law or order. Everybody took what they could. Everywhere they were breaking into stores, and I remember seeing a store from afar and I thought it was full of dummies for display—heads and arms and so on. When we got closer we found it was full of bodies, hundreds of people who had been shot and left there. It was the most horrifying sight. Everything was shiny . . . frozen . . . and people were looking for their own, to bury their relatives.

The Russians liberated Budapest street by street, house by house. When the first one came into our building my father was so happy; he had a little welcoming speech prepared in Russian. But the first thing the soldier did was to take his watch. He had about fifty watches on his arm. He was crazy about watches, and drunk. You had to be drunk to do that kind of work—just to control the fear. Later my father said, many times, "I saved the watch from the Germans and the first Russian took it." It was not that he cared about the watch, it was just the idea. I must say the

Russians were friendly and tried to help people; they gave us bread. But the girls had to hide, just as before from the Germans. By that time I was pregnant but they stopped me and tried to take me just the same. Luckily a young girl came along and they took her instead, and you have to understand that a lot of girls didn't mind because they gave them food and vodka and everybody was hungry.

We were very anxious to get out of Budapest. Three times we started out with a little bundle on my back and each time the Russians stopped us, took the bundle away and sent us back. Then we heard there was a train going through a few miles out of Budapest and we picked ourselves up again, the fourth time. I was five months pregnant and we walked a whole day to the railroad. We found a bunch of people waiting and we waited with them.

The freight train came the next day. It went very slowly but it didn't stop. People started to jump on it. One pulled the other and my husband was yelling that they should help me. He was pushing me and the people were pulling me and I had a big bundle on my back and my stomach was popping out—and then suddenly there was a big trench and he fell into it, and the train was going . . .

I didn't know if he could get out. I didn't know if I would miscarry from all the pushing and pulling. I hadn't been to a doctor; I didn't have the food a pregnant woman needs. Really, I didn't know what would happen. The train went for two days without stopping. Finally at the first stop I heard my husband screaming for me. He had come out of the trench in time to get on the last car. We got out in a big town that had already been liberated for a few months. We had brought clothing from Budapest to trade for food and we exchanged with the peasant people and went on traveling back to Rakamaz, my village. It took us a week and I already told you the welcome we had, but we stayed in the empty house to wait for the baby to be born.

We were the first Jews to return. There was no doctor in the village. I figured out when the baby was due, and when it was close to the time we rented a horse and buggy and drove to the nearest hospital, over two hours away. The doctor examined me and said I had a month to wait yet. I began to cry because I was afraid to go back, afraid they wouldn't sell us food, afraid they might even hurt us.

The hospital was full of soldiers and there was one doctor

and an intern to take care of them all. But I cried so much they let me stay. I was in a room with a Russian woman soldier and her comrades were visiting her all day and night. They were there when I came back from the delivery room and I'll never forget how this Russian picked up my little girl, just born, and began dancing with her. He put her in his boot and played with her as if she was a toy. I was so afraid and started to cry, and everybody told me to shut up and be quiet because he was drunk and just trying to be friendly. I couldn't wait to get out of there. Two days later my husband was back with the horse and buggy.

We stayed in my old village for a year, waiting and hoping for the papers to come to America. Our relatives wanted us, but the Hungarian waiting list was the longest. They first took the people who had a mother or a sister and we just had uncles, so we were at the end of the list. The only solution was to go to a DP camp in Germany, and we went and waited in Landsberg for three years. Under the Truman administration we came as displaced persons, not as Hungarians. By the time we got on the army boat to New York there were four of us; our son was born in Germany in 1948.

Ora Kohn from Turin, Italy, resisted official and family pressures to convert to Catholicism and hid from the Germans on a small rabbit and chicken farm in an isolated village. She escaped to Switzerland in 1944. After liberation she worked with refugees in Milan.

We lived with the conflict of going to school and listening to the indoctrination, being automatically enrolled in the Fascist Youth and having to take part in all the big demonstrations, and then going home and hearing the other side. The Fascist youth activities were compulsory. You couldn't say no, you didn't apply to join, you were just automatically part of it. So from a very early age I learned at home to be careful about what I said in public.

The Italians I grew up with, however, used to disapprove of anything the government did, and the ones who had a little background at home knew there was more than stupidity in it. We knew it was not just nonsense, but that there was cruelty and murder and the abolition of freedom, and we felt more strongly than the others. I don't remember anyone among my friends, Jewish or non-Jewish, who was really full of enthusiasm for Fascism. We also knew that even the people who were known as Fascists were not ardent Fascists. For the Finzi-Continis it was live and let live. It was enjoy your life as it is.

In 1938 it was as if we were struck by lightning—it was so different from anything that had ever happened to us. I don't want to talk about the material things. Of course the routine of life changed. But the really traumatic change was that you suddenly saw that you didn't know what tomorrow was going to be like . . . that it is bad today but it can get a lot worse . . . that what you heard about in Germany is coming . . . is here.

We knew what was happening in Germany because the family was taking in people and giving them food and shelter until they found a place to go. We felt sorry for them as individuals when we met them, because as individuals they were nice people. But there was also resentment against these German Jews for coming in and creating a Jewish problem where it didn't exist. A German Jew was still a German and there was a great deal of dislike for Germans. So many people felt that what was happening in Germany did not concern them. On the other hand there were the active, worrying people who were saying that what happens in Germany can happen here. "Of course it's coming here," my aunt said, but she had been involved all along. She was not surprised like the rest of us.

Toward the end of 1938 Jews were excluded from public school, from having a business and having a maid, and then the Catholic church got busy. There was a provision that said that if you had converted to Catholicism before September 1, 1938 you were okay if one-fourth of your blood was not Jewish. We could have been in that category because my maternal grandmother was not Jewish.

My mother's sister and two brothers and all their children converted. I remember how my cousin, who was my age and more religious than I, really enjoyed her Hebrew prayers, and when her parents told her they were going to be Catholic the poor kid went right on being religious with another set of prayers. Anyway, we were under great pressure to do the same, not only because it was a way out but because it was a worry for my two uncles and aunt to have a sister whose family did not go over to the other side. Mama felt we might as well do it and get finished with this "curse" and be thankful there was a way out. Papa refused to influence us one way or the other. I was seventeen by then and my brother was twenty-three and Papa said we were old enough to decide for ourselves. My brother and I had lots of discussions from every point of view and we said we couldn't. We just didn't feel we could do that, and we were ready to take the consequences. We were Vitas of Turin, and we could not give up the background we grew up with, the religion and values and the tremendous respect and appreciation that we had. And to all of a sudden say, "No, I don't belong to it anymore because it isn't convenient"—we just don't do that.

It was a personal decision; we didn't resent the relatives who made a different one, and eventually they learned to accept the way we felt. They were able to keep their money and had more time to make arrangements. When the time came and we all had to run away they got to Switzerland and didn't live in refugee camps, they lived in hotels. Most of my cousins married non-Jews and solved the problem for their children and grandchildren.

It was a time of crisis. People didn't know what to do and grasped at whatever was available. My brother had graduated from a law school and couldn't practice. In 1938 he went to raise chickens on a small farm. When I graduated from the British Institute in 1940 there wasn't much that I could do so I joined my brother on the farm. Boy, did we work! We had chickens and rabbits, angora rabbits and pigs. We had some cows. I was very good at milking cows, I loved that.

The farm was on top of a hill and down below was the little town of Fondotoce. The innkeeper was the only one with a telephone and if we needed to call we had to walk down to the inn. They were nice people and we got to be friendly with them. At that time it was not wise to divulge the fact that we were Jewish so we did not let it be known. At the time we thought we had them all completely fooled. Years after the war my brother went back to see what had happened to them and they told him they knew we were Jews and were keeping an eye out for us and were ready to tell us if we were in danger.

In 1943, my brother left to hide at a farm in Canzo, close to Como, and I remained and tried to sell the farm in Fondotoce. I eventually sold it and joined him; my father and mother also came from Milan, where they had been all the time. The Germans were close by, and the killings and deportations had begun.

We were terrified. A couple of times we had to leave the little house and go into the woods because villagers came to warn us that Germans were around. Mostly we couldn't do anything because we didn't know what to do. We just lived from day to day waiting to see what would happen. One day a priest came and offered to smuggle me to Switzerland under some vegetables, but I didn't like that. Some of our anti-Fascist friends brought me false identity papers. I became Miss Vittoria Bianchi. Then a friend of my brother's offered to hide us at an inn in a little town near Como. We had one room for my father, mother, brother and myself and it was our hiding place until February 1944. I was the only one with false papers so I went out every day. I went to church every morning and got calluses on my knees from kneeling so much.

One day I came home from church and found the innkeeper and his wife arguing about us. She wanted our room for some other purpose and said she would turn us in if we didn't leave. So it was time to go again.

I found another anti-Fascist friend to hide us for a while and began to contact some relatives who were preparing to cross into Switzerland. Our friend was a schoolteacher who lived in Milan. He was a wonderful person. He and his family could have been shot for hiding us, but they took us in until the arrangements were completed. When we left for Switzerland, we left from their house.

Getting to Switzerland required a great deal of money and involved a great deal of danger. The frontiers were patrolled by the Germans and Italians in turn. The trick was to cross when a particular Italian patrol was on. We were part of a whole band of people. There were my parents, my brothers, myself, an uncle and aunt, a cousin and a few others I had never seen before. Some of them came late so we had to spend the night in a barn within hearing of the German patrol. We were hidden there in the dark for twenty-four hours until the Italian patrol came on. We knew that any change in the plans would trap us. If we were caught we would be sent to Auschwitz. This had already happened to two of our relatives.

We were lucky and made it to the other side. Later I found out that the young Italian officer of the patrol received no money from the deal. It went only to the smugglers who took us up the path. We were also lucky that the Swiss did not send us back.

They sent many people back. As a matter of fact the most frightening part of the crossing was the few hours after being found by the Swiss patrol. They took us to the police station and we had to wait until they decided whether to let us stay or send us back to the border. Those were very long hours.

It was also our luck that the Swiss already saw the writing on the wall. They were very good businesspeople. The Allies had landed, and they probably thought it wasn't a bad idea to save a few people. The earlier groups were mostly turned back. They took us to an old school building for quarantine and delousing and then sent us to a camp. It was pretty horrible physically, but the captain directing it was a very nice man. It wasn't so bad to sleep on a pile of straw if you were treated like a human being. Later they sent us to another camp where besides making you sleep on straw they locked you up at night, and if you had to go to the bathroom it was too bad. My parents were sent to Lugano. The older people were put into an old hotel up on the hill. Eventually I was also sent to a very nice place that was only for young women. The only trouble was that the director was a homosexual and there was a lot of unpleasantness, but it was one of those things.

They kept us busy. Either we could work outside and help the farmers raise vegetables or do chores inside. There was a kitchen group, a housekeeping group, a knitting group making socks for the refugees in the men's camps. I chose to work outside until a farmer sprayed me with fertilizer because he hated capitalists and thought I was one of them. Then I moved in to the knitting group. After some time I was sent to Lugano to be with my parents, and that's where we stayed till the end of the war.

Gastone Orefice in Livorno was sixteen when he was told he couldn't be both a Jew and an Italian. Some of his relatives converted to Catholicism, but he chose to remain Jewish.

Some people came from Germany after 1933. We didn't know them; they were strangers and they were Jews. That was already something. I was very young but I was already beginning to be a Jew.

The problem first came to me in 1938, when I was told I couldn't go any further in the public school. I was sixteen and in the second class at the lyceum. At the same time my grandfather was very worried because he was not permitted to run his pharmacy. It was the most important pharmacy in the town and had been in the family for a hundred years. My father, meanwhile, was having so much trouble conducting his business that he decided to leave for Corsica, where he had some clients. He was not a Fascist and had never been a Fascist. My grandfather, however, was a very nice, honest person, a very old-style person, and until 1938 he was sure that Fascism and Italy were one. When the Fascists told him he wasn't a good Italian anymore and that he couldn't be a Jew and an Italian at the same time, he had problems with himself.

My mother, brother and I had a lot of new ideas to consider. First there was no school. Friends didn't call us anymore. We belonged to a beach club but the panel that said "Dogs Not Admitted" was changed to read "Dogs and Jews Not Admitted." I had to look for a job but it was illegal to give jobs to Jews. But I found one and I started working and thinking. We began meeting with cousins and friends who were Jews. Sometimes at a party I might meet some of my old non-Jewish friends and they would tell me they hated what was going on but they did not call and I was too proud to call them. I knew they didn't want to be involved with any problems.

And then I had a big shock. A cousin of mine whose mother was Catholic disappeared for some time and then we heard that she had been baptized. So we started talking. We spent a lot of nights with my cousins and Jewish friends—there were about twenty of us between the age of fifteen and twenty-two—and the urgent question we had to answer was, Are we right to be Jews? Do we have to remain Jews? Is this just a position of pride, of tradition? Should we renounce this position which put us in such a bad situation for centuries?

After all, there are maybe forty-five million Italians, nearly all Catholic. There were maybe fifty thousand Protestants in northern Italy and thirty thousand Jews. We were not strangers but we were certainly unusual. Why should we remain different? Is there any reason? Are we better? No. We can't rationally accept that we are any better. We are Jews. We have a tradition. We have a religion. But if that means to be persecuted every twenty years, let's convert ourselves and renounce this kind of pride. And if we say that we have to remain Jews the second question was, Should we remain in the Diaspora? Or should we go to Israel and stay there? We had to decide. It was very important.

All of us decided to remain Jews. Half decided to go to Israel (then Palestine) to have a Jewish life and feel at peace with themselves. I had a different opinion. I was in favor of Zionism and a Jewish state in Palestine but I didn't think all the Jews should go there. It was my opinion that we had to maintain Judaism everywhere in the world, that we have to remain where we are and see what happens, even if we are persecuted. I feel now that I was right. Because of this very persecution some of us are again Jews now.

The majority of the Jews were more Italian than Jewish and thought they were living in a good regime—until the persecution began. Then even Italians who were not Jewish realized that they were mistaken about Fascism. They did not accept the persecution. They were not as disciplined as the Germans—they were more human and more rational. I can only remember one friend who did something bad to me. There were many, even Fascists, who helped me at different times.

We found help from the population and from the church, even with the Fascists. The bishops of Florence and Livorno helped me hide for a month in a home for old priests in Florence. I was with my brother and cousin. After a month the director came to us and said, "You know, children, since last night the Germans are looking through the religious houses around here, and I am afraid they will come any moment. Stay if you want to, but I am not sure it will be safe anymore." And when we were moving on we were in a train station and a group of SS and four or five Fascists started checking identity papers. First of all they could have asked why we were not in uniform—people of our age were soldiers. We, of course, had altered our papers; my name, Orefice, had been changed to Ortona. But it was very obvious that we were frightened. The Italian Fascist looked at our papers and looked at our faces and told the Germans it was okay. He saved our lives. That Fascist in uniform was a nice guy.

The Jews in Italy were part of Italian life. Very few had positions of influence. There were no Jews in politics. There were doctors, lawyers, scientists, and the ordinary people and the priests had nothing against them. The political and church authorities had to be Fascist and when it came time to be against the Jews they were against them, but at the lower levels there was no basic anti-Semitism. I know about a priest in Livorno who went to the Jewish community's old people's home to bring flour so they could bake *matzo* for Passover. He had some special flour that was for the consecrated wafer and he brought it to the old Jews so that they could at least have a symbolic *matzo* for the holiday. After Livorno was bombed all the Jews had to leave, and there was no one to take care of the old people. This same priest came with a wheelbarrow and one by one took them to a house outside the city where they were safe.

This was the kind of life we had until the war was really lost. My father came back from the camp at Urbisaglia after Mussolini was arrested on July 25, 1943. Our house had already been bombed and we were living up in the Apennine Mountains, at Castelluccio di Norcia. It was a small village in the center of Italy which was completely isolated in the winter when it snowed. There was no road so you could only get to it by walking. We didn't have any money with us and had to do a lot of things to earn our food. My brother, my cousin and I set up a small improvised theater and performed Grimm's fairy tales, and we gave lessons to the children in the village. There was no doctor in the area and although my father had no medical training he was able to help people with some of his knowledge. Even in those hard times Jews were in the Italian milieu. We were different but we were not outsiders.

Martin Berliner, born in Warsaw, was working as an engineer in Paris when the Germans arrived. He fled to Lyons, then to Spain and Portugal, and left Europe on the day the United States entered the war, on the very last boat to leave.

When my work in Hamburg was completed I returned to France, and then I decided to go back to Warsaw to see my parents. I had an offer of a very good job in Warsaw for a company making ammunition but I was afraid of staying in Poland. My father was angry with me because I couldn't justify my refusal to take the job, but I just had this strong feeling that I had to return to France. I went back and forth from Paris to Warsaw many times but I can remember one particular time when my father and my sisters took me to the station. I told my sister Guta, the sister who was later taken to a concentration camp and killed, that I had a feeling I would never see my father or mother again. I left for France with a very heavy heart. It was 1938. Germany had already taken over the Sudetenland; the intrigues with Czechoslovakia had begun.

I worked as a welding engineer making instruments similar to those I had installed in Hamburg. Poland was soon invaded. My parents, sister and brother were obliged to move into the ghetto. They were in a room in which eight people lived together. At this time we were allowed to send small packages to Poland, half a pound of food. I sent them daily in my name and the name of friends. When we lost contact we wrote to them through the Red Cross. Later I learned that they had received very few of the packages.

In Paris, meanwhile, I was contacted by the French and English intelligence services, who wanted information about the Hamburg refinery where I had previously installed the instruments. It was a very important industrial center for the Germans and the refinery was bombed over two hundred times. I did my best to help them.

In 1940, just before the Germans marched into Paris, the company I worked for moved to Niort but after the Germans took Paris they came to Niort as well. In January of 1941 I was back in Paris. I married the Swiss-born woman whom I had met in Paris and who had come to Niort when I did. At this time France was divided in two parts and we were in occupied France. They asked all the Jews to register and we made a foolish decision. We thought at first that it wasn't necessary for us because it was hard to tell a Jew from a Frenchman; on the other hand, we felt we would not be true to ourselves and our heritage if we didn't register. So we foolishly decided to be in the same situation as all the other Jews in Paris.

The concierge in our house warned us that some French and German gentlemen were looking for me and left a message that I was to remain in the apartment and wait for them to return. I understood immediately that it was time to leave. I put a few things in a briefcase, and my wife and I went to her cousins, who were Swiss citizens and still safe from the Germans. We stayed with them until we found someone from the French underground to take us to unoccupied France. I had very dear friends in Lyons and I knew they would welcome us.

A man took us to Bordeaux and from Bordeaux by car to a given spot in the woods. We could look up and see two Germans walking with dogs and when they were distracted we crossed over the road and quickly got into a waiting car and started driving at full speed, changing roads so it would be hard to follow us. We paid quite a bit for this help. There was an older couple with us; the man was a music director. He and his wife and my wife were very frightened. I was the only one who was calm. Then we went by train to Lyons.

My friend in Lyons was the brother of an engineer who had worked with me. He was married to a Frenchwoman who was without religion, a woman who helped many refugees to get to Spain and did marvelous things for Jews. They were very good to us. They shared their bread, even though everything was rationed and we had no coupons.

Our objective was to get to the United States. My wife's mother was in New York where she had a large family. As soon as we were married she went to the American ambassador to ask for visas for both of us. Actually I had gotten a visa in 1937. I had a brother who came to the United States in 1920, and he had sent me a visa, but I just didn't want to leave France. I loved France. I had schooling there and my work and I didn't want to get too far from my family in Warsaw. As long as I was in Paris there was some hope that I could help them. Once away from Europe I would leave them entirely without hope. In Lyons, however, we saw that they would also be gathering up the Jews there and that there was nothing to do but leave the country.

Unfortunately the American embassy in France, which had our documents, was closed. Everything we had done to acquire visas was obsolete. We had to start all over again—while hiding in the apartment, afraid to go out lest we were stopped and questioned. Even when the American visas arrived we still had to have an exit visa, a Spanish visa and a Portuguese visa because the boat we were supposed to take left from Lisbon.

It was hard to get a French exit visa unless you could find a doctor willing to give you a false certificate saying you were incapable of doing military service. They knew that French people and Jews would try to get out to join the English army. The doctors who gave the certificates were frightened; one had been put in prison. I was in a desperate situation.

I got in touch with the Polish underground and convinced them to get me a Spanish visa because of my work with the Polish miners. For the Portuguese visa we contacted a friend of my wife's mother who worked at the Portuguese embassy and he arranged it for us. The only obstacle was the French exit visa.

One morning, entirely desperate, I left the apartment without telling my wife or my friends where I was going. I went directly to the chief doctor of the Department of Rhone. When he received me I told him that I was a Jew, and that I had everything ready to leave but the French exit visa and if he could give me a certificate that I was not able to do military service I could leave. If I didn't leave, he knew what would happen to me sooner or later.

He got very mad that I dared to ask him to do something illegal. He threatened to call the police and have me arrested. I told him I thought there were still a few Frenchmen who understood and were willing to take some chances to help people like me and that I was terribly disappointed in him. I didn't refuse any assignment when I was working while the French were still fighting and we were doing things for the French army. And then I started to walk out.

Suddenly he called me back and told me to sit down. He didn't speak for a couple of minutes. Then he pulled out a picture from the drawer of his desk and looked at it for a few minutes before showing it to me. I saw a very beautiful young girl. He told me it was his first wife who was Jewish, from a little Polish town. She died soon after their marriage and he remarried and had children with another woman. He said that he was sure that if she were alive it would have pleased her very much if he would help me. And because of this he told me to get undressed to see if he could find something.

I was perfectly healthy so it wasn't easy, but he detected little varicose veins in my legs and said that he would use them as an excuse for a certificate saying I was not able to do military service. He wouldn't accept a penny from me. I was very grateful. My wife and my friends couldn't believe my daring, but when one is really desperate one tries everything.

We went to Spain without problems. A friend had arranged a

deposit of two hundred dollars for me in a Portuguese bank, which was very important, because we could only take out ten dollars in French money and we couldn't survive on that while waiting for the boat. As soon as we got to Lisbon we found an organization that would send packages to Warsaw. It was so sunny and warm in Lisbon I was tempted to stay a while and relax before taking the boat but my wife, fortunately, said, "Nothing doing," and we left. It turned out that we departed on the last American boat. During the night while we were at sea the lights were turned out. We were told that Pearl Harbor had been bombed and that the United States was at war. It was what we were waiting for. We knew that the Germans would be punished if the United States was involved.

Sam Berry was thirty years old when he, his wife Betty and their new baby were sent to Shordilla from Sosnowiec. From there Sam and Betty were transported to Buchenwald, Auschwitz and Ravensbruck.

We really didn't believe it was going to happen. People made fun of Hitler in the beginning. They said he was talking big and had paper tanks.

I was always getting into fights with the billie-boys, the young hooligans who'd grab an old Jew by the beard and knock him down on the street. I couldn't stand to see those things. I beat them up and sometimes they beat me. I would have been happy to leave Poland in those days if I had the chance.

I had a chance but it came too early. In 1928, a year after my father died, a cousin of my father from Rio de Janeiro came to see us. She'd left the town more than thirty years before, married in South America and become very rich. She wanted to show her husband where she came from and brought gifts for all of us. My mother and sister each got a diamond ring.

These cousins had no children and wanted to adopt me and

take me back where I could have a comfortable life and be safe from Polish troubles, but I wouldn't leave my mother. She wasn't well and I was the only one home. I didn't leave until I married Betty in 1939. Then my mother went to stay with my married sister.

And then the war broke out and the Germans came in and everybody began running. My wife's family set out for Kiev, where they had family, but I thought we'd be safer in my mother's house in Sendiszow, about a hundred and twenty kilometers away. I thought the Germans wouldn't bother bombing a poor little town like that. So we took a few things and left.

First we took the train but the soldiers threw all the civilians off. We tried another train but the tracks were bombed, and we had to go on foot like everyone else. The roads were jammed with people. The planes were over our heads, dropping bombs, and we kept hiding in the ditches at the side of the road.

But we made it to Sendiszow and found the family all together in my mother's house. The only trouble was that the Germans had gotten there before us. The first night after we arrived there was a knock on the door and a few German soldiers came in and began snooping around, seeing how scared we were. One said he didn't like the way I looked at him so he put his pistol to my head as if he were going to shoot me. You can imagine the scene. My wife and my mother began crying and screaming. They settled on just giving me a few slaps, and left. We thought it was a miracle we were left alive, but it was the way in the beginning to scare people.

We stayed crowded in with the family for a few days and then went back. The Germans were everywhere. There was no place to hide from them. My wife and I organized a horse and wagon with another family and bought some flour and meat so we'd have some food when we came home. We walked behind the wagon most of the way.

They had already killed a few hundred young people in Sosnowiec. Anybody on the street or on a balcony who looked suspicious was finished—Jew or non-Jew, they didn't know the difference. Then they called all Jewish men to the marketplace and marched us down to one of the factories that had a big hall and kept us for three days. They wanted to know who represented the Jewish community and nobody had the courage to speak up.

Moshe Mein volunteered. He was kind of a playboy, a different type than the rest of us. He came from a nice family but he was one of those who took advantage of every occasion. And so he and his helpers became the big bosses. They were not Jews anymore; they had privileges nobody else had. They were in charge of the Jewish militia. Its job was not just to keep the bagel peddlers off the street but to get information for the SS, which gave the orders, and to do their dirty work for them. The Jewish militia knew who had money and jewels, where there were warehouses full of food, candy and other things, and they delivered the two or three hundred people a week for the labor camps. Those who didn't have the money to bribe them were sent away. The Germans would give them an order, for example, for twenty pounds of gold, or all the furs, and the militia got it for them.

Right away there was a curfew and we couldn't walk on the sidewalk, and then we had to register. My lumber business was taken over. My mother-in-law had a lot of merchandise from her business in her apartment where we were staying. So we began selling the stuff on the black market. We sold everything, little by little—jewels, watches, and diamonds, it all went to buy food. I took all kinds of risks to see what I could do. I would take off my badge and take the streetcar, which was forbidden, to get to people I knew who would make a little deal. And since I look Jewish—couldn't look more Jewish—my heart was always pumping very hard from fear. But the main thing for me was to protect my family.

Then one summer day there was the big selection in Sosnowiec. The Jewish community people came with all kinds of propaganda, willingly or unwillingly, to tell us nothing bad would happen, that there would be no problems, that we just had to have our papers checked. I myself didn't believe them, but they finally convinced us to come together in the square. Thousands of people, families with children and old people, and when we got there we were surrounded by SS with machine guns and they began separating people into groups. Some were released and went home. Most were kept and sent to Auschwitz. That was the first awful experience we had.

I worked in a shop for a *Sondercard,* the blue piece of paper signed by a German official that was supposed to save me from deportation. We got no pay and plenty of beatings if we were not fast enough. But if we were lucky we could unload a truck and get a bag of potatoes for our work, or a few sacks of coal. And we had a little community working near the railroad for the little bit we could take home. But then the Nazis decided to clean out the Sosnowiec ghetto and move us all out to Shordilla, about ten miles from the center of the city.

Shordilla was a settlement of little houses where poor working people lived. They moved them out somewhere and we had to move in. Me, my wife, the baby, and my wife's mother were given a room with another family. The other family was a mother, two grown-up girls, a married son and two babies.

We all had to use the same toilet, the same kitchen. That was the way it was. And in the center of Shordilla they built a barrack where the Jewish community organization moved in and all around us were tents for the German police, and the barbed wire went up around us, and there was nothing we could do. We knew what would happen to us but all we could do was live from day to day.

We built bunkers under the steps, in the basement and up in the attic. We had our own guards day and night. When they saw the police coming our way, we got a signal and would hide ourselves. We had sleeping medication for the children because it was terrible if they began to cry. You have twenty people hiding in a bunker and some kid starts in and everyone is lost. Those who didn't have children didn't want them in the bunker. Children were smothered so they wouldn't make any noise. When we would try to give our son the sleeping medicine he would say, "I'm not going to cry. I know the Gestapo is upstairs." You can imagine the feeling when your two-year-old tells you he knows the Gestapo is upstairs.

Some people committed suicide but my wife and I believed that the front was coming closer and closer and we would survive. In August 1943 my wife's mother, sister, and brother-in-law were taken while we were hiding in the basement with the baby. When we came out after the action was over, I took the child and ran down the hill to a hospital. I had heard that the nurses there took children and cared for them and I wanted to bring him to safety before we were taken in the last transport. And just as I came to the hospital, the truck came in front of me, and the soldiers threw me on and pulled the child from me. I can't forget that moment. I went through the misery of the Shordilla ghetto, and then was dragged off to Buchenwald and Auschwitz. I was in Buchenwald in the last days, when the strong survived by stealing the last crumb of bread from those too weak to defend themselves. I dug ditches in the cold without clothes, without shoes, knowing I'd freeze to death if I stopped for a moment. But whatever I went through, and with all the miserable things still bleeding in me, the biggest loss in my life was when they took that baby from me, that baby crying so loud, and smashed it on the ground.

What kept me alive was the wish for revenge. That gave me the will to live, that and the hope I'd see some relative alive. I was able to work. They sent me out to work in the coal mines, and then somewhere to build a synthetic rubber factory and I thought, "If I work I will survive, and if I survive I will take my revenge."

When the Russians were so close we felt the ground rumbling the Germans made us walk to Gdansk. We walked the whole night long in wooden-soled shoes, skidding and sliding in the snow. When we stopped to rest for a few hours in a farm, I and a few others crept to the haystack and stayed there overnight. We thought we were going to be liberated. But the front didn't move and we were caught and taken to a cattle car where we were locked up seven days without food. The only reason we survived is because some people threw us bread and rolls when the train stopped. In Czechoslovakia people threw bread down on the train from the bridges when the train went underneath. About half the people in my train died. I escaped three times from the groups going to Buchenwald. I was walking and there was a little barrack on the side. I just moved away from the others and crawled under the barrack. And the SS saw me and beat me up so badly—see that spot I have? It's where he hit me with a rifle —and I just lay unconscious for I don't know how long. I and another fellow were lying there in the mud under the barrack and we crept into a hole and lived there the last four days till we got liberated on the eleventh of April.

The moment of liberation was one of emotion and happiness —the most emotional feelings a person can imagine. But the Germans ran away and left hundred of bodies to bury, and those of us still alive went looking for food and clothes. We didn't have any money. I was in such bad condition I was put in the hospital. I wasn't sick with a disease, I just couldn't walk. I stayed in the Buchenwald area for about six weeks. The Russians came in and the Americans pulled out. I was organizing the food the Americans left behind. I worked in the warehouse to get food for the kitchens. Rations came in by the carload, good things we had never heard of. The stuff was worth a fortune. But then I got a message that my wife was alive and I left everything behind and took off to find her. It took me about a week to get to Sosnowiec, by train, by bus and mostly by foot.

Something pulled me back to Sosnowiec, where I was born and raised. I found that the grandparents left some property there, land and buildings and everything. But going back was foolish. The neighbors surrounded the house and wanted to kill me. I had to jump through a window to get away. Then I found my wife. She was working with some children that had survived, that had come from the camps and the hiding places. There was no one to take care of them, so she with some other people got them together in a big house and fed them.

I had a thousand dollars when I left Poland but I didn't go into the black market. I just started to live a little bit. We had enough food and we had parties and played cards with our friends. I just relaxed until the money was gone. Then this fellow came along and asked if I wanted to make some money, and he took me to a place where they were mixing alcohol and putting it in different bottles. He was getting ten dollars a bottle for this "mixed cognac." I bought ten bottles to sell in the black market. I got six or seven dollars a bottle and the people who bought from me sold it for ten.

Then I got the idea to do my own mixing. I organized some alcohol and coloring and old bottles from different places, and I was used big pots and pans we had in the house. I made myself a little factory. The night my wife went to the hospital to have our baby I was up the whole night mixing whiskey because buyers were after me and waiting for it to be ready. I even mixed in the bathtub because my pots weren't big enough. There were three of us in it and finally we decided to go to Frankfurt and get a license and open a distillery, a legal business so we shouldn't have to worry. I made a very good life out of it, had a chauffeur and a maid, all the goodies. And we had our daughter Ann, born in 1948.

My wife wanted to go to Israel. My way of thinking was that I'm a Jew with all the trimmings, with heritage and other things, and I thought for me it's better to go to America. I had lived through the camps. I had had enough of a rough life. I wanted a little easier and better life. I didn't want to raise my kids in Germany and I didn't want to miss the chance to go to America. I heard it was a free country and that if you want to work you can make a life; you don't have to be afraid of your religion or your upbringing. Understand, I'm not a believer, I'm not an Orthodox Jew—I have to be honest, I never was.

When we heard that two hundred thousand refugees would be permitted to come to the United States we registered. A few months later they said they found a place for me in Richmond, Virginia, to work in a lumber mill. We left from Hamburg on a troop ship full of refugees. We were with a lot of people and a lot of hopes going to a new world.

> Stanley Bors from Sosnowiec was forced into the
> Warsaw ghetto. He and his wife managed to
> escape the ghetto with the help of friends. They
> survived in Poland with false identity papers.

I graduated from college in 1939 just in time for the war to begin. It was not a surprise. The years we spent in college were the most political years of our lives. We did not have sports—sports were considered a waste of time. But we spent all our spare time at political meetings, all of us, Jews and gentiles. We knew the war was coming.

In October 1939 I married the girl I had known as a student in Warsaw. She came from Lublin. We were married by a rabbi in Lublin and then wanted to spend some time in Slonim, a town in eastern Poland where my parents were living. It was when we were returning to Lublin that we were caught in Warsaw and forced into the Warsaw ghetto. We called her parents in Lublin the day before they were taken to Treblinka. Later we were told that my father-in-law, who was the president of the Jewish community, was punished for refusing to follow some German orders.

I did nothing in the ghetto. My wife worked for the post office. We lost all contact with our families and were just two more Jews among the million in the ghetto. After a while the Germans began to go street by street and pick up the people they were sending to the liquidation camps. My wife at that time got a job in a fur factory repairing and making coats for German soldiers on the Russian front. This job saved her life. Without it we would have been sent away with the others. I fortunately met a college friend with an uncle who owned a bakery and he gave me a job selling bread. So this gave me the right to stay in the ghetto. Actually it was no longer a ghetto but a labor camp, and the only people left were those who were working for the Germans in some way. There was a request for a group of Jews to work on the farm that adjoined the airport and I was asked to be foreman of the group. Trucks came to pick us up every morning and they brought us back to the ghetto in the evening. The work was not too difficult and the air force soldiers were not the SS, and treated us like human beings. The danger was in going back and forth in the open trucks. Young Polish people threw stones at us all the way, and many of us got hurt. The irony of it all was that the German soldiers were protecting us from Polish people.

All through this we were trying to figure out how to get out of the ghetto. If the Polish population would have been willing to help, many thousands could have survived. The Polish population not only did not help, but if they knew of Jews living outside the ghetto they informed the Germans. Some of my friends got out but didn't survive because people informed on them.

I had a good friend of my family who had been a maid in my aunt's house before the war. She was a gentile person but willing to help us because of friendship and also because she expected some money. My wife also had relatives, her mother's uncles, who had converted many years ago. We were in contact with them and they were also willing to help us. They were wonderful people and offered to do anything they could. Our first plans to get out of the ghetto, however, involved my aunt's maid. She came into the ghetto to visit us a few times. It was illegal, but she was smuggled in. The arrangement we made with her was that we would jump out of the truck as we were going back from the airport where we worked—the truck drove right through her neighborhood—and the plan was that she would wait for us and take us back to her apartment. The trucks were very crowded and moved very slowly. The soldiers guarding us were not from the Gestapo or SS. An SS man seeing someone jump off the truck would kill him on the spot, but an ordinary soldier might let him go if there were no witnesses. Our soldiers were just young boys, talking to each other, and didn't give a darn if a Jew escaped. Anyway, the gamble was not that great because we knew we'd be killed sooner or later if we remained in the ghetto. We were no heroes, we were just trying to survive. We got out only a few weeks before the ghetto was liquidated.

Everything went according to plan. Our only worry was that our friend lived very close to the ghetto, and that was a very dangerous place to be. At the time of the liquidation the Jews left in the ghetto started to escape, mostly through the sewers, and the Germans were constantly searching the buildings in the area.

If you wonder why we weren't part of the underground I have to explain that we knew nothing about it. I would have joined if I knew about it but I didn't know of its existence. We were strangers in Warsaw. The underground was a small secret group of people, the Zionist-oriented youth who knew each other well enough to trust each other. It was the only way they could operate without being discovered by the Gestapo. The ghetto had its own police, post office and employment agency. The president was an honest man and didn't want to cooperate with the Germans. He committed suicide. But there were others who did collaborate. And the only idea of an underground movement we had was that Jewish collaborators were shot every now and then.

My wife's uncle who lived in Rembertow, a suburb of Warsaw, was very concerned for our safety and came to take us to his house. That involved a trip by streetcar with a few close calls with Germans, but we finally made it to the suburb. He was living in a single large room in a villa that belonged to a Polish colonel, and there were two other Jewish families hiding out in that villa. That Polish colonel was a very unusual person, and helped a lot of people. He himself was hiding from the Germans and could be sent to a concentration camp if the Germans found him. In the time he had before he was caught he not only hid Jews but also arranged to get them false documents.

One day a boy came to the house to say that the Gestapo was on the way. We left immediately. We owe our lives to that boy. They came ready to kill everybody. They executed a couple with a seven-year-old child. The Gestapo brought a priest along to interrogate people and see if they were really Catholics—everybody was pretending to be Catholic. My uncle was not recognized as a converted Jew, because he knew about the Catholic religion.

We ran away to my wife's other uncle, the one who was married to a gentile woman. They lived in Grodzisk, another suburb of Warsaw. We were able to stay with them till the end of the war. The family consisted of the uncle, his wife and his young daughter. We were six people in a two-bedroom house. All our relatives were gambling with their lives by helping us. We had false birth certificates and passports obtained by the colonel through his contacts in city hall, but any priest would know we were Jews from our lack of knowledge about the customs and traditions of the Catholic religion. The priest in that neighborhood didn't report us. He was a good man and didn't want to cooperate with the Germans. There were some Polish Catholics who behaved as human beings. All people who survived had to be helped by somebody.

My wife's uncle was a teacher in his seventies. His wife was about the same age. They were married a long time and had lived in Lodz. When Hitler came they came back to Grodzisk, where his wife's family lived. Everybody knew my uncle was Jewish but no one reported him to the Gestapo. He was a very nice man and always helped the family. His wife's family was very liberal, old-style socialists, which was why she married a Jewish man in the first place. During the war they were in the underground. It was also hard for gentiles to survive the war. They had to deal in the black market, they were involved with smuggling; it was a dangerous life. But this family of my uncle's wife, these were very unusual people. Most of the Poles I met during this period were highly anti-Semitic. Since I was pretending not to be Jewish, people spoke very freely in my presence, and I saw that they were happy about Hitler's solution. Except for that family I never spoke to anybody who was sorry about the liquidation of the Jews. Even the people in the communist underground hated Jews. I was always trying to find some sympathy for Jewish problems, but I never did.

One day the Germans were going house to house looking for somebody and we hid in the garden behind the house. To our surprise we found the people living next door also hiding. We immediately recognized each other as Jews and became friends. Mostly Jews didn't want to know each other. Everyone had false papers and changed names. It was better not to know in case the Gestapo came looking. I once jumped off a running streetcar because I spotted somebody I knew in school. He was a Jew but I didn't know if he worked for the Gestapo. Later, after the war, I met him in Warsaw and he told me he jumped off too because he was afraid of me. That was how it was. Some people didn't want even their family to know where they were.

Eventually there was shooting in our neighborhood and we hid in the basement until the Russians pushed the Germans away. Finally we were liberated. Nobody asked if we were Jewish. We didn't volunteer any information.

We immediately went to Lublin to see if my wife's parents had survived. It took us a week to get there by train. It was a very tense journey thanks to a drunk Russian officer who was looking for Jews and promising to kill any he could find. Naturally this was done by an individual, it was not government policy, but it was nerve-wracking just the same.

When we got to Lublin we learned that my wife's parents were dead. We went back to Sosnowiec, where I had friends and relatives, and I almost immediately found a job in the Agricultural Department. They gave me an apartment and a car. The new Polish administration needed people and all the specialists they could find in order to get started. I was sent to Katowice in Silesia and we were living peacefully again until the Polish Underground, former resistance fighters, began killing Jews. In 1945 they began murdering the liberated Jews, the handful who had survived the Holocaust. They also began to investigate people and arrest them without provocation. In the office where I worked someone was arrested, nobody knew why. People began to be afraid to talk to each other. A friend of mine who was a doctor was killed in his office. They just came and killed him.

Immediately after the shootings began we left Poland. I didn't believe we had a chance for a peaceful life in Poland. I was identified as a Jew. I was born and raised in the area in which I lived and many people knew me. There was no way I could hide being a Jew, and I didn't want to anyway.

At the beginning of 1946 the borders were not established or closed. People were crossing them, going west to West Germany. We didn't have any specific plans so we went to Berlin. We stayed there until the Russians started the cold war with the Americans. In 1947, still in Berlin, I found the addresses of some relatives in Chicago. It was a wonderful discovery because these relatives, George and Hattie Bernstein, were very fine people and gave us both financial and moral help that made our lives much easier. They sent packages to us, things we could exchange for food and other goods, and they also were trying to bring us over to the United States.

We left Berlin to live in Munich. Munich University had an experimental chicken farm and I worked there without pay to learn about chicken farming. Three of us, my wife, our daughter born in 1946 and I, were able to live on the packages that came from Chicago.

We stayed in Germany from 1945 to 1949, expecting every day to hear that some place would let us in. We knew we didn't want to stay in Germany. We saw a murderer in every German we passed in the street. We kept to ourselves and had no contacts with Germans. We didn't go to movies or concerts. I spoke German, of course; I was born and lived close to the German border in Poland. But I knew no Germans even before the war. I associated only with Jews. I was in contact with the Joint Distribution Committee but didn't need their financial help. Our family in America was so generous we were able to help other people ourselves. But in order to emigrate you had to be registered with a Jewish agency. They gave us back our identity and all the documents and certificates we needed after the years of false papers. They verified my education and diplomas. As it happened I had all my original school documents but most people had none. Mine had been buried in a glass jar all through the war and I was able to dig them up and find them in good shape. The hard thing was to wait four years hoping to hear from Israel, the United States or Australia. If the Truman administration had not agreed to admit displaced persons we could still be waiting for a place in the Polish quota. We came with the second hundred thousand that were let in. We were on a preferred quota because my cousin Archie Bernstein had a friend who was a farmer in South Haven and he sponsored us to come to the United States as farmers. He was another extraordinary man in my life. He was not Jewish but he helped bring about fifty people in, taking the risk that he would have to support them if they couldn't make a living.

Helene Frankle and her parents left Kolo, Poland,
after their mill was bombed. Her mother was shot
in the Warsaw ghetto, but father and daughter
escaped through the sewers of Warsaw.

I remember that an uncle came to visit us from America. He had no children and he begged my father to let us go back with him. My father would say, "I have an America here." There was absolutely no question about leaving Poland. We lived in a fool's paradise.

About two years before the war broke out there began to be changes that disturbed us a little. My father had been a representative to the chamber of commerce and he wasn't anymore. We began to see signs, "Buy only in Polish stores!" This was government propaganda, not a local effort, and it became really scary. There were many Jewish businesses in our town and they suffered. My father had one of the biggest mills in the district so he was not affected.

I had many Polish friends and always felt like one of them, except on occasion. For instance, they would go to the girl scout camp and I couldn't go because Jews were excluded. The universities were an open slaughterhouse. You really took your life in your hands when you enrolled. The Jewish students were physically attacked, and seriously wounded sometimes. A boy who was a friend of ours was thrown from the third floor and was hospitalized for months. There was a horrible story about a young man killed in the university, and then there were beautiful letters in the newspaper written by Polish women saying how ashamed they were. The majority of the people were not in favor of the violence, but they were also not against it.

I was not at the university. My sister left school to get married, but people did not leave because of the fights. It was so difficult to get in that no student would leave because he was afraid of being hurt. Many of my sister's friends studied medicine in Italy because it was impossible to go to medical school in Poland. But when they came back with their diplomas they couldn't get into a hospital and they couldn't set up private practices. If they didn't have parents to help them they would be ushers at movie houses or wash dishes in restaurants. I tell this because it explains why they were hoping for a war. They thought a war was the only solution and that it would bring some kind of change. There was a tremendous amount of anti-Semitism, sometimes covered up, often not covered at all. And all the time we didn't see what we didn't really want to see.

When it became clear that war would break out we also suddenly began to be afraid that something would happen to us. The feeling was that a Jew was not really a Polish citizen, and that first feeling of being Jewish and not Polish came upon us the first day of the war. My father's mill was next to the railroad station because they had their own railroad outlet and my sister was helping him because many people were leaving and everything was unsettled. I don't remember what day of the week it was, but it was the first of September and I remember being in the bedroom with my mother and hearing the planes. And I went out on the balcony and began counting them, sure they were ours, and all of a sudden the bombs started falling. They were bombing the railroad station three miles away and someone came by yelling, "Your mill was hit . . . the station was hit!"

It was the first day of the war in a town of twenty thousand people. We were absolutely panicked. We didn't know what was going on. The telephone wasn't functioning. The hospital wasn't equipped to handle such an emergency—more than a hundred and fifty people were injured. We didn't know whether my father and sister were among them. It was a fantastic, difficult situation and immediately we had the feeling of not belonging, of being unwanted strangers.

Eventually my dad and sister came home, unharmed, but the exodus to the east had begun. The roads were full of people, carts, cars, buggies and horses. My father left. My grandfather stayed and kept his mill running. He kept on producing flour. He was eighty-one but full of strength and thinking he was dealing with the same Germans he dealt with in the First World War. He thought it was a good opportunity to feed the town and make himself some money. He was probably the only Jewish man in the whole city until the other men, including my father, came straggling back, because there really wasn't any place to go.

Then the Germans came. My brother-in-law was caught in the part of Poland that belonged to Russia and he tried to get my sister to join him. By December the horrible things were happening around us. The Gestapo was rounding Jews up and beating them. The Poles immediately became informers and we saw we didn't have many friends after all. Some were friendly but that put them in danger. I'm not so enraged at those who didn't help, because it really was dangerous, but I cannot forgive the ones that were pointing you out and turning you in. No one in my family looked Jewish, we were all blond and had blue eyes, but everybody in town knew us so there was no way we could say we weren't Jewish. And then there was a shortage of food and Jews were not permitted to stand in line. The Poles would show the German soldiers who the Jews were and they were pulled out.

At one point my father was arrested and we were all in hysterics. They kept him in jail a few days and beat him badly. We decided then to leave Kolo. We couldn't stand the fear. When my father was released he managed to get to Warsaw and I began making trips to Warsaw. Not looking Jewish, I could buy a train ticket and take a few things. I was away when they came to deport the Jews of our town. They came in the middle of the night and put them all in the temple, my grandfather included. My sister found a German officer who agreed to take her and my mother, who could no longer walk very well, to Warsaw. She paid him some money. He was in the regular army, not the Gestapo, and kept saying how thoroughly upset he was about the whole business with the Jews. My mother, in her trusting way, gave him a little bag of jewelry to carry. When they got to Warsaw he gave it back but a couple of pieces were missing, so we don't know if he helped them for the love of humanity or not.

In Warsaw we stayed in a big room in the apartment of friends who had gone to Russia. We shared it with other people. The only trouble was that it was winter and there was no heat, and my mother couldn't walk, and my father had no money. He was a good businessman but not good at *Luftgeschäft*, the only kind of buying and selling and trading that was possible at that time. He was very upset because he didn't know how to do it. We just barely had enough money for food, mostly acquired by selling jewelry.

My sister went to join her husband who was working as an agricultural engineer on the Russian side of Poland. She lived quite well until the Germans took the area over in 1940. She could have fled to Russia but she refused because she was afraid she would never see my parents again. My sister was the kind of woman that if she were in hell or whatever she would have gotten news to my parents somehow. So she stayed in Poland and the Germans shot her. My grandfather was shot on his eighty-second birthday.

The ghetto started in Warsaw in 1941. I'm not too sure of the date. It was a gradual thing. First we had to move out of the apartment because it was outside the ghetto boundary and then we rented another large room within the ghetto. Mother had all her friends from our hometown and they would come in the afternoon to play cards with her. I would go out in the afternoon and come back in time to help her go to the washroom. It was a difficult time. I resented being responsible for her and she resented needing my help. We were both angry and sorry and yet it was a time with some stability.

I had never done any work in the house and now I had to do the shopping and the cooking. When my sister was alive she would write letters telling me how she admired my cooking. In the afternoon I would go out and meet my friends. The ghetto was a very strange place in Warsaw. There were nightclubs and theaters. People were dying of hunger in the street but there were restaurants full of food. I was dating my husband, who came from Warsaw. One of the advantages was that he still had some money and whenever he came to pick me up my hope was that he would take me out to eat. I was constantly hungry.

So there was this contrast—being hungry and going to cabarets and concerts. You could see the best actors, hear the best pianists and singers in the Warsaw ghetto. It was very exciting. There were hundreds of little kids crying and begging for bread in the streets, and singing this tragic song, like a nightmare. We used to throw food down to them. Mother would take her little piece of bread, and when nobody would see, she would throw it out the window to the kids. You'd have your favorite kids, and then one day you'd see them dead in the street.

It was very easy to get people to volunteer for the camps. The German government promised them fresh air, an area without sickness, and two pounds of bread and lots of marmalade and other goodies. The first trains were crowded with hungry people thinking they were going to improve their lives. And then in 1942 we began to hear stories about people being gassed, killed, done away with.

Of course it was very hard to believe. An old boyfriend of

mine appeared suddenly. He had been sent to the same town as my grandfather and from there to Treblinka, with his whole family. He jumped the train and came to Warsaw. He told us it was true that the people were taken to be gassed. My mother, an extremely down-to-earth woman, very bright and aware, believed him; she had heard the tragic stories before and felt that they were true. My father, an optimist at heart, refused to believe them. I remember him as the gentlest of men, I don't remember him screaming at me three times in his whole life, but he practically kicked my old friend out of the house. He said they were lies and he didn't want to hear them. I believed him—why would he lie? But most people didn't believe.

I also had to take care of my mother while my father was working. One day she was sick. It was a beautiful, sunny day in August and I looked out the window and saw the Germans coming from building to building. Her apartment was in a corner house right next to the wall. Standing on the balcony you could see across to the Polish side, over the wall. I remember seeing the people, dressed up, sitting around drinking coffee or tea. Maybe it's a fantasy that I remember this, but I think I saw them just like that while we were waiting for the Germans to knock on the door, and I thought, "My God, they're so safe over there, and we're cockroaches waiting for the exterminator." I locked the door. I hoped maybe they'd miss us. We heard them in the courtyard calling for everybody to come down but I stayed with my mother. They came looking for us. They weren't Germans, they were Lithuanians. I couldn't understand the language. I tried to tell them my mother was sick and couldn't walk but she was sitting and she didn't look sick even though she couldn't stand up. One of them pulled me out of the room. They tried to pull her and then I heard the shot.

They dragged me down to the yard where there were lots of people, and then took us to the railroad station. Luckily one of my cousins was in the Jewish police unit. He found me there and took me home. My father was there but they wouldn't let me go upstairs.

My boyfriend insisted that we get married; he thought his paper would save me. But I was afraid to leave my hiding place even to get married. He went to the rabbi and we were married by proxy, and he came one day with a little piece of paper that said we were married.

Father and I lived in a small room in an apartment where two other families lived. I cooked for him. We had bread and a little bit of meat he didn't know was horsemeat. My new husband lived with his family. After a while we were married properly in the rabbi's house. Bernard's parents came and my father and a few strangers picked up in the street to make a quorum of ten. I remember his mother trying to tell me the facts of life, not knowing we had been living together quite a while. After the ceremony we went to his parents' house for dinner. He stayed with me overnight in that little room with my father and then went back to his family. Nevertheless I got pregnant, and had an abortion in the doctor's office. There was no such thing as birth control. Those who could afford it arranged abortions. My father gave me the money. Soon after that the ghetto uprising began. It was in another part of the ghetto. Here we were, two young people anxious to go and fight, and we couldn't get to the area where it was happening. We couldn't get weapons. We were in the building where my father had the mill. The flour was smuggled in through a sewer. We had a plan to get out of the ghetto through the sewer. A neighbor who had a nephew living with a Polish woman had fixed up a little hiding place out of the ghetto for them but they couldn't figure out how to get there. They said to me, "Look, if you can show us the way out we'll take you and your dad to a hiding place." We had the connection and it was not for free; it was a great deal of money we had from the mill and we paid it. The Polish underground was supposed to get us out. You had to have a guide because the sewers are not like you see in the movies; there was a tremendous amount of water and it was very long and very narrow. You had to crawl half the way and Warsaw is a big city; we had miles to go under the ground.

It was a horrible night when we left. There were many people in the building and everybody wanted to get out and couldn't. It was the third day of the uprising and there was shooting all over. They were looking for us with dogs. In the beginning you had to crawl and walk. My father couldn't, he just fainted, and my husband was behind him and we were going single file. When one person stopped, everybody stopped. The man who used to get the flour had his parents on a sled, and he promised to come back with it to get my father. Looking back it all seems insane—my father, my husband and me sitting there in the dark in the water wondering whether he'd come back. We heard the noise above our heads when daytime started, horses, cars, people right over us while we sat and waited.

Finally they came with a little cart for my father. We were the last people to get out through the sewer. The way was closed after we went in. We got out on the Polish side and there were already people waiting for Jews to emerge to blackmail them. We came out in the middle of the morning. I had dry shoes in a plastic bag. The gentile woman, the nephew's girlfriend, was waiting for us. We hadn't taken ten steps before a guy came along saying something about having a Jewish lady with you. He followed us until we gave him a thousand zlotys. That's how he made his living.

We went to this woman's house and there were about fifty Jews there. Little by little people came to pick them up. My dad was taken to a little room hidden behind some furniture. He was very unhappy and really wanted to be picked up and taken to a camp like the others. I blackmailed him into coming with me by telling him I would not go unless he did. The ghetto was burning by then and I felt both tremendous anger and relief to be out. You see, I never heard a word of sympathy. All I heard was the remark that "because of those Jews our city is burning." And I'd hear people say that one good thing about the war was it got rid of the Jews—I heard that again and again.

I came to the apartment where Dad was staying with four other people and the woman asked where I got the money to pay the guide, and they took the money. They hid a few Jews but they were glad that most of them were destroyed. My father and the others were afraid to move, afraid to walk, afraid to talk because someone might hear them. They couldn't go to the washroom and flush the water. It was horrendous. I felt so guilty for bringing him there.

Bernard and I had false papers. We found an apartment. The woman who rented it to us knew we were Jewish but she let us stay. We paid her lots of money. But the tragedy was that my husband's family was left behind. We saw the flames of the burning ghetto and knew they were there. I cannot begin to tell you the torture this man has gone through. I can talk about my parents with a joyful feeling. I have happy memories of my childhood, maybe made up, but I have them. He has only this tremendous feeling of sadness, all-consuming really. Not that I don't feel guilt; I do. But it has blighted his life. He knows in his head that he couldn't save them. He tried to reach them but the way was barred. All he could have done was die with them. It's a very difficult thing to live with.

It wasn't as if we had come to safety. I was running around

trying to make all kinds of arrangements. I'd give money and then try to get it back because they weren't doing what they promised. And then one day two plainclothesmen, Poles from the Gestapo, arrived. Somebody had informed them that Jews are living in the apartment. They wanted money, everything we had. It was like a nightmare. They were playing two different roles, teasing us. Sometimes they were sympathetic and seemed to be trying to help us, sometimes they were just mean and hostile. Finally they took some money and left. We had to leave as well because they might come back, but they followed us. At four in the morning they took us to the police station and by then the whole building knew the Jews had been found and taken to the police. By seven in the morning when the curfew was over they let us go. I left the gold bracelet that my husband's parents had given me and my watch.

A long story—checks for circumcision, arrangements to get to Switzerland that fell through, and finally special papers to go to Vienna as foreign workers. Unbelievable how lucky we were! When we got to Vienna we were again the last to get away with those false papers. We asked for work in a small factory and we both worked making small motors. I was the only woman. It was a nice place and the people were pleasant. Our only problem was our fear of the other Poles. They were the ones who always said they could smell a Jew, and we knew we didn't look like Polish workers. But we worked in the factory and had a little room and we pretended Bernard was an officer in the army and had to run away for something. And the landlady liked how I cleaned her venetian blinds and told us we were nice people even though Poles had a terrible reputation in Vienna. We had a good time in Vienna. We were afraid because our papers were forged, but everybody looked Jewish in Vienna so we felt safe. We worked fifty-five hours a week, eleven hours a day. On Saturday and Sunday we would take trips to the Alps. It was already 1943. Our boss was very much anti-Hitler and he had two sons he saved from the war. He was a clever man. He had had a Jewish partner in his business and had taken it over from him.

We kept our Jewishness secret from everybody, even the Russians when they took over. We hid in the cellar because we were told they were raping, and they were, but our building was safe because it had been hit by a bomb and didn't look as if anyone lived there. I was very excited that the Russians were coming because they were liberating us—raping or not raping, they were liberating us. It was not a good idea to say you were Jewish. But if you said you were Polish they would think you were Fascists because you didn't want to go back.

After two years in Vienna I went back to visit. I knew for some time that my father had been shot and there was no reason to look for anybody. My husband also had no relatives left. But I went back to my hometown to see if I could get the mill back. I went to the judge in Kolo who had been a friend of my father and asked him what I could do to claim the mill. He said, "Our people aren't getting, are you expecting to get it?" And I said, "Oh my God, all my life I thought I was 'our people' also." I got on the next train and never went back.

Dr. William Glicksman was thirty-four years old when the war broke out. Czestochowa became the ghetto for the area. His parents were deported and his wife and child killed before he was sent to Auschwitz to dig in the coal mines.

The ghetto was created around us and we couldn't leave without permission. My hometown had about thirty-three thousand Jews. They brought in people from all around until there were fifty thousand. We got used to the abnormal conditions and went on living. My place of work was outside the ghetto so I had a special permit to come and go. I went to work every day—shoveling work, slave-labor work. I came home. I ate dinner. I found I could live without an apple or an orange. We had soup, potatoes, bread, sometimes a piece of meat, everything from the black market. The poor people who tried to live on their rations died of hunger. Everything was overturned. Overnight rich and upper-class people were poor and the lower class sometimes got rich through illegal activities.

Meanwhile Jewish culture was strengthened a thousand times. We had secret schools, secret *minyans* for praying. The libraries were burned down so we shared out private books. The older people were studying *Gemara*. The secular people got together to strengthen their spiritual life by discussing Zionism, socialism, literature, anything to save us from falling into despair. I was a left Zionist myself. On November 2, 1942, ten people, including me, observed the twenty-fifth anniversary of the Balfour Declaration. We were hiding in the sewer and above our heads the SS were marching back and forth. The religious people believed that they would be saved and go straight to Paradise because they had already been through the *Gehenna*. The rest of us strengthened ourselves through ideas, whether it was Zionism, communism, socialism. Whatever we suffered, we suffered for an idea. We lived to materialize the idea that sustained us.

On September 22, 1942, the night after Yom Kippur, the deportations began. We knew already something was going to happen, so my wife and child were hiding. They began to empty the ghetto, street by street, and my street was the first to go. I was young and strong, one of the lucky few to be kept for the labor force.

My brother, by that time, was already in Israel; my sister was in France. Another sister and my parents were also in the ghetto but on streets that they hadn't come to yet. My wife was discovered and executed. I brought the child to my sister but my sister was also caught with the child and killed. My father also. My mother tried to escape from the ghetto but they caught her.

When I saw I was alone and there were only five thousand of us left from the ghetto of fifty thousand I made myself a false passport with the name Adam Kowalsky. I spoke excellent Polish and my face wasn't especially Semitic. My idea was to get across through Germany and Austria to the border of Switzerland and I made contact with the smugglers that take you over. There was a group of people and I was supposed to be a peasant coming to the market. I went on the train with the false passport and got to the German border half an hour away from my hometown. There was a friend with me who looked suspicious to the border guard. They arrested us both and turned us over to the Gestapo. A false passport meant treason against the state, and the punishment was hanging.

Instead they sent us to Auschwitz. In Auschwitz I drained swamps. I was sent to dig in the coal mines. I was in solitary confinement for seventy days and beaten to make me tell who made me the false passport. And if you wonder how I lived through it, I will tell you. Right until the last day in Auschwitz, when I was working in the Union Ammunition plant, I stayed alive through spiritual strength. We never forgot for a minute that we were Jews. We didn't need the religion. We didn't need the Hebrew school. We kept the calendar in ourselves. How did we express it? On a Friday night we sang quietly "Lecha Nerannenah," not loud, we sang quietly while sitting at our workbenches. We knew the prayers by heart like we knew our own names. On the twentieth day of *Tammuz*, 1944, right under the eyes of the German supervisor, we said *Kaddish* for Herzl's *Yortzeit*. We talked about Bialik and Achad Ha-am and the subjects we studied in gymnasium. This is how we lasted until the evacuation on January 18.

They awoke us at four in the morning and marched us—five, six thousand people. We marched from Thursday evening to Saturday morning in snow and frost. The Russians were pushing and we were on the way to Dachau, first on foot and then in freight cars. Four weeks we dragged like that, with people dying all the way. I got very sick, almost to death, and it went on and on. For a while we were in a camp in Waldlager. It was by then the middle of March and we were there until the middle of April. American and English soldiers were coming close, and again they put us on cars.

I remember I was on the floor of the car and we stopped at a station and hear all of a sudden a *rat-tat-tat-tat* and there was an American tank platoon going by on the highway on the other side of the station. We thought, "The Americans are running away and we are surrounded by German Gestapo, and it is the end of us." And then suddenly the door of the car opened and an American officer was standing there. I couldn't move but I could see the Germans put down their weapons. The officer came into the car and picked me up on his shoulders and carried me out. It was April 30, 1945.

We were in Seenhaupt near Munich, one of the most beautiful places in Bavaria. The Americans chased the Germans out of some hospital and put us in there to recuperate. In June we were transferred to a hospital in Munich. Right away the Joint came to help us send mail to relatives. I wrote my cousin in Switzerland and my brother in Israel and my sister who came from France to New York.

I wanted to get out of Germany as soon as I was well enough.

Many Jews stayed to get rich in the black market but I wanted none of that. The Joint offered me a job in Germany and I refused. I tried for papers for Israel and America and I thought that whatever came first, there I would go. The papers came from my sister through the Hebrew Immigrant Aid Society and as soon as possible I was on a boat.

Sally Grubman was teaching school in Lodz when the Germans took over. She continued working with the children in the ghetto until they were all taken away. She, herself, was later transported to Auschwitz, then to Ravensbruck and finally to Denmark and freedom.

I was twenty when the Germans came into Lodz. Until the day before they were at the border the Polish patriots were saying they were not afraid of the Germans. The slogan was, "We will not give them even a button from our pants." And then they crossed the border with better soldiers, better ammunition, better planes. We were standing on a balcony watching them go through Lodz. They were singing German songs in loud voices and patriotic Poles were greeting them with hands raised, yelling, "Heil Hitler." They were throwing flowers at them.

The biggest factories in Lodz were owned by German people. There were many Poles of German origin in the city and we later found out that they had a regular fifth column spreading rumors and creating fear. The average Polish man, who was filled with hatred for Jews, thought that we alone would be the victims. The more intelligent Poles knew that what happened to us was only the first step in something terrible. Jews, meanwhile, were very frightened because we knew that the Poles were our enemies as much as the Germans.

My sister was married to a rather wealthy man who was an electronics engineer. They had the money to run and immediately went to Russia which was welcoming Jews at the time.

Thousands of people escaped across the border between Russia and Poland.

My parents and I moved into my sister's apartment when they left. It was in a beautiful section of the city where the wealthy Jews lived. It was from my sister's balcony that I watched the Germans catching Jews. They began raiding apartments at night to search for weapons and jewelry.. They would open every cupboard and take anything they wanted and break things just out of meanness. Another kind of fun for them was to be cruel to people who couldn't defend themselves. They came in one day and told all the people to go into the courtyard and one crippled man couldn't go down the steps so they shot him and let him roll down the three flights. I saw it myself.

We tried all kinds of ideas to discourage the Germans from coming into our apartment. We used to throw ashes from the stove all over the house because they hated to come into a mess they hadn't made. They would say that Jews lived in a terrible mess and they were too clean to come into it. Then it took us hours to clean up after they left our street.

I was a teacher and I was upset because the Germans closed the schools and little children were running wild in the street, but there was nothing we could do until the ghetto was organized. Going into the ghetto was not so bad for us. We had lived there for many years and my father had many acquaintances there, including one working for the housing department who gave us a room in his two-room apartment.

I began working with the children while the ghetto was forming. Chaim Rumkowski, a peculiar old man who sold insurance and took care of the orphanage, had become the head of the *Judenrat*. He had provided the funds so we could keep the children off the streets and give them a bit of food. I remember when he was just an eccentric character, a kind of laughingstock, then suddenly he was the well groomed Czar of the ghetto riding around in a private drovsky, and with the power of life and death over the entire Jewish population. The education department of the ghetto decided to take the orphans, the half-orphans and even some children with parents out to the farthest part of the ghetto behind a Jewish cemetery, an area called Marysin. My future husband Simon was hired as a counselor–teacher, and I was hired as a hygienist. I had to live with the children because our ration cards were given at our place of work. I could visit my parents once a week, on Saturday afternoon.

The children's colony was divided in four sections, each one had five houses and a central kitchen where the food was prepared. The children were responsible for giving out the food three times a day, cleaning the kettle and bringing it back to the kitchen. They also took care of the house they lived in. They had to scrub the floors and do their best to keep the place clean.

The children were always hungry, always scared. Their biggest fear was of being separated from us because we were the only family they had. When it became cold there were not enough warm clothes and many had no shoes. We founded a little hospital with two doctors and a nurse to deal with the extreme cases of frostbite. You have to understand the practical problems of being with children twenty-four hours a day without books, without toys, without television or radio, without even pencils and paper. We taught them songs and dances and told them stories. They made plays and gave performances and wrote stories for each other. There were many good things happening even in those hard times, and we thought we could continue until the war was over.

In September 1942 we were awakened one morning at five by a lot of noise. We went out and found the whole colony surrounded by German soldiers. Some were wearing gas masks and they had their guns pointing at us. We didn't know what was going on. They told us they had lists of all the children and wanted every single one. There were two children that were closer to me than the others. One was four and I knew her from the time she was born, the other was seven, and I was very attached to them and wanted desperately to save them. I took them into a tool shed and told them to stay until I came for them. "I will pick you up in the evening," I promised. "You will be hungry. You will be thirsty. You'll have to go to the bathroom. Do everything here and be quiet because the Germans are here."

There was one child just recovering from pneumonia and I asked the German very politely if he would wrap the child in a blanket. His answer was that the child would be very warm where he was going. And I didn't understand what he was talking about. We didn't know anything about what was happening outside our ghetto.

Later in the morning, when the older children tried to run away, the soldiers began to shoot and my two children in the shed became very frightened and began calling me. The Germans heard them and opened the shed. They took the children and asked them who put them there. When they said that I did they put me on the truck with the children. They put me in the Lodz jail and told me I would be shipped out the next day.

A friend from before the war had become a police official. When he heard that I was in jail he came very quietly and released me. The Germans didn't care who they took so long as they had the right number. My friend substituted another person for me. So today I live with the feeling that somebody's mother, daughter or wife went in my place. At the time it was just one of the things that happened.

We didn't know what happened to the people who were taken. Nobody could understand that people would be taken and burned. This is something a normal human being cannot accept. But it was a very traumatic experience to have the children taken away. Only one was left hiding when the trucks left. As far as we know he was the only one to survive. He lives in Israel today.

I didn't want to work with children any longer. My next job was as a secretary to a man who was the head of a department in a shoe factory.

After I left the shoe factory I got a job as a doctor's assistant in a hospital that had been turned into a factory that made uniforms for German flyers. There was a doctor on each floor, because the workers were given very meager rations and often fainted and needed medical help. My position gave me a little edge over other people; I could get prescriptions for medicine that might be traded for some other help. I had many friends. A few were in top positions like the policeman who saved me. Some were medical students who became chiefs of departments even though they had not finished their medical training.

People were affected by ghetto life in different ways. Some became melancholy and wanted to die, and they just gave up and died. There were people with the driving force to survive under any circumstances, and they were sometimes very creative in keeping some semblance of normalcy alive.

We were allowed to be out from six in the morning until five at night. The curfew at night was very strict, so we dug tunnels between the apartment houses so that we could go visiting without being seen on the street. We would get together to have parties. Everyone brought one slice of bread, a little marmalade and maybe some hot water, and it was a party. Someone would bring a violin or a harmonica that had not been confiscated and there was music. Books were shared. New books were written and reviewed. A good friend of mine recited poetry in Yiddish. His name was Shammai Rosenblum, and he's known in Israel today. We kept our minds going. People were getting married. Some couples were very devoted to each other. Some got married only because they got an extra loaf of bread for a wedding present. I witnessed a wedding of twenty-six couples, a mass wedding. Chaim Rumkowsky said a short prayer, wished everybody luck and gave them the bread. Children were born in the ghetto even though every effort was made to prevent it. Abortions were done very, very often; doctors did them for a loaf of bread or a pound of flour. Since that was very expensive, nurses did the abortions for less.

Some could take the pressures and others became animals, absolute beasts. People who had been good fathers and mothers were stealing their children's food and killing each other. Good people became informers. The Jewish police at first had a rather high standard of morality but the longer the ghetto continued the more impossible it became for a good person to be a policeman in the ghetto. For instance, when the Germans told them that they wanted two hundred children in a week they would first save their own and then their friends' and then had to go into homes and drag out other people's children. The ones who suffered the most were people brought in from other towns who had no friends, no connections, no hope whatsoever.

There were people in the ghetto who could not be policemen no matter how much they could gain by it. There were others who were just concerned with self-preservation. And there was still another category that had to do with the parties fighting each other even in the ghetto. There were Zionists, Bundists and Communists struggling for power, willing only to help people in their own group.

Some people left the ghetto voluntarily, believing they were going to work in the Skoda factories in Czechoslovakia. I didn't. I had an old mother to take care of. My father had died. I had friends who warned me when they were coming to liquidate my street. I went to some friends when they emptied our street. Later it became a crime to take someone in; it was punishable by death, so no one dared to take in a stranger.

My friend was the manager of a factory that made dresses for German women. There were bolts and bolts of cloth. I spent three days there, hiding under the bolts of material whenever I heard a noise. My mother was not well enough to hide. I loved her dearly and had taken good care of her all through the war, but at this time I would lock the door when I left and just hope that I would find her there in bed when I returned. Luckily there was a Jewish policeman living next door and he promised to take care of her.

Then the factory closed down and some friends hid me in their cellar for a few days. By this time it was the middle of August and there were very few people left in the ghetto. For the first time there was enough food. I thought I was one of the last to stay but later found out there was a bunker in which about two hundred people hid until the end of the war.

I was with a friend when the Germans caught me. They were rather nice compared to what we were expecting. They didn't beat or shoot us, they just said we had to leave. I began pleading that I couldn't leave my old mother to starve and he told me I could go and get her. It was August 18, a very hot day. I dressed her, put on my heavy overcoat. The policeman walked with us to the jail, which was the meeting place for the people who were being deported. There were thousands of people in the court-yard of the jail. I remember that wearing my Red Cross band made me an important person; I could go into the kitchen and ask for some water for a sick patient, as if I were a nurse.

My mother was absolutely bewildered. She was mourning all the things she had left behind. We had managed to save my sister's wedding presents to the last. We had dragged the silver and china and beautiful lingerie from one place to another, fi-nally to leave it all behind.

We were pushed into the boxcars, so close we couldn't sit down. There were children, a few infants, older people, sick people who died and had no place to fall. There were no toilet facilities. We stopped several times and waited for hours. No-body told us where we were. There was no food and no water. And all the time we thought we were going to the Skoda Works in Czechoslovakia.

We must have been in the cars for two or three days before they stopped and were opened. We were high up from the ground and had to jump down. My mother was still with me. She was very uncomfortable but she was alive. The soldiers were all around us, with guns directed at us, herding us like sheep. Peo-ple didn't know whether to run or stay. Somebody began a rumor that people with children will be saved and everybody began grabbing children. The children were screaming. It was a mad-house. It was something you can't explain. And then somebody else said that people who have children will be killed with the children, and mothers began throwing small children away. I remember the infants thrown on the railroad tracks.

I said goodbye to my friend, who was with me in the boxcar. He cut his bread in half and gave me an extra portion. He said, "If we do not meet again, we'll both write to the Red Cross in Lodz." And I said, "Fine." I was left with my mother, who was not much older than I am now but looked like a woman of eighty-nine. I helped her along in the crowd of women and we took the children who had been abandoned along with us. We were still dressed and had everything we had carried with us. We came to the gate where Mengele looked us over and pointed his fingers to the left and the right. He was smiling and humming a tune. We could hear music playing in the distance. He told my mother to go on one side and sent me to the other.

And then trucks came, great big trucks, and they told my mother to go on the truck. She said, "Come with me. You're so tired. Come and you won't have to walk." But the soldier said to me, in German, "Let the old lady go on the truck. It's better for you to walk." The truck, of course, went straight to the showers where they were gassed, so I wouldn't be here if I had not listened to the soldier. I told my mother I would see her later and she drove off with the other older women, the sick and the children, who had been told, "We will give you a ride. It will be faster."

I thought my mother would be taken to a house where she would be given sewing to do; there were rumors that the older women would take care of the children while the mothers worked. We went to a place where we could shower. They examined us carefully, almost a gynecological examination. They looked everywhere for hidden diamonds. I had sewn a diamond ring into my girdle; I was sure no one would take a girdle away from a woman.

They cut our hair off, took our clothes, left us in that striped thing, without shoes. And something happened to us when we left that place. We were different people than we were when we came in. We were like dogs caught by the dogcatcher. It was a great psychological shock. Until then whatever happened to us was always in familiar surroundings. Until I went into the boxcar I had moved around in the town in which I was born. I knew my way around. I had an identity among friends and family. And now I was in a place that looked to me like pictures of Dante's Inferno. They had taken all our documents, photographs, rings, everything, and we were in this tremendous place with people who didn't talk. They just walked aimlessly around, with lifeless eyes. I thought we had been put into an asylum for insane people. That's what I thought, and I never lost the impression that I was in a great big asylum with different standards than the rest of the world.

We were taken to a long, dark barrack. It was very clean but there were no bunks and we had to sit on the floor with our legs spread as wide as possible, stacked together one in front of the other, so they could get the maximum number of women into the barrack. The woman who came to indoctrinate us said she had come four years before, when there was no shelter from the rain, no floor and no water to drink. "You have come to a paradise," she said. She told us that she had helped build the barrack, under the worst conditions, and that we, at least, would have water to drink.

The woman was a *kapo*. She was very well dressed, she had hair, she looked well-fed, and yet she talked to us as no one had ever talked to us before. She told us we were prisoners and that the smallest breach of discipline would be punishable by death. Somebody asked her why we were there and she hit her in the face till the blood flowed. After that nobody asked any more questions. A woman was shot because she fainted. It was made very clear that our lives were absolutely worthless and nobody cared at all whether we survived or not.

We lived like this for about three weeks. We could go out during the day but when we came back we were packed in again. We were expected to sleep sitting up at night. There was little food and little water. The women stopped menstruating. And then they began to tell us about the crematoria. When we were outside we could catch the sweet smell of burning flesh. At first we didn't know what it was. We thought there was a slaughterhouse in the area. Then the people who had been there for a while told us what was going on. I was always inquiring about my mother and trying to find out where she was, and the person I asked just said, "She's probably going up in smoke right now."

One Sunday in September we were told to go to a special place. We stripped completely in front of three or four very nice businessmen. We were lined up in a row and they went up and down touching our arms, our thighs. They looked into our mouths at our teeth and pulled our ears, as if they were selecting animals at a cattle show. Then we dressed and were given a loaf of bread and gathered together to wait for hours at attention. We were put into cattle cars and taken to an unknown destination.

I grew a shell around me. I told myself I would survive this nightmare and that I would be very careful about choosing my priorities. It was not clear in my mind in the form of words, but it was an attitude. I told myself that I would take nothing personally. I would feel no shame for things that I could not help.

In Ravensbruck I was building roads. First there was digging, then carrying and placing the stones and pouring the asphalt. We had no motorized vehicles, no horses: *we* were the horses. We pulled, we pumped, we dragged huge stones.

I saw people who became very, very good and people who became absolutely mean. The nicest group were the Jehovah's Witnesses. I take my hat off to those people. They were born martyrs. They did marvelous things for other people. They helped the sick, they shared their bread, and gave everyone near them spiritual comfort. The Germans hated them and respected them at the same time. They gave them the worst work but they took it with their heads high.

In Ravensbruck I was given a vocational aptitude test and they found I was very agile with my hands. I was assigned to the Siemens factory to work on small parts that went into a time bomb. By that time the war was coming to an end. We were bombed every night after eleven. But we still had our quotas to produce. I was so fast that I could help other people. The way we did it was that I would fill my pockets with finished pieces when I went to the outhouse and my two girlfriends would bring the unfinished work they couldn't complete and we used to exchange. I felt good about that because the women who couldn't fill their quota disappeared.

From Ravensbruck I was taken to a camp near Berlin. The *kapo* woman went with me. I was not handcuffed but I wore my prisoner suit and had a little red triangle that showed I was a political prisoner. I also had a yellow insignia to show I was Jewish. We went on a passenger train and people stared at me. Someone gave me an apple. No one spoke to me. When we got off the train we had to walk miles and miles till we came to a camp that was under the ground. A few days after I came it was bombed and I was sent back to Ravensbruck. My last experience there was as a guinea pig for some experiments they were doing with antidotes to frostbite. They kept injecting things into my leg. If the war hadn't come to an end my leg would have been amputated. To this day I have no feeling in the part of the leg they injected. I was lucky; some of the others involved in the experiments died of infection.

It was April of 1945. The *kapos* were no longer so vicious. The beatings stopped. Then one day all the Jewish women were called out. We didn't want to go. We hid under the bunks and made them come and look for us. The next day they took us to the end of the camp where there was a big gate from which you could leave. There were big blue buses with yellow roofs waiting for us. Inside the buses there were tall, blonde men in outlandish outfits. They had masks on their faces and their hands were covered. We were sure they were going to kill us. They gave us each a package of food and pushed us screaming into the buses. The buses smelled strongly of antiseptics and we thought it was the chloroform they were going to use to put us to sleep.

The commander of the camp told us not to open our mouths when we came to our destination and not to breath a word about what was going on in Ravensbruck. And we said no, no, we wouldn't say anything. Mostly we began to eat what they had given us, which was the worst thing we could do. There was powdered milk and chocolate, ham in cans, cold beans, and we all became very sick.

We traveled through war-torn Germany without stopping during the day. There were bombs falling everywhere. It took us three days to get to Denmark. We arrived on April 28, late at night. Denmark was still occupied by the Germans but they didn't stop us anywhere. We were put on Pullman trains and when we came out in Copenhagen it seemed that the whole population of the city was there to greet us. We were the first inmates of concentration camps to arrive. There were about seventeen hundred of us. I remember seeing people with children on their shoulders, and they were throwing flowers at us. There were photographers everywhere taking our pictures. Then they put us on an elegant ship to Sweden.

There were tablecloths and settings, and we stole everything that wasn't nailed down. We poured salt into our napkins and took the napkins and the salt with us.

We were quarantined in a school for about twenty-eight days. The people who took care of us were amazed to see what horrible condition we were in. Doctors came from all over Sweden to examine us. Ravensbruck had a big experimental station and many of us had terrible wounds.

When I recovered a little they gave me the choice of going to a recreation camp to rest or staying where I was and working in the hospitals for my room and board. I decided to stay and work in the hospital. It was hard work and they had so few people to do it, and the people coming in were such pathetic cases. I knew languages and this was important when I made the rounds with the doctors. I was also a representative of the camp when people who wanted to help us came for information. There were many representatives of the new communist regime in Poland who promised us all kinds of wonderful things if we would come back. They said Poland would just forget anti-Semitic feelings and we would be heroes and get the best jobs.

Once a very nice elderly Jewish man came. He was a very hairy man with a bushy head of white hair and he was a wonderful speaker. He asked us to go to Palestine to fight for the cause. His name was Ben-Gurion, and I had the pleasure and honor of having him in my house. He said he couldn't promise us anything except another war but he really tried to convince us to come help build a new land.

The people I was with, however, were very disillusioned with life, and communistically inclined. We didn't believe him. We didn't believe anybody. We had had more than our share of hardship.

We were more interested in repairing our personal lives. We were trying to locate friends and relatives and going over all the lists that came to us. We would write to the Red Cross for information and listen to the radio program that was devoted to contacting people.

The one thing we were sure of was that we didn't want to go back to Poland. Even in the Swedish camps after liberation we were subjected to anti-Semitic outbursts from Poles. Then we heard about the Jews who came back to Kielce, south of Lodz; the greeting they received from their Polish neighbors was, "My God, we thought Hitler took care of all you Jews already." And these Jews were massacred. The full story became known when a handful of survivors of the massacre made it to Sweden in a boat and were apprehended by the Swedish police. There was talk of sending them back since they didn't have any visas, and the Jews said they would drown themselves on the shores of Sweden rather than go back.

When I was working in the hospital people came from all the

consulates to see the patients of their nationality. They brought food and flowers and encouragement. One time somebody came from the Polish consulate and said he would like to see his Polish citizens. And I took him to a room and said this one and this one is Polish and he started to talk to them and became furious: "I told you I want to see Polish citizens. I do not want to see Polish Jews."

Meanwhile I heard from Simon, who was my friend from before the war, and we both agreed we wanted to get out of Europe. I always wanted to be surrounded by family and the cousins in Canton were writing very kind letters and I wanted to be closer to them. They sent me the affidavit and money.

Simon and I were married on July 28, 1946. It was a simple ceremony. We had a canopy made of something or other, I borrowed a dress that I had to return, and we had fish for dinner because we couldn't afford any meat. And Simon bought a thin little ring from a jeweler in Stockholm.

We had many things in common. We knew each other's families and each other's past history. The fact that we both survived made it easier to speak to each other. We could exchange our feelings of fear and we were not inhibited about expressing ourselves because we knew we would understand each other.

My family in America was pleased to arrange an affidavit for Simon, and while we waited we found jobs in a small town in Sweden. I worked in an old people's home in Torshalla and Simon worked in a factory doing piecework. There were a few other families like us, and the man who took care of us was the chief of police, the kindest, nicest man. It was a great transition for us to trust a policeman. We had always felt that anyone in uniform was our enemy, but this fine man came to our house regularly and just looked for ways to help us.

My visa came through before Simon's. The Joint Distribution Committee was very helpful in processing our papers. I was already carrying our older boy and we were both anxious for him to be born on American soil. It was an overwhelming emotional feeling. We wanted him to be a Yankee, not a naturalized citizen like his parents. We went to the consul and begged him to let Simon come with me, but there was nothing they would do about it. The only solution was for me to go alone and for Simon to follow as soon as possible. They said it wouldn't be more than two or three months. We decided we could stand the separation for the sake of our child. I put on a tight dress and set out.

You see, the captain of the ship didn't want any pregnant women on board, so I couldn't ask for any special consideration. I remember it as such a hard time. During the war we knew we were part of a tragedy and we couldn't take things in a personal way. But this time I felt myself touched by something very unpleasant. I didn't want to leave without Simon, I didn't know a word of English and I didn't have any money. I was terrified of the long journey but the doctor said if I were to go I should go immediately, or I might lose the baby.

For the eleven days of the journey I couldn't eat and was throwing up all the time. After the third day the ship doctor came, and he was very displeased with me. "We do not want pregnant women," he said. "You had no business coming on board." The only one who looked out for me was a young yeshiva student. He didn't eat because the food wasn't kosher, but he had a supply of hard-boiled eggs he shared with me sometimes. So there I was, miserable most of the time, while the other people were eating and dancing and watching movies.

Eventually the trip came to an end, and my cousin was waiting for me in New York to bring me to Canton, Ohio. I had that feeling of helplessness you get when you don't know the surroundings, when you are alone, not feeling good. And the future was such a great big question mark.

Simon Grubman was forced into the Lodz ghetto. In 1940 he worked as a counselor in the children's colony. When the children were taken away he saved his family by working in the tobacco distributing factory. He was deported to Auschwitz and then to Ravensbruck and Mecklenburg.

My parents grew up during World War I, when Poland was occupied by Germans. Two German officers were quartered in our house, and my mother remembered them as cultured and civilized people. She always told how they gave her part of their rations because she had a small child. She often said, "My God, if our neighbors would only be as nice and friendly as the Germans are to us." She actually corresponded with those officers for many years. And when I told her what the new Germans were doing, she would say, "You don't have to believe everything you read in the paper. We know how Germans are."

On the Sunday they announced that England and France declared war on Germany the Jews thought that was great news and they had nothing to worry about. On Wednesday, September 6, 1939, my father woke me at five o'clock in the morning.

"You better get dressed," my father said. "You have to leave." I said, "To leave? Where am I going?" He told me that there were rumors that the Germans are almost at the gates of Lodz and that the first thing they would do is do away with all male Jews. The idea was to escape to Warsaw, which was still in Polish hands; it was expected that Warsaw would defend itself.

My mother was crying. She said the family should stay together no matter what. And I remember my grandfather, my father's father, came, and he was banging the table with his cane and yelling at my mother, "For your selfish reasons you want your son to get killed. You have no right!" My mother yielded and packed a few rolls with salami in my rucksack and stuffed a few zlotys in my pocket.

My father was originally going to go with me but he changed his mind. He didn't feel capable of marching the hundred kilometers, the sixty miles, from Lodz to Warsaw. So I was off without him on a dark street in Lodz, just going where everybody else was going. I felt real excitement, being part of this mass of humanity heading northeast. There were Jews and non-Jews, soldiers in and out of uniform. The Polish army in the area had completely disintegrated.

About five hours out of Lodz I met a school chum who was marching with his brother-in-law and other members of his family. So there were five of us and when we got to the town of Brzeziny we thought we'd take a breather. We went off the main road and walked until we came to a house. It was a Jewish family and they invited us in for tea. And just as I started to eat one of the rolls my mother gave me—all hell broke loose. Bombs were falling. Just like that. We went out into the courtyard. And standing there at the gate was like standing in the middle of an inferno, a blazing inferno. When the bombers flew away we opened the gate and went out to the street. The town was on fire. It was all rubble and corpses and I was surprised I was still alive, and decided to go back rather than go on to Warsaw. I was ready to part with my friend when I overheard four Orthodox Jews talking about Lodz. They said there was no use in trying to go back to it; it was surrounded and no one could go in or out.

So we continued on to Warsaw. We were close to a wooded area and when we heard the bombers we took shelter under the trees. At one point a Polish soldier fired at a low-flying plane and the Germans saturated the area with bombs. The place became a graveyard for most of the people hiding there, including my friend and his family.

I was the only survivor. I found myself in a pool of blood but I managed to crawl back to the highway, where people were still marching toward Warsaw. So I just lay there with a large wound on my back and no one paid any attention. Then a small miracle happened. A Polish colonel on a horse passed by. I don't know what made him dismount and come to speak to me but he did. He gave me a few bandages to stop the bleeding and then hailed the first passing truck and ordered the two Polish soldiers in it to take me to the nearest hospital. They put me on some boxes in the back of the truck and drove off to Rawa, a city halfway between Lodz and Warsaw.

It took hours to get there because the roads were jammed and there were bombing raids all along the way. The soldiers left me on the truck whenever the planes came and ran as far from the road as they could get. The boxes I was lying on were actually cases of dynamite they were taking to blow up a bridge somewhere. If the truck had been hit there would have been one fantastic explosion.

I didn't get back to Lodz until December. By then life was more difficult. You had to stand in line to get a loaf of bread and there sometimes wasn't enough for everybody, but people said that it was to be expected in wartime. Occasionally somebody would be caught in the street for labor but it was sporadic, not organized.

In January the Germans published a plan, a detailed street plan, by house number, to resettle the Jews into the newly formed ghetto, which was in a slum area where middle-class Jews never dreamed of living before the war. People read the announcement and felt they had no choice. The punishment for disobedience was death. The trouble was that it took such a long time to get people to move and it tied up too many of the Germans who were supervising the resettlement. They found a very simple solution. They went into a few big apartment houses and shot a few people. Word spread like wildfire. Within forty-eight hours all the Jews were in the ghetto.

This was the first time the Jews in Lodz were concentrated in one area. They had always been spread all over the city. My family moved in the beginning of February, about two weeks before the ghetto was closed. We were supposed to have about a yard and a half per person. By this time they were liquidating many small ghettos in the surrounding towns and the people were sent to Lodz. The ghetto of Lodz became the center of Jewish life.

It is very important to understand that the word "ghetto" as it is used in the United States has absolutely no similarity to the ghetto in Lodz, in Poland under German occupation. You have to understand that it was a completely enclosed area, with no access to the outside world. There was a sentry every hundred feet and you could get shot by trying to come close to the wires that encircled the ghetto.

There were two positive things about the ghetto. One was that you were relatively safe from daily interference by the Germans. At least in the ghetto we were Jews among Jews. We couldn't get out but the Germans were not allowed to come in until they began to take people for extermination. The other positive thing was that families stayed together. Whoever you were with, you were with for the time being.

Everything else was negative. There was the lack of work, and the lack of food and the lack of a clear direction of what to do. In the first months I did nothing. When I started to go out of my mind because of the inactivity I applied to the education department to see if I could help in the children's colony.

Different people had a different tolerance for hunger. Each person had a ration to last ten days. So what do you do? Does a wife share with her husband who is hungrier than she is? Should she sacrifice her life? And what about growing children?

The children's colony was organized in August of 1940 and I was given the job of counselor. It was a living rather than a teaching situation. The children grew up in the street in the worst part of town, and the parents were mostly tavern owners, smugglers, people that provided the least care and education for their children. I was faced with forty boys, each one a problem for an experienced teacher or counselor, and I was not much older than the oldest boy I was taking care of. And yet in this darkest period in my life, the years between 1939 and 1945, the two years I spent with those children from 1940 to 1942 were the brightest in my personal life. Without formal education or training, I found I had tremendous capacity for love and attachment. Sally was adopted by my boys as well and she visited them often. I found how rewarding it can be to see children change in response to love and devotion.

I had read one of the books about Janusz Korchak and remembered his penal code: each punishment meted out for a specific offense was based on forgiveness. In normal times it would be very difficult to convince a group of children that you can punish somebody by forgiving him, but the idea intrigued our children and we wrote out the articles of the code and the system was put into effect. We had judges to review the cases and a complaint box for disagreements. The ultimate punishment was to be expelled from the group. This went on until September 1942, when the colony was surrounded by German soldiers. . . .

After the war we found out that all the children were taken to Treblinka, where most of the ghetto children were exterminated. This is a historical fact. We checked to be sure.

Shortly after the children's colony was emptied there was a deportation action that took thousands and thousands of people out of the ghetto. It went on for two nights and three days. It was something extraordinary. An action usually took a few hours; soldiers would come into the ghetto, take a few people and that was it. This was different. The whole population was under curfew, so you could do nothing but barricade yourself in and hope they would not come to the door. People were trying to find a pattern, because if you knew the pattern you could guard against it. If they were looking for old people, you should hide old people—or sick people, or children, or cripples. But there was no pattern. In some houses they took women, in some, men, and in some houses they took older people. What they did with them we didn't know.

We were cooped up wherever we lived not knowing what the next minute would bring. You heard the rumbling of trucks and didn't know where they would stop. You heard shots and just sat and waited. We were lucky. My family was not touched. When the action was over we went back to work. The stores opened again. You took whatever food you could get. I got a job in a cigarette and tobacco distributing factory, which turned out to be a lifesaver for me, for being able to supply cigarettes saved my family.

It's a very interesting thing about the ghetto: even when everybody was hungry and poor and scared, it developed classes, its own aristocracy, its own ruling party and its own ethical base. And the people in the ruling party were very, very powerful. You can't imagine how much prestige there was in a job that had something to do with food or clothing. The men who could make a pair of shoes or a coat became the aristocracy. You had to pay them in food. Bread was the most valuable currency.

There was a complete reversal of normal prewar society. The dregs of humanity became the lords and the people who could offer brains and intelligence, the people with knowledge and education, were at the bottom. Teachers, professors, the intelligentsia, what was left of it, were terribly wronged in the ghetto and terribly punished for their intellectual independence. If Chaim Rumkowski didn't like somebody, especially if it was a professor or a teacher, he would give them the worst ghetto punishment—they would have to clean out the outhouses and drag the barrels to the places of destination. If you had that job you became a leper. The odor would permeate the clothes and wouldn't wash off the skin.

Life in the ghetto wasn't anything to be proud of. The only thing I would say is that you cannot condemn, you have to understand. Nobody who did not live through it has any right to judge. The terrible thing the Germans did was to cause individuals and families to disintegrate because of hunger. Some ate their ten days' rations in four days or six days. I had pretty good willpower and managed to have something every day. My mother was pretty good at it, my sister so-so. My father was not, so he suffered more from hunger than the rest of us. My mother, toward the end of the time, always managed to share something with him and I would chip in occasionally, but we would all tell him that he shouldn't deprive the rest of the family because he didn't have enough self-control.

Ours was not an extreme case. I knew of families where every member had a box and a lock with his own key in which to hide the piece of bread so that no one would eat it. But you have to understand that people were dying of hunger, of sickness, and the healthy ones were beginning to swell from the lack of nutrients. We were slowly beaten down psychologically.

The rest of us might hear a whispered rumor about the horrible things in store for us, but the rumors were unconfirmed and we were in a mood not to believe. It was difficult enough to live with the hunger and misery without imagining worse. There was no uprising. There were no weapons.

When they decided to eliminate the ghetto we were a docile element for the Germans; they put up placards that said, "Due to troop movements we find it prudent to move the population of the ghetto to another location where you can continue to work for the war effort for the German Wehrmacht." There were lists of things to take along and leave behind. It was set up very carefully to make us believe we were going to another place to live and work. I admit I had misgivings but there was no life-and-death anxiety. Most of us in Lodz didn't believe the rumors about extermination camps.

Still, when it was time to leave nobody wanted to be the first to go. There was no point in rushing to leave. We hoped the war would end any day, or that something unexpected would happen. It was August 1944.

The Jewish police were rounding up the people for the transports. But there were not enough of them to search every house, every day, every hour. So we began a cat-and-mouse game to see how long we could hide out from them.

We knew that we could gain time but that we would eventually have to go with the others. It became an unbearable psychological burden to remain while the ghetto emptied—even though there was enough to eat for the first time. The beets that were planted in any little space where there was a bit of earth were ready to eat. But the air in the ghetto became too rarefied for us. We had a family conference and said, "Enough is enough. What will be will be." My father, my mother, my sister and I packed our rucksacks.

We were not caught. We picked up the rucksacks and went as a family to the jail where they assembled the people for deportation. We spent the night in the courtyard, surrounded by lots of people. It was a relief, a kind of anticlimax after the weeks of hiding, to be in a crowd of people all in the same boat. We were given bread and marmalade and told we were going on a day's journey. The next day we were herded into boxcars, about eighty of us in a car meant for five or six animals. The trip that should have taken three or four hours in a car took a whole day and a night. We arrived at Auschwitz at dawn. Everything was shrouded in mist. My father lifted me on his shoulders so I could peek out the window. What I saw didn't make much sense. There were figures, grotesque-looking people with odd hats and striped pajamas, and their movements were very strange, as if they were in a trance.

There were uniformed Germans some distance away but the people pushing us into line wore the striped uniforms. They separated the men and women and that was the last time I saw my mother and sister. My father was with me and my own bewilderment was tempered by the fact that I had to take care of him, sort of drag him along and keep him in line. We came to the first selection and for my father it was the first and last. The word selection didn't have sinister overtones to me until that time. I didn't know you could select live, normal people for life or death just because they were Jews. Until then the words "right" and "left" were about directions or political affiliations. For the first time it dawned on my that "right" and "left" could also mean life or death.

My father, in his clothes, looked very healthy. And when he had to trot in front of Dr. Mengele I sort of gave him a little pep talk. "Dad, give it your best," I said, sensing it was important, and he passed with me to the same direction. But later, when we undressed in the shower room, the SS men watching us saw that his legs were swollen from the hunger. They motioned to him to follow them and I tried to hold on to him. I grabbed his arm and didn't let go. The SS man hit me in the face with the handle of his riding crop. I lost consciousness and when I came to a few minutes later my father was gone. I never saw him again.

I learned quickly that Auschwitz was a transitional place. Either you were purchased for slave labor or you went up the chimney. There was nothing to do in Auschwitz but get up to be counted and fed. But purchasing agents came from Germany looking for electricians, lathe operators, metal workers and carpenters. The people who were not chosen for work marched back and forth in front of Mengele. I put myself down as a lathe operator and was purchased very quickly. Looking at him you would never suspect he had any bestial designs on human beings. I guess his fascination with cripples is well known. He collected people with physical deformities like others collect stamps or coins. He also experimented in genetics. He kept his human oddities in a special enclosure and treated them better than the other inmates.

The whole atmosphere was a nightmare. I told myself that I could survive. Physical strength was important only if mental health went along with it. There were many strong, aggressive people who went to pieces. You had to have the mental strength to cope with hunger and pain, with discomfort you couldn't imagine.

I was sent to a factory in Brunswick. We lived in barracks outside the city, protected from the shootings and hangings and the crematorium, but the life consisted of many small persecutions. Many times after a couple of months I was tempted not to get up. Yet when the man came screaming "Everybody out!" the last spark of willpower would push me out of bed. "One more day," I said. "Let's see one more day."

In January of 1945 daily air raids began to break the routine. Between January and May I managed to be transferred three times to other camps. First it was to the Hermann Göring Works, then to Ravensbruck and finally to Mecklenburg. We knew that liberation was close but we were in terrible physical shape and afraid we would not live to see it.

Toward the end there was no organized labor force. Food was not given regularly. We were getting weaker every day and many people around me were dying. We kept embarking on journeys to unknown places, sometimes in open gondolas, sometimes locked in boxcars. Planes strafed us as we traveled. When we arrived we didn't know where we were. There was sometimes a little work and a little food. I remember once we were in the countryside somewhere and we realized that there was no wire around us, no police to chase. We could finally run away. But where could we run in our funny uniforms? Our heads were shaven. We were immediately recognizable. How would it be at the end to be shot as a fugitive?

The job we were given to do was to take some decomposing corpses out of a basement, place them in wooden boxes four to a box and then carry them two or three miles to a cemetery, where another group was digging the graves. Half of our group was used as horses, pulling the coffins, while the other half pushed from behind. Some Gestapo men came along to be sure we did as we were told.

In the last camp we just slept on some straw on the ground. Two or three days went by without any food. The overseers began to disappear and we could escape, except that we were too weak to move. We lay on the straw and speculated aloud on the number of days we could live before we were liberated. Many were very close in their estimates and died, as they expected, on the seventh or eighth day. But I refused to play any games with time. I told myself that I had to survive to tell the world what things were like. Because if I didn't, who would tell my story for me? So I sat very quietly not moving, preserving energy for days and nights, stubbornly determined to cheat death.

On May 1 all the guards left. Some of the people in our barrack could still move around and they came to tell us that no one was guarding us anymore. Somebody said, "That doesn't mean we are free. Who are we freed by? Who is here?" Those who were strong enough to walk left the camp.

And then on May 2, at about ten o'clock, we heard a motorcycle. It stopped outside our barrack and then someone kicked the door open. In the doorway we saw a figure of a soldier in full battle dress with grenades hanging from the straps and a submachine gun in his hands.

For a few minutes there was absolute silence on both sides. We didn't know whether he was a German or not. But finally someone close to the door recognized the American insignia and cried out in Polish, "It is an American!" And then there was a babble of voices shouting in Yiddish, Polish, Hungarian, whatever—and that poor guy just stood there in the doorway. He was absolutely petrified. He didn't move. He didn't utter a sound. After a few moments tears started to run down his cheeks.

We must have looked like something out of a horror picture. When he couldn't stand the sight of us anymore he turned on his heel, jumped on the motorcycle and drove off at about sixty miles an hour.

He was a scout for an advancing column. It was May 2 and the war didn't officially end until the eighth. We waited some more. A few more people died. And then we heard the sound of trucks and a huge truck came with loaves of bread. They left the bread with us and drove off.

Later there were other trucks with medics and paramedics and Red Cross people. They took us to the nearest city and put us in the empty Gestapo barracks. That night some more people died. And that was the liberation.

My physical disintegration was so severe that I felt I was at the very end of my rope. I weighed no more than a big turkey. My skin was unpleasant to touch; it was just a bone with a thin layer of flesh. My body was completely stripped of fat and muscle. Later on, when we came to Sweden, the doctors said we were a medical mystery. They had not believed a person could remain alive in the conditions they found us.

I was among the six or seven hundred survivors who were hospitalized in Sweden. I can't tell you the delightful feeling of having a soft hospital bed with a pillow under my head and a real nurse, not German, at my bedside. It was like leaving hell and going to paradise. For the first time I felt I had a chance to be a human being again. ˙

After a month or so in the hospital with all the medical attention we needed we were sent to a summer recreation spot called Larbro. In this short time the word camp lost its sinister connotation. We were sent to rehabilitation camps and the word took on a new significance. Meanwhile we were constantly reading and compiling lists of survivors, adding names we knew and writing to those we found. This was when I found the name of my old friend Sally who was in a camp four hundred miles away and I wrote to her. When she answered I went to visit her.

I was still under the pressure to bear witness. In my race with death I lived because of this burning desire to tell what happened. In Germany there had been no opportunity. In Sweden we were the big story. We were surrounded by newspapermen and photographers, and they were asking the right questions. It was the audience I dreamed about on my filthy, lousy mattress when I was trying to give myself enough courage and hope to believe I would survive. I was also one of the few survivors who had a common language with the Swedes. Most of the survivors with me spoke Polish, Russian and Slavic languages; I could speak German and English and really carry on a conversation. And everything was so fresh—all the experiences were so close. The whole of me was open. I was speaking with blood, so to speak.

Very quickly I noticed that there was some discounting of my story on the other side. It wasn't exactly disbelief but sort of an attitude that part of it might be true but it couldn't *all* be true. I see they think the poor fellow is out of his mind. After all he suffered so much. Someone would ask me something and I would start pouring out what I thought was the answer but the response would be, "But—but—didn't this happen?" or "How could it be?" The reality of the death camps had not penetrated yet. I started to get a glimmer of the truth that would later be

261

confirmed—that the enormity of the Nazi crime was such that a normal person who did not experience it would have trouble believing it was possible. I couldn't bear to tear myself open and show my bleeding heart as long as I had a feeling that I was not being believed.

On the other hand, I understand now that had I been a newspaperman in that time and place, I might have had the same problems. People do exaggerate in such circumstances and it probably was very difficult to believe.

All of this, however, made me want to focus on rebuilding my life. This requires a man and wife. As soon as Sally and I met again we knew we wanted to be together. There were many marriages in the refugee camps. It was a natural response after our losses.

Also I was very anxious to come to America. Sally's family was very pleased that she was coming with a husband and very helpful with money and affidavits. I had no doubts about my personal ability to make a living. I had a profession and expected to be able to work at it. I wasn't coming to the United States like the mostly illiterate, unskilled immigrants at the turn of the century. I wasn't afraid of winding up in a sweatshop. I knew the language and I had been educated. I expected to be able to stand on my own two feet without the help of the family.

In Sweden I was a factory worker in a steel stamping mill. It wasn't too bad. The long wait to join Sally in America, however, wore me down. They told us it would take a couple of months for my visa to arrive; it took more than twenty months. We were on a quota system that was based on your place of birth. You could have a British or a French passport, but if you were born in Poland you had to wait your turn on the Polish quota, which was the most oversubscribed because so many people wanted to leave.

My son was born without me and was growing up without a father. My wife was completely dependent on her cousins and I was in a deep depression in Sweden. In one letter I pleaded with her to pack up and come back. After all, Sweden wasn't the worst place to live, and at least we would be together. Her letter was a vote of confidence for the United States. She felt it was worth waiting for and urged me to be patient a little longer. And she was right.

When the visa came through I was too impatient to wait for any boat. Her description of her passage was so grim I wasn't eager to experience it. I flew to Idlewild Airport at the end of October.

> *Dr. Emanuel Stein sent his wife, Rose, and his*
> *mother east as the Germans approached Krakow,*
> *Poland. He remained with his patients in Krakow*
> *until an army colonel urged him to go east as well.*
> *He was reunited with his family in Lublin and*
> *then fled to Vilna and to Moscow. They took the*
> *Trans-Siberian Express to Vladivostok, then*
> *traveled to Tokyo and San Francisco, where they*
> *couldn't disembark and had to continue on to*
> *Mexico.*

It was on a Friday morning that the war started, and by Sunday we heard that the Germans were progressing in a two-pronged offensive from the south and the west and that they would engulf us as soon as they closed the circle. Another doctor and I went to our battalion and tried to enlist, but the colonel in charge said, "No, gentlemen, you better go east as quickly as possible." We were patriotic and eager to join the army and I asked if that was an order, and he answered that it was not an order, just good advice.

I went home and told the maid to take everything in the house she could use. I didn't expect to return. I put a few things in a rucksack and set out for Lublin to join my family. I had all my papers and all my diplomas with me so I could establish my credentials anywhere in a few minutes. There were hundreds of people on the road with me. And I'm ashamed to say it, but I was very happy. I felt so free on the road, with no responsibilities.

I walked and walked. Horses and buggies passed me. Some were driven by my colleagues from the university who didn't offer to take me with them because they knew me for many years to be the Jew, but that's not so interesting. After a few days I came to a village and tried to rent a horse and buggy. I hired a young man to drive me for a while because no one was willing to let me take a horse in case I didn't return.

We tried to stay off the main road because the Germans were dropping their bombs and every few minutes we had to run for cover in a ditch. It was very slow going because the roads were full of bomb craters. Eventually I got to Lublin. It was late at night, pitch dark, and I didn't know what to do. I met up with a young man who offered to take me home with him to one of his relatives with the idea that they would tell me where to go in the morning. When I came to the place I found myself at the estate where my family was waiting for me. It was like a palace, but fifty or sixty people were sleeping on the floor. In the morning I saw how beautiful it was. The birds were singing. The gardens were gorgeous, and I turned up from another world like a ghost to bring them the news of the war.

The next day we went east to Pinsk, where I tried again to get into the army. After all, I was a Polish citizen, a Polish Jew, and I had a double reason to be in the army fighting Hitler. I argued until they said it was all right and I became a doctor in the Eighty-first Regiment of the Sharpshooters and the Thirty-first Regiment of Field Artillery. They didn't have a uniform for me and I didn't have any medicine for them, but I organized a hospital and requisitioned hospital supplies. There were more wounded than we knew what to do with.

The Russians came in on the sixteenth and the colonel in the camp came to me and said, "Doctor, we have two doctors here already and the hospital is arranged. Perhaps you will go east." He told the sergeant to give me a pass and I left. That pass saved my life. All the officers in the camp were taken and shot—all of them, including some well-known doctors from Krakow, and whether it was Stalin or the Germans that ordered the shooting we don't know.

It was a piece of luck that I got away. I left the camp at six o'clock in the evening and tried to figure out how to get to Pinsk. There were big forests to go through and I knew there were criminals and marauders there, and I didn't dare take the road through the forest on foot. Just then the doors to the camp opened and a horse and buggy came out with a peasant going home. "Wait, I'm going with you," I said, but he refused to take me. I told him I'd pay him any amount of money if he'd take me along and he scratched his head and asked if I'd give him five zlotys. I had at that time about nine thousand zlotys, which was a big amount of money, but I haggled him down to three zlotys. You have to understand my reason. He was from people who cut a match in three or four pieces to kindle the wood in the stove, people so poor they ate only the skins of potatoes. It would not go well with me to have him think I was a rich man.

Anyway, he took me to Pinsk and there I found my wife was already on the way to the Russian border, so I kept on going on foot. One night I slept on the floor of a police station where lots of other people were sleeping. When I left them I saw a freight train going east, and I ran after it and jumped on. There were lots of people on the train and they pulled me in and I was on the way to the border.

Just before the border there was a railway junction and I had to get out because the train didn't go any further. There were thousands of peasants waiting with sacks on their shoulders, ready to enter the town at dawn. I could see the city but didn't know if they'd let me go by. They were coming to loot and rob and kill, and just waiting in silence.

When it grew light they went, and I went as if I were one of them. Nobody touched me. Later, when I saw myself in a mirror, I knew why they left me alone. I hadn't shaved for days. I didn't have a bath for weeks. My hair was unkempt and I was just as dirty as they were.

The town was already deserted. A few Polish soldiers were still fighting the Russians. I went to the Hotel Levi, a little Jewish inn, to wait for the Soviet army to come in. About five minutes after I arrived, a Russian officer came with a revolver and put it to my head while he checked me for weapons. All he found was my scouting knife. He looked it over, returned it, saluted and went on. And that's how I knew the Russian occupation had started.

I had no feelings of fear. I was just very excited and knew I was having an extraordinary adventure. The experiences with the peasants were unpleasant, but I wasn't actually afraid. I was sure my family was safe and that I'd catch up with them. We'd only been separated for about a week. I went behind the Russian line and joined my wife in the little town of Laclva. There we packed ourselves into a horse and buggy and slowly went back to Luniniec.

We could see the situation was not too good. The Red Army came looking like beggars. There was no food and no place to stay, so we went very slowly to Lvov. There were lots of refugees from the western part of Poland which had been occupied by the Germans, and we kept inquiring everywhere about my father-in-law, who had not been well when we last saw him. And then in the street in Lvov we met someone who said, "You know your parents just arrived." So the family was reunited. We did not trust the Germans or the Russians and were looking for a way to get out. The southern route was closed. The border with Rumania was closed. The northern route to the Lithuanian border was still considered possible so we decided to go to Vilna.

Unfortunately I had no money by this time. The Russians came in with their currency and my thousands of zlotys weren't worth anything. All we had was a little jewelry. But I was hopeful about getting to Lithuania because it was on the seashore and I knew a little about the Baltic Sea. I thought we would get a rowboat and make it to Sweden. It was a little window that was open.

We left Lvov on Christmas in the deep snow but our plan was to go over the border on New Year's Eve, when the Russian guards were likely to be drunk. We had guides and went part of the way on horseback, part in a buggy and the rest walking. It was forty degrees below zero and we were nine people with a little child. We couldn't keep to the plan and when dawn came we were two hundred meters from the border. The Russians found us and took us all to prison. They kept us for eight days, interrogating us day and night about what we were doing and why we were going. And there was nothing to eat but a little hot water and a slice of bread. They took the diamonds and the gold; everything we had.

While this was going on, one of the officers was watching us very carefully. My father-in-law was a Jew with a beard, still an Orthodox man, and he talked with the officer who became a little attached to us, a little sentimental about an old-fashioned family, still together. He began to give us advice. He told my father-in-law to burn some shares he had among his papers so the others wouldn't know we were "bourgeois" people. He told us what to say and what not to say. "You are all working people," he said. "You do not want to go to Palestine." He told us to insist that we were going to Vilna only because we had family there.

The officer who talked to us gave us back everything they had taken from us. The money and the jewelry were returned. The officer was probably Jewish and saw a family that reminded him of his own. There were jars full of confiscated diamonds on the table that had been taken from others and not returned.

We had friends in Vilna who made us very comfortable. There was lots of good food, but I wasn't taken in by the comfort. The lesson from history was that all the wars in Europe had taken place in this area and I was determined to get away from it. We couldn't get a visa to Palestine. My father-in-law wanted to go to Greece because he thought he'd find Jews there, but I was sure the Italians or Germans would occupy Greece and we couldn't get a visa anyway. Meanwhile people were trying to discourage us from leaving. They thought it would be too hard for our parents. But my wife and I had decided that what would happen to us would happen to them as well and because we insisted everybody was saved. The other families were destroyed because they thought only the young could leave.

One day I heard that the Dutch consul was giving certificates for the Dutch West Indies and that a visa was not necessary. I immediately left for Kovno to get the certificates. On the basis of the certificates the Japanese consul gave transit visas through Japan. Meanwhile the Russians annexed Kovno and the Japanese consul stayed on the steps of his hotel until the last minute and whoever came to him he gave the stamp to go. Ten thousand people got this stamp and were saved because of it.

My mother sold her beautiful diamond earrings and my wife sold her engagement ring. We changed the Vilna currency into dollars and kept everything hidden to buy the tickets to Curaçao and Japan. But it was illegal to own foreign dollars and if you were caught it meant five years in prison. But once you were in the door of Intourist, you could bring out the dollars and it was legal.

We went from Vilna to Moscow by train, to transfer to the Trans-Siberian Express. My father-in-law, of all of his wealth, had now only two big five-carat diamonds. He took two apples and put a diamond in each one and added a few more. When the customs officer told us to put everything we had on the table there was the bag of apples and my father-in-law was very nervous. One of the customs officers noticed how anxious we were and quietly said in Hebrew that the officers understood Yiddish so we should be careful not to give them any information. He just threw the apples back at us. And the train went to Moscow and we were lucky.

We arrived on the eve of Rosh Hashanah and my father-in-law insisted that we stay until the holiday was over. We asked at the tourist office where the synagogue was, and the man was astonished. He said he didn't know, nobody had ever asked him such a question. Instead we went to a little kiosk where a Jewish-looking man was selling soda. We waited in line like everybody else and when it was our turn we asked him in Yiddish. He was from Warsaw and very friendly. He gave us the directions. It was the synagogue that Golda Meir came to later on.

There was no rabbi, but we asked the gentleman in charge for permission to come to evening services. He gave us permission. He took us into a little room and told us he was cooperating with Stalin because it was the only way to exist. He showed us papers to prove that there was a council of Jewish communities in Russia and some semblance of communal Jewish life. Though it was forbidden, he had managed to acquire twelve *lulavim* and *ethrogim,* the palm branches and citrons needed for Succoth. He had couriers ready to take them to the communities in occupied Poland when he was done with them. This man had news from all over the Jewish world. How he knew I didn't know.

The synagogue was full that evening. There was a beautiful service and an excellent choir of young people. There were hundreds of women up in the balcony, crying like in the Polish synagogues. We heard people mumbling about our clothes. We looked very well dressed to them. We thought they looked poor and hungry. They surrounded us when we went out after the service. They crowded around us in the dark asking, "How is it in Palestine?" That was all they wanted to know.

After three days in Moscow we got on the Trans-Siberian Express. We had to spend Yom Kippur on the train. The head of the dining car was a Jew and he prepared us a meal of traditional food and fed us early before the fast began and late the next day when the fast was over. We turned our compartment into a synagogue and prayed all day. People came to look and see what was going on, and the dining car head begged us not to tell anyone he was Jewish because he would lose his position. It was a good position. In Siberia at that time people were coming to the train at every station to beg for leftovers from the tables of the tourists.

We spent ten days on the train and then five days in Vladivostok waiting for the ship to come from Stockholm. We found a cargo boat that left earlier and took it. You can imagine our feelings when we passed the three-mile limit and the Russian customs officers got off the ship and we were free. We went through the Yellow Sea and came to a little port town called Tshruga. When we got off we were in ancient Japan with women in kimonos and clacking shoes. We had an extraordinary experience there with the porter. We had third-class tickets to Tokyo and no money, and the porters said we couldn't go third class. They paid for our first-class tickets and we sent them the money the next day. They said we had to go at a certain level and that was it. In Tokyo, however, we found we had serious problems. We didn't have the United States transit visa to go through Panama. All we had was a spurious Panamanian transit visa, and we took a chance and left with it. We had this fantasy that war would break out between Japan and the United States and that the American fleet would take us into their hands and our troubles would be over.

The reality was very different. They wouldn't let us off the ship in Hawaii, and the same thing happened in San Francisco and Los Angeles. We began to worry. It was, Where are we going and where do we belong and what will we do if nobody takes us?

We were allowed off the boat for the first time in Mexico. A man from the Jewish Congress waiting for his own family bribed a guard so we could have a few hours on the ground. At that time there was nothing illegal in Mexico that couldn't be arranged for a little money. We talked to the harbor doctor and he gave us some advice. I said my father-in-law was suffering from a gall bladder ailment and needed treatment. I gave myself appendicitis. We found a medical excuse for every member of our family to stay on in Mexico for six months and we took a train that went to Guadalajara and from there to Mexico City.

The Jewish Congress helped us find a room but we had no permission to stay. We didn't pay people who should have been paid and they made a cause célèbre out of our case. The papers in Mexico were full of news about nine foreigners who had disembarked illegally, and the police were sent to arrest us. We hid and didn't open the door, and luckily they were not allowed to enter a house by force. Jews brought us food through the roof and we stayed until the ship left and they couldn't send us back. By that time there were people who offered to pay the Minister of Interior the money he thought we owed him, but I stupidly told them not to. I felt we were legitimate refugees and that Mexico was a free, democratic country that owed us asylum. They saw it differently.

Though there were many Polish Jews in Mexico City from earlier immigrations we were the first of the refugees at this time. We didn't have the right to work, but Jews from Poland came to see us and tried to help us. I got an illegal position in a pharmaceutical factory as a medical adviser. And when they heard at the embassies that my wife had training as a eurythmic and dancing teacher they quietly arranged classes for children that she could teach. She never continued in her profession as a lawyer. But we were able to live on a small income. I kept saying I was a diagnostician and it was a waste of my education, but no one paid any attention to me. Then one night I was called in to see a man who was dying of something and I told them correctly that he had malaria. They gave me a hundred pesos and the word got around that I really knew something.

In the meantime we decided to have a child. We thought we were so low we could only go up. My feeling was, why not? Whatever happens, happens. My wife thought that a child born in Mexico would be a citizen by birth and able to bring the parents legally into the country. Not that we really wanted to stay in Mexico; we looked forward to going to the United States, but at that time we had no choice.

When my wife went to the hospital to have the baby I had less than ten pesos in my pocket to pay the hospital bill. But the child was born, and I found a patient just in time and earned a hundred and twenty pesos so I could pay the hospital bill. Just as soon as my daughter was born I applied for her passport and also for our citizenship. But instead of citizenship papers we got a letter from the Minister of Interior saying we must leave the country with the child within thirty-one days.

This was already 1942 and America was at war. Japan wasn't sending boats to Mexico anymore. Where could we go? I put the letter in a drawer and decided to forget about it. But when the thirty-first day came around there was a knock on the door at five o'clock; the police were there again to arrest us.

I told the officer I had no time to get arrested, that I was just on my way to meet some friends at a coffee house. He understood that I was going for money and said, "All right, when shall I come back?" We made a date for the next day at eleven and he left without being paid off. The next day I went to the Minister of the Interior and was formally arrested. They wrote out the protocol which said that I came into the country illegally and had no right to practice medicine and that I was a burden to Mexican society, et cetera, et cetera. I was supposed to sign it.

So I said, "Why are you making up stories? You know the

boat left with our clothes, that a war is going on. What is all this writing for?" I tried to make a joke of it and said to them, "Now listen, I want to have the right to be in this country and to practice medicine." And he said, "You know we are friends," and I understood that meant I had to give some money. For three hundred pesos it was arranged that my wife and I and the child had the right to be in Mexico and I could practice. In the afternoon when I came back for the papers I was accepted with great smiles and friendliness and "Doctor, sit down," and so on.

The new protocol went as follows: "In view of the fact that Dr. Stein, assistant professor in Poland, educated in the best university, who brings medicine to Mexico and therefore is of great importance to the Mexican people . . . " etc. It went on for four pages, and this protocol I gladly signed.

My sister and brother-in-law were already in the United States. They knew someone who sent them an affidavit. They went to Dr. Stephan Wise to see if he could arrange something for us but we had trouble with the vice-consul, who had the idea there were enough unemployed doctors in America without bringing in foreigners. Later the law changed and visas came from Washington, D.C., and we found some rich relatives who sponsored us.

We still had to bribe the Mexican immigration authorities on the Texas border because we didn't have the entry visa to Mexico. We had to borrow money for the train fare to New York. I remember that there were lots of soldiers on the train and they were drinking milk. And I said, "My God, this army is going to win the war? Children, all of them!" In Europe no adult ever drank milk. A soldier in Europe would have vodka with his lunch, or at least beer. We had a lot to learn about America.

Bernard Brown from Viseul de Sus in Rumania
was in a forced labor battalion that was sent all
the way to Stalingrad. He was one of the few
survivors to return to his family. Five months
after he returned, however, he was deported to
Auschwitz, then Mauthausen. When the American
army arrived, he was one of three Jews in
Gunskerchen, a camp of Russians and Poles.

We traveled to Gomel in cattle cars. From there we walked forty to fifty kilometers a day toward the front. We slept under God's heaven at night and kept on going with little rest until we got almost to Stalingrad. We were in civilian clothes with a yellow arm band, which showed that we were Jews for labor.

We began the journey in June. In October, when the snow began, we stopped in a small community. We cut bricks from the snow and made a path so the cars, horses and buggies could go through. When the Russians broke through the German lines in January 1943 we began to retreat. Two or three times we were encircled by the Russians. We tried to be captured but it was not as easy as it sounds. I was with two other boys; one was from Bessarabia and spoke good Russian. He convinced a Russian family to hide us in their basement, but after two days we were warned that the Germans were going from house to house and shooting any Hungarian or Jewish laborers who were trying to go over to the Russian side.

So we set out on our own, retreating away from the main line. This way we could get something to eat. If we went with the soldiers there was little to eat and no place to sleep. And it was very cold. Sometimes it was forty degrees below zero. In some companies only two or three boys survived. My company began with 220. After the retreat there were 30 of us left. Nobody cared. The companies sent out to Russia were marked for destruction. They wanted to be rid of the young Jews, to really destroy them. The only thing I should mention is that the Germans sometimes behaved better with the Jewish prisoners than the Hungarians. The Hungarians used us for shooting practice, as if we were birds.

In the spring there was a typhoid epidemic. They organized a hospital in Doroshit. I was lucky I wasn't there. The Hungarians burned a hospital full of Jewish boys to keep the typhoid from spreading into the army. By the time I got typhoid it was Passover. I don't remember the date, but it was Passover in 1943. I remained in the little town where our company was stationed. The hospital was gone by then.

They brought us back from Russia in January 1944. I went home to my family. They were still at the sawmill. It had been declared a war industry and a lot of Jewish boys were deferred from labor camp by working there. In March, however, the Germans occupied Hungary and things got very bad.

In May the chief of police came to our house. He excused himself very much and said there was nothing he could do. He had orders to take us to a ghetto area in Bistrita. He was very nice about it. He let us take our own horse and buggy so we wouldn't have to walk the fifty kilometers. He sat in our kitchen for almost four hours while my mother baked bread for us to take along. We didn't take too many things. The main thing was to have enough food.

There were about six thousand Jews in the camp. The region commander wanted to take the young people to work in a labor camp but the Germans would not permit it. They knew where we were going and wouldn't let anybody out. In the beginning of June they started sending us away in boxcars. I left with the third transport. I arrived in Auschwitz without any shoes.

We didn't know where we were or what was going on. I won't go into the details of dressing and shaving and all that. I remember sleeping on the hard cement of the barracks and eating like animals without dishes or spoons. At least it was summer, so it was easier to survive.

I was sent out to work in the sewers until the Russians began coming closer. Somewhere around October or November we were sent to a place near Berlin to build barracks. Then the Russians caught up with us again and we were taken to Mauthausen. In Mauthausen they took all our clothes and left us in the barracks, totally naked, for a week or so. Then they gave us clothes and took us to Gunskirchen. We were three Jews in a camp of two hundred Russians and Poles.

One morning they brought in barbed wire for us to unload and barrels of gasoline. The rumor was that they were going to gather all the Jews in the area in the camp and then burn it down. You can imagine how I felt. At the last moment a messenger came from the U.S. Army, which was close by, offering to exchange a German commander who had been taken captive for ten thousand Jews. So they made a trade. The barracks were not set on fire as planned, and the Jews were all set free.

I was in pretty bad shape by then. My face, hands and feet were swollen from malnutrition but luckily it was May 8 and the American army came in. They saved us and freed us. When I saw they wouldn't put me in a hospital I just walked in and lay down in a bed.

When the doctor came in he asked me for identification to see if I belonged there but I pretended I didn't know what he was talking about. So they kept me there and fed me rice water, just rice water without salt or anything. After a week I was tired of it and wanted to leave but they wouldn't let me out. I found a boy from my city and told him I was healthy enough to get out but had no clothes. So he got me some clothes and hid them under the bed. In the middle of the night when there was no one around I got dressed and walked out. I always said I went in without permission and I went out without permission.

I went to a camp in Wels where the food was good. I still remember the day they gave out the venison and rice. It was while I was in Wels that we heard that the United States was going to give a part of Austria to the Russians and that they will have occupation troops there. We didn't know about the Russians then; we thought that liberation with them would be like with the Americans. When they came in we found it quite different. They disbanded the camp and told us we were on our own. They gave us no food and no shelter. There was nothing to do but go home. We took any transportation we could find to get there. Finally we got to Budapest.

I was hoping I'd find my younger sisters alive. I knew my parents and my older sister and her children were lost. In Budapest I found an uncle and spent a little time with him and then continued on my journey home.

I couldn't go into the house where my parents lived, but I went up to the sawmill. I knew where we had hidden some money and that we had left things with neighbors. There was a family with whom we left a lot of clothes and silverware that I hoped I would get back. The sawmill was almost completely destroyed. The Hungarians had been searching for hidden money and gold and ripped the walls apart to see if anything was hidden in them.

I was able to get my clothes back. Then I went to Bucharest and got a company who had dealt with my parents to advance me some money so I could rebuild the sawmill. I paid them back in lumber. It took me about six months to rebuild it.

In the meantime I got engaged. I knew Libby from before. So we became engaged and then married in May 1946. We were just married by a rabbi; she was a minor and for government permission to marry she needed a guardian, which we couldn't arrange at that time. Anyway we needed each other—I was the only one left of my family, and Libby had only one sister who came back.

In the beginning of 1948 they began to build a railroad next to my sawmill and the inspector forced me to cut lumber for him. Rumania was already communist. The inspector, the manager of the railroad, was a Nazi turned communist, and very anti-Semitic. I was too young to be afraid so I told him I couldn't afford to lose all that money working for him for nothing, but he said if I didn't I would be a saboteur. We finally agreed that I would lease him the sawmill and work for the government. This went on for a couple of months and when I got my check I found I was getting about a tenth of the salary I was supposed to get. He said it cost too much money to keep the agreement. It was better for him when I cut the lumber for him for nothing. He couldn't take anything off the workmen's salaries, so he had to take it off mine. And then they put up a repair shop to fix trucks right under my bedroom window. On my property! I had acres and acres they could use but the only place they chose was right under my window. I saw how things were going and knew there was no hope for me there. Then I got a telegram from my brother-in-law and he said things were getting worse everywhere. We were living out in the woods without communication, not knowing what was happening. There was no phone, and mail was very slow.

Libby left before me with the baby. I waited for some money that was owed me, but when it didn't come I followed her. Just in time! It was while the elections were going on, and the night we went over the border to Hungary to go back to the uncle in Budapest was the last time you could do it.

In Budapest I bought a passport with a Uruguay visa and a French transit permit so I could go through Austria to France to get to Uruguay. When we got to Vienna I went to a doctor for a certificate to say that the baby was sick and we wouldn't be able to continue to Paris. There was no point in going to Paris. You couldn't work anything out there. In Vienna, however, I thought I would try. What I did was to throw my passport away and go to the police and tell them I lost my papers. They gave me permission to stay a little while longer.

Three months later, on a Saturday at three in the morning, the police came to the door and took me to the police station. They said I had to pay a fine for coming over the border illegally. But I told him I had a passport and lost it, and after a few phone calls they set me free.

The first thing I did was register to go to Australia. I said I was a farmer and wanted to get out of Europe to a place where I could do farming. In the meantime I heard there was a new law that anybody who was in Austria, Germany or Italy by January 1, 1949 had the right to go to the United States. So we decided to go over to Germany.

I had been able to make a little money in Austria by leasing a license to buy and sell chocolate. That's what I did, and I was doing pretty well selling chocolate to the grocery stores, but there was no way to get out and go anyplace.

In Munich you just went and applied for a license and got it. We were able to buy an apartment and get our own furniture. I spoke German very well—and with my looks they didn't take me for a Jew. In Munich I had an import–export business. I got a new automobile and traveled from city to city. I sold nylon stockings and goods imported from England. I did a lot of business in Germany.

My only problem was that I was an observant Jew, and eating was a big problem when I was traveling. I lived on bread and fruit, hard-boiled eggs and milk.

Then finally I had my papers in order and I got a contract through the Joint Distribution Committee to come to the United States. The United Nations Relief and Works Agency paid our way.

Lydia Brown was eighteen when the Germans occupied the town of Viseul de Sus in Rumania and made it the ghetto for the area. The population grew from seven thousand to thirty thousand almost overnight. Then she and her family were deported to Auschwitz.

When Germany occupied Hungary in 1944 we were ordered to wear the yellow star and we could no longer listen to the radio. German officers stayed at our hotel so we couldn't take any chances. I remember sitting at the window on the last day of Passover, looking out on Main Street. In other years it had been full of Jewish girls and boys walking around in their new clothes. That year the street was deserted. Nobody went out walking after we had to wear the yellow star on our sleeves.

Then the head of the police passed by. He told my father that he had received an order to get all the Jews together at five o'clock in the morning, and he didn't know where they would be taken. He told us to give him our valuables and he would save them for us. He was a nice, friendly man. Others were like dogs.

When my father came back he alerted a few neighbors and that night nobody went to sleep. We didn't have any suitcases in the house so my mother took the runners the peasants used to weave for her to put on the floor and sewed up the two ends and made bags like saddlebags we could put over our shoulders. There were seven in the family and we each had such a bag. We put in a blanket and a pillow, some clothing and a few pillow cases. It was right after Passover so we had no bread in the house. It reminded us of the Passover story, where the Jews were told to leave Egypt; we too didn't have any bread. We took the matzo that was left and preserves and boiled eggs. At five o'clock they knocked at the door and told us to go to the city hall.

They didn't take the whole Jewish population. They took only the leading families, the business people and the wealthy people in the community—about two hundred families. They kept us in the yard until noon, with all the crying children and the weak old people. We knew already that something very bad would happen to us. Some men in the community had already been interned. It was a system where a gentile person who had some little thing against you could go to the police and say you were a communist or you were in the black market, and they would take you away without a trial and send you to an internment camp.

They took us to the Rabbi Viznitzer's yeshiva, a three-story building where they kept us overnight. They let only a few women go home to milk the cows. The homes and the animals had been left unattended; we left so early the animals had not even been fed.

My father was also taken out. He was appointed to be one of the ten people to lead the ghetto that was formed in our community. The next morning we were ordered to go home. The boundaries of the ghetto had been set. Our community was to become a ghetto for the entire province. The non-Jews in the ghetto area had to move out and Jews had to collect their belongings and move in. They gave us three days to make the arrangements. Every family got a room. A five-room house became a five-family house. Our hotel was in the ghetto area. The guards of the ghetto stayed with us, and there was also room for sixteen families.

My father was put in charge of the public kitchen since he knew about food from running a restaurant. My sister was one of the main cooks. My mother also cooked. Hundreds of people were housed in the synagogues where there were no cooking facilities and were fed in the public soup kitchens. My father turned his garage into a warehouse and the people from the cities were permitted to go back for potatoes, flour and dry foods to contribute to the kitchen, so there would be enough food. We were a town of seven thousand people. When the ghetto was created, the population jumped almost overnight to thirty thousand. People had come from twelve neighboring towns and were housed in every local home. And I remember myself standing with a broom from morning till night just trying to maintain cleanliness. In such congestion the worst sickness could break out.

Four weeks after the ghetto was formed they began to take groups of people away. I don't know how they were chosen. By that time everybody was registered with the police. They put about eighty people into a freight car. It was possible to take two changes of clothing, a pillow and a blanket and some water and dry food. Everything else was left in the ghetto.

Our transport left on May 27, a Wednesday. We were among the last seven hundred people left in the ghetto because my father was responsible for the food and also because the guards were living with us and wanted us to keep the hotel clean. What I remember of that day, what stays with me most, was my mother's face. We were out in the yard with our few belongings waiting for the cart to come to take us to the place where we would be searched. My mother was sitting under a beautiful blooming acacia tree and looking at the buildings with painful eyes. The buildings were the work of my father and mother and all of us in the family. We had built up the hotel and maintained it. My mother had tears in her eyes. It was like she was saying goodbye to life.

A midwife searched us and then we walked the long way to the train. I watched the people of our community, the gentile community, standing on the side of the road with smirks and smiles on their faces. They were the people we grew up with. People we lived with, worked with, did business with, had no compassion. I don't know if they could have helped us, but there was no sign of sadness in their faces.

Our whole family went on the train together—uncles, aunts, cousins. I remember we happened to be in a corner of the train and there was a little window with shutters we could open. We could see which cities we passed. We stopped in Segeth, the main city of the area, and picked up their last five hundred people. And then we stopped in Hust to pick up the last people in the ghetto there. I remember that my father was very upset when we crossed the Hungarian border into Germany. He saw that as a very bad sign.

We were on the train for three days in terribly cramped quarters. I remember the younger girls gave up their places at night so the elderly people could put their heads down. The last night was Friday and I was too exhausted to take it anymore. When we arrived on Saturday morning I woke up with my head in my father's lap. He was holding me to give me a little rest.

When we looked out of the window we saw people in prison clothes and I remember my father saying that they must be murderers or lawbreakers of some kind. We didn't realize that they were all Jews like us. After a time the doors opened and young men in striped uniforms came in. They spoke Yiddish. They told us to leave our belongings on the train and get out. They asked the young women with babies to give the infants to their mothers. My mother was forty-six years old. She was a beautiful woman but she looked very broken-down after the hard journey. Being Orthodox, she had no hair, only a wig. The man who came on the train said, "Pick yourself up. Make yourself pretty," but she didn't realize what he meant. When we got out of the train we were lined up. German officers were telling people to go to the right or the left. Men and women were separated. I was with my sister, separated from my family.

Then we were somewhere in a line and there were men working on the side of the road, digging ditches, and they were begging us for food. All I had left was a little piece of strudel my mother had baked in the ghetto. She said that it would give us strength if we were hungry because it was very rich, but I just had a little piece left in a small cloth bag. We saved our food on the train because we didn't know where we were going or what we would get when we arrived.

They put us in a barrack. A German officer told us, "There are no questions and no answers. Do as you are told. That's all you can do." A girl who spoke Yiddish explained what he said. She emphasized that we should follow orders if we wanted to be all right. Then we were ordered to undress entirely. We were only allowed to keep our shoes and they took the laces out of the shoes.

Imagine women and girls from very sheltered areas and from Orthodox homes—what it meant to get undressed in front of these German officers and soldiers. They were standing there with their big rubber whips. We did as we were told and then we were taken into a room where our hair was cut off on all parts of our body. From there we entered another room where we had to get into some kind of solution. After that we took a shower and we were thrown a dress. We were out in the yard. It was cold and windy. We had no underwear, only that dress. And after hours of waiting standing in line we were taken through the streets to a barrack in a big fenced-in area. We were in this long building with a big chimney in the middle and two cement walks. There were three layers of bunks made of wood—just boards, not even close together. There were no blankets, no pillows. We were told to lie down on those rough boards. Later we were lined up in rows of five, counted and handed a piece of bread that was like black mud. There was a little bit of margarine on it and some warm fluid that was called coffee.

The crying and shouting that night was like something in a horror movie, something no one every heard before, and it went on for days and days. Imagine the pain! We were torn from our families. We were cold and hungry, and there was the standing in line for the roll calls in the morning and afternoon. We were given no work to do, we just had to sit like little chickens in those bunks. In the daytime we were allowed to go out to the toilet and the washroom. But there were no towels. We had to dry ourselves on our dresses. At night we were not allowed to leave the barracks, so they had just buckets. There was a Slovakian girl by the name of Hanna in charge and she was just like a wild animal. She had lost all human feelings. She used to tell us to be quiet and go look at the chimneys. And you know, we didn't know what she meant by it. We didn't know what was happening. We heard rumors that there was a place for the children and they were drinking milk and eating white bread and having it good. We still didn't know where we were or what was happening.

We spent eight weeks in Auschwitz before we were sent out to work. My sister became very ill with dysentery and I was so worried about her. I remember one day they brought some coffee and I ran to get some for her and I was bending over her when someone behind me hit me very hard with a stick. When I got up I saw it was a girl from my town. She wore beautiful boots and fine clothing. She was one of the girls taken for the men and she was given gifts. But when she saw who she hit she turned around. I never saw her again. There was another girl from our town who was the secretary in the block and she used to come and visit us. I begged her to intervene on our behalf and put our names on the list of people to leave for work and she did. We were among the first to go.

They picked seventy girls. They gave us a warm shower and even a piece of soap, and I got a little nightgown for underwear and on top a gray dress. And even a panty, so I could stop shivering. I even had a pair of shoes. Then we were given a bowl of barley with a spoon to eat it with.

We came to the town of Reichenbach late at night and had to wait in the station for a long time till someone came to get us. Our guards turned us over to other guards. We were taken down a street where the linden trees were blooming. I don't know if you have ever smelled blooming linden trees but it is a wonderful smell, and the air was thick with the sweetness of it.

They put us in a garage to sleep overnight. There were wood shavings on the floor, something soft after the hard boards and cement we were used to. In the morning a Russian lady came in. She was the doctor in the camp and also a prisoner. She examined us one by one and then we were given a bowl and a cup and silverware and taken to a barrack where there were nice little beds with straw mattresses and each one had a pillow and two blankets.

Such a change! Such a beautiful improvement! We couldn't have been happier. The next day we were taken to a factory where they made radio receivers and transmitters. We sat at tables and a foreman explained to us what we should do. I had a little machine with soldering irons to make certain wirings. The engineers used to like my work. They would come to my table and examine it, and they used to give me a bonus of a bowl of sugar when they were especially pleased. They would give me a slip of paper and I could turn it in for my reward. They were so satisfied with the Jewish laborers that they brought more girls in and then they moved us again. The camp was owned by the Telefunken company. There were lots of girls from Holland there with us.

We worked in the factory till the end of February. We heard on the factory radio that the front was approaching. We were just sixty kilometers from Wroclaw and the air raids were tremendous. The German workers and guards would go down to the shelter and lock us into the factory. We would hide ourselves under the tables while the bombs were falling and the glass was breaking all around us. When the raid was over we ran back to our camp, with the last few bombs still exploding around us. I remember that night in the camp with the blankets on the windows to keep it dark and our excitement because we thought we'd soon be liberated.

There were thousands of us in the transition camp. They just kept dragging the prisoners back from the front so we wouldn't be liberated. I think what kept us alive was that most of us were from religious homes. The hope kept us alive even when we were hungry and cold. We observed holidays the best way we knew. I don't know how we knew the days but we knew. We didn't eat on Yom Kippur and said the prayers by heart. On

Friday nights the married women used to reminisce about their families and their homes. We even composed a song we used to sing while we were marching to the factories. It was about how our lives would be beautiful again when everyone would be free and we would be with our families in nice, bright, warm homes. And this is what really kept us going no matter how terrible the times became. We kept each other up with encouraging words.

Some people have it, that kind of spirit-giving power. Some girls helped the others a lot. I remember being in a camp on Passover and I didn't want to eat bread. My sister and I gave away our ration of bread for two raw potatoes on the first day of Passover. I knew prayers by heart. My grandmother had taught me that if you say *Oleynu Lishabayach* seven times, backwards and forward, you are saved from terrible things, and I said it with all my friends and all the other prayers we knew. This gave us a lot of strength to survive.

The girls were really amazing at that time. We used to get together for sessions to try to make each other stronger. Also, when we were very hungry we used to cook in our imaginations. You wouldn't believe the recipes that were flying around. We used to say what when we were free we would make potatoes in every possible way—baked with sour cream, boiled with butter, fried with onions and so on. It was a terrible thing to be hungry all the time.

My sister and three cousins were together with me until we were freed on May 8, 1945. We were in the camp at Parsnitz at the time, digging trenches and tank obstacles. Weak as we were we had to shovel the dirt and throw it ten feet high and they were standing over us with rubber whips so we either worked or were beaten until we collapsed. They took us in open cars for two days to the town of Krazau somewhere in Slovakia, to an ammunition camp, and I was lucky to be working inside testing the metals. There was an old man, a Czech, who used to bring me little bits of food until the German guard caught him and threatened to punish him. Then on May 7 we heard the announcements on the loudspeakers. That night they took us to a steambath and put our clothes in ovens to kill the lice. The next morning the gates were opened and the guards had all disappeared.

We were liberated by the Russians. We didn't have shoes. We didn't have bread. We didn't have anything. The five of us cousins didn't move without each other. We were so afraid of being separated. So we were standing at the side of the road and a man came by on a Russian wagon with horses. He talked to us in Yiddish so we weren't afraid of him. After all, he was one of our liberators. He wanted to know what we were doing there and what crimes we had committed. We told him we hadn't committed any crimes; it was only because we were Jews that we were taken to a concentration camp.

And then a young officer came over to sit with us on the grass. He didn't say anything but threw a silk scarf into my lap. And then he took some perfume out of his pocket and began to spray us. And I became frightened. I wasn't yet eighteen and something told me there was reason to be afraid. The man who spoke Yiddish asked my oldest cousin if there were any more girls who would come back to spend the night with them. And she said, "What are you talking about? We're all sick and undernourished —don't even talk about it!" So the Yiddish-speaking man told us to go home and we went quickly, without looking back, because we were afraid they would come after us.

The Frenchmen who were prisoners in our camp guarded the women until we could leave. The Russians didn't usually ask the women with silk scarves and perfume; they usually just did what they wanted. At the camp they gave us three days to go looting through any German home we wanted. The Russians said that we should take anything we wanted, that we could break things, smash things, and they would protect us and not say a word. So we girls went, like on a shopping trip, to find clean clothes and shoes. And we finally got rid of our lousy clothes and had clean, fresh clothes on us. There was one girl from our hometown who was taking men's underwear and men's shirts and we told her not to do it—what did she need it for? But she insisted; she said her father would come home and he would need it. And you know something, when we returned home, the only father who came home was her father, and she had the clothing for him.

In Budapest the Red Cross and the Joint Distribution Committee had stations where people could come for help. So we registered our names and began looking for people who had news of our families. Someone told me that my father was back in our hometown and that he had already opened the restaurant. You can imagine the happiness. And then one of my cousins found a brother-in-law. He already had an apartment and a cook because his wife had not returned and he invited the five of us to his town and gave us a warm reception. There were five men who had put the household together. None of their wives had returned. I remember we arrived on a Friday and bathed and put on clean clothing and cooked for *Shabbat*. We made the first *cholent* in a long time and for the first time in a year we sat at a nice table and sang *zemiros* and felt human again.

Then, however, the shock hit us. Until we came home we had hopes of finding our families. We didn't know the whole tragedy of what had happened to our people; we only knew our own private tragedy. But now that we were free it was like the roof really caved in on us. All the hope that had nourished us disappeared. I learned that my father was gone, that someone else had opened his restaurant and that there was nobody of my family in our town. My mother, my grandmother, and the two younger brothers only fourteen and eleven had not survived. We just kept hoping our father might have, however, because he was only forty-five.

When we were on the way to Auschwitz my father told us where he had hidden things, even some gold. Lots of things were hidden in the attic because my mother used to say that she got married in 1918 when it was impossible to find clothing and fabric. She wanted an easier time for her girls, so she always bought cloth to put away for us, for the future. So we wanted to go home and find our things. We didn't like to take charity from anyone. We came home, and that was the worst shock of all. The home we were longing to see was totally destroyed. There was no electricity in the town. And from our whole hotel we couldn't find a single mattress to lie down on.

So there we were, two girls all alone. The cooking stove was broken. But a cousin's husband was back in the town and he was so excited that someone from the family survived that he came and fixed the stove and brought us pots and dishes. He told us that his wife had not returned and there were many men without wives who had no one to cook for them. We knew about cooking because of our father's restaurant and he suggested that we make a living by feeding the men who were living alone in the town.

I would go out in the morning, buy the meat, make it kosher and by noon we would feed about fifteen people. We had our food and weren't dependent upon anybody. I went to a peasant where we had left some bedding and linen and he gave them back to us. We opened up some rooms and brought back a peasant girl who used to help us.

We had inherited a grain mill in a small town. We went to the peasant who had taken it over and he gave us a little money. My sister went to the city and bought material for some dresses and coats. For the whole mill we got four dresses and two coats. Then we got a search warrant from the police to find the peasants who ran the hotel while we were in the camps. They went with us, the two policemen, to find the rest of the bedding and dishes and we found enough to reopen the hotel.

My sister met a young man and became engaged. I had two boys who wanted to marry me and I couldn't make up my mind. I had a boyfriend before the war and we were very much in love and I couldn't make up my mind until I knew what happened to him. When I found out that he had not survived I became engaged. Barry was one of the most eligible bachelors in the town. He found the money his parents had hidden and was able to restore a mill.

But when I think back now, I see we were not really normal people. From a community of seven thousand people, maybe two hundred returned. We had only two older people among us in the whole town. The men who survived were in the forced-labor battalions of the Hungarians. The girls were from the camps. And we used to have dances practically every evening. When I think back to our dancing and how miserable, how desperately miserable we felt, I see that we were still trying to survive. All kinds of marriages happened. Older men married very young girls. There was all kinds of mismatching . . . it was not normal.

Sometimes I would see a girl go by wearing my blouse or my coat from before the war. And I would say "Can I have my blouse back? I'd really like that blouse back," and she would say, "What difference does it make who wears it?" It was already the Russian occupation—what could I say?

I kept looking for the gold my father hid and finally found the place in the wall where the box had been left. There were two kilograms of gold. My sister sold her share and opened up a store. I kept it. I didn't need it. When Barry and I married we went to live near the mill in a secluded place in the forest. We rebuilt the sawmill and began working again. I became pregnant. I had to go to the city to have the baby because there was no doctor or hospital in our town.

In 1948 communism began to grab more and more of our area. The Communist party was not elected, it came with the Russian occupation. After a while we began to feel the anti-Semitism mixed with the fear of communism.

When the communist government was elected my sister urged us to cross the border into Hungary. Barry came home and began to make the arrangements. We went to Satu Mare, a border town near Hungary, and paid the large amount of money it cost to get over the border.

The people that arranged the crossings told us we would have to walk over the fields for about half an hour and then we would be at a railroad station. They were supposed to have the arrangements with the train people and have hot milk for the baby. We were also supposed to be able to wash our shoes, which would be muddy and give us away. It was a well-organized business and they even gave you Hungarian money, so you could pay for your tickets.

A peasant picked me up at the edge of town in a cart. I carried my four-month-old baby. She put a big bandana over me and the baby and brought us to her house. My husband went separately with another cousin who also crossed the border that evening. The woman in the peasant's house gave me some warm milk to put in the bottles and I put in a sleeping pill because we would all be in danger if he began to cry. Lots of people were caught on the border because the children started to cry and alerted the guards. When people were caught the penalty was ten to fifteen years in jail, so you can imagine the fright.

The peasant said that I had to leave even though my husband had not yet arrived or I would miss the train. This meant that I had to carry the baby in his heavy snowsuit and the baby's food and I really didn't know if I could do it but just as I was ready to go my husband and cousin arrived. I also had a basket with a kilogram of gold hidden in it under the baby food.

The half hour across the field was a three-hour tramp. The men walked faster than I did and I could see their silhouettes moving; I kept falling into the ditches between the fields. I had leather boots on and sores began forming on my feet. Then one of the suitcases broke open and the silverware fell out and dogs began to bark and we heard some shots.

We finally arrived at the little railroad station and the men stood outside and I went in to buy the tickets. A woman with a baby is always in less danger. They gave me the tickets and it was for the baggage car. In the car there was a little toilet and in that toilet we packed four grownups, a baby and our luggage. It was a regular magic trick. A few stops past the border a man came to let the men into the regular car, but I was left behind with the baby, the food and the little basket of gold. Later I too went into the regular train, but we didn't look at each other or talk or anything; just in case one person gets caught the others could at least get away. I was so afraid the mud on my boots would be noticed and I tried to wash them off in the toilet. Then, I'll never forget, a beggar came up to me in the train and I had this Hungarian money I didn't know what it was worth and I gave him such a big note he bent all the way to the floor to kiss my feet.

Finally in Budapest I could get together with my husband. We watched the guards checking the peasants' baskets and my husband threw his coat over my basket hoping they wouldn't see it. Luckily we got by. We had an address to go to in Budapest, an aunt and uncle there who had survived the Budapest ghetto. But everything was dangerous. Hungary was also under Russian occupation and if they found us we would have been sent back.

Fortunately we spoke Hungarian. We got in contact with people who gave us false papers. We were like people that come from the country to live in Budapest. We had to have ration cards to get bread and milk and butter, and we got those too. My husband's relatives went to get the cards for us so they wouldn't hear our accents, which would show we were not real Hungarians.

We were in Hungary from March to August, and all the time trying to get papers to cross into Austria without going through the same ordeal as we had coming from Rumania to Hungary. We were determined to leave the communist countries. And my personal goal was to be reunited with my sister, who was already in Germany. It was 1948 and we had already heard that Israel had become a state; it was a big happiness for us. But our first thought was to find a place where we would feel safe.

We got a Rumanian passport in Hungary and a visa to Uruguay and then we asked for transit visas to Vienna and Paris. This way we could leave Hungary and come into Austria legally, with a passport. In Vienna we lost our passport and went to the American embassy. We declared ourselves stateless and they gave us a piece of paper.

It took two years before we could leave Vienna. My husband did some business and I started to learn to be a hairdresser. Meanwhile my sister left Germany for America with the help of the Joint Distribution Committee. In 1950 they sent her to Portland, Oregon. From that time we knew that we would keep striving until we could join her.

*Angela Yaron's family survived the war years in
Rumania with false identity papers. When they
came out of hiding they returned to Dorohoi and
found the anti-Semitism unbearable.*

There was always anti-Semitism and segregation but we were
not too aware of what was happening. My parents traveled a lot
but didn't understand what was going on. In 1932 they were in
Germany and really envied our cousins in Berlin. They thought,
"They have it so good," and my father was ready to leave Rumania and settle in Berlin. The only reason we stayed was because my mother hated to move.

We had this isolated, sheltered life until the war came in
1939, and everything broke loose. Suddenly there were posters
all over town showing how horrible Jews were, and we would
go to my dad and ask if it was true: was that really what we are?
And he would say, "That's their problem, not yours. You are
okay. That should be enough for you and hold you up."

My brother, who was fifteen, wanted to become a Catholic.
Dad blew his top. He said, "You can't do that. You're Jewish."
But my brother said that it was too hard to be a Jew and he had
had enough of it. "Okay," my father said, "go try it out. See if
you can become a Catholic if you want it so much." My brother
took some courses with a priest and then never mentioned the
subject again. Later on he wanted to join the Communist party
and my dad was against that; he didn't talk to my brother for
nearly a year because of that.

Meanwhile we felt the overwhelming Nazi propaganda. We
were kicked out of the Rumanian community as undesirable,
untouchable, totally unworthy people. They took us out of school
because they said we were not fit to be with other children. Kids
we used to play with threw us out of their games. They told us
we were animals and that they didn't play with animals. It hurt
us a lot. If we weren't altogether dehumanized by it, it was be-

cause our family was so supportive and my mother and father made us feel good about ourselves in spite of everything we heard.

My dad did another sensible thing that saved us. We did not have to wear the yellow star in our town, but our name was just like a star, telling who we were. He arranged to have an uncle of ours with the un-Jewish name of Balus adopt us. So our name was changed to Balus and we had identity papers with the new name, and that was very important.

It was in 1941. I remember a very rainy day and my mother, dad and I were at home. My dad could not work in his profession so he was always at home. My brother was off with a friend studying for an exam. At that time we were going to the Jewish ghetto school. It was a fantastic school with even kindergarten taught by college professors.

It all began in the Jewish cemetery. Dorohoi was only fifteen minutes from the Russian border. A Jewish soldier who had died at the front was brought to the cemetery for a military burial— Jews at that time were still serving in the Rumanian army. Even though he was a total stranger, the rabbi conducted the funeral and some representatives from the Jewish community went as a sign of respect. After the man was buried the lieutenant and the handful of soldiers who were there turned on the Jews around the grave. My uncle was there. He survived, and told us how the soldiers picked up their guns and said, "None of you Jews can leave. You will be buried with him." They forced them to turn around and began shooting. My uncle was wounded but he got away.

When the soldiers were finished with those at the cemetery they went from house to house in the Jewish district killing and torturing Jews. When they found Jews with beards they set fire to the beards and then killed them. In two hours half of the Jewish population of Dorohoi was wiped out. Then they went to the non-Jewish district to look for Jews. They went from house to house, and I can remember how they came in and looked us over. There was my father, my mother, myself and a neighbor with her two children. She had heard the shots and thought the Russians were coming.

The killers were not from our town. They did not know who was Jewish and who wasn't when they were out of the Jewish district. My father had taken off the sign that had his old name, and the new one was not yet ready; there was only the mark on the wall to show something was being changed. We told them we weren't Jewish and showed them our new identity cards. Then they went across the street to the courthouse and asked the janitor about us. He was just an ordinary peasant but he did not give us away. He told them we were not Jewish.

My brother was also lucky. He decided to leave his friend's house when the shooting began. He was afraid my mother would worry. So he started walking down the street and was stopped by the killers. They asked for his identity card and he pulled out the new one that he had had only two days and showed it to them, and they let him go. When my brother came into the house my mother just fell on him with kisses, and he didn't know how narrow our escape was.

That night the chief of police came to tell my dad that the Rumanian police were going to take hostages from among the Jewish population and that he was at the top of the list. The idea was to get ransom money, but the excuse they gave was that the Jews were to blame for the shootings because they attacked the soldiers at the cemetery. Ridiculous as that sounds, since the Jews had no guns and no idea of defending themselves, that was the excuse.

We left Dorohoi the next day. We just walked out of our beautiful house will all the lovely things in it, and all we took were two suitcases that mostly had my mother's jewelry and a few things to wear. We paid the conductor to get a double compartment and he locked us in so no one could throw us off the train—Jews were not allowed to travel. There were just the four of us. My uncle refused to come. His refusal cost him his life. When they took the Jews they beat him up in the police cellar, and after that he had stroke after stroke. He was a beautiful man, kind, loving, thoughtful, but unlucky. He accepted persecution. He never learned to defend himself.

We went to the granduncle who had adopted us and given us his name. He was a doctor in the town of Targu Jiv. He was not married and he let us stay with him until we could figure out where to go. Dad couldn't work and he was also upset because my brother and I weren't getting an education. He could stand everything that was going on, but life without education for his children, that he couldn't accept. We moved from one small town to another. We lived in boarding houses and sold pieces of jewelry to have money for rent and food. Meanwhile we told ourselves and each other that the Germans would soon be defeated and that we had to stay sane and keep ourselves going until the crazy time was over. I must have been very unhappy because I've blocked off much of those wandering years. I remember lots of details from the time before we left but there are three years that I cannot remember.

I do remember living in Bucharest during the war. We had a small apartment on the third floor with one room for my parents and half a room for my brother and me. I remember thinking it was cosy to be together in such close quarters. I slept on a chair that opened into a bed at night, and went to a fantastic ghetto school with marvelous teachers. My father worked in the legal department of a textile factory owned by Jews. In Bucharest we were in the Jewish district. We had the Jewish stamp on our cards. We were no longer pretending.

We lived a sheltered life, in self-imposed segregation. We had no political power. We could express our feelings by not going to a concert in which someone like Walter Gieseking was playing. We would be careful not to support anyone who accepted the Nazi regime. But really we had no power, except to continue our private life without attracting attention.

The way we identified as Jews was in our search for education. I was a good student. It was my way of showing I'm okay. I enjoyed learning. When the war was over Jewish kids could go back in the Rumanian schools, but on the quota system, which was a merit system. There were very hard exams to pass. The Jewish faculty on the community board decided to send some kids back into the public school to show that we were ready to forgive them for expelling us in the first place. They came to me and asked me to take the tests. I talked with my dad and he said he couldn't tell me what to do. So I had to make up my own mind.

I didn't know what I was getting into and he didn't either. I had no idea that I was going into a real stress situation, into shocks and dramatic events that demanded more than I could give. I wouldn't wish the experience on my worst enemy today.

It began in a normal way. I took the exams and they accepted me and one other girl. I went for two years and nobody talked to me. There was no counseling, no backing, no support to fall back on. Once I left the Jewish school I lost all my ties there. I should have kept them and gone back for support, but it didn't occur to me. Instead I decided to study and that's what I did. The teachers were afraid to relate to a Jew. The kids in the class would sit by me at exams and tests because they wanted to copy my answers, but there was no other contact. There were awards given at the end of each year, and at the end of the second year I displaced the girl at the top of the class; they really ostracized me for that. But there was no other way I could show them I'm okay, because no one would talk to me. The image of the Jew as a beast, created by the propaganda, was too strong.

At the end there was the big college entrance exam, the prestige examination, and all the schools came together to take it. I didn't want to go to the assembly where they announced the results. I didn't want to go to graduation. I told a boyfriend I had that there was no sense in going. I didn't belong there. All the years in that school were a mistake. He insisted that I had to go to graduation and finally I got on my bike and he went with me to keep my courage up. It was about an hour's bike ride, and when I got there the principal scolded me for being late and told me to sit down. And what do you think? I had taken the first place, and they were waiting for me to start the graduation. I was the first of the 132 kids in the class. But they never allowed me to be a person and relate to and socialize with them. I didn't have a friend for two years. I don't know if I'd send a child of mine to do that.

Then I went to college, and that was really a bad trip. We had to go to college, as middle-class kids, but the fees were enormous and we didn't have the money. And being Jewish was a stigma you couldn't escape.

Then I met my best friend's brother who came back to visit from Israel. He had left Rumania when he was sixteen on a children's transport and I'd never seen him. We met and fell in love and decided to leave Rumania. We were very young, and I said, "Where you go, I'll go." I was twenty years old and in my first year of college, and I applied for a visa to go to Israel. It wasn't easy for me to decide to leave my parents, but I thought I could study in Israel and it was very important for my husband to leave Rumania. The Rumanians kept us waiting for two years, telling us from week to week that we would get the visa but not giving it to us. I was at the department of immigration every week. My husband meanwhile registered at the Rumanian Polytechnic Institute, and he actually finished his degree in Rumania while waiting for me to get the visa. I had almost finished my requirements as well, but I didn't have the teacher's training. Not letting me go was pure discrimination and harassment. The clerk in charge of immigration one day committed suicide, hanged himself above his desk on a hook. His successor let me go.

We went to Israel in 1949. We had no money. I didn't know the language. I was sick. I had a son and then got a slipped disc. I had to work and there was no one to take care of the child. I remember days and nights with the baby crying and my husband working twelve hours a day. I just couldn't adjust to it.

Then my parents came and moved in with us, all of us in a little room with a balcony, just one little room without a bathroom or a kitchen. My parents didn't say they were coming. They just sent a wire from the boat. It was not a time of immigration so there were no support systems for newcomers and no housing. We managed that way for a year. We used kerosene lamps. We had no refrigeration, just a little box with ice melting away. And my mother—I remember like it was today—used to wash the clothes by hand in a bucket in the toilet, and the sheets too, because we had no money to send them to the laundry. In Israel we hit the bottom of physical comforts. It was hard to imagine us as the family in the large house with beautiful furniture and servants and everything. We lived in conditions of poverty, but didn't feel like poor people. You see we were only economically poor, we were not culturally poor.

My father learned Hebrew and passed his bar exams in Jerusalem. He was fifty-two when he came, so that was no small accomplishment. My husband Ted was really accepting of the whole thing. It was just the way it was and we had to make it, and we did—in a very beautiful spirit. I am surprised at myself now when I think of it, because I never thought I was so giving, but it was the kind of situation where you needed to prove your strength and love your family.

I went to an Ulpan and learned Hebrew. I never reached a level where I could say I was educated. But we had wonderful friends who were in the same position as we were. On *Shabbat* we would dance and talk and get really close to each other. We were really enthusiastic about Israel and hopeful that everything was going to be well. We never thought of leaving and would have a big fight with anyone who suggested it.

But it was so hard, one thing after another. At first it was my being sick and having to stay in bed. And then it was feeling responsible for my parents. Ted was working two jobs, one as an engineer and the other as a teacher. And with it all we could only afford one chicken for the week and one stick of margarine and a fish fillet. Food was rationed. We did not go to a single concert in six years. We never went to the theater or to a restaurant. We never had a vacation and of course had no car. Some of our friends had parents who had lived in Israel for many years. Some came from Egypt and had a little money and decent furniture. We had nothing but responsibilities.

Then Ted got a scholarship to come to America and get a master's degree in industrial engineering. I left the baby with my mother and came with him just for six months. It was the first time Ted and I were together alone. We started thinking of the kind of life we had in Rumania and in Israel. We were never Rumanians but we couldn't say we were Israelis either. When we came to Israel Ted was very much a Zionist, I was not. I came because I was a Jew and I hated the Rumanians and the communists. As for the Nazis, I still had trouble believing they had actually killed six million people with the world standing by.

I wouldn't trade my experience in Israel for anything. It was a fantastic gift. I learned in Israel to raise my head—to say "I am what I am and that's all." This is the Israeli concept of being Jewish: you're not proud and you're not ashamed. Living in Israel, whether you remain or not, is a very special experience. It gave me an identity. I think if I were born again and had to choose whether or not I would want to be Jewish, I would have a hard time saying that I would prefer not to be a Jew, in spite of the sufferings and hard times, if I could be guaranteed that I would live through it. I would have to admit that it did me good. I acquired strength and coping tools. I have resources that I wouldn't have had if I hadn't gone through all my troubles. I might be willing to pay the price if I had to choose.

My brother and my friends who did not pass through Israel do not share my feelings. Something is missing for them. I'm sorry for my brother. He feels very awkward about being Jewish; he was hurt much more. When I look at my brother I see how much Israel did for me. It was a redeeming experience.

In America with my husband I was exposed to new opportunities and I couldn't resist the chance for a better life. When we decided to stay it was in another frame of mind. I was ready to adjust. I wanted to make a permanent home. I was ready to be shaped and changed by America.

Life
In
America

America for some survivors was "the blessed land," the ultimate refuge. They arrived with expectations that all their dreams of freedom would be fulfilled. Others came with the idea that it could be no worse than Europe, perhaps better. America was the first country to issue a visa, or where they had found a relative willing to sign an affidavit or a Jewish community prepared to sponsor a refugee family. Many had applied to several countries while waiting in the displaced persons camps and had no preference, needing only to put some distance between themselves and Europe.

Some had picked up ideas about America from pen pals and the Americans who liberated them. Sender Wajsman from Vilna thought he knew what to expect because he had read Sholom Aleichem's Yiddish stories about New York. Some were dazzled by their first sight of New York, but most were confused and bewildered by the crowds and the noise, by streets "full of dirty papers and neon lights that burned the eyes." They arrived physically and mentally exhausted, anxious about being in a strange land without money, family or friends.

Some of the newcomers received warm welcomes from generous and supportive families, but many were totally dependent upon the Hebrew Immigrant Aid Society (HIAS), a refugee relief organization funded by American Jews. The Jewish Family Service provided them with temporary lodging, clothing, pocket money and job information. The service made free medical care and counseling available and also paid for transportation to the cities that had agreed to accept refugee families. Refugee families were dispersed throughout the country to encourage their Americanization and divide the burden of their support among many communities.

Social workers made the arrangements for the people they

called "new Americans." They urged them to learn English as quickly as possible and to take on American fashions and values. They found them housing they could afford and menial jobs as dishwashers, stock clerks and factory hands. Women who had had servants became servants and cooks. Men who had managed factories worked on assembly lines.

In later years, most of the survivors would have only praise for the help they received, but there were also harsh memories of their first experiences in America. The social workers were not interested in the personal needs of their clients and were not prepared for the maturity and complexity of adolescent survivors who had lived by their wits since they were orphaned at a young age. Survivors who had gone to university or medical school before the war hoped to continue their studies in America but were not encouraged. Those who had been professionals knew they would have had less trouble making a living and keeping their place in society if they could have overcome their revulsion to Europe.

America in the late forties and fifties had many problems to solve, and survivors who came with idealistic expectations of equality and justice found the realities disturbing. The engineers discovered that engineering companies discriminated against Jews. Medical schools had their quotas and restrictions. Newcomers who went to Southern cities were alarmed by the segregation of black people. Divided buses and segregated washrooms frightened and offended the survivors. Another source of anxiety were the McCarthy trials in the early fifties, in which they heard overtones of the dangers they thought they had left behind.

The individuals and organizations that welcomed refugees expected compliance and appreciation, not complaints and criticism. The survivors were well aware of what was required of them. Those who had been in the camps had learned to be responsive, to dissemble easily, to say only what people wanted to hear. They felt isolated among relatives who had no conception of what they'd been through and little understanding of the magnitude of the adjustments they faced. When they were urged to put the past behind them and forget the horrors of the Holocaust they understood that they were being asked to protect Americans from facts they couldn't face.

Survivors also quickly sensed that Americans looked down on refugees and foreigners. Americans found it hard to believe that European Jews might be better educated and more sophisticated than they were. The European refugees, in turn, thought Americans were childish and spoiled, unable to face reality. The traditional Jews from Europe were especially critical. They were certain that they had the authentic blueprint for Jewish life and that American Jews, as a whole, lacked knowledge, culture and discipline.

The Jewish communal structure in the United States seemed strange to those who were accustomed to the European pattern. Newcomers were shocked to find there were guards at the doors of American synagogues on Yom Kippur, the holiest day of the year, and that tickets were required to enter. They remembered that synagogues in Europe were open to all but forgot that the rabbis there had been paid by the state and that all Jews supported their institutions through a special tax. Observant Jews learned that American synagogues and temples were open and free every day of the year with the exception of Rosh Hashanah and Yom Kippur and they adjusted to the American system of supporting its religious institutions. Newcomers who were ambivalent about attending religious services gave the need for tickets as their excuse for not going. "It's only a money business," said one survivor. "If I come to pray they shouldn't turn me away because I have no ticket. A synagogue is not a concert hall."

Though cultural differences and practical problems distressed some of the newcomers, there were many young optimists like Herman Herskovic and Robert Spitz ready on arrival "to be reborn" as Americans. They had plans for education, work and service and were brimming with energy accumulated during the years of their confinement.

One by one survivors tried to come to terms with their feelings about themselves, their pasts and the challenges of creating a new life in America. Gradually they assessed the damage done to their bodies and minds and struggled with the psychological problems they had suppressed while their lives were in danger. Some were overwhelmed by physical and mental exhaustion and unable to work for a few years. Men and women who had seemed fearless in the most dangerous times began to tremble uncontrollably and have terrifying nightmares in America. Feelings of rage, suppressed during the Holocaust years, became overwhelming for some survivors. They could not accept any more frustration or delay, not even the normal confusions that were part of making a new life in an unfamiliar country.

Most of the refugees tried to become Americans and wanted

to be accepted in their communities as quickly as possible. Hilda Branch spoke no German to her daughter in the hope she would grow up with an American accent. Claude Cassirer avoided contact with other German refugees, seeking only American friends. At the age of sixty-three, Arthur Herz still plays baseball with his young sons and is a den father for their boy scout troop in order to feel like a real American.

Acceptance, however, has been hard to achieve. Many survivors complained of their feelings of isolation from Americans. Claude Cassirer was perplexed by the social barriers that separated Jews and Christians. He discovered that when American Jews spoke of a mixed group they meant Jews and Christians; for the newcomers a mixed group meant Americans and Europeans. Arthur Herz poignantly bemoaned his lack of friends: "I don't have a chip on my shoulder. I have a whole family born here, and I do a good living. I love this country but I have no friends whatsoever." Looking for reasons, he added, "Maybe my English is lousy but I'm not a dumb person."

Americans responded to refugees as strangers, aliens with funny accents, equally foreign. The foreigners, however, were acutely conscious of their differences from each other. Jack Goldman, explaining his aloofness from fellow survivors, said that the Holocaust did not weld the people who experienced it together. There were many survivors with whom he disagreed violently. He understood what they were doing but disapproved of their life-style, their philosophy and their attitudes toward life. Simon Grubman, telling of his lack of friends among survivors said, "We're not friendly with them here because we wouldn't be friendly in Poland. We have nothing in common and we never will no matter what country we live in." The clubs organized for "new Americans" were no comfort to those who chose solitude and isolation rather than the company of fellow survivors who they felt were not their intellectual or social peers.

Success in the business or professional world was often easier to achieve than social ease in a community. Well-trained doctors struggled for a time but reestablished themselves as physicians. Other professionals became involved in business or sold insurance and real estate. The women who came to the United States with university degrees or who acquired them when they came with student visas did very well. They became sociologists, psychiatrists, social workers, artists, and had the advantages of knowing several languages.

Many men and women, however, were not able to summon the energy or interest to make American successes of themselves. They struggled along with part-time jobs, restitution payments and the help of relatives. Surviving the Holocaust was the climax of their lives. Anita Magnus Frank watched her parents flounder and decided that immigration was marvelous for the children but terrible for parents. She had come as a teenager, had graduated from Washington University in St. Louis in 1958, received a Woodrow Wilson Fellowship at Harvard in its Russian program and gone on to become a Russian expert for the Rand Corporation. She thought, however, that America should be described as "a very hard country where immigrants work their tails off and live under poor circumstances with no guarantees of success and affluence." She compared her own accomplishments to her parents' struggle. In another time or place her father might have been a university professor rather than a gardener and custodian. Her mother might have been a teacher, a nurse or a businesswoman instead of a cook and a nurse's aide. Her father, Felix Magnus, described himself with less bitterness. He thought less about what might have been in the best of circumstances and more about his actual choices. He was happier working as a gardener in Los Angeles than he had been as an unsuccessful businessman in the Netherlands.

Eugene Weissbluth, a school principal and political figure in Hungary, was another survivor who didn't regret his loss of status. He worked as a box-maker when he came to Cleveland and later sold insurance to fellow Hungarians. He said he was respected in Hungary for his official position but he preferred the honor he received in America as a man and looked back on his early struggles with pride rather than bitterness. There were others like him who boasted that they "worked like horses to pull themselves up" and were grateful for the opportunity to struggle in freedom in an open society.

A few of the survivors in the transcripts could not adjust to American life for a variety of personal reasons. They compared the best qualities of life in Europe with the worst aspects of life in America, denying even their reasons for leaving their homelands and the severity of the cruel years they had survived. They were all men and woman who were not sent to concentration camps and who had never identified themselves as Jews in a Jewish community.

A Frenchwoman, born in Paris, explained that she had never

become an American citizen because she could never "divorce herself" from her strong feeling of being French. She had strong anti-French feelings but felt that her language, values and cooking made it impossible for her to be an American. She had difficulties with her daughter who insisted that she was Jewish and American in spite of her education in a French lycée. Another Frenchwoman who did become a citizen never lost her fear of being visibly Jewish. She would not join any Jewish organizations and said that she didn't "accept obligation and commitment as positive values." Still another Frenchwoman echoed her feelings. "I hate religion," she said. "I hate all organizations. I don't want to belong to anything. I belong to myself."

An extreme case of rejection whose story does not appear in this book was that of Ludwig Markevits, who was born in Satu-Mare, Hungary, and graduated from the University of Budapest in 1937. He came to New York in 1958 with a ten-year-old son. He was a businessman without money or connections who spoke five languages but not a word of English. He stayed only long enough to get his green card. New York terrified him. He convinced himself that "all countries are the same" and that America was as dangerous and anti-Semitic as any other place. He lives in Vienna and was interviewed while visiting his son, now grown, who does not share his father's feelings. His son, Andrei, lives in New York and believes that all of Europe was poisoned by the Holocaust. He thinks of America as a unique and precious place in which he is at home. He knows that his grandparents died in Auschwitz and that his father survived by bribing his way into a job in a military factory and he can't understand how his father can remain so attached to a world that wanted to destroy him.

Peter Bloch from Frankfurt, Germany, was another special case. His story also does not appear, but it revealed an unusual personality. He's a bachelor who lives with his mother in New York, still nostalgic for his privileged childhood in a wealthy family of doctors. He is a United States citizen but has never voted. He claims himself to be "too intellectual and too steeped in European culture to adjust to America." He mocks German-Jewish refugees who have adapted themselves and calls them "conformists, red-white-and-blue Americans who shamelessly wear their Judaism in their buttonholes and speak English rather than German."

Peter Bloch speaks of himself as a Jew but was never circumcised. His family had not converted, but they were stridently anti-Semitic. His father was killed by the Nazis while resisting arrest and he had some close calls before escaping, but he would still be pleased to go back and live in Germany if he could find work as a lecturer or a writer.

He was the only one in the collection of transcripts to express such feelings. Most of the survivors not only adjusted to America but fell in love with it. The longer they lived in America the more critical they became of the countries they had left. "Here the rights come from the government," said Stanley Bors. "There our rights were taken away by the government." They thought that America meant more to them than to the people born in it and they took nothing for granted.

Survivors do not measure their success in America by how much money they earn. They boast instead about sending their children to college, about marriages and grandchildren. Success in America is a Jewish wedding to which survivors can invite fellow survivors from all over the world to celebrate the contin- uation of their families, their real victory over the Nazis.

Involvements in the philanthropic efforts of their Jewish communities are another great source of satisfaction for survi- vors. They remember the support they received from fellow- Jews after the war and feel the obligation to help others as they were once helped. It is not unusual for women to belong to every helping organization in their city without regard for political, ideological or religious differences. "Whoever approaches me for a donation will get it," said one woman after another. "I pledged myself after the war that no one will ever leave my door empty-handed." Those with modest incomes meet in private liv- ing rooms to collect seventy-five cents a week for refugee chil- dren in Israel. Affluent women sign checks for thousands of dollars for the same purpose.

Men are more competitive than women about raising money. They are not embarrassed about soliciting funds for good causes. They give their share and explain they come as refugees who know what suffering men and women can endure. Some are not comfortable speaking about their personal experiences and pre- fer historical explanations, but they pride themselves on their ability to persuade people to share their resources. A survivor who was once a *kapo* in a concentration camp now boasts that he never spends an evening at home because of the pressure of meetings and fund drives. He rests only on Saturday, when he closes his business and goes to services. Nathan Sobel, the acerbic New York City planner, takes pride in his ability to raise a quarter of a million dollars for Israeli bonds. Another survivor in New York spends 60 percent of his time selling real estate and the rest on philanthropic projects. Working for the Jewish community is his way of relaxing, and he claims that he looks forward to the time when he will be able to spend 40 percent of his time on business, leaving more hours for "relaxation."

This sense of obligation touches even the survivors who have trouble with what Anita Magnus Frank called her "self-concept." She explained that she had always been ashamed of being a Jew and didn't admit to it when she went back to Holland at the end of the war. "The Germans in some horrible way got to me," she said. She saw being a Jew was something that caused you to be killed, and she yearned to be safe. She avoided the Jewish community in Albuquerque, New Mexico, where she lives with her husband and son, until they needed a Russian interpreter to help with emigrés from the Soviet Union. The need to be of help finally allowed her to come to terms with her identity and she offered her services. "Religiously," she said, "I'm not Jewish, but I guess emotionally, I am."

Working for the Jewish community gives survivors a way of remembering without being overwhelmed by feelings of bitterness and helplessness. Few survivors seem able to reconcile their wish to forget with relentless, uncontrollable surges of memory. They may say, "Enough is enough, I want to forget the past," but they cannot forget. Martin Berliner, who doesn't believe in looking back and has never spoken to his sons about his past, cannot resist documentary films. He scans the screen with great intensity, searching for the faces of his murdered family.

Survivors say that they've put the past behind them, that it has been put away and locked out of sight, but waves of emotion come unbidden. "When my oldest daughter was married," said Leon Bergrin, "I went under the canopy with her and before my eyes had my whole family. I didn't see anybody in the hall, only my lost family."

Restitution payments from Germany challenge forgetfulness. Survivors say it is easy to take money for lost property or time spent working in concentration camps, but it is very hard to take "blood money" for lost relatives. Many were sickened at the thought and did not come to claim what was offered. Survivors also found it hard to spend restitution money in ordinary ways.

They set it aside to pay for their children's Hebrew education, gave it to scholarship funds for children of survivors or used it to buy Israeli bonds. In any event the checks kept memories of the past alive. Germany remained a presence and a problem in their lives.

Robert Spitz, who visits Germany regularly, deplores the "victims of emotionalism" who are still phobic about Germany, but most survivors claim that they cannot stay overnight in Germany or Poland. They do not want to own anything with a label that reminds them of places they want to forget. They discourage their children from studying German in school because they hate the sound of it. Sally Grubman, who is proud of her adjustment, described a pathological experience in the Frankfurt airport that told her she was still vulnerable. A German woman working for Traveler's Aid asked her if she could be of help but the woman wore the boots and uniform that reminded Sally of concentration camp. "As soon as I saw those boots," she said, "I began to tremble. I was shaking so I couldn't answer her. It was the boots that upset me."

Whether survivors express overwhelming hatred for the countries in which they suffered or just see them as places where they are not welcome and have no wish to be, they argue against stereotypes and reject the damning of a whole country. Bernard Brown remembers the "good Germans" he met in the Wehrmacht. Others speak of the Russians who helped them, the Polish peasants who fed them, all the exceptional people in every country who saved them from total despair. They make it clear that the new generation in every country cannot be held responsible for the sins of the past. Robert Spitz was encouraged by the new generation of long-haired, bearded German soldiers who had little in common with the immaculate, disciplined soldiers he remembered from the war years.

Though survivors hope that the younger generation in European countries will be different from the old, they hope to persuade their own children to follow the traditions and values that they learned from their parents. Many tried to direct and control their children as they were once directed and controlled. There are many old-fashioned mothers and fathers in the transcripts who expected their American offspring to go "in the footsteps of their parents."

The children of survivors were caught between their parents' conflicting wishes and needs. The parents wanted happy, guilt-free, American kids, enjoying the kind of life they missed, and at the same time also wanted obedient, diligent and respectful children who would continue the parents' mission as teachers and witnesses of the Holocaust. The relationships between survivor parents and their children were fraught with all the difficulties and conflicts that beset other parents, magnified by the vast differences in life experience, value systems and expectations of these two generations.

Survivors are obsessed about continuity, not only for Jews but for Judaism. They see it as the last stage of their resistance and measure their success as survivors and parents by whether their children remain Jewish, marry Jews and raise Jewish children. "If, God forbid, my kid married a non-Jew," said Chaim Schepps, "then he wouldn't be my kid anymore."

Many of the survivors' children did not marry Jews and caused their parents great pain. Rene Molho and his wife regarded their son's marriage to a "very nice, very excellent girl— but not Jewish" as a personal defeat and betrayal; Molho felt that what Hitler "couldn't do to me with killing, [my son] has done." His survival seemed meaningless without future generations to confirm the value of the struggle. It was difficult for survivors to accept the possibility that Jews could endure the ordeals of the camps only to be obliterated in America by comfort and freedom. The enemy in America was assimilation, ignorance of Jewish history, intermarriage, lack of marriage, childlessness, all avenues that led to Jewish disappearance.

Orthodox survivors came to America with the idea that freedom for Jews meant the freedom to be Jewish. They were determined to keep their identity and control their children. They did not think it necessary to give up their religion and culture to become Americans. They were convinced that immigrants were Americanized when they ceased to be dependents and could contribute to American culture. They worked hard to rejuvenate dwindling congregations and declining institutions. They created new Jewish schools where none had been before. The Steins from Krakow, the Browns from Rumania and the Goldmans from Germany were among those who wanted to be "a counterbalance in a time of assimilation." They went to great lengths to bring their children up in traditional ways and felt that they succeeded when their children married other observant Jews and sent *their* children to Hebrew day school to ensure their loyalty for another generation.

308

There were liberal parents with equally strong feelings about continuity but without control over the interests and life-styles of their children. They hoped their children would respect their feelings but could not exert as much influence as they would have liked. Claude Cassirer was one of many parents who said that their children had no interest in their past and refused to listen to anything they had to say about it. Parents often blamed themselves for their children's defections. They wished they had been less liberal and that they had given them better Jewish educations, found better ways of inculcating loyalty. The stories of the children of survivors in the tapes are not included in this volume, but their responses to the pressures of their survivor parents offer some clues about the mixed messages they receive. Some saw their parents as heroic figures whose values and attitudes they were obligated to adopt. Others seemed ashamed of their parents and looked for ways to separate themselves from them, refusing any special responsibility that might be conferred upon them as the children of survivors.

Some young people compare their lives to their parents and feel guilty for "having it so soft," for having so few struggles. Jack Goldman's sixteen-year-old daughter heard her father lecture about the Third Reich at her high school. He taught history lessons without revealing his personal experiences. She said that she knew that she was not to ask questions about his past at home. Some of the children committed their lives to keeping "the heritage alive," to "keeping faith with the Holocaust" by marrying as their parents wished. Others were true children of the sixties and seventies. Some dropped out of school to the distress of parents who had been forced out of school by anti-Semitic laws. They postponed marriage and put off starting families in spite of their parents' desire for grandchildren. In Felix Magnus's family, the three daughters married non-Jews and his son converted to Christianity and became a minister. The daughter of a German-Jewish survivor who twice married non-Jewish men, however, chose to marry an Orthodox Israeli and settle in Israel. There was no way to predict what the next generation would do or be.

On the tapes with interviews of both parents and children one found strikingly different descriptions of the family realities. Survivor parents comparing their children to themselves see them as "typical American kids," untouched by their parents' conflicts and anxieties. The children meanwhile are acutely aware of the foreignness of their parents, conscious of every nuance of behavior that separates them and their family from other American families. Some find strength in the difference, others only uneasiness. They have many problems with their peers. A fourteen-year-old in Ashville, North Carolina, makes a fuss at school because a classmate has scribbled a swastika on her locker. She doesn't think the scribbler knows what a swastika means, but as a child of survivors she does know and must protest. Sometimes people ask her where her grandparents lived and she tells them they were all killed. "They listen," she says, "as if I were telling a horror movie." She wishes that the Holocaust was taught in school because she's tired of explaining things. "I can't go around educating all those people by myself. I try. But who's going to listen to me?"

The children of survivors can't escape their parents' values. Their parents have sensitized them to injustice, to signs of anti-Semitism, to the dangers of apathy. A young man in a Quaker school found an anti-Semitic texbook in the school library and went all the way to the president of the school to complain. "I think of myself as a Jew standing up for myself," he said without embarrassment about attracting attention to himself. The parents speak with pride about their children's involvement in civil rights, in antiwar demonstrations, and in the Soviet Jewry rallies. They send the children to Israel so they can see the country as a response to the Holocaust as well as a place where it is normal to be Jewish.

Survivors who spent time in Israel before coming to America remember mainly the positive aspects of being there and they often send their children to Israel to study so they too will have what their parents found a therapeutic experience. For Leah Schepps it was the place where she learned to hold her head up and recover her pride. Lydia said she "felt like a newborn person after three days in Ein Harod." She pitied her sister who missed a time of recovery in Israel and never felt whole or secure in her life. Survivors are pleased when their children settle and marry in Israel, and it is a solution for the children who never get over their feelings of alienation among their American peers.

Israel provides a powerful focus for survivors. They live in America to feel physically secure but need Israel for "spiritual security." Their loyalties are not divided; their needs after the Holocaust are just more complex. Survivors feel implicated in Israel's future whether they want to live there or not and whether they approve or disapprove of its policies. They see it as the only evidence that the Jews are not a broken and defeated people. If they were Zionists, the Hitler years confirmed their distrust of the nations of Europe and their belief that Jews had to have a country of their own to survive. If they were not Zionists before the war, the Hitler years convinced them that they should be. Israel and the Holocaust seemed to them to be two aspects of the same event in history.

There were, however, assimilated Jews who were opposed to a Jewish state before the war and who were not changed by the events. A Frenchwoman feared any ghetto-ization and imagined Israel only as a place where Jews would be "concentrated" and wiped out. A Czech physician still thought Kenya or British Guiana would make a more sensible home for Jews. He came from a family that observed no rituals and he couldn't understand any emotional attachment to the Jewish religion. He said, "I don't see why anyone would want the historical, emotional part of it. Jerusalem and all that! I don't think you should shape your future for the sake of history." Peter Bloch from Frankfurt identified with the Arabs and didn't think Jews belonged in the Middle East at all. Such views, however, were exceptional. Most survivors speaking of Israel shared Sally Grubman's feelings. "We had to go through the fire to get it. It was a big price to pay." Israel is now too valuable to lose for those who know how many lives were lost to pay for it.

Survivors tend to see themselves as teachers and witnesses. The most "Americanized" of them play a role in their communities as sensitizers and guardians of peace and freedom. During the years that Americans resisted confronting the facts about the Holocaust the very presence of survivors kept memories alive. They built memorials and organized services and raised money for Jewish schools in America and Israel. In out-of-the-way places like Williamsville, New York; Walnut Creek, California; Fort Worth, Texas; and Canton, Ohio, there were opportunities for survivors to explain who they were and what had happened to them. Sometimes they irritated friends and relatives by telling them more then they wanted to hear. Sometimes they struggled with unsympathetic members of their communities who couldn't understand their yearly memorials. A survivor who brought a placard advertising the Warsaw Ghetto Memorial Program to leave in his local butcher shop was dismayed to be asked, "How long are you going to go on with this? Are you making a business of it?"

Remembering, "keeping faith with the Holocaust," acquired

a religious aura for survivors, and they and their children felt threatened by those who did not share their feelings for the dead. Connie Lerner, a devoted daughter of survivor parents, said she found those unwilling to hear about the Holocaust "less human," even dangerous because their apathy might lead to a catastrophe in the future. "I think they have no compassion," she said. "All they care about is themselves."

Survivors found many different ways to keep the faith. Sender Wajsman from Vilna directed a Yiddish school in Cleveland to keep vestiges of the language and culture destroyed in Europe alive in America. Fred Veston in Albuquerque, New Mexico, painted pictures of Polish Jewish life. Survivors carried on their personal vendettas against prejudice. They would never be able to understand why Nazis must be permitted to picket in front of the temples where they held memorial services for their dead. "This isn't freedom of speech. This is permission to hurt people," said one survivor. Another wanted a law passed against prejudice in public places. "You want to hate someone? Go down in the basement and hate them to yourself but don't come out in the street with signs and demonstrations."

Survivors told their stories in Hebrew and public schools. Their children went to the library to ask for books the librarian might not have planned to buy. When Elie Wiesel first began teaching about the Holocaust most of his students were children of survivors trying to find out what their parents had been through, and when courses in the Holocaust were expanded many of the teachers were children of survivors.

Many survivors kept the faith in the most traditional way. "I prayed in concentration camp that I should survive," said Arthur Herz, "and now I must go to synagogue every Saturday and give Him the thanks." Simon Grubman noted that after the camps survivors either became very religious or completely irreligious. "You could either say, 'God saved me and I must therefore believe in Him, or 'How can God exist . . . if innocent children have their heads smashed against walls.' " He did not describe himself as a religious man but his story reveals him as a religious seeker, a spiritual person in spite of his disbelief. His wife, Sally, showed her divided feelings by maintaining in one conversation that she had no faith to lose but saying in another part of the transcript, "Before, during and after Auschwitz I believed in a merciful God."

The survivor stories unfold with unpretentious answers to

the unspoken question behind all the questions. They tell how people live *after* Auschwitz and how they see themselves and their fellows. A survivor from Sobibor says he lives but has no appetite for life. "I have deep feelings for other survivors but basically I believe most people are rotten." A women who escaped with him has another nature. "I'm happy and content," she says. "I like my life and my self. I'm not depressed." She says her will to live was so great that she is still showing the world she could do it "and be normal and fit into society."

Survivors respond differently to violence. "If somebody hits you with a rock," says Elizabeth Mermelstein, "throw him back a piece of bread." A survivor of Sobibor says, "Fight if you have the strength. Don't give in. Don't bend your head if you're a Jew. Only fighting back can give you honor and respect." Most survivors, however, admit that they have no strength for physical or even verbal violence. They do not like to read violent novels. Claude Cassirer couldn't even cope with a cowboy movie.

Survivors, examining their own lives, illuminate the problems that face all people who have lived through ordeals and also those who try to move from one culture to another. Their memories of life before and during the Holocaust help us imagine the lives of the millions who were lost. When they describe their adjustments and maladjustments in the United States, however, they catch the contradictions, the strengths and weaknesses of Jewish and American life as well as their own needs. Their passion for survival and strong feelings of identity foreshadowed the recent concern in America for ethnic roots, and also the understanding that individuals as well as nations must come to terms with the past in order to gather the energy to create a future. Survivors, after living for thirty years or more as Americans, still have the distance to notice what native-born Americans might miss. They know what is great about "the blessed land" they chose and also what they think is missing, unfinished and waiting to be accomplished.

Marika Frank Abrams from Debrecin, Hungary,
survivor of Auschwitz and Bergen-Belsen, came to
the United States in 1948 with a scholarship to the
University of Washington arranged by the Hillel
Foundation. She married, became a painter and
settled in Seattle, Washington.

We came on a small army transport boat in very bad weather. My cousin and I were determined to fight the seasickness. We would get up at five-thirty in the morning and run up and down the deck breathing fresh air. We were sleeping in large areas with people seasick all around, so it was a hard fight. And then we came out in New York, and it was depressing to feel so anxious in this glowing city.

We stopped in Chicago on the way to Seattle to visit the Foreign Student Service of the Hillel Foundation. Then we went west on a beautiful train, the Olympian Hiawatha. We had done a lot of research to inform ourselves about America—we had never heard of Seattle until we got the scholarships. And we had a whole delegation meeting us, and I knew right away that it was a wonderful thing that was happening to me.

My experiences with the Americans at the consulate had been very humiliating. We were treated with such suspicion and animosity that it was one more experience with cruelty. Here we were, two little girls out of this inferno, and they were accusing us of lying. They wanted a paper for everything we said. They wanted me to chase up my concentration camp certificate. I came to Auschwitz in the summer of 1944, when they were killing so many people they didn't bother to tattoo us. And when a representative of the Joint Distribution Committee came to intercede for us it was made even more obvious that we were unwelcome and unwanted in the United States. So I had reason to be afraid. Actually I never believed I would be able to come.

Being here seemed such a dream, so unreal, so unbelievable. And the Hillel scholarship offered us everything. It paid for transportation, living costs, tuition at the University of Washington, transportation back to Europe—everything. The United States government wouldn't have granted us a visa unless somebody here promised that we would not be a public charge at any time.

The Jewish sorority paid for our room and board. We were told that it was their contribution to Hillel, not to us personally, but it was all very mysterious because we didn't know what a sorority was. It was quite a surprise to find ourselves among a bunch of girls who weren't very well educated or especially interested in doing anything but going to parties. The standards at a European university were much higher, and also my cousin and I were both twenty-three and the sorority girls were eighteen and nineteen. But I was ready to ignore anything unimportant. I was concerned about the possibility of studying fine arts and delighted to find that the university included an excellent school of art. I had all the requirements from my gymnasium education and I was free to study drawing and design. I was a painting major and took all the painting courses available. My main problem was understanding English, but after a few weeks I had the hang of it. And I also had a part-time job in a costume jewelry factory downtown: for seventy-five cents an hour I set little stones with glue for two or three hours. It gave me a little pocket money. I didn't need much. I had one skirt and one coat and that was that.

The sorority girls never became my friends. They were nice girls but we had nothing to talk about to each other. They were not at all aware of what the war meant to the Jewish people. They were really not aware of anything except their tiny, tiny little lives, their clothes, their boys and things like that.

I don't blame them. Their parents were no better. Once I was invited for a weekend by a girl who was the president of the sorority house and her father told me that the Jews in his town had a very hard time during the war. A window was even broken in the synagogue. He was perfectly serious and I was just speechless.

The girls also became jealous when the boys rushed me. And I thought, my goodness, how could anybody in the world be jealous of me? Coming out of the kind of life I had—how could they ever? But it was all new for me. We didn't date in Europe. Social life was group life and not this dating—somebody calling you up and asking you out and paying your way. The good manners I learned in my family taught that you couldn't refuse; it was the polite thing to accept because the person was so kind. So I went out with many boys I really didn't care for at all.

The close friends I made in the school of art were all non-Jews. They didn't even know I was Jewish. I didn't say I was and they didn't realize that my accent and experience and the way I look and feel couldn't be anything else. My Jewishness is so important to me that I didn't realize they didn't recognize me. My closest friend was a woman much older than I, a Catholic nun, who came to take her master's degree. We talked quite a bit about my past and she was very interested in me.

One of the lucky things that happened to me in school was that the Nieders and the Sameths, two outstanding families in Seattle, took me under their wings and taught me what it was to be an American. They were very positive people, great fighters, with a strong social consciousness. I became very much involved with them and their friends and they made me very happy to be here.

You see, when I came here I thought to myself, "People are people. The world is big but people are the same everywhere. They have the same kind of standards and desires and dreams and I will be able to get along in America just as well as anywhere else." Fortunately I didn't know enough to be afraid. I learned gradually, by alienating people who were shocked by my behavior.

For example, the way to make friends with someone where I had lived was to ask the person personal questions and then tell all kinds of personal things about yourself, and give advice about what the person should do and expect the person to give you advice, discussing issues in detail—very open and friendly. When I tried this method in this country I really shocked people who were not accustomed to such openness. When I realized that they were upset I became very anxious to change. I loved America and I wanted to be part of it and to be accepted. So I tried hard to dilute my Hungarian enthusiasm. I kept on trying until I thought that I wouldn't have anything left of myself if I didn't stop.

I'm a very open person and need to communicate. The society in which I grew up had some very valuable traits which it would be a pity to lose altogether. There are always misunderstandings where people never speak their minds. I hate that, I really do. I think you waste your life if you don't show yourself.

There is a very beautiful poem by a famous Hungarian poet, Endre Adi, in which he says, "I want to show myself so I can be seen seeing." It is a feeling I know well.

And yet when I first came I didn't want to speak publicly to students. I used to watch another Hungarian, a very handsome young man who could speak on any subject, and I really didn't want to do it. I had a feeling that people weren't ready to listen, and I also didn't know whether I was good enough to take on the responsibility.

In 1948, shortly after I came, the new Displaced Persons Act was passed and I was able to apply for permanent residence. My status changed and by that time I was also married. My husband, Sid Abrams, was one of three Seattle boys who went to Europe to help bring immigrants to Palestine, and were involved in Aliyah Bet activities in Bulgaria, Italy and France. He came back to Seattle just after I arrived. We were introduced, fell in love and were married in two months. It was a very foolhardy thing to do because we were both so young and inexperienced, and we naturally had a very hard time. We're married twenty-eight years so I guess we worked out our problems, but it was really hard.

We were both in school and both had part-time jobs. After I got my Art School degree I found I could be quite successful as a painter, but not make enough money to live on. I was represented by the best gallery in the Northwest but it was not a dependable way to make a living. Ten years after I left school I went back to get a master's degree in library science, and while doing that I was engaged in designing sets for two operas. It was the good old times when I could work sixteen, eighteen hours a day and love it.

I can look back on moments of great pleasure. In 1953, just after my son Eddie was born, I became an American citizen. I can remember that I had just learned to drive and I drove around with the baby in the car, being an American citizen. I felt like the queen of the world!

In 1962, when we had the World's Fair in Seattle, I designed the sets and costumes for the opera *The Dybbuk*. It was a completely new experience for me and I had terrible nightmares about getting it right. It turned out to be a roaring success. When the curtain went up the audience burst into applause, which was for me. I started crying. An artist never has such an experience. And then I was asked to design the sets for the Seattle Opera's first production, a very exciting experience for me.

A kind of sadness, however, is always with me. I didn't know that others could see it until my son, only five or six years old, asked me once, "Mommy, why is your smile so sad?" And I realized that he divined my real feelings. I was always sad.

I used to go through periods of "violent witnessing." I would push my witnessing on people and be repulsed and very unhappy. And then I would give up and not say a word for a long time. You see, people say, "Oh, we don't want to ask you about your experiences because it must hurt to talk about it." But of course this is not true at all. They don't want to hear because *they* don't want to be hurt. I'm always hurt; I think about it all the time.

I have a close friend, a very charming, intelligent, very unusual person. He's a lawyer. He and his wife are excellent people, very social conscious, very responsible, always wanting to do the right thing. She comes from a Quaker background in Virginia and he is from Texas. She is president of Planned Parenthood and involved with the school board. They care about a lot of things. When I tried to talk about the Holocaust, my friend said, "Don't talk about it. I don't want to hear it. I love you but I don't want to hear it." And I thought to myself, "How could you possibly love me if you don't want to hear? You don't know what love is."

I learned from my friends that social consciousness in this big loving country of ours doesn't include the Jewish experience. People get excited about going to the Peace Corps to work in Nigeria or Guatemala. They want to build a new Cuba and get very upset about the blacks and the Puerto Ricans. But the Jews, never—after all, who are the Jews? There are two hundred and ten million people living in this country and only six million Jews. It is hard to meet Jews; there are millions of gentiles who have never met a Jew. And they grow up feeling very ambivalent and have very confused ideas about what Jews are.

Finally after all these years a course in Jewish history is being given at the University of Washington. The Jewish community fought for this very hard, and even paid for it for a while. There is even a course on the Holocaust and, amazingly, over seventy students are enrolled. I was invited to speak to them; it was the first time that anybody wanted to hear what I have to say. All the societies in the Western world lived with Jews, legislated for Jews, against Jews, used Jews, killed Jews. The history of the Jews throughout the world is a touchstone. But nobody every says a word about it. It is traditional to ignore Jews.

The Holocaust couldn't have happened if this wasn't so. The Germans did it, but they couldn't have done it without the backup of all Western civilization. And in spite of all this, thousands of us are leaving to be part of the gentile world. All the children in my husband's family have married non-Jews. They are just not interested in remaining Jewish.

I feel this sense of aloneness. My husband is in business and politics and is also a kind of unofficial ambassador to Israel from the Northwest. He's very involved with Zionist activities and the Jewish community. I enjoy his involvements because I have to be alone most of the time. Being a painter is a very lonesome kind of life. When you work you have to be alone and when you don't work you have to be alone to plan your work. I love people and I'm very social, but I am alone most of the time.

So it's been very gratifying for me to suddenly meet people who are studying the Holocaust and Jewish history in a scholarly way, people who know much more than I do about it. I'm particularly pleased with Professor Alexander at the university. He introduced me to the poetry of Abba Kovner, an Israeli poet who writes about the Holocaust. It's a relief to know such people, because more often than not people are uncomfortable with me because I care so much about Jewishness. On the other side, I often feel very sad when people to whom I have been friendly and sympathetic have anti-Israel attitudes.

There is really no place in the community where I am really at home. Our family belongs to the Reform synagogue but I do not belong. I don't like it even a little bit. I like the Orthodox services but feel completely out of place there because I'm not an Orthodox Jew. I'm not an observant Jew and I'm not a religious person.

My son Ede enjoys being in a small synagogue where the people perform the services themselves, but there isn't any in our area. He speaks Hebrew and lived in a very religious kibbutz when he was in Israel for six months. When he came home he told me how nice it was to observe the Sabbath and he wanted me to introduce this in our household. I just couldn't, however. It would have been completely artificial. His father would not abide by it. So I said that he was free to observe and I would assist him, but he is just a little too weak to do it on his own. He had an unusual Jewish education. It began with private lessons with Arthur Lagawier, a rabbi and scholar from Holland. He was a man who dealt in diamonds until his retirement and then devoted himself to teaching young people Hebrew and Jewish history and philosophy. And then he had instruction in religious observance at the kibbutz.

I love Israel. I am very uncritical. I'm too old and tired to live there but I love it with all my heart. If I couldn't have come to America I would have gone to Israel. But once here I liked it so much I stayed. It is very hard to change and change again—you know, I changed so many times; I really am tired. But in Israel I spoke all my four languages all day long. The Oriental Jews spoke French and I spoke German to the Yiddish-speaking Jews and there were lots of Hungarian Jews speaking Hungarian, and of course English.

We do the best we can here. My son is eager to learn and so am I. When he was little it was hard to give a child a good Jewish education. One of the reasons I didn't sent him to Sunday school at the temple was that I looked at the books they used and I thought they were the most God-awful, poorly written, dull, unimaginative things, and I didn't want Ede to be exposed to that. I wanted him to be a very enthusiastic Jew. Now there is a Hebrew academy, an Orthodox school, but I question the wisdom of sending a child from a modern nonobservant household to such a school.

On the High Holidays I buy tickets to the Bikur Cholim, an Orthodox synagogue. I adore the cantor. He is a real, old-fashioned Eastern European who survived the war by being taken to Russia—a great musician with a magnificent baritone voice. This year my husband didn't want to come. He stayed at home and observed the holiday by reading.

I guess I'm always searching for ways of understanding society and values. I lost the people who created me and the world I was created for, and America took my life over. The influences of my parents remained with me, however. My mother was a very positive sort of person, a very modern, very sophisticated woman: beautifully dressed, very chic, a good dancer. But she had a simple faith in God and gave us a lot of love. She had a sense of continuity and a feeling for justice which she gave to me especially. I remember on Sundays my father and mother would hire a horse and coach and go to the cemetery to visit the graves. She would put little stones on the graves of her beloved father and mother and aunts. Later I found out it had to with a *Chasidic* legend that the souls come out at night and when they find a little stone they know their loved ones were there visiting them.

When I lived in Hungary I came from a small group of people

320

with a certain vision of themselves as Jews and Hungarians. Now I have an entirely different concept of what it is to be a Jew. I feel guilty when I realize that I became what I really ought to have been thanks to the tragedy that befell all of us. If nothing had happened and the world of my childhood hadn't been destroyed I would never have become an artist. So here I am, flowering on the devastation.

Painting to me is living. I paint very naturally. I have never been able to incorporate my survivor experiences into my work. I failed every time I tried. I think it is because I paint from a depth which is more encompassing than my later experience, from the depth of my personality, which has been altered and affected by the Holocaust but not created by the Holocaust.

Painters paint because they see things. I go through life looking at things very intensely. Everything I see effects my creative imagination. I always have a very definite idea of what I want to paint. Sometimes it requires very large space, sometimes only a sheet of paper. I often fail. Sometimes I succeed. I usually have so many, many ideas that more than half get lost because I don't have the time, the physical ability to pursue them all. My Holocaust experiences have not given me visual inspiration. I receive my visual inspiration from living in the Northwest.

When I look back over my work I see the same shapes, the same compositions, the same structure, redone, reworked, superficially different but actually the same. I paint from a very basic personality and that's what I've got, for better or worse. I paint very often from inspiration from the Bible. There is one especially strong image that I paint over and over. It is when Moses went up to the mountain and the Lord told him to look at the land. Here is the man who brought his people out of slavery, and they are going into the promised land and he has to die. This just breaks my heart; I cry.

I don't know if I'm right or wrong, but I just can feel those genes chasing in me down through the ages. I really believe in that continuity as my mother did. And I brought my son up in my—our—image. I think that German people my age who grew up in the Hitler Youth must be bringing up their children in their image. I hear that Germans have changed and that they are a better people, but knowing what parents do I can't be sure. I realize sometimes that I don't buy German things because I don't need objects around to make me think of Germany. I remember too much as it is.

I'm very lucky to be in America. I think the United States of America today is the best place for a human being to live. We are as free as it is possible for a citizen of the world to be. My good friends that I met when I first came to this country told me I had to have faith in the American people and that I had to believe that the majority of the American people would stand up for their freedom and decency. There are times when that is hard to believe, and I want to recapture the tremendous feeling of relief and hope and optimism we had at the end of the war. Not only we Jews who were in hell and then freed, but the world in general: that all this is over, evil is defeated and only good and constructive things will come from now on. But the things we expected didn't happen. The countries are not governed by statesmen dedicated to righteousness. The deals go on as before. Our country plays games just like the others. And I look at my friends and think, "These nice, nice people whom I love don't even know that their hands are dripping with Jewish blood." And they don't care to know of their responsibility in the Holocaust. And they have to understand it if it is not to happen again. My God—I certainly hope it couldn't happen again.

Joy Levi Alkalay came to Portland, Oregon, with her husband in July 1950. She had lived through the Holocaust years in touch with her family, guarded by friendly Italians. At the age of twenty-seven she added English to her knowledge of German, Italian, Ladino, Spanish and Serbo-Croatian.

We didn't come on an UNRRA boat because I didn't want to go through Bremen. I said, "I'm not going to Germany. I don't want to see that land." Since we had worked and saved some money we decided to pay our own way from Genoa. We went on a small boat called the *Atlantic* and most of the passengers were non-Jewish German refugees, ethnic Germans from Yugoslavia, Rumania and Bulgaria who were coming to the United States.

We arrived in New York on July 5, 1950. Our friends were waiting for us at the dock. And with them was my former rabbi and teacher, the Sephardic rabbi from Vienna. It was a very good welcome, but the first impression of America that I will never forget is standing at the top of the steps on the boat and it was very steep and I was afraid to go down. I'm a scaredy-cat when it comes to heights, and I had a coat over my arm and a small valise, and I just couldn't move. My husband Joe was behind me but his arms were full and he couldn't help me. Then this big burly policeman came and said, "Don't be afraid," and he carried me down. This was the first time in my life I saw a policeman as a nice, friendly person, a helpful person not to be afraid of.

And then this lady arrived from the United Service for New Americans. She introduced herself and said she had our tickets for Portland; we were to leave from Pennsylvania Station before midnight. Our friends pleaded with her to let us spend a little time with them but she said we just had to go. I guess they had had some bad experiences with people wanting to stay in New York and we couldn't assure her that we had no intention of staying. So we had a hectic taxi ride from the docks to Penn Station and the train was almost leaving, and we were pushed on with the luggage without even saying goodbye to our friends.

We had never been on an American train and didn't know what to expect. A woman from the Traveler's Aid met our train in Chicago and drove us to another station where we got the Union Pacific to Portland. It was all done nicely. And so we went through Wyoming and Idaho. We crossed the Idaho-Oregon border early in the morning and I saw Multnomah Falls. The consul in Naples had told us that the scenery in America was like Switzerland, but he didn't really prepare us for how beautiful it was. And at seven o'clock in the morning there were two ladies to take us to the apartment that the Service for New Americans had prepared for us.

We didn't stay there very long because an old friend wanted us to move in with her. I immediately got a job as a typist. It was all quite confusing and frightening. They put me in a cubicle with a telephone. The phone would ring and I would hear somebody dictating something. I never saw anybody. I only lasted two days.

After that I got a job with the regional director for the Anti-Defamation League, and I did bookkeeping and secretarial work for him for six years. I found out about voting and registering. I worked on the Neuberger political campaign and the civil rights bill in Oregon.

When the office was closed in 1956 I was hired at the Congregation of Beth Israel, where I've been ever since. I started as secretary to the rabbi and gradually took over the administrative responsibilities. I supervise building maintenance and office personnel and work with the investment committee, the religious services committee and the insurance committee. I'm involved with education, the religious school, and I represent the congregation as administrative affairs director.

I was lucky to be involved this way, because my husband had problems with his health. When he came to Portland he got a job in the warehouse at White Stag; there was a bit of a recession at the time and he had trouble finding something better. When he got a job at the Schnitzer Steel Company he stayed with them until he passed away in December 1975. He was very interested in mathematics and chemistry and he had studied to be a chemical engineer before World War II, but he didn't have much opportunity for technical knowledge at his work. He was a deep person and quite lonely at times. He was not one for small talk and had difficulty making friends. If we had had children we might have made contacts through them, but the only people we knew were the ones we worked with.

And then there were his illnesses: he had a thyroid operation in 1952 and he suffered from high blood pressure. In the middle sixties he found he had arteriosclerosis, and then in 1973 he was operated on for a melanoma. He was in and out of the hospital until the end. . . .

We have to say that we were lucky, the way we arrived, and that we had an easy time under the Italians compared to what was going on in Europe.

And I can still remember my excitement about becoming an American citizen. We had a few disappointments but really no bad experiences in this country. Sometimes I worry about the new interest in the Holocaust. I read the books. I know that many people think, no ill will intended, that it is all exaggerated. They know it happened but it is beyond their comprehension. Sometimes I wonder whether all the talk is not going to help someone get ideas, you know . . . of starting some Jewish persecution. I think people are very easily led, and my husband, when he was alive, was always concerned that if economic conditions were to deteriorate in the United States the first person to be blamed would be the Jew, and a new surge of anti-Semitism could start. We've seen it before in other countries.

That doesn't mean that I don't think that the American system is the best that exists in the world. It is only I'm afraid that we're going back to a certain isolationism, and that might be bad for us and other countries.

Martin Berliner, a Warsaw-born, French-educated engineer, came to Hoboken, New Jersey, in 1941. He knew no English and found it harder than he expected to adjust to America and find work in his profession. He eventually succeeded. He and his wife settled in Forest Hills, New York, and raised their sons without speaking of their past.

Our families were waiting for us when we arrived in New York. It was a very emotional time. My mother-in-law brought us to her house in Hoboken, New Jersey. We were received with great joy and many questions. Everybody was interested in us. But it was in America that my troubles began.

I loved France and I never wanted to come to this country. I never made an effort to learn English. So I found myself in a sad situation. I couldn't talk. I couldn't work. My wife tells me that she found me once sitting at my bed pulling my hair. Maybe that's why I lost it all!

In France I was a specialist in repairing American-made instruments used by petroleum refineries and big companies like Renault and Citroen. They came from the Brown Instrument Company, which was part of Minneapolis Honeywell, or Moore Pressure Gauges. I used to meet their engineers in Paris and they always told me that they would be happy to have me if I ever came to the United States. I was sure that one of these companies would offer me a job immediately.

I got someone in the family to write letters for me, giving my experience and credentials. In them I said that I didn't speak

English but I didn't mind accepting any menial job as long as I could make a living and learn the language. So I was shocked to get answers saying that they couldn't do a thing for me because I was not a citizen and they were not allowed to employ noncitizens while the United States was at war. The family, however, was not surprised. They told me that Jews had difficulty getting into big companies, especially as an engineer.

It was very sad for me. I found that Jews were not better off here than they were in some countries in Europe before the war, and this depressed me very much. At one point I thought I had a job with a company in Bridgeport, and my cousin felt very strongly that I ought to let them know I was Jewish before going to see them. When I found a way of telling them, however, they immediately wrote to say the job was taken and they didn't need my services. This was very shocking to me.

I made some decisions. We moved out of my mother-in-law's house. My wife found a job in a French laboratory in New York for twenty dollars a week and I decided to learn English. I devoted myself to it day and night, listening to the radio even though I couldn't understand, going to movies, and after six weeks I could make myself understood and begin to understand other people. All that time, however, I would carry little cards with me to help me ask people directions, to ask about trains and stations. I would pull out a card to show people and they would guide me.

I had an extraordinary experience during this period. I met a Frenchman, an old friend, who was an officer on the *Normandy*, which was the most famous ocean liner in the world at that time. I knew a lot about it because I was one of the engineers who had examined the boat before it was ready in France. Now they were changing the boat into a troop carrier, and they needed someone to rearrange the electrical connections to the instruments; the generators didn't work and there was a mess in the engine room. My friend asked me if I could rearrange the control installations and I said that I could. It was a very good offer with an excellent salary. The very next day I reported to the vice-admiral who was in charge of the work and he assigned a young engineer who spoke French and English to be my interpreter. I immediately went on the boat to examine all the controls. To get down to the engine room I had to use a narrow stairway to go down four floors. I saw immediately that a lot of work had to be done. I went back to the vice-admiral, asked for my translator, and told him that he might not know that the boat could be electrically separated in three parts. There were metallic doors which opened and closed by pressing a button, and the first thing that had to be done was to get the generators in order and the elevators running for the sake of safety and so that there would be enough light to do the work.

The vice-admiral became very angry and told me he didn't need me to give him advice and that I was just there to check the instruments. He gave me a badge and dismissed me. I was really depressed because I didn't know if I hadn't understood or the translator was at fault. It was also very distressing to see the woodworkers destroying the beautiful wood paneling on the boat to make space for bunks, and I was very nervous about the steelworkers with blow torches working so close to the woodworkers. When I went down to the engine room, in the lowest part of the boat, I knew that if anything went wrong five or six hundred people could be trapped.

A strong desire came over me to run out, and after fighting with myself for a while I started to run as if someone was chasing me. I ran up the four flights and got off the boat so fast I forgot to return the badge.

When I caught the train to Hoboken, I sensed a big commotion. People were agitated and talking and discussing, but I couldn't understand what they were saying. When I got back to an aunt's house where my wife was waiting for me everyone started to cry and kiss me and say, "Thank God you're alive." And then they told me that a fire had broken out on the boat, and almost five hundred people were caught. If I had remained another half hour I would have been trapped in the engine room where I was supposed to have been working.

When I finally accepted the fact that I couldn't get an engineering job because I was Jewish I went to look for help from a Jewish organization and through that organization got an assembly-line job in Trenton. It was in a huge hall with long tables and about fifty young people on a mass-production line. I was given a place at the table and all I had to do was make one move with a screwdriver and pass the piece along. It was good for me because the people all around me were speaking English, and little by little the voices became clearer to me. After a while I even dared to make some suggestions to my boss about improving the operation. As my English improved I sent out more letters and eventually got a job with a company that manufactured thermometers. After that I was hired by a company in Long Island City which manufactured pressure gauges for war needs. There I had all the authority and help possible, right until the end of the war. Then the company was sold and I was offered the job of manager.

The amazing thing was that the factory was moved to Bridgeport, about two blocks from the company which once refused me because I was Jewish. There I was, so close to them, and the only competitor in their field. And even more astonishing was that one day I got a letter from that company, from the man who had turned me down, inviting me to dinner. Not only that, he offered to pay me a lot more than I was getting if I would join his company. I reminded him that he refused me the job when I needed it very badly because I was a Jew and told him I am still a proud Jew, and in spite of the good offer didn't want to work for him. That was a great satisfaction for me!

I was well aware that I was the only Jew in my organization and I must say that I never felt any antagonism. I really felt absolutely comfortable. And I was glad to hear that the situation was changing in the country and that many companies had Jewish engineers.

The problem with my work was that I was alone in Bridgeport all week and came to New York to be with my wife only on weekends. Eventually I started my own company in New York. I must admit I'm a better engineer than a businessman.

I preferred living in New York, however. When I had a job opportunity in 1962 in western Pennsylvania I went walking around the streets to see if I could find some Jewish names; I went through the telephone book, looked over the stores and doctors, and decided not to move there. I had two young sons then. My son Tom was seventeen and I wanted him to be close to Jewish activities, to a temple. My parents were religious people who sent me to *cheder* before I went to the gymnasium. I also had a Jewish teacher who came to discuss Torah with me a few times a week, and I wanted my sons to share my Jewish sentiments.

When I lived in France I did not practice. There were no temples and no Jews. I didn't fast on Yom Kippur. I was more interested in what the Zionists were doing. In 1936 I was even involved with getting weapons to the Jews in Palestine. I don't consider myself a very good Jew. I was never active enough. I did what I could, but maybe not enough.

I do not like to think of the past. I lost four sisters in concentration camps. My oldest sister went to Russia. We heard from her occasionally when we were in France, but then they asked us not to write anymore so we lost contact. In the early forties and fifties, when they had lots of documentary films on the war, I used to sit at the television and search for familiar faces. I read every book I could find that described what happened. I thought I would feel better if I knew more. But then I found that the realities were more horrifying than anything I could imagine. So I tried very hard not to remember, not to think. I didn't speak to my sons about what had happened. I didn't want to go back to the past. I was trying to live for the future.

My sentiments toward the Germans will never change. I've owned a Volkswagen, but that doesn't mean anything. It's just that if Israel does business with Germany I feel that it is time to change.

*Stanley Bors from Sosnowiec and the Warsaw
ghetto was brought to Chicago in 1949 by
American relatives he had never met. They helped
him settle on a small farm in Hebron, Indiana.
He now makes his living selling real estate in
Crown Point, Indiana.*

We landed in Boston and then went by train to Chicago, where our relatives gave us a wonderful welcome. We found ourselves surrounded by lovely people. They brought us into their large apartment only a few steps from Lake Michigan. And it was very impressive to see the fantastic standard of living. Even in Germany, where the standards were higher than in Poland, there was nothing like it.

George and Hattie Bernstein were sister and brother. We had never met them until we arrived, and yet they greeted us with so much love and confidence that it was almost unbelievable. They offered help in finding a job, buying a farm, anything that would help us settle down in America.

I accepted the loan for the farm in order to get out of their house. I felt like a parasite sitting, eating, sleeping and doing nothing. They kept telling us to rest but we had had enough rest in Germany for four years. Part of my problem was that I spoke little English. I went to the universities for advice because I had a master's degree in agricultural studies, but they had no idea of what to do with a foreigner.

We bought a small chicken farm in Hebron, Indiana, about forty miles from Chicago, and sold eggs in Gary and Chicago. My wife and I worked together. There were about a thousand people in Hebron; we were the only Jews.

We became friends with our neighbors and also the local minister and priest. They didn't know we were Jews, but were curious about us. They expected us to join a church, and eventually we told them we were Jews. We had an unusual visit from a bishop with a Jewish name who came and talked to us in Yiddish and tried to convert us. He told us that he was from a small town in Illinois and had converted, become part of the church, and that it was only because he was a Jew that he couldn't be archbishop.

We joined a Reformed temple in Valparaiso and drove ten miles every Sunday to bring our daughter to Sunday school there. Meanwhile we lived like all the other farmers. We didn't make much money but didn't need much money. We had a comfortable house and enough food, but after five years we began to feel the hard physical work. I began to have trouble with my back and we were also worried about our daughter growing up without any Jewish children to play with.

When she was nine we sold the farm and moved to Gary, the nearest town. We met a few more Jewish people. I began looking for a job in my profession, but nobody knew where to place me. The university was paying very little in 1952 and my degree wasn't worth anything. I went to the steel mill and lasted only one day; the noise was unbearable. Then, because I was involved in trying to sell my farm, I learned something about real-estate people and answered an ad for a real estate salesman. That's how I started to make a living.

I would be much happier in my own profession. I'm not a businessman. But I make a good living. I left the first company I worked for when I found their attitude toward Jews was anti-Semitic, and later set up my own office. I joined the temple, the Federation and the B'nai B'rith. I was very impressed with

American Jews. They are more generous and better organized than the Jews in Poland, and ready to help the poor. The rich Jews in Poland never shared their wealth as American Jews do. I see that American Jews really do good, and if they squeeze people a little it is for a good cause.

We also find gentiles in America altogether different from the non-Jews we saw in Poland. When we lived on the farm the Christian minister was our witness for obtaining citizenship. He was a very fine young man and never tried to convert us. My wife worked at the Methodist Hospital for many years and we made many friends. I know that occasionally there are anti-Semitic incidents but our experience has been with good people who were very friendly and helpful to us.

In spite of this, our experiences in Europe make us strong supporters of Israel. We can't foresee the future in America, but we know that if, God forbid, things go badly we would have a place to go to. When we visited Israel we were very touched and impressed with what we saw. I would go every year if I had the money. I just didn't realize it was so well organized, with cities and hotels and streets full of people. I expected poor little houses and a much harder life.

If I would be born again I would go to live in a kibbutz. I think it is a wonderful way to live and I would not have to worry and fight from day to day to make a living. If I were not as old as I am, I would go, because I think they have a wonderful life.

We are also here because we do not want to lose touch with our daughter and our grandchild. She is separated from her husband and lives in California. I do not know what her feelings are about Jewishness. We did everything we could to give her Jewish feelings and education. She went to Sunday school and sang in the choir. She knows that by some miracle we survived Hitler. We didn't tell her all the details of our past experiences. Maybe we should have told her more.

In our temple 20 or 30 percent of the people have intermarried. I don't know if that is good or bad. Maybe it will be better if in thousands of years Jews disappear and there will be no Jewish problem and no one will suffer from being Jewish. Personally, I would not like to see it happen. I can't explain my feeling. It is just that I was born a Jew. My home was Jewish. I feel good in Jewish company. My wife and I will drive an hour to Chicago to be with our Jewish friends.

Sometimes we need to talk about the past, to recall the relatives we lost. We can't talk about it every day or life becomes miserable . . . I'm sure none of us will sleep tonight. Every person who lived through the Holocaust never forgets it. Sometimes I hear people compare the situation of black people in America to that of the Jews in Poland, and when they do that I see they don't understand.

I remember when I first came south to Florida and Georgia and saw the signs "For whites only"; it shocked me. We knew it from books, but seeing it was different, and also seeing the poverty and the segregation frightened us. But now the blacks are in a much better situation than the Jews ever knew in Poland. They have the right to government employment. In Poland no Jew could work in the post office, in the school system, in any government office. They took two or three Jewish students out of a thousand for high school. Here the rights come from the government; there the rights were taken away by the government.

I am very optimistic about this country. It is so rich and so good I think it will survive all the tumult and all the changes. It is the best place in the world. When you think of it, who wants to emigrate to Russia, to China, to Poland? Everyone wants to come to the United States. It is a beautiful country with a democratic government and one of the few places in the world where you can feel free. I'm grateful for my good home, my good friends, my good life. All I need is continuing good health and seeing my daughter and grandson happy.

Dr. Hilda Branch from Essen, Germany; Verona, Italy; southern France and Brussels came to the United States in 1941. She went to Women's Medical College in Philadelphia and presently practices psychiatry in Los Angeles.

We left through Portugal in May 1941. We had to bribe our way on to a little Portugese boat. I came with my husband and daughter and a friend who escaped the French internment camp with my husband.

We landed in New York, where my brother-in-law and his wife were waiting for us. They took us to their apartment in Kew Gardens, and I remember my astonishment at all the food that was available and my horror at the way they wasted bread. But a much more serious discovery was that I could speak English very well but couldn't understand a word.

I guess I got over that quickly, because I enrolled in some courses at Columbia that summer. I had decided when I was in Italy that I would study medicine. It was not possible there but I was sure I could do it here in the United States and I immediately began to make up my premed requirements. I learned very quickly that it was very hard for women to get into medicine, but I was accepted at Women's Medical College in Philadelphia in September in 1943, just after I got my bachelor's degree from Columbia.

My parents by that time had settled in California. My husband was all over the eastern United States working at different businesses. We had grown apart and were divorced in 1951. He kept all his connections with people all over the world, and even managed to get back most of his possessions in Germany. But the problem at the beginning was that we had come with emergency visas and once the war broke out we had to wait until March 1944 to be examined by the State Department in Washington and then had to go to Toronto to reimmigrate. That was an unpleasant experience, because the consul in Toronto was pro-German, but it was worth it because then we could take out first papers and begin to become citizens.

I thought of America as the land of the free, and soon found out how unfree it was. I found the anti-Semitism horrifying and the anti-Negro attitudes very distressing and disappointing. I was also very unhappy to find that friendships between men and women were impossible. It was the attitude of, you know, "If I take you out, you are obligated to go to bed with me." And I found the separation of men and women at social gatherings very annoying. If I talked with a man for two seconds his wife would be there to protect him.

The social behavior in America was very different from what I had been used to, and as you can see I didn't need women's liberation. While at Columbia I wrote a paper on women as doctors. I had applied to at least twelve medical schools and at my interviews they would say, "You're a woman. You're married and have a child. Why do you want to go to medical school? Why don't you take care of your family?"

That was not the only issue. A few weeks after I came to the Women's Medical College I was asked whether I had trouble because I was German and I said no, my trouble came from being Jewish. I could feel anti-Semitic animosity rather than anti-German animosity.

I graduated from medical school in 1947. I had an internship at Michael Reese Hospital in Chicago. I was planning to be an internist but while I was there I became very interested in psychiatry and psychoanalysis. It began with my own psychoanalysis, but the more I dealt with patients and heard them pour out their problems the more I began to feel that 90 percent of their troubles needed psychiatric help. In 1949 I went to the Veterans Administration hospital to do a psychiatric residency.

While all this was going on my daughter Veronica was growing up a little lost and rootless. She had started speaking French in Belgium but I wanted her to learn English without an accent, so we spoke English to her and sent her to nursery school. At that time we were so grateful to be here I wanted only to assimilate as quickly as possible. I did not speak to her of my experiences, but I think she felt that she didn't belong anywhere. Until we moved to California when she was seven she had no roots, and this really bothered her. I think it led to her interest in Judaism and Israel. I wouldn't say that she is a Zionist, but in the last eight years she and her first husband supported Israel, especially during the the Six-Day War. She has taken her children to Israel to visit and at the age of thirty-six she herself had a *Bas Mitzvah*. Both her first and second husband were Jewish. My approach when she was growing up was not religious. Her Jewish identification came after her marriage. My second husband is not Jewish. I, of course, have never been a Zionist, but I have been interested in Israel and sympathetic to it since 1933. I have great admiration for what has been accomplished there. My best friend, the girl I lived with in Verona, is married and lives in Tel Aviv. I often think of what it would have meant to Jews if there had been an Israel to go to when Hitler came on the scene.

I still have problems with Germany. I can't stand it for more than a few days. I don't mind the young people, but with people my age and older the idea of "What were you doing at the time?" is always uppermost.

I should say that there were a few people in Germany who didn't disappoint me. Mostly they were the simple people: my parents' maid, my piano teacher, an old friend who sent me my university papers from Munich. When my parents went back in 1949 they found many sympathetic people. They heard that the Catholic church in Cologne had been more helpful to Jews than the churches in Frankfurt and Düsseldorf; the city was supposed to have behaved somewhat better than others.

I think I've resolved by now even my hatred of Germany. I am able to analyze Germans and the people who had no part in it, but I couldn't objectively analyze somebody who was a Nazi. My psychoanalytic training has helped me understand the guilt of some people who were saved and also the incredible passivity of the Jews.

My parents came back to Los Angeles after making their economic arrangements in Germany and they made a good adjustment. My mother, in particular, did well. It was harder for my father, because he was thirteen years older and the language was hard to change.

I, of course, have also changed. I admit that America, relatively speaking, is still the land of opportunity. I saw in medical school that it was not only doctors' children who could go. The experiences in Germany have also emphasized my liberalism and my sympathy for the underdog. Being in the United States has increased my appreciation for the life I have. It's hard to forget that I could have been dead for almost forty years if I had not been given that emergency visa. I do not forget it.

*Bernard Brown, from the Carpathian mountains
in Rumania, survived Auschwitz and Mauthausen
and married another survivor from his hometown.
They came to Portland, Oregon, in 1951,
determined to help create new Orthodox Jewish
communities in America.*

I had an idea about what the United States was, but when I got off the ship on March 22, 1951, I could see I hadn't imagined it

335

the way it was. Libby and I went to the Joint [Distribution Committee] to register, and they told me I had to go by train to Portland, Oregon. My sponsor was from Seattle. I ask how long it takes and the woman says four days. So I said, "I'm not going. I don't ride on the Sabbath." And she tells me, "So young and already a fanatic." I told her she can call me anything she wants, but I'm not going.

Then she asks if I would go by plane. She tells me it takes six to eight hours. So I say all right. But after this they don't let me out of their sight. They want to send me right out from New York because they're afraid that if I find out I can stay in New York they'll have problems with me.

I really have to thank the Service for New Americans a lot, because they took good care of us. You see, when I came I was not used to manual labor. But they sent me right away to a doctor, and he told me to jump twenty times on one foot and I did. And then they put me in a factory which made lift trucks, on a hydropress to straighten out the lines. In the beginning they gave me a small truck and I could do it, but then they started with a big truck line and I had to pick up lines which weighed a hundred and fifty to two hundred pounds. I didn't know how to lift and nobody showed me, and I just couldn't do it. I knew I had a wife and child to take care of—what can I do? I just kept on working until one day I couldn't move. They sent me to the doctor and put me in traction in the hospital for ten days. Then there was a brace, and the doctor says I can't work. I got so upset my ulcers started in. And this went on and I was sick for a year and everything going down, down, down. I could see there was no end to it. And the Federation was taking care of me.

We came not knowing even how to say "bread and water." Mostly I learned being among people. One thing about the people in the United States: they are helpful in every way they can be. They don't ridicule somebody who doesn't know the language.

In the beginning, when I started peddling scrap metal, there were a few people who, after I told them I was a Jew, didn't do any more business. On the other hand, I had some very nice people who knew we were Jews and they couldn't be more considerate. If it was a Friday night or a holiday and I couldn't come they would take care of everything and save it for me for the next day.

We applied right away for citizenship. I went to school and took the exam. I had no problems whatsoever. But I remember my son when he went to school came home and said, "Dad, teach me English, because some boys beat me up." You see, he didn't understand what they were saying to him. So I said, "How can I teach you when I don't know myself?" And he answered me, "Dad, you are a father. You must know." This son is now twenty-eight years old, married, a father himself, with two children. He is an attorney in Cleveland. He had a good education. We sent him to a Jewish day school in Seattle when he was eight years old. After five years there and high school, he went to Yeshiva University and after that to NYU Law School.

We have four children altogether, all of them now out of the house. Our second was a girl; she is married and has a two-year-old boy and lives in New York. The third is twenty years old; he goes to Yeshiva and to Brooklyn College at night. Our daughter, you should know, went to the day school we organized here in Portland. Then she went to regular high school here in Portland and then to Stern College in New York. Our youngest son went to the Yeshiva Torah Va'daath high school in Brooklyn. Miriam, our baby, is now in the Cleveland Day School. In school they were all straight-A students. We laid a lot of emphasis on how important it is to learn, and we were lucky to have children who want to learn and have the minds to do it.

We didn't speak about our past. Libby, my wife, would have terrible nightmares if the subject came up, so we avoided it most of the time. I have the tattoo on my arm, so I sometimes have to speak of it when someone asks me what it is, but I know that it is something which no one can understand if they didn't go through it.

And when I tell anyone that I am the only one left in my family they listen as if I were telling them a story, a story that goes in one ear and out the other.

I felt very bad when the United Nations said that Israel and the Zionists are racists. I thought we should be used to such things from way back. As Jews we always had to suffer—really very few like us. So we have to keep helping Israel until everybody gets used to the idea that it is here to stay.

In 1948 we considered going there to live, but after the camp I didn't feel strong enough to expose myself to a war again. And I was afraid of going and having to leave. There is a curse in the Talmud for anyone who leaves Israel, and I didn't want to be involved in such a possibility. But I hope to go there to retire when all our children are settled.

In the meantime I work for religious causes and do the best

I can for people here. When I first came to Portland lots of people, Jewish people, were kidding me because I was so Orthodox, but I let them know that I accepted them on their terms and I wanted them to accept me on mine. And that's how it's been. We go everywhere and take part in everything, but when it comes to eating, we eat only at home. I live walking distance from our synagogue. We are about twenty blocks away, but I can do it in half an hour.

For the last ten years I've been the president of the synagogue and the treasurer of the Hillel Academy. I also raise money for the *mikvah*. If Orthodox people come to Portland they know to come to us. We have only kosher meat and bread that is baked by Sabbath observers. And our synagogue is the only real Orthodox synagogue, with separate seating for men and women and a *bima* in the middle and the women have to cover their heads.

I should explain that I was not always so religious. During my youth I went through a rebellion, just like the youth today; I tried the other way. But then I came to the conclusion if you don't have religion then you really have nothing. When I came home after camp I didn't want to do anything that was Jewish. I didn't keep kosher. I didn't lay *tefillin*. But after a while it all came back, little by little, until I ended up more religious than I ever was.

I am happy with our way of life, and our children are happy too. When our oldest son was considering marrying a nonreligious Jewish girl, the reaction was swift and positive. We refused to meet her. We felt that if we meet her we have to find fault with her, and his reaction would be to defend her. By refusing to meet her there was no problem, and thank God he accepted our reaction in a good way. He married a real religious girl and thank God he is very active now in religious organizations. He is on the board of the yeshiva in Cleveland and on the Board of the Jewish Federation, and he works for the day school and other Jewish organizations.

So I am very satisfied with how things have turned out. I have a busy life, not only with making a living. I like to take out the Talmud and learn a little bit, and on Friday and Saturday to do the Torah reading. I am the rabbi for the congregation and lead the services. Now I also go to college to study business administration. My son took the course and he thought I would be interested in it too, and he was right. In the first test I had eighty-four and in the second I got a hundred. Thank God, I don't complain; I've done pretty good for myself.

What pulled me through during the war was that I knew I had two younger sisters and I felt it was my duty to come home and take care of them. Too bad—they never came back. My commitment now is to work for Jewish causes and to try to help the unfortunate. I know what it means to be hungry and not to have clothes. I know what human suffering is.

Lydia Brown returned to Viseul de Sus, Rumania, after her liberation from Auschwitz. On May 18, 1945, at the age of nineteen she married Bernard, the most eligible survivor to return to her village. When the Communists were about to nationalize their lumber business and threatened to arrest the owners of factories and businesses they escaped to the west and began the difficult journey to America that ended in Portland, Oregon, in 1951.

Our processing to come to America started at the end of 1950, and it was like you had to go through hell's gates, with all the paper work, the interrogations and the examinations. We were in a displaced persons camp; we already had a son and I became pregnant with my daughter Dorothy.

The trip on the boat was terrible. It was in March and the ocean was rough, and I was so sick. We were in big rooms with hundreds of people. I couldn't eat anything but a little tea with a cube of sugar in it. The only kosher food they had was potatoes cooked in the skins and sauerkraut, and I don't have to tell you that a person who is seasick can't eat either one.

I'll never forget the lady from the Joint [Distribution Committee] who met us at the boat. We told her we were religious and hadn't eaten for eight days, so she took a cab and brought us to a kosher restaurant in Williamsburgh. It was Purim and we ate a beautiful kosher meal that I never forgot. That same evening they put us on a plane with a slip of paper that said we were newcomers and didn't speak the language. It was nighttime and my husband fell right to sleep, but I was sitting up so hungry that I finally called the stewardess, and all I could say was "Eat, eat." And she brought me a ham sandwich with cheese. I shook out the ham and ate the bread; I figured a pregnant woman can allow herself this transgression.

When we arrived in Portland it was already Friday. My sister met us with a German-speaking lady who drove us to my sister's house. That first night sleeping on a soft American mattress made me seasick, but we had a beautiful *Shabbes* with my sister. Then on Sunday the Service for New Americans brought us to a nice, clean apartment they rented for newcomers. The first thing was for my husband to find a job. All we had were two Leica cameras that we sold for a few hundred dollars. But the New Americans Service gave us twenty-five dollars a week and paid the rent for us, and I was resourceful and saved a little. We had lots of problems with health, but we had an angel of a doctor, and people were wonderful about helping us. We also had the drawback of being Orthodox Jews and my husband couldn't take just any kind of employment because he wouldn't work on the Sabbath and holidays. When he was better and got into the peddling business it was possible to make a living and keep the observances.

It was a hard time, a time of adjustment to the language and the food, to the way of life and the mentality of the people. And our bodies gave out after we arrived here. A lot of time was wasted in sickness the first two years. I had all these pains but they couldn't find anything wrong physically. It was just probably from all the pressures and hardships we had gone through before.

My husband didn't go into the lumber business as he planned. He found it easier to make a living with the scrap metal. We bought a house for $12,000 with a small down payment, and I cannot describe the happiness that we had our little home. I used to work in the garden with so much love it was the showplace for the whole area, and Bernie painted the outside, and the children were happy in it.

Our second boy was born in 1955; we made a beautiful *bris* and the whole community was invited. We were already used to inviting all the orthodox people in our synagogue for a *Malave-Malke*, the special Saturday night gatherings. We saw there was a need for religious expression in the community and we realized that if we want to make ourselves a part of the community we have to take the initiative and not wait for others to come and cater to us.

Five years after we came to America we were naturalized. My husband went to school for language classes but I had to stay home with the children, so I used to just let the radio run as though it would go sideways past my ears. And then suddenly one day I realized that I could understand what was going on. It was one of those soap operas, and I had learned English by listening to "My Little Margie" and "Ma Perkins" while I was washing and ironing and taking care of my children. It was like an awakening after living in a vacuum. It had been peaceful for a time because I didn't know about war, about crime, about anything outside my little house, but it was wonderful to wake up and be part of the world.

When our little boy started to go to kindergarten and first grade I learned how to read by following his books. I never went for formal classes, but I learned with my children to read the English language.

Giving the children an American education was not a problem. Our difficulty came with our wish to give them a Jewish education. It was not that there weren't any Jews in Portland. When we came twenty-five years ago there were already two kosher butcher shops and a kosher bakery and six or more synagogues. We could go walking on a Sabbath afternoon and find people to say a "Good *Shabbes*" to. There was even an afternoon Hebrew school. I found out to my dismay, however, that children started Hebrew school at the age of ten or eleven. In Europe we sent a little boy to *cheder* when he was three or four. The first thing he read was Hebrew prayers. Then he went to public school at six. So here we are with a boy of seven and we take him to Hebrew school and we're told he's too young to start. And my husband says, "What do you mean too young? He reads already English." He did go for two years but we could see that this was no way to get a Jewish education, and we began to investigate other possibilities. When our son was nine we went to Seattle to see the Hebrew day school there, and then we had to find a family where he could board. I used to come home from Seattle crying all the way on the bus because it was a hard emotional decision to send our young boy away from home.

It was hard with each of the children to make the decision, but we sent them away to school in order to maintain the religious spirit we wanted for them. Thank God we've had no problems. They know their background. They know their goals. They have the same religious outlook as my husband and I do.

Our older daughter Dorothy was lucky enough to be able to go to Hebrew day school in Portland. Then she went to the public high school there. Being a religious girl set her apart from the others. She used to come home and tell me, "Mommy, it makes me feel like a creep because I'm not part of the Jewish crowd shopping and skating on *Shabbes*, or the non-Jews either." When there were holidays at the Jewish Center, she was supposed to explain things and arrange things, but she would always come home disappointed because no one paid attention.

It was very odd; my daughter's best friends were sweet gentile girls with whom she didn't have the conflicts she had with the Jewish boys and girls her age. So it was important for her to go to Stern College where she made friends and started to date Jewish boys with religious backgrounds. Knowing she is happy, I'm happy myself, even though I miss her.

I'm very pleased with the way our children grew up and married, but I'm never smug about it. I always pray. And we still have two that have to go through their schooling and find their place in the world. Our oldest son in Cleveland is raising an observant family and he has a responsible place in the Jewish community and on the board of the Telshe Yeshivah. Our daughter who lives in New York is married to a lawyer. They are also observant and she works for her Mizrachi group. Our two older children were brought up in the European way: the father was the law in the family and whatever he said went. The older ones had this fear and respect for us. The younger ones have already expressed their individual needs and individual decisions. We too have become Americanized, and think they have the right to make their own decisions. We are not the same parents to them as we were to the older ones. And I don't know if they will make the sacrifices to please us that the older ones did.

In the beginning we didn't talk about our wartime experiences at all. I had to put like a lid over my experiences and my feelings. We just went on with present-day living, with the problems, the plans, and with keeping busy and never looking back. Now the children are older and they themselves want to know.

Sometimes on a Friday night, when the family is relaxed, an article brings something up and we talk more. The children want to find out about their grandparents. It pains them not to have grandparents, aunts, uncles, cousins like other people do. Our oldest son avoids the questions the most. Our older daughter asks sometimes. My youngest is the most emotional. She doesn't want me to read books that will upset me. I think sometimes that I'm already immune and I can finally do it but when I try I find myself crying hysterically.

I'm very lonely here in Portland. I came here because of my sister. But she has moved to New York in order to be able to bring her children up in a more religious atmosphere. So I feel quite isolated. We have a wonderful group of friends in Seattle whom we met when our son was in school there, and we share each other's celebrations like family. I also belong to organizations like Hadassah and Mizrachi and work actively giving time and financial support. I work for the *mikvah* and the day school, which is a part of my life even though I don't have children going there anymore. In a community where there is very little orthodoxy, one must fight for it. There are only forty members in our synagogue and not too many workers.

American Jews are not threatened by anti-Semitism or communism, but they are threatened by apathy and too much well-being. They're not enough concerned by their lack of education and their beautiful empty synagogues. We had a religion given to us on Mount Sinai that we still have to prove. Every Jewish child should have the opportunity to learn the history of his people and the *Halachic* laws that helped us survive so long. To make things easier everything is diluted more and more, until there's very little flavor left in the end.

There are only four or five religious families of the forty or fifty families in Portland who were saved from the concentration camps. It's sad for me to think that they were saved from those terrible things to disappear as Jews in the United States. I meet these people and invite them to our house but they are always worried about inviting us because they know we don't eat in their homes. The hostess calls and says, "Libby, what can you have?" And I say, "Fruit and your company is all we want." Some people invite us on those terms. Others are not comfortable.

I have not had many contacts with non-Jews except for the people my husband has business contacts with and the ones I meet by helping the March of Dimes and the Cancer Fund. When they hear you speak with an accent they ask where you came from and when. And when I tell them they respond with shock. They do not know what transpired in Europe during the war.

Even though I could not speak about it in the early years I believe it has to be told to the young generation. It has to be brought out in its entirety. The Hitler regime must not be turned into some kind of heroic part of history.

I can remember when we were grasping for any bit of hope that help would come from the Allied forces. When Roosevelt wished the Jews of America a Happy New Year we thought in our village that it was a promise we would survive. My father would go to a neighbor and listen to the clandestine radio under the covers so no one would hear. When we think of those days now and make demonstrations for Russian Jews, it is easy to be bitter and wonder where everyone was in those bad days.

I love this country. I love Portland and the warmth of the people who welcomed us and cared for us when we came. There were still elderly Jewish people here then who were more observant, and they made it easier for us to adjust. It was the realization of a dream I had as a little girl. I had friends who immigrated to America and wrote me letters about how beautiful and rich it was, and I dreamed of coming.

Now we worry a lot because the mentality here is so different. We still think that if there's something we can't afford, we don't buy it. We see the waste of clothing, food and energy. You can't close off rooms for heating, because they don't have doors. I wish American people would face realities. We should have more national feeling and face our problems together and solve them. And we need more religious feeling, more feelings of responsibility and respect. I think the young people are losing out. Families are breaking up. Quality education is missing. There is great ignorance of Jewish ways of helping the sick and the poor. No one knows what a *chevra kaddisha* is, even though it's in Jewish law—things like that. I would love to see more Orthodox Jews come to this part of the country to strengthen the Orthodox community and be an example for the others.

I thank you for giving me the opportunity to express my thoughts. I hope it might even help future generations who may listen to the recordings. I am an optimist by nature. I hope that the dedicated Jews who identify with Israel and work for the Jewish community in America will be strong and come back to religious feelings as well. It's the only way we can survive.

*Claude Cassirer from Berlin came to New York in
1942. He was twenty-one years old and had
survived the Holocaust by "keeping a step ahead
of the Germans." He came into the country sick
with typhoid fever and was helped by the Jewish
agencies that looked after refugees. He settled in
Cleveland, Ohio, after his recovery, married and
became a professional photographer. He became a
committed Jew, had a* Bar Mitzvah *at the age of
forty and tried to raise his adopted children to
share his commitment.*

I sent a cable to a friend of my father's, the photographer Roman
Vishniac. "I'm very sick," it said. "No money. Pick me up at the
pier." And he did come, and took me to Mount Sinai hospital,
where they were horrified to find I had typhoid fever. All sorts of
doctors came to see me because they were amazed that anyone
could get into the country with the disease, and also because I
was a rare case they had never seen. It just happened that the
doctor was not on board the day I came through.

The Federation took excellent care of me at Mount Sinai, and
then sent me to a convalescent home in Yonkers, New York.
From there I went to a special home for refugees in Manhattan
where I could live while I looked for work.

I had some hotel training at a school in Nice and thought of
going into the hotel or restaurant business, but the best job I
could find through the Federation was to be in charge of the
ladies' room in Longchamps in New York. I then worked myself
up to be a busboy, but I didn't really have any expectations. I
was taking each day as it came. I found the city overwhelming
even though I was born in Berlin and had lived in London and
Paris. I wanted to leave the city. This was 1942. The Jewish
agencies were very helpful, very understanding. I would take
the menial jobs they found for me, but then leave because they

were so unpleasant. I realized I had to do jobs I didn't enjoy. There was no question about having to work. I never left one job until I found another. They all paid thirteen or fourteen dollars a week. I kept on living in the house for refugees, paying my way as soon as I was able to.

Some cousins I met in New York helped me find a job as a stock clerk in Cleveland. I still had so little money that the Jewish agency had to pay my bus fare to Cleveland. They were glad to do it because they were trying to get refugees out of New York. I was relieved to leave New York but apprehensive about coming to Cleveland. I had no idea of what it would be like. As it turned out, the department store was of low quality and Cleveland was not the most beautiful city, but I found a boardinghouse where I could rent a room and got started.

The boardinghouse was very confusing. Some people worked during the day and others at night, and the same room was rented to two people: one who slept during the day and the other at night. I enjoyed this more than living alone. The people had cars and we would go to Euclid Beach and meet girls and go dancing. They were hillbilly types and not very intellectual, but I enjoyed it for a short while. Before long the merchandise manager invited me to live in his house in exchange for babysitting. He lived in University Heights in a very nice home and this was a chance to have free food and board; I had nothing to lose from such an arrangement.

In 1943 I received a draft notice and I was very anxious to go. I told my boss I was leaving and they gave me a going-away party. Then when I got to the induction place they turned me down. I didn't pass the physical because of a hernia. I was so disappointed. I went back to my stock clerk job and tried to give back the presents. I was so ashamed of coming back.

It was not a job I enjoyed. They promoted me to the floor and promised that I would someday be an assistant buyer, but I really wasn't interested. I had always enjoyed photography and was looking for an opportunity to get into the field. I answered an ad and took a job even though it paid less than I was getting. My boss was very decent about it. He let me continue living in his house even after I stopped working for him.

I started as the assistant photographer and after a few weeks the chief photographer was fired for drunkenness and I was given his job. I stayed until after I was married and ready to try photography on my own.

346

I met the woman I married on the train to New York. I was going to visit a girlfriend and she was visiting a boyfriend and we happened to sit next to each other. I was very quiet and shy in those days and she wasn't. She heard my accent and began asking me questions. I was excited about meeting a Jewish girl who was intellectual and well-educated. She was impressed because I asked her to have breakfast with me after we had talked all night long and I got up and shaved and changed my shirt so I would look right for her. My father had warned me that American women were very anxious to get married. In Europe it was customary for boys and girls to have relations before marriage. It was only in America that you got married before you had relations. On my first date I told her I didn't want to get married before I was established. On the second date I asked her to marry me.

We actually got married a year later. What I found very interesting was that I wrote my father in New York to tell him I was engaged and his first question was, "Is she Jewish?" When I didn't answer quick enough, he sent me a telegram asking the question again. Here was a man with no Jewish interests whatsoever, and this was his only question. He didn't ask "Does she have money or education?"—only whether she was Jewish. This to me is a very interesting point. I finally wrote and told him she was a Jewish-American girl from Cleveland.

I married into a wonderful family with a great relationship between the children and parents. They had the kind of conversations, arguments and discussions I had never had. I enjoyed the whole family. The children could argue with their father, have different political views or just take the opposite view for the sake of discussion. No one pressured us to get married. Her father was opposed to our marriage. He wanted his daughter to marry a doctor, not a photographer earning twenty-five dollars a week. In fact, Beverly earned more than I did.

Meanwhile I was consciously trying to get rid of my British accent and also to learn to like American food. I wanted to join the American mainstream. I had no wish to be with other German refugees. I was independent in many ways. For example, today there is all this talk about woman's lib and men doing chores; my wife and I always had this. She helped me with my photography and I helped with the housework and the children. I was able to care for the house and the children. It was part of my feeling of independence.

I learned this from my father. Maybe because I didn't have a mother. By contrast, my American-born father-in-law is absolutely helpless. He couldn't pour himself a glass of water. But he introduced me to other things. I was made aware of Jewish holidays, of Jewish food. I had never been in a synagogue before my wedding. I was in a completely different world and I accepted it as just another experience. I didn't disapprove of it but I didn't feel cheated because I never tasted a bagel or fasted on Yom Kippur or eaten *matzo* at a *Seder*. Actually I had heard about *matzo* because my great-grandmother on my mother's side was married to a Hebrew teacher in Munich and she ate only kosher food that was brought from a special kosher restaurant.

I shared with my father, however, this feeling that it was not a good idea to marry a non-Jew. Maybe it was because of the unpleasantness of the mixed marriages during Hitler's time. I haven't gotten over it. As a photographer at weddings I still feel uneasy and awkward about mixed marriages. Politically and socially I'm a liberal man, but this feeling hangs on.

I'll tell you something that amazes me. My wife and I come from very different homes and yet we are so close, so much in love and have so much understanding of each other. The only way I can account for our having so much in common in spite of the difference in our upbringing and background is that our values are the same. Basically we both have good Jewish values.

After our marriage we moved into a Jewish neighborhood and I felt very comfortable about it. And then I gradually became involved with the synagogue and the Federation. I was determined to do my share for the Jews of Europe. I did not respond to the building programs. People were more important to me than buildings.

I was very anxious to have a family, but we had trouble having children. Our daughter was adopted after seven years of marriage. She was born in 1951. Our son was adopted in 1954. I was determined not to be like my Germanic father and went overboard being soft and lenient. Whenever I punished them for doing something wrong, however, they would accuse me of being too strict, too European and Germanic. I know I don't have the warmth and family feeling that is taken for granted in my wife's Russian family. I don't know if I can generalize about that, but I did have very different early experiences that deprived me of the fantastic warmth that I enjoy but can't quite radiate myself.

I've been a little disappointed in my children's disinterest in my experiences in Europe. They have sometimes heard my speeches for Federation but usually decline politely. My youth is so far in the past for them, so irrelevant. They are not curious. They seem to resist my influence. I also regret that they lack drive and are not pursuing things with more diligence. Their moral and ethical values differ quite a bit from mine. My wife is equally disappointed.

Both children have turned away from everything Jewish, in spite of the fact that our son was *Bar Mitzvahed* and our daughter was confirmed. Our son is very musical and actually conducted the youth services as a cantor, but he has drifted away from such things and seems to have no interest in them. Our daughter, if anything, has turned a little anti-Jewish and has joined a Christian group with some of her Jewish girlfriends. It's the kind of mild group that meets with a minister who speaks very well of Jews but is trying to persuade them to become Christians. It is as if our children seem determined not to do as we do. Perhaps they have all the problems that children have today with the additional ones that come from being adopted. Psychiatrists tell us that adopted children always resent having been given up by their real parents and take their resentment out on their adopted parents. There seems to be nothing we can do. If I really let my Prussian background come into this I would say, "You will do as I say, like it or not," but I'm more inclined to take the psychiatrist's advice and say, "I hope some day you will feel differently." I truly hope they do.

My work, however, has given me much satisfaction. I was happy to pick an honest profession. There was never any reason to cheat anybody. I created something that gave people a lot of enjoyment. My pictures are kept in albums and hang on walls. I'm one of the few photographers who doesn't sign wedding contracts. I want to satisfy people and I usually succeed. Many of my customers become my personal friends.

I don't have a studio because I didn't want to be out minding the store. My wife and I always worked together. She has not only done the promotion but also kept the books and done the secretarial work. Our friends don't understand how she can tolerate a man around all the time, but we actually miss each other if we're not together at lunch. Working together made our marriage even more successful.

I regret a bit that 99 percent of our friends and clients are Jewish. I'm a bit curious about the non-Jewish world with which

I have no contact, even though we are very lucky to have wonderful friends. I'm not comfortable with men's organizations. I like women and enjoy being with them. My other involvements are with political campaigns. I'm also a member of the Federation's Speakers Bureau. I feel I have a message to give. I'm sensitive to anything that reminds me of Germany. When they had this no-knock law, for example, that was too close to Gestapo technique for me—or that certain books were to be banned, or sterilization of groups of people. I'd like people to think of such things carefully and see the frightening implications. I want to resist this feeling of hopelessness that people get. They think they can't change the course of history. That's not true. I think there are people who have the guts and courage to do things and we should help them. I don't think we can dare to take our liberties for granted.

Anything can happen here. When I saw the faces of the people in the South preventing the black people from going to certain schools and using German police dogs and fire hoses they looked no different than the Nazi stormtroopers with their dogs fighting the Jews. People are people. The Germans are no worse than others. If the government becomes immoral and sanctions such things there is danger for everyone.

I was very much afraid during the last oil crisis that Jews would be blamed. I was pleasantly surprised that the American public was sensible and reasonable. I don't want to be pessimistic, but I feel I have to be realistic. Even though I say this, it's been my personality to put unpleasant things aside and try to forget them or overcome them. I don't read books about the Holocaust or see movies on the subject. The first time I went to Israel I found it impossible to go to Yad Vashem. The second, I tried to go in but found it very difficult. I see no sense in getting involved with gruesome things even though I speak to prevent such things happening again.

I was in situations of utter helplessness myself with no protection of any government and I know what it's like, but what sense is there for me to dwell on the fact that some of my relatives were turned into soap? I don't forget what happened but I'm not fascinated by it, except to be sure that such conditions can never happen again. This is why I get involved in communal work. For the last eight years I've been director of public service, which means anything from snow removal to sewer cleaning, to street paving, to handling citizen's complaints and requests for service. I learned about city administration and the use of equipment. I had some innovative ideas about picking up rubbish and learned a lot about public relations.

There's no end to learning. My wife and I originally planned to take an extensive trip in honor of our thirtieth anniversary, but after the October War we felt that most countries had been so miserable to the Jews we just didn't want to go and spend our money there. We decided instead to further our education right here. Neither of us had been to college; my wife graduated in the thirties during the Depression and had to help support her family, and I was at that time running from Hitler. So we both enrolled in a couple of courses to see if we could do it. We took elementary psychology and a philosophy course in contemporary values, and we enjoyed it and did well. My wife decided to go full time to John Carroll University, and I'm taking as many courses as I have time for. I get a minimum compensation from the German government for their interruption of my education and I'm finally putting it to worthwhile use. I'm not the student my wife is, but I like the atmosphere on the campus. Our brains are working a bit.

I guess it's my nature to try to make up for what I missed. When I was in my forties I decided to become *Bar Mitzvah*. I don't want to give the impression that I went from a self-hating Jew who was very uncomfortable being Jewish to an ardent Orthodox Jew. Nor did I do it because it was the "in" thing. It was that I began to feel very comfortable at the Park Synagogue and to have a very good feeling being there on a Friday night. I was involved in establishing the adult education program. I learned a little Hebrew and I wanted to be part of what was going on. It was like the next stage of my life. I felt the time had come and I was doing something I wanted to do. Maybe, thinking about it now, it had to do with the great loneliness in Europe of being an isolated Jew, of knowing I was Jewish only because of the *J* on my passport. I needed to feel the strength of unity, of seeing myself a part of a community. It's only here in this country that I felt comfortable as a Jew.

My grandmother came to visit us for a while and she couldn't understand how entertainers and public figures on the radio and television would proudly say they were Jewish. She couldn't understand why they used Jewish expressions. She still thought it was something to hide. Maybe it would be in Germany or France. She reminded me that we were once anti-Zionists. I admit that I wouldn't want to move to Israel now, but the truth is I wouldn't want to move anywhere. I've moved enough. I would not like to uproot myself if I could avoid it. But I know that Israel is good for us.

If there's any hope of survival for the Jews they must unite and stand for what they believe. They must not hide. I found that out when the Jews of Germany said they were not Jewish, and Göring said, "I'll decide who's Jewish."

I have confidence in this country. It is as good a democracy as one can find. That's why I was so disturbed when the Nixon thing happened. The other aspect that troubles me is the crime and violence. I abhor the aggressiveness. I don't watch cowboy movies, with people hitting and shooting one another. I see no sense in such things.

Nevertheless, I'm delighted to be here. I like the friendliness, the outgoingness of American people. Very few countries accept foreigners easily. The French are terrible with strangers. The British take a long time. The Germans we need not mention. My father does not like it in America. He feels it is a highly uncultured country and he is not comfortable here, even though he admits it is the land of opportunity. But he was critical of France and England as well. He could have come to the United States before World War I but he didn't want to. That was his mistake.

I may wish for some things to be different, but there is no other place I wish to be. I hope to do my little share to improve things a bit—even if it's only to tell people not to throw up their hands and say it's hopeless. We have to do the best we can.

Maurice Diamant, born in 1922 in Germany of Polish parents, spent the war years confined with his family in Italy. They escaped to Switzerland just before the Germans arrived in 1943. He met his wife in Lugano and they were married just before the war ended. He loved Italy, but problems with his health and difficulty earning a living brought them to New York City. They eventually settled in Denver, Colorado, where he makes a living as a type compositor for the Denver Post.

I met my wife in the camp in Switzerland—she had escaped from France—and we were married in Lugano just before the war ended. It was a strictly Jewish marriage and the Swiss authorities didn't consider it valid. At the end of the war we crossed the mountains and went to Milan. The city was so disorganized that we went back to the small town where we had been interned. My father was there. He got a few machines, got some merchandise on credit and we went into the fur business.

About a year after we settled down in the town I began getting severe pains in my spine. One physician recommended a warmer climate so my wife and I went to Naples, where my sister was living. We had contacted people in America before the war broke out. It was, of course, impossible to leave during the war. Then when the war was over we thought we would stay in Italy. I felt very comfortable there—fond of the people and the language. I felt a tremendous affinity for the language. I was good at it. I loved it.

At the same time Europe had bad memories, horrendous memories we wanted to leave behind us. We thought of going to Israel but were not ready for new struggles and pioneering. We wanted normalcy. We wanted stability. The United States sounded good to us, not only because it was the land of opportunity but because it was far away, in a different world.

Meanwhile I was going from one doctor to another, fearful I had some terminal illness and wearing a brace. All this had profound influence on my life, the way I saw things and the way my wife and kids saw me. But I eventually found a physician who was optimistic about my problem. He assured me that it would improve and that I could live a long, productive life if I didn't let it get me down.

Our papers were arranged by relatives in New York who came at the turn of the century. We sensed in our correspondence with them that they were willing to help us but didn't want any emotional involvement with us. We were the "poor remnants of the family after the Holocaust." They were sorry for us but not interested in us.

It was hard to leave Italy because I had many friends who had been in the camps with me. We would have long, heated discussions in a small café in Milano and people passing by would smile to hear us shout and argue. One was a communist. Another was a Christian Democrat and another a socialist, and each one of us had a theory about the future.

And then there was the landscape and the pace of life we loved. Before we left Naples I remember going to the upper part, where you can look down over the bay. It was a nice, sunny day and I said to my wife, "If I could only find some decent work in this city, I would never, never leave."

We used to think of that day when we came to New York and were nostalgic about Europe and wondering whether we should return. We thought of going back and considered the pros and cons until we came to the conclusion that Europe was like a gorgeous apple with a huge worm in it. My wife Helene had lost a brother and a father. We knew that there was more to Europe than strolling in the pleasant streets and sipping coffee in a café. We would always be homesick for that easier pace of life, but we made up our minds not to go back.

We were grateful for the help of the Hebrew Immigrant Aid Society in getting here. We arrived without a penny and they found us a little apartment in Brooklyn, paid the rent and gave us a small allowance until we could get on our feet.

My brothers came before us but they were horrified by the life in New York, and went back to work with my father. My sister came with her two children. Her husband, with whom she had gone through the camps, was supposed to join her, but instead he found another woman and left her here alone.

I was the only one of the brothers to remain. My wife and I knew we would have to work hard, but we were a little intoxicated by the thought of being on our own. As much as we were attached to our families we were ready to cut the umbilical cord. Even on the boat crowded with Jewish refugees we were already turned to the future. Nobody told stories of the past, though everyone had a story to tell. There was expectation of new things in the air.

We came to New York in a fog so thick we never saw the Statue of Liberty. I remember calling our relatives and finding that they were not interested in meeting us. We told the people at the agency that we were ready to be on our own and become self-sufficient as quickly as possible. I was trained as a furrier and my wife was prepared to be a seamstress. I spoke enough English to manage with coworkers; my wife spoke French and Yiddish and she too could manage.

My wife became a member of the Amalgamated Union of Clothing Workers and got a job at one of the clothing manufacturers. I worked in a small shop making fur toys. They paid less than the minimum wage, maybe fifty or sixty cents an hour. But with the two of us working we were quickly independent of the agency. I was very impressed by the way they handled us. We didn't want to be dependent and they helped us to be independent. That was good.

New York, however, looked to us like a madhouse. On the one hand we were exhilarated by the freedom of going around without carrying papers, without worrying about being stopped and asked for working permits. On the other hand there were things that frightened and disappointed me. I was an avid reader of newspapers and went through *The New York Times* on my way to work. I quickly found out about McCarthy and was really horrified because I saw overtones of the things I thought I had left behind. I remember one morning noticing that the man sitting next to me had hidden his *Daily Worker* in the pages of a *New York Times*. Coming from Italy, where everything was out in the open and there was freedom to discuss every philosophy and political possibility, I was not prepared to see people in free America scared of believing in some things.

In the meantime we had our personal lives to worry about. I changed my job when I saw a better opportunity. When we saved up a little money we bought a small house in Newark, New Jersey. My wife stopped working and we had a baby. And then there was another. So we had a boy and a girl and I was one of the commuters from Newark to Brooklyn, getting more and more dissatisfied, wanting to do something better with my life.

I thought for a while of teaching languages. I knew German, Italian, English, French and Yiddish. Yiddish was quite important when I met Helene. She came from a family that had migrated from Warsaw to Paris when she was little. She grew up in Paris speaking French but her parents spoke Yiddish, just as mine did when I grew up speaking German. For a long time we communicated with me speaking Yiddish-German while she spoke Yiddish and French. When we came to the United States we were speaking French. I went to New York University for counseling and found that my dreams were not quite realistic. They encouraged me to go to college but I was not physically capable of holding a full-time job to support my family and being a parent to my kids while going to school. And I was always fighting my back condition. Yet I didn't want to spend the rest of my life cutting animal skins as a furrier.

It was suggested that I try to get into the printing field, since I enjoyed the printed word in all languages and reading and books were so central to my life. I enrolled in a linotype school with classes three nights a week. After a year I left my job in the fur toy business and worked in small nonunion shops in New Jersey to get experience. I knew the chances of getting into Local 6 in New York were small. It was a kind of father-son thing I was up against, mostly Irish-American and German-American and closed to newcomers.

One of my brothers had come back to the United States. Finding New York an impossible place to live he moved out to Denver, Colorado. He brought his family and opened a furrier shop and really liked it. We came to visit him in the summer of 1962 and fell in love with the mountains.

I went back only to quit my job. I found out there was no problem in joining the union in Denver. I left my wife to sell the house and went west by myself. It turned out to be a harder time than we expected. It took a year before she came with the children.

Coming to Denver changed our lives completely. We were not involved in synagogue affairs in New York. I was never comfortable in a very Orthodox synagogue and felt even more uncomfortable in a Reformed setting, so we remained aloof from congregational activities.

I was still working out the conflicts of my childhood. Since my parents came to Germany from Eastern Europe we knew that we were looked down upon in school as the children of East European Jews. Assimilated German Jews had contempt for their eastern brothers. And I remember wanting to be proud of my parents and yet feeling ashamed of them. I wanted to be one of the German Jews who talked about German culture, about Goethe and Heine and Schiller and music and everything. I was always torn by the feelings of conflict, by despising and loving at the same time.

As a teenager I was always questioning, fighting the concept of God. My personal experiences of life in Europe and what was happening in Europe said no to all this stuff. Where was the world? And if there was a divinity, why wasn't there any response to our plight?

I mention all this because it accounts for my inability to affiliate myself with Jewish institutions while I was in New York, in the city where Jews were so easy to find. When we moved to New Jersey I made some friends who belonged to the Ethical Society. They were humanists and the group was nondenominational. They were concerned with man's behavior toward man and totally uninterested in supernaturalism. There were very attractive people in this group and we were pleased to join them. The children studied comparative religion and were taken to different places of worship. Our children knew they were Jews. Our son was circumcised. He even had a *pidyan haben,* a ritual for firstborn sons, but that was to please my wife, who had grown up in an Orthodox family and was a bit cheated by my indifference to Orthodox customs. The only Jewish custom I practiced was the lighting of Hanukkah candles.

Occasionally on holidays I would take the children to a small synagogue in our area in New Jersey, but I never quite recovered from my first effort to enter a synagogue on the Jewish New Year. When I got to the door of the huge reformed temple I found a whole battalion of ushers with flowers in their buttonholes and they asked for my ticket. "I don't want to go to the theater," I said, "I want to go to the services." When they told me I had to have a ticket to come to pray I told them I was new in town. But that made no difference; they turned me away. That experience turned me off and I didn't pursue it any further.

So then I came to Denver and everything changed. We had already left the Ethical Society because it had become too churchy for my taste. Trappings of Protestantism crept in that bothered me. It was not a matter of theology, but mannerisms and mores. So I was not looking for a similar group in Denver. First my Yiddish-speaking mother-in-law came from Paris to stay with us; then my parents joined us from Italy. My father was not at all pious, but he had a great deal of feeling for Judaism. He insisted on joining a congregation. It seemed strange to see my father standing there, reciting the Hebrew things he had been taught as a child and enjoying it so much. It seemed that it was not so much religious belief but feelings of warmth and security— childhood memories—that made him feel good.

Then my twelve-year-old son announced that he wanted to go to Hebrew school and have a *Bar Mitzvah*. So we joined Temple Emanuel and both of our kids went. Some of the instruction was appalling. They were often bored, but some family sense of belonging seemed to have touched them. My father was very pleased and my son's *Bar Mitzvah* gave me a lot of personal pleasure. It was an affirmation of continuity, a link in the chain, and I was pleased that my son was part of that link. It was telling, in a way, those who had wanted our destruction that we were continuing.

Over the years my wife and I had tried to tell our children about what we had been through. And they always evaded the discussion. They really didn't want to hear. We didn't force it. When they were ready they asked questions. Only in the last two years or so. My son comes to me with a book about the Holocaust and asks questions. Until now, however, they didn't want to connect us with pictures they saw and the things they heard.

I see my children affected, however, by the tensions we brought from Europe. I think they are less secure than their friends. They seem more sensitive to injustice. They've both been involved in protesting the Vietnam War and helping blacks, politically active to redress injustices. I'm pleased to see them like this, but also apprehensive. I don't want them to get hurt.

Our daughter met her husband in the Jewish Center. My wife and I were pleased with her marriage to a Jewish young man. My son, on the other hand, lives with a girlfriend who is not Jewish. This disturbs my wife very much. It disturbs me too, I must admit. I blame myself for not giving him more Jewish direction. I blame his poor teachers when he was studying. I admit that he didn't get good examples at home. It's only in the last few years that I've become involved with Judaism myself. The funny thing is that I think my son is pleased about this.

About three years ago I saw a program on the educational channel in which they were interviewing a few people who were Reconstructionists. I had never heard the term before. It appealed to me and I made some inquiries. Ultimately I found a group of people who formed a fellowship, called a Havurah, that was part of the Colorado Federation of Reconstructionists.

We've had wonderful experiences with it. I'm a humanist, a universalist, but I'm also a Jew with a sense of tribal pride that is like the pride of a family. Reconstructionism serves as an anchor for me and Helene as well. I learned that I have to anchor myself to a special part of humanity without renouncing the broader sense of brotherhood or sisterhood.

We do our own services, taking from Orthodox and modern sources. We have the kind of closeness that is possible in a small group. Some services are held in the park in the summer. Our son came to that and met our friends.

I realize I do all this rationalizing about belonging that my father didn't seem to need. I was puzzled by him. He became very involved in Judaism toward the end of his life. It wasn't senility or infantilism; he just found this feeling of pride in who he was. He went on a trip to Israel and that must have been the highest point of his life. He came home . . . lyrical.

I feel like an American, not an average American but still an American. My European experiences left me with the feeling that I have to follow through on my beliefs. In order to live with myself I can't just let things happen. I have to participate. I need to make my opinions heard, write letters to editors, take active part in election campaigns, things like that.

I've been working as a type compositor for the *Denver Post* for the last twelve years. I have no tremendous ambitions to be a supervisor or make a hell of a lot of money or to own a lot of things. I think it's more important to have time to look at yourself and the world, to think of your connections to other people.

I would like to see a change in America, toward stressing what I consider true values rather than material things, achievement as the only goal in life, the grasping for money and power.

I guess that sounds un-American, weird. My fellow workers call me a weirdo because I'm not interested in football. But sometimes I find another American like me and then I get a good feeling. One Sunday afternoon recently my wife and I were driving to Washington Park. We had the FM station on and we were listening to *La Traviata*. We parked the car and sat there listening and smiling. And right in front of us was another car with another couple listening to the same thing with the same expression on their faces. The man rolled his window down and I rolled mine down and he called across, "How'd you like that touchdown?" And that was very nice in America. I knew we weren't average, but we weren't alone.

Edmund Engelman from Vienna helped smuggle Jews into France before leaving Europe. He came to New York City in 1939, just after the invasion of Poland.

Poland was overrun while we were boarding the ship. When we arrived on Ellis Island they wouldn't accept my wife's student visa and insisted that she had to return to Poland. I couldn't intervene because we were not legally married and it would seem I had brought her on false pretenses. She spent nine days on Ellis Island while lawyers were trying to get help from Mayor La Guardia, from Washington, until she was released on a $500 bond. Then she went to New York University and we were legally married. In order to immigrate legally, however, she had to leave the country. Canada wouldn't take Jews so she had to go to Cuba. The cruelty of the system! They wouldn't tell us how long she would have to wait in Cuba. The American consulate in Cuba had to request the quota number from Berlin. It could be a week or five years. Fortunately she got her visa after a few days and came back.

The first thing I wanted was a decent apartment. We had lived through so much deprivation I felt we deserved some comfort. So we rented something way above our means on Washington Place in Greenwich Village in New York and tried to save pennies by walking. And as soon as I went looking for a job I saw the resentment against immigrants. I was told, "You come in and take someone's job away." And I would say, "I also create a job because I rent an apartment, buy food, have my shirts washed and so on." But this was still the time of the Depression and there were ten million people out of work.

Meanwhile my wife and I were very depressed. The war had broken out. My parents were in Vienna and hers were in Poland. We heard no news from anyone. And at the same time we are excited by the fact that we could walk in the street and nobody could do anything to us. You cannot imagine what it meant to have the protection of the law. We were outside the law. In Germany and Austria anyone could beat us and there was no place to go to complain.

At first when I went looking for a job I didn't think of anti-Semitism. I had my credentials as an engineer. Everything would be fine till they noticed how I filled in the space for religion. I could have passed for a non-Jew but I wouldn't. I wanted it to be known that I was Jewish. I didn't want to have to hear anti-Semitic remarks. It pained me too much.

I took a salesman's job in the photographic field. Then one day I met an engineer who wanted to know why I was wasting my time selling. At this point the government specified that you couldn't be asked your religion. He helped me get a job in a company working for the army and air force. I worked several years there developing electrical equipment for combat planes.

I felt, however, that I was treated as a Jew. I was not invited to engineering meetings. I put out patents that I assigned to the company. I got twenty dollars for each one minus four dollars for tax. My boss put his name next to mine and later my name was removed. I left then for another job.

I was sensitive to anti-Semitism, but I found it much less painful than in Europe. I didn't feel that they were out to destroy the Jew economically or physically in America as they were in Europe; it was just a matter of excluding Jews from certain professions.

We didn't let the cultural prejudices hurt our feelings. Our friends from the start were Americans. My wife didn't take to the Viennese refugees, and we met few Poles. We found new friends who helped us integrate into this country. We spoke only English.

After two years we bought a home in Queens in the Forest Hills area. We had two sons. We sent them to Hebrew school. We didn't practice religion in our home. The boys were not *Bar Mitzvah.* If there had been a Reformed temple in our area I might have felt differently, but I couldn't find a place for myself in the Conservative Center.

Nevertheless I had a strong sense of identity. My parents were Orthodox. Not that my father wore side-curls, but I grew up in a kosher house and my father pushed his customs of praying and observing on me. I rejected these practices. I kept, however, the Jewish passion for education. I wanted the very best for my children.

It was a tremendous financial sacrifice but they were both enrolled in the Walden School on Central Park West. I had become a freelance consultant for photofinishing plants and was able to manage the tuition. From Walden my oldest son went to a small Quaker school in Richmond, Indiana. We were inexperienced and didn't give him the right direction.

Some interesting things came of it. One day he found an anti-Semitic book in the library. He wrote to the dean of the School of Religion and was brushed off. Then he wrote to the president and was brushed off. He called the American Jewish Congress. The whole thing got rolling, and finally the school had to add another book with an opposing view to the library. I'm telling about this to show how he maintained his identity even without religious observance. He later got a Ph.D. from Washington University. He wrote his thesis on Dietrich Eckhart and the origin of Nazism. He learned German, which he never heard spoken at home, and did his research in Munich. When he came back he taught at Hofstra University for four years. At the moment he's out of work and writing.

One of the unfortunate fringe benefits of his trip to Germany was that he met a young German woman who has since come here to study psychology. She is a very nice, very capable young lady and they are living together. It's very painful for us. My wife is especially distressed, because her parents were killed by Germans. The young people feel they are a different generation. We are not responding rationally, but we can't help our feelings . . . and we cannot interfere.

Both our sons have been to see Vienna. They've seen the places of my youth and heard the story of what happened. They both have strong feelings of Jewish identification, but they have both chosen young women who are not Jewish. I have a strong regret that I did not pursue the actual practicing of religion. It might have strengthened their feelings of belonging to the Jewish group.

There is something about Jews that is different. We have until now preserved our identity. I hope it will not end. It pains me to think it might be over for our family. I am not a racist, but we had kept our purity for thousands of years. At the same time we identified with the oppressed. When we came I was terribly upset by the treatment of Negroes. In educating my children I stressed the need to help. My older son was very much involved. He worked for integration with his closest pal, Andy Goodman, the one who was killed in Mississippi. It was just an accident that he was not with him at the time.

We had many adventures and many traumatic experiences. My wife has undergone psychoanalysis to overcome the shocks of the loss of parents, the feelings of aloneness. She came out of it a very strong and creative person. She is a psychiatric social worker. Out of her inner turmoil and the need to help herself, she has matured into a helpful person. She enjoys life, has a lot of zest and interest; she functions on a marvelous level.

We have chosen the best place there is. We didn't suffer personally, but we suffered seeing what was going on, and we had the fear that what happened in Europe would happen here. We count on the free press to save us. All kinds of rotten things go on but they do come out. That's very important.

Helene Frankle, the mill owner's daughter from Kolo, Poland, was married while confined in the Warsaw ghetto. She, her husband and her father escaped through the Warsaw sewers and made their way to Vienna, where she and her husband had false papers and worked in a factory. They were brought to the United States by relatives in Chicago, Illinois. They settled in Chicago. She has three children and works as a professional in a social agency.

I had an Uncle Abe in Alabama and an aunt by the name of Wasserman in Chicago. I had no addresses. In Vienna I went to the services on the High Holidays. The soldiers came from all four occupation forces. I was sitting and crying my eyes out and some American officers began to talk to me. One of them said he would write to his parents in New York and find my relatives, even though I had no addresses.

One day he arrived on the scene with a suitcase full of letters from people I didn't know who were my cousins and one from my Uncle Abe. He even sent us money, which we didn't need. My husband was working as translator for the Polish and Russian consulates while he was enrolled in medical school, and I was enrolled in the University of Vienna's chemistry department. We had made a sort of life in Vienna while trying to decide what to do with ourselves.

Everything was for the moment, for whatever the day would bring. It was strange and exciting—a kind of reaction to the war. The first months were terrible because we knew what we had left and what we lost. And it was like getting drunk every day and going to theaters and nightclubs, and we were with all our close friends, living in a kind of commune. But we were strangers and knew in Vienna we would be strangers all our lives. And I had such a yearning to be part of something.

To get all those letters at this time was intoxicating. The idea of a family was overwhelming. I remember writing to them to explain exactly who I am and how it is I'm alive; I tell you, it was the most difficult letter of my life. All of a sudden I found myself terribly defensive because I survived. You know, how come everybody was killed and I wasn't? It was the beginning of working through this feeling of "Why me?" that I'm still working through.

We got the papers from my uncle and two affidavits, from my cousin in Kentucky and an uncle in Chicago. We went from Vienna to Bremerhaven on a freighter that took about three weeks. We were in our early twenties and sleeping on the floor and carrying on. I remember the ten days in Bremerhaven mostly for being hungry. Then they put us on the *Lilly Marlene,* a soldiers' transport, dormitory style, the women on one level and the men on another. Mostly I remember nearly dying of seasickness.

We came to New York with a suitcase of worthless things. It was 1947 and all my clothes were too short; I looked funny and felt terrible. I knew maybe ten words of English. My husband felt very positive about being here. He really felt this was the place for him. I was more pessimistic. I felt I didn't really know anybody. I felt isolated and miserable.

My cousins in Paducah, Kentucky, arranged for us to come to visit them. After a few days in New York someone put us on a sleeper to Kentucky. They were lovely people, but the wife was from Alabama and spoke with a Southern drawl that was absolutely impossible to understand.

We were the first displaced people to come to Paducah, and we were taken around as a kind of novelty; my husband kissed the ladies' hands and they nearly died on the spot.

It was soon agreed that we should go to Chicago, where there were more opportunities. So off we went to live with an aunt. She was an old lady from the old country whose every sentence began, "Here in America . . ." She took it upon herself to teach me new ways of life, and I was very resentful because I didn't think my ways were so bad. She left Poland twenty years before I was born and she was sure nothing had changed. She would say, "Did you ever have bananas?" I would say, "Surely." And she would say, "Don't tell me. I lived in Poland and there were no bananas." Silly things like that would drive me crazy. But she lived in Regis Park, close to the lake, and we were in a beautiful area.

I was desperately looking for a job so we could be on our own. My husband found a job as a salesman selling cemetery monuments. I finally got something at the National Food Store. My uncle was willing to help us financially but I didn't want to accept the money. I was also going to school to learn English and typing, and also to the Americanization classes. After a while we found a terrible apartment in one of the rooming houses, with bars all around. It was a room with kitchenette and a bathroom to share with a thousand others. My aunt cried because she didn't want us to live there but it was like paradise to move out and be on our own. Later on we found a better place. My husband had to watch the obituaries to sell his monuments, and the same technique worked for finding an apartment.

He always managed to make a living. While selling monuments he met a man who owned a lamp factory who was looking for a salesman and so he started to sell lamps, and then he got into selling furniture and became a manufacturer's representative. I couldn't recognize the young husband I had in Vienna who lived high and spent every penny without a thought of the future. The moment he came to this country he was a different man. He became tremendously goal-oriented and future-oriented. He was determined to have a business of his own. He gave up the idea of going into medicine. The whole idea was to become independent as soon as possible.

I had my own thoughts. I wanted to become Americanized, but I was homebound. We had one child and twenty months later another, and I was miserable and bored. We were living very modestly and trying to save some money, so there were no babysitters. Finally I just couldn't stand it any longer and decided to go to school. I took a course in pronunciation at Northwestern and met a woman who changed my life. Her husband was a counselor at a junior college. I did not know what a junior college was, but they convinced me that I could do it and I began taking courses at night. My oldest boy was seven, the younger one was five.

I realize now it was part of my identity problem. I needed to prove to my dead parents that I really wasn't such a dunce after all. Good grades came easily. I think people were nice to me because I was foreign and older than the other students. Now it's not unusual to see older women in school, but twenty years ago I was unique. I found a few others and they became my friends.

I began thinking of social work. I like people, and it seemed appealing to me. I transferred to Roosevelt University. I began to want to finish, so I took some courses at Northwestern at night and some at Chicago University during the day. I was like a miser accumulating credits. If you woke me up in the middle of the night I could tell you how much I needed.

By this time the boys were in school and my husband was doing well. He was the sales representative of a large company and had a little business of his own on the side. Then as soon as I enrolled at Roosevelt University on a full-time basis and I was coming close to graduation—I discovered I was pregnant. David was nine. Larry was seven. I told my husband and he said, "Marvelous!" He loved kids and wanted a big family. And just at that time he was planning to really go into business for himself. My uncle had died and left us a little money and he had saved a bit.

Everything was happening at once. I was going to school with my big stomach and determined to get A's. If I got a B I would be ready to commit suicide, which was so stupid, but I guess I was still trying to prove something. I had my finals in January and in February my son Mark was born. And right from the beginning he was an easy baby, a sheer delight. My husband was working a lot and money was coming in. I still didn't have my B.A. When the baby was a year old I went back to school and finally graduated. I immediately enrolled in the University of Illinois School of Social Work.

I did a lot of injustices to my children because I was away so much.

I did fulfill my obligations at home and took care of the children and drove them to Hebrew school and did all the suburban things. But the boys kept telling me I was an intellectual snob, and probably I was. It was always the question of time. It was not just that I wasn't in the kitchen baking cookies but that I wasn't friendly in the neighborhood. I had many friends from school but I was too busy for the coffee-klatching. We lived in a development where everyone was desperately looking for friends but me—and if I was, my neighbors were not the people I would choose.

You have to realize that my husband and I were both in mourning all the years our older boys were growing up. I mourned my friends by working all the time, creating pressures for myself. My husband went through all kinds of depressions. Every High Holiday was a nightmare in this house. Going to the synagogue was a mess. The kids went with their father because they could see he was upset and depressed and in no mood to take any crap of any kind. Last year we went to Israel for the holidays because I just dreaded being here so much. It was like a nightmare to go through the same motions year after year. All of this gave the kids the message that being a Jew was not the most wonderful thing in the world.

They would get very angry with us when we tried to tell them that being Jewish was something special . . . something better. They were growing up in the humanitarian era, when we love everybody and people come first and being Jewish is second. I guess we kept trying to tell them that they may think so but one beautiful day they will find out it is not always so and it is better to be prepared for that. They find that hard to accept. We have many conversations that turn into loud discussions, with a lot of screaming and yelling.

Our oldest son is now twenty-five and it's much easier to talk to him than it used to be. He was one of the rebels—involved in all kinds of strikes at the campus and God knows what. So you can imagine what went on with my husband, who has a great feeling of gratitude to this country and really feels that every citizen is obligated to serve his country. For the kids "military" is a dirty word. They are very critical and my husband doesn't always take to criticism. Meanwhile the kids think it is a cop-out to compare what happens here to what went on in Poland or

Germany or Russia. They keep saying "You made it here," as if that was his only reason for defending government policy. And he kept saying, "They gave me the opportunity."

The worst time we went through was when our second son Larry got a number forty for the draft. It blew my mind, because he is a very gentle person and would never want to go to war, especially that war. It blew his mind because somehow he blamed his father, who was the Establishment and responsible for everything. Luckily the year of his graduation the draft was discontinued so he didn't have to go. Now he's going into law and it will be as a public defender or in Legal Aid. He's not going into it to make money. Isn't that serving the country when it comes down to it?

It's a kind of joke with us. Our oldest will graduate from medical school in a few months. The youngest also plans to be a doctor. They are all good students. I never came out and said, "Listen, you better or else," but the message was there. I used to worry that I was too permissive and sometimes too protective. It was, especially in the beginning, the feeling that this is the only family I've got, and there was a tremendous amount of ambition to succeed. I'm sure my son's decision to become a doctor reflects my husband's original wish to be a doctor. They knew he didn't like this business of selling. He hated it with a passion. Every morning he dreaded going to work. They grew up with this.

Three years ago our oldest son married a girl whose mother and grandmother were practicing Catholics. There were some feelings on our part that she wasn't Jewish and we were very outspoken about it, but we were not about to stop it. The girl was disillusioned with Catholicism and they were married by a rabbi. I was very moved by her parents. Her grandmother tried to persuade her to convert to Judaism. I didn't know what was going to happen. I just had the feeling that my son wasn't ready for marriage. The girl was also very attached to her family and didn't want to be far from them. They are now in the process of a divorce. I'm sorry about the hurt feelings. She's a lovely girl. Her parents are the nicest people.

My youngest son is different from his older brothers. Mark is sixteen and I'm very worried about him because he is so nice. There are none of the rebellious episodes we had with the others. He loves to please and is also being pleased constantly, because I'm so happy with him. He has many friends and doesn't feel so threatened by being Jewish as the others. I guess I was a very different mother to him. He got the least attention but is the most independent. He really made it easy for me and never made me feel guilty for what I did or didn't do. I guess I was no longer so depressed when he was born. I really felt his birth brought us good luck. Everything was nicer and easier after he arrived.

Dr. William Glicksman from Czestochowa survived Auschwitz and came to New York City in 1946. He edited a monograph about his hometown, married and had a son. He is now the principal of a Yiddish school in Philadelphia and teaches European history at the Hillel Foundation at the University of Pennsylvania.

I came to the United States with three dollars in my pocket. The Hebrew Immigrant Aid Society gave us each ten dollars but I spent seven on candies and Coca-Cola, not having tasted such things for so many years. I was wearing these torn pants because I didn't want anything from the Germans. They offered clothes and all I would take was an old suit. I remember once going on the trolley car in Munich in my hospital pajamas because I didn't want to wear their clothes.

In New York, thank God, I didn't have to worry about money. My sister was not rich but her home was my home. I came on a Friday. Ten days later I was earning money as a translator, translating Polish into Yiddish and Yiddish into Polish. The first thing I bought was a shirt. I was hired to be coeditor of a historical monograph about my hometown. It was called "Czestochowa Yiden" ("The Jews of Czestochowa"). Each *landsmanschaft* prepared one of these living, printed memorials for the people we lost. I did the research, sitting long days in the building of *The Forward* on East Broadway, where they had lots of documents, and I also worked at the Joint [Distribution Committee].

I did not know English when I came but I couldn't go to

school. Life in a regimented group in concentration camp left me psychologically incapable of sitting in a group commanded by a teacher. I knew the difference between a teacher and an SS man, but I had to be free, by myself. I was fortunate in finding a high school teacher who came to my house and gave me private lessons for $1.25 an hour. He taught me English and I also taught myself. I put away the Polish and Yiddish newspapers and read only the *New York Times*.

In February 1947 I married a woman who had been born in Russia and came to New York in 1921 or so. In 1953 we had a son. He is now a third-year student in Temple University majoring in American history. He is, thank God, a good student and very active on the campus, a nonreligious good Jew.

I taught him a lot and he inherited a lot from me. He belongs to an Orthodox congregation in spite of his religious attitude. He's an American Jew but he took some ingredients from me. I am a historian by profession, and he knows Jewish history, and not only because he took a course in it at Temple. We can talk to each other on a very high level.

I have written a number of studies on the history of the Jews in Poland and the Holocaust which were published by the Yad Vashem in Jerusalem and YIVO [Yiddish abbreviation for Yiddish Scientific Institute founded in Vilna in 1925] in New York. My first book was my doctoral dissertation, *The Economic Life of the Jews in Poland as Reflected in Yiddish Literature, 1914–1939*. I got my degree from Dropsie College. My second book is *A Kehillah in Poland During the Interwar years: Styles in Jewish Community Organization*. I just finished a study called "Jewish Social Welfare Institutions in Poland from the Earliest Times until World War II, Reflected in Memoir Literature." I write in Yiddish and the studies are translated into English.

I no longer belong to the Zionist movement or any political or social organizations. My connection to the community is as the principal of the Folkshul, the Yiddish school for children on Haverford Street. I've been principal since it was founded in 1951. The children come three times a week and they learn Hebrew as well as Yiddish, but not from a religious viewpoint. They will not be scholars but we have a fine school.

I belonged to the organization called New Americans, made up of refugees from the camps. I joined in 1958 and I was very active in the beginning, but after a time it did not give me satisfaction. The survivors fell under the impact of American Jewish life so quickly they were completely swallowed by the synagogue. They became just one more society with a New Year's party and a memorial service once a year. That is not enough to keep my interest.

The overall picture in America is assimilation. Christianity has had a great influence on American Jewish life. The religion has become institutionalized. You are a Jew because you pay $500 to a congregation. Outside of the congregation a Jew is not a Jew, he's an American. There was assimilation in Eastern Europe too. It is the result of being exposed to external forces. But we also had a counterforce, from Orthodoxy and from the Bund, the Zionists and the other secular Jewish organizations. In my hometown of about thirty-four thousand Jews it would have been hard to find a hundred really assimilated Jews. Yet I took good things, intellectual things from Polish culture. Here the assimilation is to the cheap things, the vulgar things, that give nothing spiritual, nothing intellectual. For example, Halloween is observed with such enthusiasm and devotion and Purim is forgotten. They were not strong enough to resist the influence. You cannot have Jewish education until you have Jews.

Understand, I have nevertheless found many good things here, tremendous things on a high level. In a country of two hundred million people it would be absurd to say there's no culture. But it is a materialistic culture, and the cultural life is a result of the economic, social and technological conditions. The American Jew doesn't aspire to anything spiritual. The rabbi fills his religious needs. I call the *Bar Mitzvah* and *Bas Mitzvah* not confirmation but deformation, not a *mitzvah* but a transgression. But I'm a realist and I know that without these symbols it would be a complete wilderness. My son was *Bar Mitzvah,* but he brought to it a strong Jewish awareness that I seldom see in others.

In spite of what I say, understand that this is a great country for a man like me who has lived in a semidictatorship in Poland and then under the Germans. It is a fantastic thing to be in a country where you can express yourself.

I see American Jews thriving physically and economically but not culturally. There is only one Hebrew magazine for over six million Jews. Yiddish is losing its newspapers, its readers, its strength. In my school I have eight or ten parents I am teaching Eastern European culture. I tell them that I don't fit in the American Jewish community; I'm a Polish Jew living in the United

States. You can't expect a man who comes here at the age of forty with such a full background in Jewish life to get accustomed to such ignorance and reckon with it. Can you turn day into night? Do you understand what I say?

Jack Goldman from Mannheim, Germany, survived Auschwitz, Sachsenhauser and Dachau. He came to the United States in 1946, and lived in New York and Santa Barbara, California, before volunteering to serve in the U.S. Army in Korea. He currently lives in Denver, Colorado, with his wife and children, and makes his living as a photographer.

I had expected New York to be something huge and mammoth, so my first impression was that it was not as big as I thought it would be. But a few days later when I actually stood in front of the Empire State Building and my head went up and up and up, I got this closed-in feeling. It was May and I couldn't see the sun, and everything looked gray and drab to me. After coming from a beautiful place like Heidelberg, New York was a disappointment, and I told myself right then and there that I wouldn't stay.

I did stay for a few months. I got a job in a sweatshop as a floor boy, cleaning up, sweeping, turning belts inside out. It was a dull, boring job. I lived with the relatives who brought me to the States. They had come from Eastern Europe years and years ago. Then I lived with a cousin I knew from Germany, and then another cousin invited me. I got tired of taking advantage of their hospitality and wanted to be on my own. They were very generous; I didn't have to pay for food or rent. One of my relatives took me to the bank and showed me how to open an account, and that's where most of the money went.

The problem was adjusting to freedom. And about that time I began to feel this incredible hatred for Germany. It became apparent to me how much I lost as far as youth, life, education, not to speak of family and material losses. It was life itself they had taken from me. And I didn't want to speak German. When people spoke to me in German I would say, "Please, you're living in America. Speak English."

Then I was always uncomfortable when people would expect me to be the emaciated, depressed survivor every minute of my day. "Oh, you look well," they would say, surprised that a year after liberation I no longer weighed eighty pounds, as I did when the Americans rescued me. And having a dull job and loving music, I used to whistle or hum a tune, without even knowing I was humming or what the tune was, and people would say, "How can you whistle after all you've gone through?" Such questions seemed so ridiculous to me.

I didn't mind the questions, the real questions of what happened and was it really true and all that. But after a while I didn't want to speak about the Holocaust at all. In part it was because the questions were so silly and insensitive. In part it was because American soldiers who had not liberated camps were coming back with stories that were very different from what I was telling. They were saying that Germany was a beautiful, clean country, well organized, much nicer than France. And when I would hear them I would feel as if I were a liar, telling some exaggerated story. Why should people believe me, when their sons came back with altogether different stories? So I just decided to give up, to forget everything and avoid anything that had any connection to the past.

What was more important was that I shouldn't remain a floor boy in a sweatshop the rest of my life. I quit the job and spent my days filling out forms in the state employment office. The trouble was that when they found out I wasn't yet a citizen they couldn't help me. GIs were returning and they were supposed to get the jobs. They sent me to the Joint [Distribution Committee] but I didn't want to go. I had never taken anything from any of the Jewish organizations; I felt they were for needy people. As long as I had two good hands and a head on my shoulders I felt I should take care of myself. Eventually I had an offer of a job from people who were friends of my parents in Germany. They had a small novelty manufacturing company and I worked for them until I left New York.

I had a friend who was going to live in Denver, Colorado, for his health. He asked me to come along and I jumped at the opportunity. Arriving in Denver was absolutely beautiful after New York. I fell in love with it the minute I arrived.

My friend had been a rich industrialist in Germany before Hitler. His wife and child had died in camp. So he too was alone, and he had an idea about starting a company to weave blankets. Unfortunately he became too ill to carry out his plans, and I didn't know enough to do the work without him. So there I was in Denver without a job and without much money. When I realized that I was subject to the draft I thought I would just as well enlist for the minimum time and get it over with. I didn't know that the war in Korea was about to break out.

I can't say I was enthusiastic about being in the army. I wasn't a citizen yet and when I got my first notice I really hoped they would let me off after all I'd been through. And they were very nice and gave me a deferment, but I knew I couldn't get off forever. I felt the obligation even though I had had enough living in barracks to last me my whole life. I got in in 1948 and out in 1952. At the time I should have been getting my citizenship papers, I was in Korea.

Soon after I got out of the army I got married, and in 1954 I went to school in Santa Barbara, California, taking advantage of the GI Bill. We really enjoyed Santa Barbara. I went to school during the day and did odd jobs at night and on Sundays. I worked in a drive-in theater as an usher and had gardening jobs on Sundays, mowing lawns and weeding, and then we met some people in the Jewish community and I got a job teaching Hebrew school. My wife, meanwhile, was hired as a homemaker for one of the members of the congregation. We had a baby, by then, so it all worked out very well.

We came back to Denver when my schooling was finished. It was hard to find a job as a photographer but I went out on my own and struggled and managed to make a living. My wife worked during the early years and for a time earned more money than I did, but that was only until I could build up the business.

We have four children, three daughters and a son. We started them all in Hebrew day school, not necessarily for religious reasons but so they would get a good Jewish education. We didn't speak of our experiences until they asked. I didn't make them feel that they had to live in the past and suffer because I suffered. They knew my background and they knew there was a Holocaust. Our oldest daughter goes to Hebrew University. The youngest children, aged nine and eleven, came with me to Yad

Vashem. I didn't want to spend much time there because I felt they were too young but I couldn't get them out of there. They went from display to display, asking questions, noticing things I had missed when I was last there.

Last year when we were picketing the Russian exhibit in Denver our kids were in the forefront. They knew what it was all about. On the other hand my kids are more American than I could ever be. My son loves to play baseball—his team won last year—and when football is on he teaches me what's going on in American sports. They're American.

We are not living in a ghetto. We have contacts with non-Jewish people. I was the first man to be president of a Parent–Teacher's Association in a public school and my wife and I were involved with the Human Relations Committee. Actually we were cochairmen and we had black people and Chicanos, moderates and radicals, and we worked together for the betterment of the school. And because of this we have many non-Jewish friends.

This doesn't mean I wouldn't feel very badly if our children married non-Jews. That is very hard to take because I happen to be proud of what I have and want to retain it. I don't want my people to die out. I would like to keep alive as a people and I hope my children will feel the same. If I'm opposed to interdating it's not because I say I am better than anyone else; it's just that it leads to intermarriage, and I'm opposed to that.

I had gone away from religious Judaism during the war. But as I got older and started rethinking my philosophy I realized that if I live in exile I have to show my Jewishness and involve myself in Jewish activities, including the synagogue. So I've been active in B'nai B'rith and the Anti-Defamation League and the Soviet Jewry efforts. I belong to the Mideast Public Relations group and speak to groups who are interested in the problems of the Middle East.

I don't put a sign on my door that I am a survivor of the Holocaust but people find out and they have questions and they wonder if we could prevent such a thing from happening again. I am not a belligerent person but if I hear a slur against Jews I might still grab somebody by the collar and threaten to punch them in the nose. As I told someone once, "I wasn't afraid of the Gestapo and I'm certainly not going to be afraid of you."

I believe you have to be positive about Jewishness. You can't run away from it. You can't hide it. We have Friday night suppers with lighting candles and making the blessing over the wine. It's a night of no rush, relaxed, the whole family at home. On Saturday morning I go to services. I don't force the kids to go every week. I learned that many Jews turned away from religion in this country because their parents forced them. Luckily I'm in a business where I can keep the Sabbath.

I feel it's my responsibility to do what I can to avoid a recurrence. I tell people, "If you are asleep, it can happen again." If we discriminate against one group, blacks for example, we can discriminate against another. Everyone has the right to live as good as they can.

I have not been back to Germany, even though I've been right to the border. But I have never condemned every German. The country as a whole is guilty, but I knew Germans who spent more time in camp than I did because they opposed Hitler. And I would never condemn young people for what their parents did. I had a German camera, but not a Volkswagen or a Mercedes; they are too symbolic for me. If I were to boycott, I'd have to boycott the English and the French. There'd be no end to it. I think boycotting is only for education—to make a point, to explain an issue.

I think a lot about life in this country, which has so much that is good but also negative qualities. Is it a good life because we have big houses and two cars in the garage? I liked in Israel the way people walk and if they pass a friend's house, they stop to visit and talk. Here everything is planned, weeks in advance. Not that I regret coming here. If I had gone to Israel I would have learned other things, had other experiences. Jews in Israel are lacking qualities, just like American Jews. There are Israelis who are not aware that they are Jewish. They study Jewish history but not Jewish values. Just to have a nationality is not enough.

My experiences left me with a great love for life. I place great importance on the meaning of life, the value of every human being. When I fought in Korea it made me ill to see that a donkey had more value than a person. I want to stop talking about the Holocaust because what's the use of talking about that, when something bad is happening at this moment—whether it's Vietnam or Biafra or Ethiopia or Afghanistan or things in this country. You don't have to go far. Right under our own eyes we have things not going right. To me personally it's a frustration. The war in Vietnam is a frustration, because I have to ask myself what would have happened had America not become involved in World War II. I can't compare the Nazis with what is happening in Vietnam, but are the people in Vietnam less involved with their freedom? There is no simple yes-or-no answer to things.

It's like the big question, Why am I here and my friends and relatives lost? Why did they have to die? Why did I survive? And how did I manage it? When I speak at a lecture I tell people that they can talk to ten people who survived the camps and each one will tell a different story, and each one will be true, a hundred percent true. I think we should learn from our guilt feelings if we have them. We should get something positive out of it. To keep on living as Jews is the main thing.

This should be uppermost in our minds. Why do we have to cry about the six million, if we're dying out here on our own? So I see the only reason for talking about the past is if it can be used to reawaken Jewish people to their responsibilities as Jews and human beings. It's our responsibility to keep the world from forgetting what happened, so that it doesn't happen again.

Sally Grubman, the schoolteacher from Lodz, Poland, survived the Lodz ghetto, Auschwitz and Ravensbruck. She came to the United States alone while her husband waited for his visa in Sweden. They settled in Canton, Ohio, where she still teaches children and adults and is a spokesman for survivors.

The whole family was waiting for me in Canton. I was a touching sight for them, a reminder of their past and the family that was lost. I stayed with my cousin, and she said that relatives she hadn't seen for years came to see her because of me. These were all people who had come as young children after World War I. My father was the uncle who had the great family feeling, and he had helped them out. Now they had done well in America in the liquor business and the tobacco business, and were a prominent family in Canton, Ohio. And I was reminder of their childhood in Poland.

Thinking back, I realize it was a sad and lonely time for me, in spite of all the visitors. There was no progress with Simon's papers and I became very worried. The family started writing letters to senators and congressmen but all they could tell us was that we had to wait.

Two weeks before my baby was born I found an apartment. That was the hardest thing. People had no confidence in me: no husband, no money, and I knew only the few words of English that I was learning at the night school classes. But a Jewish landlord took pity and rented me a little walk-up apartment in a run-down area of the city. The rent was forty dollars a month, but it was the first privacy I had, the first time I could cook what I wanted, eat when I pleased, be on my own. To me it was a palace.

The family gave me a monthly allowance, some used clothes and furniture. And then the baby was born on July 20, 1947. I think the doctor is shaken up by the experience to this day. When I woke up from the anesthesia I thought I was back in camp. Having seen so many children killed right after the delivery I thought that was going to happen to me. My mind was very clear and I explained it to the doctor in German. "I swear this baby is not mine," I said. "It's a Christian baby, even though I'm Jewish. Doctor, you know this is not my baby. So don't kill the baby." I yelled, I screamed. I made them bring my sister as a witness that it was not my baby. The doctor thought I was in a postnatal shock, and called my sister because he didn't know what to do with me.

My sister told the doctor to humor me. She said to me that everything was arranged, that she had signed as a witness that it isn't my baby, and I calmed down and went to sleep because I knew the baby was signed as Christian and she had the Christian papers. This was twenty-some years ago, and I remember it so exactly . . .

When I brought my son home everything was fine. Nothing bothered me. I settled into the routine of taking care of the baby. I was the youngest in my family and had never had anything to do with a baby. I used to lie awake at night listening to hear if he was breathing. I was afraid of breaking him, as if he were a doll.

By this time I was reading newspapers and listening to the radio to learn English. I never managed the King's English that

Simon spoke but people understood me. Twenty months went by before Simon arrived in New York. He came on October 20, 1948. My sister came to stay with the baby and I went to meet him.

When I came to New York the first time I was so sad and anxious I couldn't pay attention to where I was. The second time I was so glad to be with Simon that I could just as well have been in the middle of a desert for all I cared. After three days we went back to Canton to introduce my son to his father. It was hard at the beginning for him to accept this strange man in the house taking my attention from him. Some of the strain stayed with him as he grew up.

When my son was about three years old the Jewish Center asked me to work in the nursery school. I accepted the job because I could take him with me. It was a perfect job. I spoke very poor English but had good rapport with the children. Later I became a regular teacher and eventually director of the whole nursery school, which I converted into a well-run Montessori school.

Before that happened we had our son James. In between the two births was a miscarriage, which I remember because of another strange episode. I was sorry but not frightened by the miscarriage until my sister wanted to call a police ambulance to get me to the hospital. And than I became frantic. I remember jumping up and down and saying that they will never bring me back if they take me in a police ambulance. I'm well adjusted but it took me long time to cope with the sight of a policeman. I crawl into a shell. I'm just afraid.

I see policemen on the street. I ask directions and they are very nice. A policeman saved me from a fire once when I was alone in the apartment over the bar. But sometimes this terror overcomes me—not so much now as it used to.

I went back to work after my son James was born. It was very important for me to be working. Canton was a sleepy little town where everybody knew everybody else. If they didn't know your grandfather you were a newcomer. I had the feeling I came from a test tube because I didn't know anyone and nobody knew me.

To have a well-adjusted life you have to have common memories or backgrounds with the people who are your friends. That has made me a permanent outsider. It might have been easier in a city with many different ethnic groups and immigrants from different countries. Our friends are Americans but I feel the bridge between our background and theirs cannot be crossed. Simon and I are the only family of immigrants involved in the community.

My connections have been through my work. I'm a good teacher. I never went looking for a job. When I did a good job with the nursery school I was asked to teach Sunday school. I was a second grade teacher for many years and now teach fifth and sixth grade. This is my twentieth year of teaching.

All through these years I've felt that American Jewry has been very patronizing towards immigrants. They feel superior to people who were not raised in the United States and they have made us feel as if we were touched by leprosy or something. They may admire some qualities in us and may acknowledge some superiority of intellect or whatever, but they don't understand us. We come to their homes, they come to ours, but we do not share the camaraderie they have with each other. It is almost thirty years since we came and we are still "the refugees."

There are times when, even if you have a good husband, you want to sit with a girlfriend and talk things over. And I could never open that much to the women I knew, because my responses were colored by my experiences and they would never understand.

I've joined the organizations that I feel are worth my time, that have a humane base, not only a Jewish base. I belong to Hadassah, the Sisterhood Board, B'nai B'rith and the Council of Jewish Women. I'm on the board of the Planned Parenthood Association. All of this has helped us acquire many acquaintances.

My closest friends are only two couples. One is Israeli; she is a *sabra* and he is Polish-born. The other people are from Poland also. I was the second newcomer to come to Canton. The people that came after me came on affidavits sent by organizations or relatives who were not as concerned with them as mine were with me. Most of them were on a low intellectual and educational level, and they were also in a bad financial position. I met them while I was working at the Jewish Center. I could interpret for them and help them in many ways, but I had nothing to do with them socially.

We separated ourselves from them because we have a very different outlook on life. I feel that I owe this community just as much as the community owes me. The other newcomers do not feel part of any area of American life. They are just Europeans living in Canton, Ohio. They don't support any organizations. They don't contribute even to the United Jewish Appeal, and this puts us off. We felt that to find ourselves we had to open ourselves to the outside world.

What's happened in Canton, however, is that we've become representatives of the whole Holocaust group. Whenever something comes up we're called upon by Jews and non-Jews. We're not professional speakers. We're sick of talking about it, because the subject makes us sick. We're used by all kinds of Jewish organizations, however.

There is a tremendous interest in the Holocaust that we didn't see when we came. I get these frantic calls from twenty-five-year-old teachers. *The Diary of Anne Frank* is required reading and the children are asking questions and they want me to explain why normal, good people are living hidden behind bookcases and closed doors. So I come and talk, on different levels depending on the age of the children. I'm also one of the panelists on the Panel of American Women, an organization to combat prejudice on any level. It is composed of a few blacks, a few Jews, a few Catholics and a Protestant moderator. I am forever telling my story, and describing my life here in the United States. I talk about anti-Semitism in this country and I'm surprised at the ignorance of middle-class, non-Jewish audiences. There is still a great deal of prejudice and resentment toward Jewish questions. But even with Jewish audiences I've been asked, "Why were you in a concentration camp?" They would say, "You must have done something. What did you do?" And all I could say was, "What we did was, we were born Jews." And where do you go from there?

In recent years I've had the feeling that there is a change in American Jewry. I see an awakening of consciousness, but also some confusion about the reality. American Jewish teachers invite me into their classes to speak, but they do not want me to make the Holocaust a sad experience. They want to turn us into heroes and to create a heroic experience for all the survivors. There is this book they use, *The Holocaust: A History of Courage and Resistance*, but the Holocaust was never a history of courage or resistance. It was a destruction by fire of innocent people, and it's not right to make it something it never was.

We are not heroes. We survived by some fluke that we do not ourselves understand. And people have said, "Sally, tell the children about the joy of survival." And I see they don't understand it at all. If you're in a canoe and your life is in danger for a few moments and you survive you can talk about the joy of survival. We went through fire and ashes and whole familes were destroyed. And we are left. How can we talk about the joy of survival? Then sometimes I am asked why Jews didn't defend themselves. And I've learned to answer without getting emotionally involved and without being shocked by the lack of understanding and sensitivity. I've changed a lot in my expectations.

Sometimes the question of God comes up, and whether I lost or found my faith because of the Holocaust. I have to say that I never had much of a religious faith even before the war. When I was a little girl I used to go to a very Orthodox *shul* with my father. That was when people believed in what they were doing, but I was just a little girl going along. Still, before, during and after the war I believed in God. And that was a great comfort to me. In spite of everything I believe in a merciful God and I don't believe in a vengeful God, punishing us for our sins.

I don't think we express our religious feelings by going to the temple, even though we do belong and do go. It's more important to give donations to the right causes and to be nice and good to people. I try not to refuse anybody, no matter how hard it is. And I try to help people by listening to them and trying to understand, and helping people from other faiths as well as our own.

When I talk with American-born Jews about anti-Semitism they think of being excluded from a country club or a residential area. Such things don't bother me at all. I wouldn't want to go where I wasn't welcome. The important things for me are equal rights in education, in politics and economics. I'm a registered Democrat. I vote. I have never missed voting in an election. I like to work in an election, to make a contribution and see how the political system works.

I should explain that my need to participate in different areas of life in Canton is a consequence of the size of the town. There are advantages to living in a small town. Life is easier, simpler, more comfortable. You are not an insignificant pebble in a sea of humanity, and if you take part in the community you can become known and respected. On the other hand, Canton is a culturally deprived little town, even though it's much better than it was twenty-five years ago. It's not like a university town that has educated people coming and going. It's clannish and groupish, and whether you belong to one group or another depends on where you live and how much money you make, and it's not open to strangers who come from thousands of miles away. In a big city I might not have had to work so hard to find an accepting group of people.

I used to think we would have had a more enjoyable life in California, in Los Angeles maybe, but our financial security is here and I have made peace with myself. Coming to the United States, living the way we have been able to and raising our children here has been a great opportunity. There's no other country I would want to live in. I'm not sure that I'm integrated in the community, in spite of the fact that people know me and I've tried hard to contribute to it, but I am adjusted, and grateful for all the good things. I have a good husband, wonderful children who've never been in trouble. If I lack certain things . . . so?

Simon Grubman from Lodz, Poland, survived
Auschwitz, Braunshweig, Mecklenburg,
Ravensbruck and a twenty-month wait in Sweden
for his visa to America. He came to the United
States in 1949 and settled in Canton, Ohio, where
he worked as an executive in a steel company.

I felt completely at home the first day. I had left nothing on the other side but misery and tragedy and horror. It was like emerging from the ashes like a phoenix, and with this exhilarating feeling of freedom. The tragedy was in me and would stay with me, but for the time being this was the rebirth of Simon Grubman, a new man who doesn't have to worry about the police unless he commits a crime. He doesn't have to carry a passport unless he's going on a trip. I felt like a hunchback with the hump somehow removed, who can straighten out and walk like a man.

After a few days we went to Canton. I was ready and willing to adjust myself to my son the first day, but he was not so willing. I was no daddy to him, I was a stranger who came into the house and changed his life. He cried if I tried to pick him up and I had to fight my feeling of rejection. It was a gradual thing. I wheeled him in his buggy. Eventually he took my hand.

After the second or third day in Canton I was anxious to get to work. I had no fear about my situation. I had a profession. I spoke English. I expected to be able to stand on my own two feet without any help from Sally's family. I just assumed there would be textile mills in Ohio and I would find them.

I discovered quickly that the textile mills were either in New England or down South, and also that the textile industry was in the dumps in 1948 and 1949. Sally's cousins owned a scrap metal business and they suggested that I try working for them on a temporary basis until I found something in my profession. I didn't know what their business was about or what they expected of me but I went down and started doing clerical work, things that didn't require any great ability.

The scrap industry was booming at the time. What began as a boring job became more and more interesting. My cousins found out that I really did know English, even though they had urged me to go to night school and were put off by my refusal. The weeks turned into months and the months to years and I got deeper and deeper into the business, and didn't even think of going back to textiles. It worked out very well financially. The only problem was that Sally and I were big-city people. Canton, Ohio had many advantages, but it was a provincial place.

In the beginning everything seemed just beautiful to me. I had absolutely no criticism of the life in the United States. I thought it was just great. I couldn't understand why Americans griped about high taxes or inconveniences. I was a very appreciative newcomer and saw no faults.

The urge to bear witness was still with me, but even in the family I would hear, "It's over and done, let's not wallow in it." The women would say, "Don't give me nightmares. I'd rather not hear about it."

I was nagged by the idea that American Jews had not done their share during the Holocaust—not even as much as we now do for Russian Jews. But I was a realist and didn't force people to listen to what they didn't want to hear. In the beginning the only thing I criticized was the educational system. I couldn't conceive of a system where the education of children depended on the voting of money by local groups, and I couldn't understand the fear of control from Washington. Anyway, I realized I had had a better education than one could get here, and I found

I could do anything any American could do and maybe better and faster. It may sound conceited, but it's just a matter of fact. I started to climb the ladder of success. My cousins thought it would be a few years before I would be of value to their company. It was no more than a few months.

It was not that I liked the work, but it was no trouble to learn and I became good at it. After a short time I became an assistant manager. That was my job for eighteen years. I left in 1966 because there was no place to go any higher, since my cousin was the manager.

It was a good move. I am now a vice-president of a successful corporation and I have the kind of financial independence that gives me peace of mind. In the beginning my earnings were modest, and I felt very insecure about the future. I wanted to be able to protect my family against my sudden death or incapacitating sickness. Now I can relax a little. I'm not rich, but I'm not insecure.

I am a self-sustaining person. I can live with my records and books. I don't need many people around. I'm not a social butterfly. My Holocaust experiences left me with an ability to cope with life to a greater degree that I had before. I see things more clearly. It gave me a tremendous sense of value—a feeling about what is important and unimportant in life. In a way it made me philosophical rather than emotional. In order to pick up the pieces and continue through life, not as a cripple, but as a human being, I had to build some kind of shell around me. I didn't isolate myself, but I tried to temper any hurt that might come out of an emotional issue with another person.

I have many acquaintances but few friends. I have respect for them and they for me, but I don't bare my soul. Many of my acquaintances are not Jewish and I feel an invisible wall between every Jew and non-Jew. I felt it in Poland. I still feel it here. It has nothing to do with the Holocaust. I just feel that a Jew with a Jewish soul is something of a mystery to a non-Jew.

I'm not a joiner. I belong to the National Association of Manufacturers. I'm on the Board of Federation and I've been on the board of trustees for the temple brotherhood. My involvement there is administrative, not religious.

We didn't join the Reformed temple for religious comfort. We weren't looking for answers to spiritual questions. The temple here is very different from anything we remembered from when we were children in Lodz. I had learned Hebrew and had a *Bar*

Mitzvah but resented reading from a prayer book without knowing the meaning. The only good experience I remembered was when I was between thirteen and fourteen and went to live with an uncle who was a professor in a Jewish gymnasium. Hebrew was taught there as a language and I had to work hard to catch up with his class.

Organized religion in a Reformed American congregation seemed to me to be a social organization. People joined because it was the accepted thing to do. We joined because otherwise if, God forbid, one of us were to die we wouldn't have a place to be buried. And the second reason was to send our kids to Sunday school to give them a feeling of belonging. We were conformists. We wanted to belong where the rest of Sally's family went. The service appealed to us. It was dignified. We see ourselves belonging to a people rather than a religion. So the Reformed congregation suited our needs.

After the camps you either became very religious or completely unreligious. You could either say, "God saved me and I must therefore believe in Him," or you could say, "How can God exist when things like I have witnessed are permitted to happen? Where is our merciful God if innocent children have their heads smashed against walls?"

I was not one to be thankful for my personal survival. I was the one that found it difficult to believe in God after the Holocaust. When I look for a philosophical answer, I only come up with the idea that God gives man a choice of life and death and says "Choose life!" and doesn't interfere with what happens on earth. If God interfered then man would be absolved of his personal responsibility to live by the Commandments. If you can accept this you can remain religious and understand why God didn't act in the Holocaust. My wife has the image of God suffering with his people in the camps. She sees the establishment of Israel as the reward for the suffering. I think the price was too terrible.

I don't know how my sons feel about all this. I think they have deeper feelings than we or even they know. Their feelings of heritage, of belonging to a people, have not yet been tested. When our older boy was growing up our stories overwhelmed him. He didn't want to listen. When our younger son came along we could look at our experiences in a more detached way. We could feed it to him in more controlled doses and he took it much better. He showed more interest and understanding.

The strange thing to me is that now, after all these years, our older son, a man of twenty-seven, is bringing up the subject of the past. He lives in Chicago and during one of his infrequent visits recently he asked me for the first time to tell my story from beginning to end. He remembered snatches of happenings that we had told him when he was a youngster and wanted me to put it all together in a more coherent way, which he was never willing to hear in the past.

The hypothetical question of their marriages is still ahead. Neither seem to be ready, but I've let them know how I feel about intermarriage. I am well aware that it is possible and even likely in the society in which we live. I've told them I won't disinherit them or denounce them if they marry someone non-Jewish, they will not stop being my sons. But I cannot possibly approve of it. I cannot possibly be happy about such a possibility. Sally feels much the same way, except that she feels their happiness is of great importance and she would accept more easily whatever makes them happy. She hopes they will marry nice Jewish girls, but anyone who would make them happy would be welcome in her house.

Our children have marvelous friends. They have a much broader, more humane approach to humankind. Some of their friends are Christian, some are Jewish, and some they don't even know what they are. They haven't asked and it isn't appropriate to ask. So anything can happen.

As the years go by people are more aware of us as Simon and Sally of Canton, Ohio rather than Lodz, Poland, and it's understood that it is better not to ask about our past because the story is unpleasant. Once Sally talked a little to the panelists on the Panel of American Women. It was just informal conversation in someone's living room and the people were so shaken they called me to say they had never heard such a tragic thing in their lives. It was really too much for them.

In a way it is also too much for us. We've both felt that we had gotten over the hurt when we spoke publicly in recent years, but this interview has dragged out many, many painful memories and brought us to a point where we just feel that we've done our share. I'm ready to say enough is enough and also ready to be absolved from any future discussion. I began with wanting to bear witness. Sally and I have seen the tendency to turn survivors from pariahs to heroes. Please don't be shocked. In my opinion survivors are not the best people, not the most noble or the most good-hearted people, or the most ethical. The decent, the superdecent, nice people, the kindest and gentlest were the first to die. They absolutely couldn't cope with what happened. The less sensitive survived . . . with a few exceptions here and there.

If this puts Sally and me in a bad light, we might say that we like to think of ourselves—let me speak of myself—as an error, a mistake. I like to feel that I was also a good person, but according to my own definition I shouldn't be alive today. It's just that death had so much to do, it overlooked a fellow here and there, and I like to believe that I am one of those overlooked.

Now for the remaining years we have I mean to pursue what pleases us most. We would like to travel. We'd enjoy taking courses in a university, not for credit but for the pleasure of learning. We love music and theater and ballet. We've been culture-starved all these years in Canton. Now we'll drive all the way to Cleveland to see the ballet. And we go to New York to get saturated with the things we miss in Canton.

In the last ten years we've traveled to many different countries abroad, and every time we came back here it was with a feeling of relief and a deeper understanding of how fortunate we really are to be in the best country one can live in. Everything is not wonderful and democratic for everyone in the United States but we are far ahead of other countries.

Personally, there is a circle we are now closing, from the horror of what happened, to the liberation, through the busy years of building and raising a family. Now that the children are out of the house and we have the financial security to enjoy a few pleasures, the enormity of what happened starts to dawn on us. It may seem strange that the terrible feeling of loss of our fathers and mothers weighs on our souls much heavier now than it did all the years before. It now hits us that our parents went to their deaths for no good reason, and what a nice life they could have had here with us—in the first country where we've had the feeling of patriotism.

Herman Herskovic was twenty-four years old
when he came to Cleveland, Ohio, in 1945 to study
at the Telshe Rabbinical Yeshiva. He quickly
discovered he was more suited for work as a
businessman than for being a rabbi. He became a
success in the business world and fulfilled his
early ambition in Humenne, Czechoslovakia,
where he had hoped to go to university to study
business administration.

I filled out all the forms and one day received an affidavit signed by a Jacob Saperstein in Cleveland. I was twenty-four years old. I had saved enough money for the journey, and was permitted to take only ten dollars out of the country. I first took a plane to Sweden and then a boat.

I stopped in New York, visited a cousin in Brooklyn and went on to Cleveland. The rabbis in the yeshiva there really treated me royally. But I soon realized that even though I enjoyed the study of Torah I was not cut out to be a rabbi, and that I better think seriously about my future.

Meanwhile the communists had taken over Czechoslovakia and the prime minister of Czechoslovakia had escaped to Washington. When I went to extend my visa at the end of the year I was told at the Czech embassy that they would not extend it, and that I was to return to Czechoslovakia immediately.

I had no intention of going back but I needed to find a way to remain here. I wrote and asked the Czech prime minister what I could expect if I went back and he answered that I would be seen as a suspicious person and jailed. At the yeshiva they told me to take his letter to Senator Taft in Cincinnati and see if he could help me. And it didn't take long before I received a letter from his office stating that he had introduced a bill which would allow me to remain in this country as an alien. I will remember his deed as long as I live.

It didn't take me long to realize what a beautiful and good country this is. I mean, what a pleasure it is to come to New York and nobody asks for your identification card. When I came to Cleveland I had a picture taken of myself and went to a notary public to notarize that the person in the picture is Herman Herskovic. I couldn't imagine living in a country that didn't ask for identification.

I went from Cleveland to New York. The first job I found was selling vacuum cleaners door to door to Slovaks, Bohemians, Russians and Hungarians. I knew all the languages and I did all right. Then after a few months I thought I'd like to try Washington, D.C. It was a holiday, so I checked in at the YMCA and went to *shul*.

You could tell from my clothes and my pronunciation that I was a greenhorn, and a man next to me introduced himself and invited me to his house for lunch over the holidays. He was a very fine person and though I wasn't in the mood to go to a stranger's house I accepted his invitation. We ate together and talked together, and he wanted to know where I was going to work and who I knew. When I told him that the only person I knew about in Washington was President Truman, he admired my courage. He told me his father-in-law was in the supermarket business and that if I wanted a job he could get me one.

The next thing I knew I was behind the counter in a meat market. It was a marvelous job. I had all the salamis and other stuff; my breakfast, lunch and supper were right there and I didn't have to spend anything on food. And in my position, every penny counted. But in a few months I got restless again and decided to seek my fortune in Houston, Texas.

There again I checked into the YMCA, looked over the ads in the paper, saw an ad for people to sell home repairs and I just walked in and sold myself to them. I told them they didn't have to pay me a salary, I would just take commissions. So they gave me two weeks' training and I was out selling home improvements.

Again I did very well and one day I received a letter from the yeshiva saying that the immigration office was looking for me. I came back to Cleveland and by this time Senator Taft's promise had become a reality. I had permission to stay as a regular alien and I could start to seriously plan my future in this country. I decided not to go back to Houston but to make my home in Cleveland.

You see, I met a second cousin in Cleveland from my

mother's side. He came in 1937, ten years before me, and had a little drygoods store. I saw how he was doing business and suggested that I would be willing to go in as a partner with him; we could take turns peddling and do better than he could in his two-by-four store. We peddled curtains and bedspreads and then when people began to have confidence in us we would get them a coat, a fur coat even, and then it was a bedroom set and a dining-room set. These were Bohemians, Italians, Germans and Hungarians; we spoke all the languages and each thought we were one of his people. Then we made connections with certain stores and we would take people to wholesale furniture and appliance stores and then the stores began to extend us credit.

In 1950 I went to the Kane Furniture people and asked if they would extend us credit if we opened a store for furniture and appliances and they did. It was a profitable business for them and for us. And we're still there. We have enlarged until we are occupying three-quarters of a block. My cousin and I are partners now for twenty-six years, and thank God our relationship is very strong, and we hope to be good partners for another twenty-six years.

In 1952 I married a very fine, American-born young lady who didn't appreciate my hard working hours. She felt it was important for me to be home at six o'clock instead of nine-thirty or ten, and that I should leave in the morning at nine-thirty, not seven. She didn't want me to interfere with her social life. But I felt I had to rely on myself and the time to make money is when you're young. Therefore I suggested we should part ways, and we did.

I married again in 1963, this time to a wonderful woman, an angel. My wife's family is also in the furniture business, so she knows what it involves and what it means to be successful in business. We have now a beautiful relationship for eleven years, and she has made me very happy.

I am a very practical person. I knew from the moment I came to this country that this is no place for a dreamer. I asked myself right away, What is the secret of success? What are the ingredients? How much perspiration? How much inspiration? The only thing I was sure was that the possibilities in this country are enormous and it is up to the individual to apply himself. Nowhere in the world is a person more able to make something of himself than in this country.

To be successful in Czechoslovakia one had to come from a rich family. A person from a poor family had no opportunity to elevate himself. I have proven myself that in this country a person who wants to work can succeed. But there is something you have to remember: always be contented, but never be satisfied. I was not one of the people who were afraid to take the risk of being without a job for a few weeks. I wouldn't remain in the same place if the accomplishment was going to be zero. I felt I could do better than just make a living. Courage and confidence is the important thing—and always to look to the future. I visualized that it would be a good idea to spread the money around, and instead of putting everything in furniture to invest in real estate. I'm happy to say we were able to acquire some nice pieces of property, which I call our "pension fund." God willing, once we go out of the retail business we will have enough to take care of our needs.

I see myself as a man living on borrowed time. I made a vow when the boat sank that if I ever get out of that mess I would do whatever I could for my fellow human beings. As soon as I was able to support myself I tried hard to involve myself in the community. I grew up, after all, in a strict Orthodox home. My home today is hundred-percent kosher. Due to the fact that I am in a business which requires that I should be open on the Sabbath I cannot be classified as a hundred-percent Orthodox Jew. I belong, however, to an Orthodox synagogue and I am happy to say that I'm just finishing my seventh year as its president. And, God willing, as soon as I'm out of the retail business nothing would make me happier than to be a *Shomer Shabbes* Jew. It will be a pleasure to go to services in the morning and come hone to a fine meal and a nap, and then go back for more lectures and services —a pleasure.

But right now I cannot afford the luxury. I admire and respect the business people who close on the Sabbath but I cannot do it. Rosh Hashanah and Yom Kippur I close. I make it my business to attend services during the other holidays, but the store is open.

I am a strong believer in Jewish education and serve on the board of directors of the Hebrew Academy and the Telshe Yeshiva. I'm delighted to say that I was a cochairman of the committee that raised a quarter of a million dollars to liquidate the mortgage of the Hebrew Academy. I'm proud when I see seven hundred Jewish children getting a beautiful Jewish education there. I am also serving as the national vice-president of the Union of Orthodox Jewish Congregations of America and the board of governors for the Bonds for Israel. Nothing is too much. Whatever I can do, I'm delighted. My real pleasure is derived from the causes which serve the Jewish community.

My customers are all non-Jewish and people sometimes ask if I have problems with anti-Semitism. I have no problems. If you want to stay in a location for a long time in a word-of-mouth business that doesn't advertise you cannot take advantage. I believe that if I treat my customers honestly and fairly and give them a lot for their money I will have no problems.

I learned a long time ago to stick to business when you're doing business. Once you get personal or bring in religion, you ask for trouble. You can make conversation about the weather and sports but never religion or politics or anything that brings difference of opinion.

When I come home I don't bring my business problems with me. I have a beautiful library with *Mishnah* and the Talmud and the *Encyclopedia Judaica*. I don't read fiction; I have no patience with it. I go into facts. I read current events. I have nice records and tapes to listen to. I enjoy looking at the beautiful old glass I've collected from all over the world, also ceramics and figurines.

When we travel we seek out the treasures of whatever country we're in. Instead of running around after strange women I run around to bring something home of lasting value. And then we can look at the lovely things, and each piece has a story and brings back memories. I enjoy traveling because I can speak all the languages. In Naples I say my father was Italian. In Vienna I say he was Austrian. I feel at home everywhere, not like other tourists.

My thoughts and mind are strictly American. I cannot even visualize myself in Czechoslovakia. This blessed country is the best for me. I hear people say that success is all due to luck. *L-U-C-K* to me stands for Labor Under Correct Knowledge. There is also the factor of being a European and not having anyone to rely on but yourself. You will find Europeans in this country achieve more success than the native-born. I don't want to knock the native-born, but he has the protection of a father, a mother, an uncle and he doesn't have to work so hard.

At the end of the war I had a lot of trouble with myself. I was very bitter toward Germany for what they did, that nation with high intellect and people who knew better. And I was angry at God. When I came home and thought of the fine, religious people who performed all the good deeds, and then vanished the way they did! My Judaism was questionable at that time. I was very weak and I couldn't justify what happened to my family and the people around me.

And then little by little I realized it wasn't the first time. It happened a hundred years ago and two hundred years ago. In our generation it was just on a bigger scale. I just let time be a healer. You cannot live and have grudges forever. I don't bring anything German into the house but I don't see a German as worse than a Frenchman or an Arab. It's all a different generation.

I am not the young dreamer who took off on the boat with five hundred kids to try to get the Palestine. I had no personal ambitions then, no desire to accomplish something for myself. My plans were to live on a kibbutz and help the Jewish cause. Later, as I grew older and wiser, I realized that to do justice to others you have to do justice to yourself, and I began to make plans. After thirty years in this country I know only that this is the only place I could have such a success, and I'm grateful first of all for being an American citizen, for being part of the American Jewish community, and I'm proud that I was able to work to continue the Jewish causes and the Orthodox community.

Ora Kohn from Turin and Milan was twenty-six when she came to the United States in 1948 with a scholarship to the School of Social Work in Cleveland, Ohio, arranged by the Council of Jewish Women. She married and remained to raise an American family in Cleveland.

When the war was over it was a matter of returning to Italy and picking up the pieces. The town we came from had been bombed, and we didn't know if we'd find a roof over our heads. My brother returned ahead of us and got us permission to stay in a remodeled barn on the farm where we had been before, which my brother was now managing.

I wanted to go to work. My father didn't approve of it, but I was adamant. He finally talked my uncle into giving me a job as a stock clerk in his clothing factory. I didn't like it at all. Then I got a job with the Joint Distribution Committee in Milan. They wanted someone who knew shorthand and typing and I asked them to give me six weeks and I would learn. I wasn't perfect at the end of six weeks but it was adequate and I began working. I stayed with an aunt, and then when a relative moved to Israel I bought her little apartment. My brother, mother, father and I lived in this apartment; my mother is still there.

My parents had no wish to leave Italy. Only the Zionists went to Israel. My father did a little consulting here and there but never had a serious career again. My brother didn't get back into law; he managed a paper mill. I meanwhile worked my way up from secretary to assistant to the director for northern Italy. He was involved with rebuilding the Italian-Jewish community and helping Jews en route to Israel, South America, Australia, wherever they could go. We were also tracing missing people, reuniting families and helping the camps that were training people for life in Israel.

One day my boss brought me an application for a scholarship from the Council of Jewish Women for the School of Social Work. He thought it would be a good idea for me to go to the States, get some education and come back to work with him at an even higher level.

My poor mother made the mistake of saying, "Over my dead body." It just made me very stubborn. I was twenty-five years old and I had been deprived of an education, and this seemed an opportunity too good to miss. My father, meanwhile, encouraged me, but he told me not to tell my mother that he agreed that I should go. The only stipulation was that I promise to write every blessed day, and I kept my promise.

Actually I had to postpone leaving for a year, because a large new group of refugees from the concentration camps had come to Milan. These were the toughest group of survivors and they really needed my help. So I didn't leave until 1948.

I was very anxious to go, and had a very idealistic image of the United States as a symbol of freedom, liberty and equality. I wasn't thinking of it as a permanent place to live, because I wasn't planning to separate myself from my family. I thought more about moving to Israel, because of the contacts I had at the Joint Distribution Committee. I worried a lot about the people from the camps going to Israel. They were maimed, physically, emotionally, morally . . . and not at all desirable people, no matter how sad and sorry you were for them. And there was no place for them but Israel. My friends who were taking them to Israel would tell me not to worry. "Their children will be our asset," he said. "They will be a burden now, but we want them." That was very moving, and I wanted to be part of it because that was where the hopes for the Jews were.

I thought very often about going to Israel, but I knew I would have difficulty with my family. Coming here was very different because it was supposed to be for only two years. There was another factor involved that had to do with my tremendous Jewish identity. It was a new kind of self-awareness that developed after we decided not to convert. My sense of Jewishness became so strong it affected me, the way I raised my children and the way I move in a community as a Jewish person. It was not in the form of ritual but a strong feeling of belonging. Whether I was working in a refugee camp or hiding and running like a rat or coming back, having nothing, I knew who I was. No matter what anyone said, I knew for myself, and this carried me along no matter what the circumstances were.

Then I arrived in New York, early in September. I was expecting to be awed by the Statue of Liberty, and all I saw was a little, old, dirty, green lady, completely dwarfed by the great skyscrapers. I was so disappointed. It was like a bad sign that modern materialistic values had taken over and the Statue of Liberty had lost the value and meaning it had in my imagination.

I spent a few day talking with the Council of Jewish Women and then went on to Cleveland. I was put in this family service agency and you know, they give you clients right away. It was pretty funny, because I could speak English fluently with anyone who spoke it like I did, but I had never heard a southern dialect before and found it terribly confusing. I had also never seen Negro people. I remember getting on a bus and there were Negro people and children. The children were so absolutely beautiful I couldn't get over it. All I could do was concentrate on those faces with those great big, black eyes. I was so busy looking at them I forgot to get off at my stop.

I lived in a rooming house near the university with other students. Everything had been arranged for me. I had been afraid that I would be much older than the other students, but this was after the war and there were many older people in the

Graduate School of Social Work—also other foreigners. My only disappointment was that the school itself was extremely boring. It was like kindergarten. We just got a smattering of ideas from psychology, psychiatry, statistics and all that, and didn't go into anything in great depth. I guess my life experiences had matured me beyond the introductions they were offering.

My only problem was listening to and reading a foreign language for twenty-four hours a day. By the end of the day I used to feel that my head was ready to bust. There was also the great difference in approach I had to get used to. I was used to thinking about the problems of hundreds of people, thousands of people. Here I was concentrating all of my ability, knowledge and interest on the problems of a single person, one person struggling over a marriage, a divorce, children's problems, contraceptive information.

I had some innate, undeveloped ability to listen and be supportive. I had learned what was called "interviewing techniques" through life experience.

I was making friends with American students and in a way interpreting what an Italian Jew was. When I thought it would make a difference I fought against some of their values. I was often very shocked by their values. One of the worst shocks was in the house where I lived. I expressed concern for my parents and one girl said, "What are you so concerned about? I'm not concerned about my parents. I didn't ask to be born." This "I didn't ask to be born" really showed me two entirely different ways of looking at the world. I didn't ask to be born either, but there is a certain concern you have for the people who have been concerned about you.

I was very upset when I realized what was happening to Negroes and to Indians and when I spoke about it that was not liked. I remember going back with my roommate to Dallas for Christmas vacation and becoming so incensed by the segregated restrooms and fountains and buses and all the separations of whites and blacks. What annoyed me even more was the "We've come a long way and give us time" response. I didn't think they'd come a long way, and it all hurt me personally. It was as if it were done to me, not the other person. Anything that infringes on a person's freedom is done to me again—this I carried with me from those war years.

In 1950 I finished my studies and packed my trunk to return to my family. My reservation was made. I had really avoided romantic involvement because I knew I was going back and didn't want to complicate my life. Whenever I was invited to dinner at the home of a friend of my boss at the JDC in Italy they would have a young man pick me up. We saw each other on and off this way for two years, with nothing serious between us. Then just as I was ready to go back he decided that we should get married.

You have no idea what a difficult decision that was. I cried so much I got an ulcer in my eye. I called my parents and wrote to them. My mother was very angry. My father wrote the most pleading letter, begging me not to do it. My brother came for the wedding to see what I was getting into. We were married in Minneapolis where his family lived. Fortunately my brother approved of my new husband.

I remember how annoyed I was when I was a student and people would say, "I bet you'd like to stay." And I would say, "No, I want to go home." Then after I was married people would ask about my family and I would say, "They are all in Italy," and they would say, "I bet they would like to come and be with you." It was hard to convince people that they wouldn't. This was not heaven on earth. I was not a refugee. There are many things here that I don't like.

I've never gotten over my distress at the disintegration of family life. I see Jews imitating Americans and depriving themselves of relationships, and parents too busy to spend time with their kids. Howard and I have tried to combat this in our relationships with our three children, but I'm afraid that the American way will affect them and their children and reflect on their Jewishness and their values. I see the denial of responsibility and interrelationship as a kind of spiritual impoverishment.

I realize now that I responded to my own separation from my parents by creating an adopted family of friends as substitutes. I chose sisters, cousins and aunts that became very dear to me because I needed a family. Then, once my parents got over the shock of my marrying a foreigner, they came to visit me every summer. And when my brother married, his wife and children would come too for a family reunion every summer.

One of the problems was that our guests spoke only Italian and our two older boys did not speak Italian. When they were born I purposely spoke only English. I had to be more American than the Americans. When our daughter was born, I spoke Italian to her from the very beginning. She spoke it very well but didn't like it. When she started kindergaretn, she said, "No more." I had to work with what I had, which was my memories, my values and my love. Later, on their own, they learned in college. Both boys went to Italy after graduating and stayed with my family. By now they're proud of their Italian background. They're very nice children. The oldest is twenty-four and is going to graduate from Yale Medical School soon. He is very bright, individualistic and maybe most like me. He was the one who applied for conscientious-objector status and in his application stated how deeply he had been influenced by his mother's attitudes and reactions to what happened in the war.

Bob, the middle one, is twenty-two. He is working for his doctorate in mathematics at Princeton University under a National Science Foundation scholarship. He is very much like his father: bright, kind, thoughtful, sensitive and quiet. His sister Lucy is eighteen, a freshman at Indiana University. She is a bright girl who gets straight A's but has to work for them. She is also sensitive, thoughtful, very capable in a quiet way, also like her father.

It was a kind of pity that none of them enjoyed religious school. They found the classes a terrible waste of time. We had a young Israeli student working at Case Western Reserve give them private lessons and both boys were *Bar Mitzvah*. It was a superficial education, however. Nevertheless, Norman, the oldest, has become an Orthodox Jew. When he was in college at MIT he was influenced by a number of friends and a Rabbi Pollack at the Hillel. He was in a crisis of identity and met a lot of Orthodox people that he respected.

When he came home from college he asked me why I don't keep a kosher house and I told him I didn't know how. I didn't know much about ritual and it didn't seem honest to do it when it didn't mean anything to me. But I told him I would learn and do it for his sake if it was important to him. Anyway, he keeps a kosher home. He's not rigid but he feels right about his decision. His brother is more of a Conservative Jew, but deeply Jewish. He observes all the holidays.

I don't know how much my past has to do with all this. I've always been honest with my children. I've tried to communicate the idea that it was not only part of me but something that has to continue with them and go on from them. You don't just wipe the past out. You try to make something positive out of the negative experience. If you can't pass something on to your children and grandchildren then it has only been for nothing.

I don't know whether my American friends feel this. It's like the way they take for granted that you grow up, you get married and you have children. For too many years I didn't expect that to happen. I see it as something so terribly, terribly precious. For example, I had to raise my kids. I couldn't go to work and let someone else raise them.

I worked at the Family Service until the children were born and then kept on as a volunteer when I could get help. I worked setting up libraries in the ghetto schools and with Women in Community Action through the Council of Jewish Women. I wanted people to know that I, Ora Kohn, am Jewish and can do a good job in the community. I'm always a little surprised that social life in America is so polarized, that one has contact with non-Jews only by deliberately working outside the Jewish community. There was another unpleasant surprise when we were looking to buy our first house and the real estate agent told us that he couldn't sell us the one we wanted because of a "gentleman's agreement" not to sell to Jews. This was very foreign to me. I was more embarrassed than angry because my parents were with me and such a thing did not happen in Italy.

I object to many things in American life. I cannot generalize about anything, but I see something sad in the materialism and the chauvinism and the showing off of possessions. But nowhere else would a stranger be accepted as readily as Americans have accepted me. I will always be surprised by the openness with which I am accepted, and of course I try to reciprocate.

There isn't even a word for "volunteering" in Italy. The concept is impossible to translate. Here it is a way of life. I'm not a clubwoman in any way, but I support the Council of Jewish Women, who brought me here, Hadassah, ORT, Technion University and the Museum of Natural History, the Nature Center, the Youth Center for Shaker Youth, the Museum of Art, the Institute of Music. This is the only country where this would happen.

And I am very much a part of it. I feel very much American. The only thing I have in common with other refugees is that because I am a new American it means more to me and I don't take it for granted. Because I care so much I can become very angry and upset about the things that aren't right.

*Felix Magnus and his family were hiding in the
Netherlands during the war. They all came to
America in 1952 when he was fifty-two, because
his wife, disturbed by her experiences during the
war, wanted to leave Europe. They struggled to
make a living first in St. Louis, Missouri, then in
Los Angeles. They now make their home in
Orlando, Florida, but are still unsettled.*

In May of 1945 we could leave our hiding place and go back to
Breda. The government furnished a rent-free house because we
had lost everything and we brought the children back from all
the places where they had been hidden and they went to school
where we were. My wife, however, was still upset because the
baby, hidden with a wonderful family in Lisse, had died of diphtheria. We heard when she got sick and my wife went there and
held her in her arms. But before she died she asked for her other
mommy and died in the arms of her foster mother. So that was a
very hard thing . . .

We went back to Breda to find there were no houses. All we
could find was a bombed place with a little piece left. And there
were no windows and no water and no gas. Cats and dogs went
through the wall downstairs, and there were no doors whatsoever. We put our belongings down without permission because
we didn't know what else to do. It was like sleeping in a tent,
only a little higher off the ground. The head of the council that
was trying to help the people who had suffered from the German
occupation took my father-in-law into his own house because
there was no place for the old man in our primitive situation.

Later we got a nice house and I went to Germany for an
interpreter job. I worked for the English in the post office, examining the mail to find out who the Nazis were. And while I
was away my wife started to think she wanted to leave Holland
and come to the United States. There were some bad experi-

ences with people who didn't like Jews, and she was afraid for herself and her children.

I agreed without thinking. I was fifty-two years old at the time and if I had any idea of what life would be I wouldn't have dared to go. We had to sell our furniture and things to get the money for transportation. I had a sponsor, Henry Koster, who took my daughter to California to be a babysitter for his children and my wife had family in St. Louis who were willing to help out.

We arrived in New York on December 7 and then went to St. Louis. Again we were separated from our children, in three different families, and I went to try for a job from the Jewish Council. They sent me to a paint factory to pour paint from big containers into small. I was there for eight months until the lead poisoning made me so weak I couldn't stand on my legs. Not being familiar with the laws I took my dismissal and didn't get paid for sickness.

Then my wife and I got jobs in a private school. She was cooking and I was to rake leaves and pick children up in a station wagon. But I was still so weak I would lay down to rest where I could and I made a bad impression; after fourteen days we were fired because of me. Then I met a Dutchman who was a custodian in a public school. He was going back to Holland and he arranged for me to take his job. By then I was stronger and could do it. And my wife had a job as an aide in a hospital.

I tried to do a little business importing tulip bulbs and I bought a little land for a display garden but it was my luck that the land was flooded, so the display was under water. But there were other bad things at the time. I had thyroid trouble and took bad medicines that made me very sick, and then there was an irregularity of my heart.

Six years we lived, struggling, in St. Louis. My two daughters, Helga and Ingrid, became nurses. They visited their sister Anita in California and decided that we should all go there and they would work and take care of me after all the years I took care of them.

We rented a U-Haul wagon and put it behind our '52 Mercury, and we packed it full of the German crystal and porcelain we brought with us and other heavy things—all very stupid. They said we had to have booster springs so we got them and everything went fine till we came to the California freeways. The radiator blew up and the brakes gave out, and most of the time my daughter Ingrid had the wheel, and she had gotten her driving license only a few days before we left.

It was a terrible experience. Instead of going in three days we traveled ten days to California, and the worst was when we came to the desert and the car overheated. When we came to California we sold the car for twenty-five dollars and all we could say was that we were lucky we were still alive.

We lived a quiet, isolated life in California, not knowing people outside of the family. I worked from morning to night as a gardener. I liked that but my wife missed people to talk to, people you could invite to dinner and who would invite you back. She was upset and very nervous. She likes very much to talk but she and I have a completely different philosophy about life. We can talk about things of the day but if we get into a real discussion we differ too much, and one of us gets angry.

The fact that I have been all my life such a bad businessman was a big disillusionment for her. Her parents were big businessmen and she was brought up in surroundings so different from where she has had to live with me. She is a very clean, neat person. Everything has to be just in the right place at the right time. She needs cozy surroundings. And we are always in turmoil, everything in boxes and cartons. We are now living three years in an unfinished house and she is sick from it all. We cannot move because we are dependent upon our children and that of course is my fault. She looks at me as . . . a nice man but a schlemiel.

My needs were so different. I needed more affection than she could give. She thinks kissing a husband is a little dirty . . . you know, and this was hard for me. So I have kept busy. I have a hobby of making rugs and pillows. All my children have their homes full of things I made for them. I no longer have a driver's license because I lost the sight in one eye, but that is not a tragedy. I can manage still to do many things. I am just sad that I cannot give my ideas and opinions. I cannot even say how unfortunate it is when people look only at the things that are bad and the beauty of the other things gets lost. Before the war my wife was always full of joy and happiness, and I don't know what made her turn to the other side.

She is still a great figure, even though sick, and she never lost her strength in organizing and helping out, in seeing things for the family in the right way—and saving us through the war. Without her we would all have been killed. She was a wonderful mother and is a devoted grandmother, and our children are the best you could hope for. She goes to Boston to help Helga when she needs her and to Albuquerque when Alan is sick, or anywhere she is needed.

She is, of course, critical. She gets upset with her American-born son-in-law who didn't have a proper upbringing like in Germany and has ideas and qualities she finds childish and repulsive. And I tell her she is wrong to feel this. He is a very good man, a very helpful, capable man, but she cannot approve of him.

I think it would be easier for my wife to be at home in a Jewish family than a non-Jewish family but none of my four children married Jews. This was, of course, because I didn't go to synagogue. I believed, however, that there was a Jewish inheritance, something inborn, whether we follow the religion or not. There is a common experience, common feelings that are precious. So I regret that I never put a religious stress, or any stress, on my children.

Only once in my life did I talk of such things, and that was with my daughter Helga when she came to tell me she was becoming a Christian and wanted my opinion. I explained to her why I could personally never do such a thing and then she decided not to. My son, however, didn't ask me. He not only converted but became a Christian minister, and his children know nothing of his background.

They are all good children, without bad thoughts and hatreds, and I am very happy about that. I know that they will try to help anybody who asks for their help and they will never go to prison, never do something against the law, never have to be punished for this or that. They received from their parents a good education and love and care, and they will never do anything to disappoint us.

The United States has been good for our family in spite of our isolation. Perhaps I would not have been so alone if I could have gone to a synagogue or a church where people come together, but I could not pray. Praying is something I cannot do. I cannot hate either. That is another thing I cannot do. I cannot believe in a power who would be pleased if I put a *tallis* on my shoulders or ate this or that. I hate to do things in which I do not believe completely.

My wife hated the Germans with a passion, but I couldn't. I don't know if this is a weakness, but I cannot hate. When the Germans were shooting the rockets over our heads I would tremble. It was a sickness of trembling that I couldn't control. And my wife then was so strong. She had no fear, only hatred. Later, when the war was over, she suffered depression and trembling. She couldn't believe that it was peace and she always said to me, "You got rid of your sickness with the bombs when I had no fear whatsoever, but now I have it and can't get rid of it."

She is still hating, but I think it is stupid to hate a people. In Germany people live as you and I. I hope they get educated in a better way than they have been and don't do harm in the future. But I cannot hate them.

The world doesn't get better when you hate. You have to forgive and try to reconstruct and rebuild and do things better than those who have been doing the naughty things and been criminals. Nobody should hate anybody else, whatever they do or have done. I think that is my religion.

People are so stupid, thinking of this moment and not looking to the future. There must be an end to the inhumanity. It cannot go on. Little Holocausts are occurring all over the world every day. When I was a boy I believed there was a God but after the Holocaust I said, "If there is a God who allows such things, let him go to hell. I don't want such a God." But now I see I have to find some people to converse with, share my feelings with . . . Now maybe we'll go once to the synagogue and see what it is there with senior citizens. You know, I am seventy-five years old . . .

Rachella Velt Meekcoms was born in 1928 and was hidden by her Dutch neighbors before she was deported to Auschwitz. After her liberation in Denmark she visited relatives in England and met Daniel Meekcoms. Two years later, when she was nineteen, they were married. In 1952 they came to America with two children and settled in Portland, Oregon.

I said to my husband, "Please let us go to America," and this was the first he heard of my promise to my sister. It was at a time when he wanted to fly for the Israelis. It was really quite strange, because he had lost his parents at an early age and had not been raised as a Jewish boy at all. He was the only Jewish student in his school, but he always spoke up as a Jew and if there was any derogatory remark made he was in with his fists and got many a bloody nose for his trouble. So when he heard they were looking for boys to fly for Israel he was quite ready to help them.

I didn't want him to go. I had just given birth to our first child and was not ready to go through any more pain and agony after all I'd been through. I just felt it would be much better to go to America. He said that it was okay and we'd go. We applied for visas and my sister was our sponsor. Three years later we were on our way.

Then Grandma and Grandpa said, "If you go, we go." They were already in their sixties and I didn't think it would be easy for them to start a new life at their age, but they had never had children of their own and we were their family and they were determined. They sold their home with everything in it and went to Brussels to wait for their visas so they could join us.

We arrived in America in New Jersey, June 7, 1952. We had about a hundred dollars in our pockets, not enough for the fare to Portland, but my brother-in-law paid for plane tickets and sent a friend to take us to the airport and away we flew.

We arrived in Portland on a beautifully clear, sunny day and I really felt I was in a new life, where we belonged. I felt so happy and I can't tell you the reunion with my sister. It was that we are together forever. This is it and we will never move anymore.

We found a little apartment close to my sister and I settled down with my little babies. My husband began looking for work. He had a chance to go on the road as a salesman but I wanted him home. Then Grandma and Grandpa came and we had a houseful of people, and I was home taking care of them and the two boys. When I lived in England Grandma was in charge; in Portland, I was in charge. My husband went into the cabinet-making business, and so we were all together.

At first I was very uneasy about identifying with the Jewish community. I always came out to say that I am Jewish and people could see the number on my arm, but I stayed away from the Jewish community for many years. My husband left it up to me. He was not the strong Jewish influence in our life. But when I became more sure of myself, I changed. I thought to myself, "Be

406

liberal, be nothing." I can't be a nothing. My father lost his life because he was a Jew. I could never forget that.

I decided that I want to identify, I want my children to know they are Jews, I want a feeling of continuity in my family. In 1960 I became a member of a temple. My husband did not like me to tell the children about my background. He would say, "Don't start about that again, Chella. You have had so many nightmares." But it was in my head and my soul. I felt it was important for my children to know their mother as a human being.

Sometimes I think I made a mistake by telling them at too early an age. They turned away from all the pain and I could see why so many Jews turned away from being Jewish after the war. I could no more turn away from being Jewish than I could turn away from being a woman. I wanted my children to have that feeling of not being afraid, of being secure in what they are. At first they would walk away or change the subject, but when they grew up they could listen.

They went to Hebrew school and we observed the holidays. We were not very religious Jews but they learned a lot from me and their school, their *Bar Mitzvah* and their associations with the Jewish community. And I always told them that my life was saved by non-Jews and they had friends from all walks of life and all different backgrounds.

I love people. I've had beautiful experiences with people out of my religion. But when they say, "wouldn't it be better if the Jewish people just integrated with everybody else so there would be no Jews and no Christians, only human beings," I cannot agree. I would like Jewish continuity. I'm a strong supporter of Israel. And I tell my children that for Judaism to survive it's terribly important for them to marry Jews. If we don't continue our Jewishness and raise our children as Jews, it will be as if Hitler succeeded. "If you forget you are a Jew, then you forget your mother" is what I say, and I made my son cry and we both cried because it came so from my heart.

I've tried to explain my experiences to my non-Jewish friends and they could never grasp it. I tried to make them understand that I was a Jewish girl growing up in Holland. I was like the little neighbor girl next door, and it was a democratic country like America. We were free as the birds and there was no such thing as being different. And then the Germans came in and destroyed a people, and my whole family was destroyed. My sister and I and my aunt in Holland are all that is left of a family of sixteen people. And the people who opened the ovens in the gas chambers were ordinary people, and they have to think of that. And when people get upset about what I tell them I say that I want them to be upset, so they should be alert to what goes on in government and see to it that such things can never happen again.

In spite of the things I tell my children they are normal, healthy individuals, quite happy with themselves. They are not scarred. They have a good sense of humor. My daughter Yvonne was a normal teenager, having the enjoyment and fun I missed when I was her age. I never had any teenage years.

I was never sorry that I came to America. Life was good here. We had security and love and a nice comfortable home. I found America a fair country, where we could make a living and spread our wings and make something of ourselves, which we could not have done in England or Holland. My husband is in the building business. Though we've been hit severely by the state of the economy and taken tremendous losses we hope to come out of it. I think we can pull out of it.

I enjoy the high-caliber Jewish people I have met here and especially enjoy my work with the National Council of Jewish Women. I'm the chairman of the senior citizens at the Jewish Community Center. I spend a lot of time with them. I was sorry that my kids didn't enjoy the Jewish organizations but they have Jewish friends.

Vietnam was in full swing when my children were at Kent State and they were actively involved in the marches. I was with my son in his ideas but I was very worried that nothing be done in a violent way. He changed to Portland State and his life was actually in danger. There were vigilantes in the school, really threatening his life. My son was emotionally upset about what went on in school. He talked so much about our government and the Hitler government and the atrocities we were guilty of in Vietnam. There were thousands, maybe millions of youths who felt that way without mothers who went through what I went through, but my experiences definitely had an effect on him. The Kent State killings frightened him to death, and he dropped out of school the next year. Then his number was up to go into the army and he volunteered for the Navy hoping that would be easier. In six weeks he was on a ship off the coast of Vietnam and that's where he stayed for a year. Actually I was not as worried about him there as I was when he was in college. He was in a group growing very radical and I was afraid he was going to be too involved with the radicals. He was very confused. You know the Navy wasn't bad for him. He learned a lot and came out with quite a level head. It put things in perspective. He found that the government wasn't all bad.

I pointed out to him that things could be brought out in the open in America. Watergate was a very important lesson. I watched it very intensely, and I thought it was wonderful how it all came out and the highest official could be thrown out. That is not possible in a lot of countries. The important thing for me is that we can speak out. No matter how dissatisfied we are, we don't have to keep still.

My sons always say about me that if there is something on my mind I tell it as I see it. It's a release I didn't give up even in the camps. Once on a Saturday a bunch of us, Dutch and Hungarian kids, put on a little show for each other and I was the master of ceremonies. We mimicked top overseers and I did impersonations about camp life and somebody did a little tap-dance, different funny, crazy things. The overseers slipped into the barracks while we weren't looking, and instead of giving us a punishment they were laughing their heads off. I couldn't believe it: one day they were hitting us black and blue, and then there they were laughing while we made fun of them. But, you see, in spite of all our agony and pain we never lost the ability to laugh at ourselves and our miserable situation. We had to make jokes to survive and save ourselves from deep depressions.

But when I tell my stories it is not to be funny. If I tell young kids about the atrocities that went on in a civilized nation in a civilized world, with civilized people knowing about it, it is so they should not sit back. They must be active in government and realize what goes on because of what can happen to intellectuals in a civilized, educated country.

Some people became very devout because of what happened and some lost their Judaism altogether; I came out of it very outspoken as a Jew. Whoever knows me, whoever touches me knows that I am a Jew and a survivor. My father used to say to me, "Chella, when you stand in front of a mirror, do you like what you see? Ask yourself. You have to live with that. And do you give of yourself what you really are?"

He taught me a lot in the weeks and months we spent hiding together. The days were long and the nights were long and I learned a lot from him. And when I stand in front of the mirror, I ask myself . . . and most of the time I like what I see.

> *Elizabeth Mermelstein from Viskovo,*
> *Czechoslovakia, went to Prague after liberation*
> *but then fled the Russians. Her sister had been*
> *killed, and she married her brother-in-law while in*
> *a displaced persons camp in Germany. They*
> *applied in Munich to go to America and Israel,*
> *willing to go wherever there was a place for them.*
> *They came to the United States in 1949 and settled*
> *in Oak Park, Michigan, where she operates a*
> *pastry shop.*

When we came to New York there were lots of people welcoming people and we sat like two orphans, with nobody claiming us. Then we heard the loudspeaker calling our names. It was a girlfriend, also a distant relative, who had come three years before and a friend of my husband's who had come ten years before. My girlfriend had a beautiful apartment. My husband's friend leased the Parkside Hotel on Park Avenue, and he brought us there as his guests. And I thought, "Well, this is America." We were so pleased with what we saw we didn't want to continue on to Detroit.

But after two days I wanted to visit some friends. I had addresses somewhere on the Lower East Side. I went there and cried and cried. After two years they still lived in a two-room apartment. The bathtub was in the kitchen, covered with a board, and there were no windows, and when I saw the condition they were living in I wanted to shoot myself for coming to America.

My sister-in-law, her husband and my mother-in-law were already on the way and I couldn't imagine them in this mess with the rubbish piled high outside. They had been wealthy people before the war. They had a six-room home with a cook and a maid, and my mother-in-law was this dainty kind of woman who never put her finger in water. And now they were coming through the Hebrew Immigrant Aid Society and didn't have even a hundred dollars.

They just didn't allow us to take any money. All we had were the two trunks full of things that seemed like treasures in Germany. I'll never forget coming to Detroit with those trunks. New York was such a hectic experience. We had to go to Broadway and the Jewish theater and Radio City Music Hall, and all I really needed was a good night's rest. My husband's cousins all came to the train station to meet us. There were maybe thirty people and they gave us a real warm welcome. They were very curious to see what's in the trunks and we didn't open them for a while because there was so much going on. And finally we opened them to show them what we had *shlepped* across the sea. It was army towels and army shirts and ragged clothes too old-fashioned to wear. They laughed and laughed at our treasures.

We stayed with an aunt for three months. It was awfully hard to get an apartment, and we just started to work. I got a job in a cookie factory. I wouldn't wish it on my worst enemy. It was an assembly line and you couldn't even straighten your back. And my husband got a job in the stockroom of Sam's Department Store for thirty-five dollars a week.

Both of us, meanwhile, improved our English. I was completely lost when I came. As soon as my husband improved he got a job in a linen supply house, where he has worked to this day. Then I stopped working when I became pregnant—except for baking cookies in the basement.

I didn't consider myself a baker. I didn't know how to roll the dough when I was married. I didn't even know how to boil an egg—this is the honest truth. I never liked the kitchen. I knew how to make only one pastry that I learned from my upstairs neighbor who was Hungarian. And everybody who came I offered them the pastry. That's the kind of *berrieh* I was.

My husband's boss's wife always visited with me and one day she said that her son was being *Bar Mitzvahed* at Temple Israel and she wanted me to do the baking for the party. She insisted that I could do it and that we could maybe start a little baking business in the basement. And I said, "You must be out of your mind."

She asked to see my recipe book and I said, "Who has a recipe book?" So she brought me her recipe book and orders for about five thousand pieces of pastry. And then she sent over a freezer and a stove and installed them in my basement and told me to take the cost off the payment for the pastry.

I called up all my Hungarian friends and asked, "What's your specialty?" Everybody had a specialty, and I packed up my flour and sugar and went over so they could show me how and that's how I learned, and in two months I made the five thousand pieces of pastry. It was nothing professional like we do now but it was beautiful, elegant, home-baked and delicious. Everybody wanted to know where the pastries came from and that's how I started my business. Everybody was calling me up, and I never went out for work or to look for clients or anything. The kosher caterers came to me because they knew I was kosher.

Then there was the cute little place, like a Viennese or Budapest pastry shop, that I was in with a Hungarian couple. They couldn't cook or speak English, but they were swindlers. As soon as I signed a contract it was "You're going to dance the way I'm going to fiddle," and I was in bad trouble. He was a sick man and there was a lot of yelling and hollering. I got out even though I lost my money. So I went back to my caterers, and I built my own business up really quickly.

If I wanted to push it I could have made much more out of the pastry business. But we're very contented people. Neither my husband nor I are aggressive about financial what-have-you. Whatever we have, we're comfortable and satisfied. We take things in stride. It's only money. We had everything, we lost it, we climbed up again where we are. As long as I have a roof over my head I don't care what my next-door neighbor has. Maybe these people who are striving to get to the top had a very poor childhood and family life, so they want it. But I was on the other side of the fence. The diamonds and things don't faze me. They just don't mean anything.

My mother had gorgeous china and gorgeous sterling and gorgeous satin damask. The damask was in the linen closet and the china was in the china cabinet and we never ate on the good china because it was saved for company. And everything was left with the maid. Now I use everything I have and it doesn't make any difference.

When we were told to leave they gave us three days. Remember? I made my bed before I left, I swept the floor. I wanted to leave a clean house, so that I would come back and find it neat and dusted, so help me God. And when I came back all I found was a ripped-up house and an older man lying on the floor, dying. And we had this beautiful garden and the wheat was as high as I was and all the flower beds were overgrown with weeds. So I don't want to remember that, I want only to remember how it was before we left it.

You can't always pick what you want to remember, however. I didn't talk about it at all to my daughter when she was a kid. She was always very emotional and I didn't want to burden her with stories from my past. I never even told her that her father had been married to my sister. And then she found some pictures and she was hysterical about it. "Why didn't you tell me?" she cried. She was about eighteen and I told her that she takes things so hard I didn't think she was ready.

I don't like to burden anybody with my problems. Not even my husband! He is a different type, *kvetching* over every little thing. We both have had problems with health. I developed ulcers in Germany and when I came here I was already living on Maalox. Once I was so sick they had to bring me on stretchers to the hospital and I thought it was enough that my daughter remembers me with a hot pad lying on the floor. And then I had the miserable surgery for a gastric ulcer they thought was cancer. But ten days later I was driving a car. And ever since, knock on wood, I didn't have as much as a headache or a cold. But my husband had everything—you name it, he had it. And he wasn't even in Auschwitz. He had kidney stones and gall bladder and a slight coronary and a bleeding ulcer that they couldn't find the ulcers and two years ago surgery for a tumor. But otherwise he's all right. All this was hard for my daughter. Then there were the difficulties with her older sister. She had been in an incubator and had an overdose of oxygen. That was permanent damage.

So why should I have told our girl all the horrifying things? Why give her the pain and agony of Auschwitz? Sometimes if I'm together with friends and something comes up she walks out of the room. I don't blame her. I don't want to hear it either. The way I see it, she knows everything.

She was a very happy child, a big ten-pound baby, and I never had a day's problem raising her until we moved into a gentile neighborhood. And there she was, a Jewish girl with foreign parents speaking Hungarian, and the neighborhood kids making remarks. She had the roughest time in the junior high. There were a lot of anti-Semitic kids, Arabs and Catholics. That's where she started to feel the discrimination. But when I came to the graduation the teacher told me I could really be proud of her and that some day we would all hear about her because she was so brilliant.

Meanwhile religion was her other problem, a big one. My husband happens to be a religious Orthodox Jew. He keeps the Sabbath, and that kept her from doing things and going places. And that's why she just turned the opposite way and doesn't want to know anything about religion. She's a good Jewish girl. She is very American, but she knows her ethnic background and now is old enough not to be so upset about it. Maybe she's even a little proud of it. She gave her daddy her word that she would not marry a non-Jewish guy. I have nothing against gentiles, I really mean it, but I think we have enough problems to iron out without adding any extra.

I don't hate anybody. Believe you me, I don't even hate the Germans or the Arabs. I just feel pity for all the sorrows . . . and I remember how happy our neighbors were when they were taking the Jews away in Viskovo.

Odd that those memories made me an even stronger Jew. They really did. I know people who converted because they didn't want their children ever to have such experiences, but for myself it only made me very Jewish. But I'm not religious. My husband is religious; I'm just a hypocrite, dancing after him. I keep everything but I don't know if I believe in everything. Sometimes I'm sorry we didn't move to Israel. My husband's sister in Israel doesn't keep a kosher house or what-have-you but they're Jews and it's easier for their children. I wish they would settle down and have peace. I feel like they would be my own sisters and brothers. Everything that happens there affects me.

My father once taught me something. He said if somebody hits you with a rock, throw him back a piece of bread. And it once happened just like that. When the Russians came and we were liberated from Theresienstadt they stripped the Germans of their uniforms and they shaved crosses on their heads just as they had done to us and they were in this courtyard under our window, hungry and crying. And I took a piece of bread and threw it down to them. The girls in the barrack were yelling, "What are you doing? Are you out of your mind?" And I said, "It's nicer to give than receive." And I've never forgotten the Germans grabbing for that piece of bread. That's how I feel to this day, and that's what I taught my daughter: not to fight fire with fire, not to hate.

414

*Ernest Michel was born in Mannheim, Germany,
in 1923 into a middle-class family that had had
ancestors in Germany for four hundred years.
Their efforts to leave the country began in 1936,
but they had no relatives in the United States and
even letters sent to the President were not
answered. He was nineteen when he was deported
to Auschwitz and spent five and a half years in the
camps before escaping from Buchenwald. He
found work as a farmhand until he was captured
by American soldiers who thought he was a
deserting German soldier. When he explained who
he was and what he had lived through he became
the mascot of the unit that had captured him. He
came to the United States in 1946 at the age of
twenty-three. He lived in Chicago, Detroit and Los
Angeles, married when he was twenty-five and
settled in New York, where he has raised his
children.*

Can you imagine my feelings? In April of 1945 I was a prisoner
in concentration camp, hardly knowing if I was going to live or
die. Five months later, on November 20, I'm a reporter for a
German news agency testifying and reporting about what had
happened. I became pretty well known at the trial but the Russian prosecution decided that they couldn't use my testimony
because I was German. You see the trials were conducted by the
United States, the Soviet Union, England and France and each
country took a different area. The Russians were assigned the
concentration camps, which was why they interrogated me about
Auschwitz. The Nuremberg trials that began in November went
on until May or June of 1946, and I covered them from beginning
to end. But during that time I decided to leave Germany. I heard
from my sister who was in Palestine, but I decided to go to the

United States. I was twenty-three years old. I had eight years of public school education. I was offered the job as head of the Berlin office of the German news agency and made friends with people who were important in government, but I still decided to make my life in the United States.

I was one of the first immigrants to come under the Truman Displaced Persons Act in 1946. I came with no more than six or seven dollars in my pocket. When we arrived in New York there was all the commotion that goes on when an immigrant ship arrives, and suddenly I heard my name called. The mother of a lieutenant that had befriended me when I first came to Mannheim was waiting to meet me. I had written to tell him I was coming and he sent her to see if she could be of help to me. He was off on the West Coast somewhere.

I knew immediately that I didn't want to live in New York, and after a few days I told the people at the National Refugee Service that I wanted to go to Chicgo, where I had a friend. They were willing to pay my fare to Chicago but after that I would be on my own. My friend in Chicago wanted me to go to college and offered to lend me the money for tuition, but I didn't feel I could accept his help. I decided to get a job and found one on a newspaper in Port Huron. They paid me twenty-five dollars a week and I went there to live. I learned more about America, its history and way of life in Port Huron than I could have learned in a hundred years in New York.

I really got my feet on the ground and started to know what America is about and how the people live. That year I spent in Port Huron I also was going with a non-Jewish girl whose father wanted me to become a Catholic, but I knew it was impossible. From Port Huron I went to Detroit, where I also had some friends. But I didn't stay long. What happened was that I entered a short-story contest and won an automobile. And once I had an automobile I went to California to see what kind of life I could find there.

In 1948 in California I began giving lectures for the United Jewish Appeal and involved myself in Jewish work. I met my wife. In spite of my early feelings we settled in New York, and raised our three children there. I consider myself a very lucky person. I am one of those who survived and was able to put into practice the deep conviction that I want to do anything I could to see that what happened never happens again. My working life, my private life and all my free time is absorbed in this.

It's regrettable that I have no contact with non-Jews, but it is a fact of my life and I can't seem to do anything about it. I have such good feelings about this country and don't think what happened in Europe could happen here. I see it as a young country with many opportunities for diverse views and backgrounds. Many immigrants have found great opportunities here, including those who came after World War II.

I watch the response of my own children to my experiences. They are not religious. They went to Sunday school, not to yeshiva. Our son lives in Israel and will probably be going into the army there. Our older daughter is very much aware of my background and is considering joining her brother in Israel in a year or two. Our younger daughter is not the least interested in Jewish questions, even though she grew up with the same education as the others.

After the war I refused to speak German. I didn't want to have anything to do with anything German. But I found I couldn't live with hate all my life. The people living in Germany today are not those who were responsible for what happened in the thirties.

In 1960 there was an Auschwitz memorial dinner. Among those who were in the camp were Norbert Wilheim, a Jew who decided to file a suit against I. G. Farben, our employer in the camps. I. G. Farben agreed to settle out of court if Norbert Wilheim was willing to represent all the other survivors of the camp and if they would be willing to accept a one-time settlement. The offer resulted in a payment of $5,000 to every inmate of the Auschwitz Buna concentration camp who could prove he had been there any time during World War II. The list amounted to several thousand people living in the United States, Canada, Israel and other countries. Once they agreed to the settlement a few of us decided that we could not take the money for personal use. We decided to create the Auschwitz Buna Memorial Scholarship Fund, dedicated to the memory of those who died but created to give scholarships to the children of survivors who had no parents to pay for their education. The money was turned over to Bar Ilan University.

The scholarship was announced at that dinner. It was a very emotional event. It was the first time in fifteen years that survivors got together. It was also our opportunity to express our thanks and appreciation to the president, the Congress and the people of the United States for making it possible for us to create a new life here. But none of us had the strength to do it again. It just took too much out of us. It was especially difficult for those of us who are committed to the teaching and public relations in the Jewish community that keep the memories of the Holocaust alive as an ongoing commitment.

I know how much I have changed over the years by my ability to go to Germany. I have been back many times and I feel no more uncomfortable than in any other country. I will never forget what happened. It will always be with me. But I cannot live with hate all my life.

Rene Molho, from Salonika, Greece, survived Auschwitz and Dachau and was in the displaced persons camp in Landsberg until November 1945. He tried to return to Greece to finish medical school but was too overwhelmed by mental problems. He married Tillie, his childhood friend, in 1946 and they decided to come to America for education and opportunity not available in Greece. They were sent to Oakland, California, where he took a menial job at Sears Roebuck where he still works.

I was in the Displaced Person Camp in Landsberg near Munich and worked in a hospital, in charge of medical supplies, until November 1945. But I began to suffer from depression. It was odd that I didn't have any mental problems while I was in concentration camp, only afterward. There were the bad dreams and the cold sweats, and I had this idea to arrest the doctor who had killed my brother. I tried once to kill him and I couldn't. It's easy if you have a gun but to try to knife somebody, to hit him until he dies, is not so easy. I couldn't do it. But I traveled around looking for him in Germany and Italy.

Then I went back to Greece. I was penniless. My father was dead. I was twenty-seven years old. My uncle, my father's partner, took care of me but I didn't want to be a burden on him. I went back to medical school to study dentistry and was drafted into the Greek Army. And all the time the dreams were getting worse. In 1946 I married Tillie, my old girlfriend, and we both agreed I needed to change my surroundings. I thought I could start over again in a new country where nobody knew me, where it didn't matter that I had no money even though I once was from a rich family. I didn't want to be in Salonika, where there were only two thousand Jews left of the community of seventy thousand.

Our transportation to America was arranged by the American embassy, where I had a job, and we also had some help from the Joint Distribution Committee. They gave us some money when we arrived in New York and then gave us tickets for the train to Oakland. This was the three of us: my wife, my son and I.

Oakland made a very bad impression on us. I thought to go to school to finish my studies, but instead they got me a job as dishwasher, and my wife had a job in a factory. And when we went to the grocery store the grocer took twice the money he should when he saw we didn't speak English very well.

After two weeks as a dishwasher I went to a warehouse to be a shipping clerk. It was a hard time, with us both working and our little boy crying in nursery school because he couldn't speak English. Then I got the job at Sears, where I am to this day.

We settled in. We became citizens. I joined the Reformed Temple Sinai and we found three or four other Greeks to be friends. Once a year we got together with Sephardic Jews in the Sephardic Temple in San Francisco, all survivors, and also with survivor friends we have weddings and *Bar Mitzvahs*. We also have American friends. And at my job at Sears people take me for a Frenchman. They don't know enough about Judaism to recognize me for a Jew. But I tell them right away that I'm Jewish and Greek, because if I hear an anti-Semitic crack I get very, very mad and I don't want to hear.

Our son grew up here in California. He had the usual Jewish education and went to college. He's a very intelligent man and very successful in his computer work. He is just like all his American friends. He was always ashamed of me. I had an accent. He refused to speak anything but English with us, so he never learned Greek or French like he could have. He could never understand our experiences. He wouldn't listen, really.

He didn't marry a Jewish girl. He doesn't think Jewish. What we need is another Hitler and a war . . . for about a month. You think I'm kidding? There is a French poet by the name of Alfred de Musset, and he wrote that in order to feel and to live, man needs tears in the same way plants, in order to flower, need water.

There is a lot of bitterness for us about our son. What Hitler couldn't do to us with killing, he has done. My daughter-in-law is a very nice girl, a very excellent girl—but not Jewish. But what could we do? He was twenty-six and on his own. That's why we say maybe we need a little more anti-Semitism in this country, so people wake up before it is too late and we are all gone. We don't see much anti-Semitism here. My son never saw any. People make a fuss that four Nazis are marching in San Francisco. They don't disturb me. Twelve people? Twenty people? I see them as crazy people who belong in a mental hospital. When I see the uniforms I shake a little, but I try to give my logic to it. Maybe if there were eighty I'd worry, but just for a handful I don't upset myself.

I'm against violence, any kind of violance. I can't condone violence because I've seen too much of it. And it has had its effect on me psychologically. I know I'm not normal in my reactions. They are more normal now than when I came out, but that life for years, and somebody having the power of life and death over you every minute, and the torturing . . . and then you are out and you have a son and he does something bad and your reaction is too strong. The traits of the people who hurt you come into you, and in order to keep it under control you have to be very, very strong. And the more educated, the more sensitive you are, the more affected you are. I'm sure our problems with our son are because of this. I'm sure. And my wife too has felt this.

Another sadness for me is what happened to the United Nations—that the body that stands for brotherhood, and logical people, learned, intelligent people, should say Zionism is racism. Maybe it will wake people up. I don't want anybody to be hurt. I am really a pacifist. But sometimes a little anti-Semitism is good for Jews.

I went to Israel six years ago. I would like to go back. I have the feeling there that it is the only country in the world which I can think is mine, where I really belong to something. Even my son felt kind of Jewish there. But it was a mistake for me to go to Yad Vashem. My son practically carried me out.

But I don't hide from it. I read books, in French, Greek and English. I began to read *Exodus* at six-thirty at night and read through the whole night till the sun came up. And there is another book I liked very much, *The Painted Bird* by Kosinski. I read all his stuff. He is a very strong writer.

I wish I knew how to write. The books about the Holocaust I've seen so far are too mild, much too mild. Americans cannot imagine it, and they do not feel guilty about allowing such slaughter. And the crimes were mostly greeted by silence, not just by the Americans, by the English government, the Vatican, most of the world.

I really became strongly Jewish because of the concentration camp. And I am happy I am here in America. I may criticize what is wrong but I couldn't live any other place. I am changing over the years. I am less liberal than I was when I came, less anti-German in terms of the new generation, but not less Jewish. I understand when people say they are Americans and not Jews and they think they are protected by forgetting their identity. It happened in Germany before Hitler. We knew many people who did business with my father and they would say, "I'm a German, not a Jew."

I understand it, but I don't agree with it. I think it's stupid. When someone tells me that's how they feel, I say to them, "The day will come when somebody will remind you that you are Jewish."

Tillie Molho, the wine-dealer's daughter from Salonika, Greece, was hidden in Athens by Greek friends during the German occupation. Her family survived, though her father never recovered his business. When she was nineteen she married Rene Molho. All of his relatives died in the concentration camps. He had lost everything and had no place to go. She persuaded him to go to America in 1946, expecting him to finish his dental school training. They were sent to Oakland, California, however, where they had a hard time adjusting to a new language and a new life.

After the liberation we walked in the street, finding our friends, kissing and screaming. A big thing! We survived!

And we went to the house we used to own and a Greek family was living there. They were collaborators with the Germans. And we told them the Germans had gone and we were going to live in our own house, and they didn't want to leave. My father said, "What do you mean? It's your house? This is my furniture, my dishes. Everything is mine." The man offered to settle for half and my father said, "Nothing doing. You have to get out of here." And then we found some other Jewish people who were liberated and they came in and said, "Either you go or out you go over the balcony." So they left, and we moved back into our home.

Then my father went to his Greek partner in Athens. They were close as brothers; the families would stay at each other's houses and eat together. And when the Germans came, my father made false papers selling his part of the business to him so the Germans wouldn't confiscate it. Now my father went to get his share of the business back and said, "Thank God, we survived and we're here." And his partner, who had been like a brother to him, greeted him with, "What do you want?" He said he had my father's signature and that the papers weren't fake to him. My father couldn't take him to court because he had trusted him and signed the business over.

So we started from nothing. I went back to finish high school. I lost two years but I had studied by myself and just took the examination for the diploma. I was eighteen. My boyfriend came back from the concentration camp and we took him into our house. He didn't have any place to go. He had lost everything. When I was nineteen we were married. My little boy was born when I was twenty.

It was a very hard time. My father borrowed some money and tried to start a little retail business. It was like my father and brother had a pair of shoes between them, so they could go out only one at a time. And people were coming back from the concentration camps and we opened our hearts and our home, and anyone could stay with us until they found a place.

It was my idea to go to America. My husband wanted to be a dentist in Greece, but he could get a priority on the quota because he lost his whole family. I kept saying, "Let's go. Don't be afraid. Don't worry, we'll work and make a go of it."

So I left my family in Athens and we went. It was very hard at the beginning. We stopped in New York to visit an old aunt of my mother's and it was very, very cold. It was the end of January and I had to stay in with the little boy.

And then we went to Oakland and this old couple met us at the train and took us to an old, old apartment house where we had one room and a little kitchen and a bath we shared with lots of people. It was a very run-down, depressing place and we didn't know a soul. My husband could speak English so he began calling people about jobs, with no luck whatsoever. He went to the Jewish Federation and they gave him his first job, as dishwasher. He kept saying he was a dentist and that he never washed a dish in his life.

And then they asked about me and what I could do. They sent me to a factory where they made ladies' coats. I didn't know a word of English, and all the way there the woman was teaching me, "Needle, needle, needle . . . thimble, thimble, thimble." They gave me a job sewing buttons for seventy-five cents an hour. It was my first job and I was very excited. I didn't know anything. I didn't stop for coffee breaks because nobody told me anything. I brought a sandwich wrapped in newspaper. I didn't know about wax paper. I didn't know how to go to the market

423

and buy things. Later I met a German Jewish girl and she took me and showed me. I became her protégée.

Everything I did was wrong. I came to work in my beautiful handmade Greek dresses. I had no sloppy clothes. I was in a factory all dressed up like for a party. I couldn't communicate with anybody. The first thing we bought was a radio. And then my husband was a European man, and didn't do any housework. So I worked all day and then came home to do the shopping and the laundry and clean house and take care of the baby, and he wouldn't move to help me.

One of the girls in the factory told me to tell my husband to vacuum the house, so I went home and said, "You better vacuum the house." He said, "Me?" And I said, "Yes, you." He said he never did it before. I said I didn't either. I don't believe in the women's lib, I'm against it, but I had my experience in those days to get my husband to help with the housework.

It was very hard for me. I had come from a nice family. We had a maid. I had never worked in the house. And suddenly I'm in a strange place, I don't know the language, and it was like finding myself in the gutter. And I knew it was all my fault. I didn't want to cry or complain to my husband. I knew he would say that I wanted to come. So I swallowed my tears and wrote my mother all kinds of lies that we are living in a beautiful house. I didn't tell her my little boy was sick and we were in one room and the window is broken and the heater doesn't work.

One miserable Pesach I wrote and said, you know, that we were invited to the nicest people and had the best holiday and it was all fabulous lies, because we were alone and had nothing really. But I was very strong, believe me. My father had told me before we left, "Listen now, you want to go, I don't have the right to stop you. But if you don't like it, if anything goes wrong, you come back here. Here is your home and we are here and don't worry about a thing." But I didn't want to go back like a loser, like, "Here I am, we couldn't make it." And we did make it. I have never regretted coming here. I love America. I've been back to Greece many times, and I know we did the right thing. You never know with that government. My father really supported the king, but the Jews in Greece don't mingle in politics. They have to go with the changes in the wind.

So I went to night school to learn English, and I also learned to use the comptometer machine. And then a friend of mine came from Greece. She knew English very well and was working for Blue Cross and she got me a job there. Rene went to work for Sears and that was better for him. We had friends and we bought a little old car and a television. It was much, much better.

My son, however, had a hard time, poor thing, like my husband. We had to send him to nursery school and he didn't know the language and couldn't ask for anything. I used to leave him there in the morning, looking out of the window, waiting for me to come home. He had been so spoiled, growing up in a house with grandparents. He was a little king in their house. Then suddenly we drag him away; it was bad for him.

We did the best we could. We joined a temple and prepared him for his *Bar Mitzvah* and he went to confirmation class and postconfirmation and had lots of Jewish friends. It was just after he went to college that he became less and less Jewish.

He never made fun of us. He came on Pesach and Yom Kippur to please us. He just got the idea that religion is something that separates people and that it's a business to make money. "It's money, money, money," he would say, and show us how rich the Mormon church was and the Catholics and all. And if I said, "Sam, look at what your father went through for being a Jew," he would say, "If everybody was the same, they wouldn't have to kill all those people."

I don't know, we lost him somewhere. The little girl he married doesn't believe either. She's from a Catholic family and went to Catholic school and everything. I was hurt, but not as much as my husband. I felt I had to pretend it's a normal thing. I had to be the diplomat.

I try to help him not to be sick. When we first married he had these terrible nightmares and used to wake up with sweats. I used to say, "Come on, it's all right. You are here. I am here. Don't worry." And then it got less and less. Now he gets together with his friends from concentration camp and they talk for hours. "Do your remember when they did that to me? And the soup!" I've heard those a hundred times. I don't know why they do it— to punish themselves? But I listen. I never interrupt. I never say "That's enough!" And he reads all those books about it, I don't know why. I like to read happy things and funny things. I like nice books, not depressing things.

If anyone criticizes America during the war, I feel the only thing I know is that they liberated my husband from a concentration camp and that's good enough for me. I think it's a good system of government and if anyone doesn't like it they should go someplace else and see the government. I'm not kidding. They can go anyplace and they'll see if with Nixon we're not the best off. My husband and I don't agree with politics. Whatever he tells me, I do the opposite. If he says vote for this guy, I vote for the other one, and that's it. Actually, he used to be more liberal and became more conservative, and I used to be more conservative and am more liberal. So the truth is we're coming together.

We are lucky to have many good, close friends from Greece and from America. We are like a family with our Greek–Jewish friends who were in the camps, or hiding.

A few years ago we went to Israel and I felt real high and tall and it was a place to walk with your head up. But to go to live there seemed too hard. I feel a little sorry for the people who live there. I guess I am more an average American housewife, except maybe that I am always for the loser, for the underdog. Even watching a football game, I am for the losing team. I was always like that.

But the main thing is, I'm glad I'm alive. I wish everybody could have survived. I guess I was one of the lucky ones. I couldn't prevent what happened. I was hiding because of Hitler. He was there when we were there and that was it. It was a long time ago and I'm adjusted to America. I feel good because we live in this country, and America has been good to us.

Rose Rosenthal from Paris and Aix-les-Bains came to New York City in 1942 with her family. She learned English quickly and went to City College to study psychology. She presently lives in Houston, Texas, where she teaches French in a high school.

When we were in school we heard that the United States was in a very bad way, that there were no cars and no gasoline and that even President Roosevelt took his bike to work. We didn't know he was a cripple who couldn't get out of his wheelchair. That shows you the kind of propaganda that was used. But even so, I expected everybody to be wealthy and live in huge buildings like the pictures of New York City. But mostly America represented freedom. It meant life instead of death.

We were still afraid to go. Our friends said they wouldn't dare take a ship because of the submarines and the mines and all. And my mother kept saying, "I would rather we all die together than be separated." Yet when the visas came she said it was our one chance and we should go no matter what: "If we die, we die. That's it." I thought of going as a tremendous adventure, and I felt we would be safe.

We took the train to Marseilles and then went to Lisbon. I remember one night sitting up in the railroad station on the border, and it was very cold because we were in the Pyrenees. In Lisbon we came together with other Jews and everything was arranged by HIAS. We left on the last neutral ship to leave Europe. My father paid $500 apiece for us, from the money my mother had sewed in the clothes.

We went first to Dakar and then to the Canary Islands and then Bermuda. From Bermuda we came to Baltimore and were taken by bus to a camp. Everybody cried when they saw America. This emotion you read about that people feel when they come to America is true. But that camp they took us to was the worst psychological thing that could be done to anybody. We had been three weeks on a ship, seasick and miserable, and we couldn't get off when they stopped. My parents expected that we would put our luggage on a train and go right away to New York when we landed. Instead there was all this confusion, pushing us on the buses, and no one spoke French or Yiddish to tell us what's going on. We went into this camp with two huge houses, and the men and boys went to one building and the women and girls to the other; with the two buildings separated by a chain-link fence with barbed wire. And it looked just like ae pictured work camps to be in Germany.

Here were people who escaped from everything bad and they are brought to a country that is free and are put in jail. We were in one big room with cots. This is where I learned to make hospital corners on beds; the guards taught us how. But they couldn't communicate. They spoke only English. Everything was in sign language. They were rough, cold people doing their job, not understanding our feelings.

Downstairs in the basement were the bathrooms. There were twenty toilets lined up, with no separation between them; there were showers lined up without curtains. The people had come from a civilized country and were used to social graces. To sit on a toilet in front of twenty other people was the message that we were in jail. Also, the only time we saw the men was at meals.

They said our luggage and papers were being processed, but it was the atmosphere that frightened us, the uncertainty of not knowing what would happen next. Each day some people left, but we didn't know if they went someplace in the United States or were being sent back or taken to a work camp. We stayed about a week or so, and in that time some people went insane. The children felt it and didn't play. We just sat around, waiting.

Then finally everything was checked out for smuggled things and for spies, and we were taken to Baltimore in a car and the Red Cross took us over and things were fine. But that week was my worst experience. I have never been able to stand a chain-link fence because it reminds me how frightened we were.

We came to New York in July 1942. I was thirteen. My uncle came to meet us in the most gorgeous car I had ever seen. It was so black and shiny, and I thought to myself that everything I imagined about the United States was true after all. He took us to his home in Seagate, where his family stayed in the summer. He was a very wealthy dress manufacturer and owned apartment buildings and things like that. He and my aunt, my mother's sister, had come from Poland thirty years before.

My uncle lent my father the money to buy a small grocery store in East New York and we moved to the neighborhood of Howard and Pitkin avenues. I went to junior high school and luckily met a little girl two doors down from my apartment who spoke Yiddish, so she took me under her wing until I learned English.

My parents always spoke Yiddish. They still do. Okay, my mother speaks French, but when she speaks French it's 50 percent French and 50 percent Yiddish. When she speaks English it's also 50 percent Yiddish. If you understand English, French and Yiddish, you can understand my mother—otherwise you don't understand her.

I learned English in a few months. The most difficult thing for me to adjust to was having boys in the classroom. In France the boys went to their own school far away, and you never mingled. If you did you were a loose girl. And suddenly I'm in junior high school and there is a boy sitting at the next desk. I don't think I stopped blushing for the first three weeks I was in school.

The eighth grade is very strange. You have some students who are big and grown-up and some who are still little. I was one of the little ones and I made friends with another little girl who spoke French. There were no other immigrant children. Later, when we moved to Washington Heights, we met German Jews.

My parents had a hard time starting a new life. My father learned English quite well. He depended on my uncle for quite a long time. He and my mother worked like dogs from morning to night. My sister and I at one time decided not to speak French anymore. But when my friend Fanny came from Aix-les-Bains it all came back to me. She was the only survivor of her family. She stayed with us and I introduced her to my friends and made blind dates for her. We compared our educations because we had both graduated from high school. Hers was greater, because French schools are much harder than American schools and go much deeper into the subjects.

I went to City College and majored in psychology. My friend Fanny got a job with Air France. I met my husband while I was at school. I had many friends by then. Being French gave me a certain status. Everybody was Jewish, but this was something special. And my parents by then had quite a nice grocery in Washington Heights, so there was no reason to be looked down upon.

I was married in 1950. My husband's family was surprised that he chose a refugee. His father's family had been here for five generations. They lived in a small town in Middletown, New York, and went to a Reformed synagogue. My husband had no Jewish education and he was brought up to think that native-born Americans were better than refugees.

We settled in Queens and I had a child a year and a half after my marriage. I didn't speak French to my daughter Vivian but I did try it with my son Larry, who was born two years later. But it made her jealous because it made him different, so I stopped.

My friend Fanny settled in Houston, Texas. We went to visit her on vacation and liked the city so much we decided it would be a better place for the children to grow up in than New York. Five years later, in 1956, we moved to Houston. It was a big change. Suddenly we became conscious that we are Jewish. In New York we never had to think about it. We went to all the synagogues and picked one to join. And the funny thing was that my unreligious parents became religious after they retired. They began going to synagogue on Friday and Saturday and celebrated all the holidays. Most of our friends in Houston were Jewish, though my husband's business acquaintances were not.

Our children went to Sunday school and Hebrew school. Ms son was *Bar Mitzvah*. They are both very conscious of being Jewish. They have gone out with non-Jews but there was never a question but that my daughter would marry a Jew. They're very conscious of my experiences. I never sat them down and told them the story of my life, but they heard things and I told them things. One of my father's childhood friends came and told that no one was left in their town. My father's brother was in Auschwitz, and my aunt was saved by a convent orphanage in France.

They would hear my violent discussions with people who could not understand why the Jews do so much for Israel and the ones who said that they never heard of anti-Semitism in France. Our feeling about Israel came to us gradually and became especially strong in Houston, because our identity as Jews became much stronger. I really believe that Israel is the only hope for the Jews. If there is to be persecution there should be a place to run to.

My daughter wants to live in Israel. She went for seven months and came back very idealistic and very convinced. Her husband, however, is not yet sure. So she is trying to get him to change his mind. You know, I don't personally want to live there, but it has to be there as a haven. My parents can't understand my daughter. They think Israel is a wonderful place but life is so good here, why go there?

I remember my mother's first reaction in New York when she turned on the radio and out came a program in Yiddish. To her, this was the utmost in freedom. This couldn't happen in France, in Poland, anywhere she had lived. The idea that she could go down the block and get a Yiddish newspaper and nobody would call her "Jew" was something incredible to her.

My own feeling of appreciation has to do with citizenship. I was a citizen of France because I was born there. I renounced this citizenship when I became an American citizen, but I was always conscious of the fact that my parents were not citizens in France. They couldn't vote. They had to carry their papers with them at all times. And I remember how hard it was for them just to make a living.

I get so upset when people don't vote, when they don't accept their responsibilities as citizens. I feel much more strongly about America than the people who were born here. Americans think everything is coming to them and don't really appreciate what they have.

I've been very busy teaching. I teach French to sixteen-year-olds. In the morning when I am standing up to salute the flag I can't stand to see the kids slouching around, not wanting to stand up and show respect. I get very angry with them. I'm not against disagreeing with the government. I thought it was wonderful in the sixties when we had the protest against Vietnam. It showed that here is a country where you can show your feelings and speak against the government without thinking you're going to be killed. Where else can you do this?

It's alright to challenge the government for a cause. But these kids slouching around, thinking they're so smart, have no cause.

I try to tell them about France and Germany so they can make comparisons. They are quite interested in how I escaped from France and the whole business with the underground and going to unoccupied France. They like to hear about our playing cat-and-mouse with the Germans. It's for them something exciting, like a James Bond movie.

Even though I'm not observant I make a point of not teaching on Jewish holidays. I want the children to know that I am Jewish. They are always surprised that I can be French and Jewish, and I explain how it is. I think children must be made aware of what happened so they do not take American freedoms for granted. And I think they should be aware of the possibility of Jews being killed for no other reason that the fact that they are Jewish and different. I think all students should see the films of the camps and read the books and know why Israel is so important.

Last year we had an American Field Service student living in our house. He came from Argentina and was Catholic. We welcome anyone except a German or an Arab. We belong to the Institute of International Education and foreigners are frequently guests in our house. It worked out very well. My son went to visit the boy's family in Argentina. They enjoyed each other. But this year two foreign students came to the school, one from France and the other from Germany. The German girl was in my French class. I introduced her as "Gisella, our new foreign student from Germany," and the kids immediately gave me that look to see how I felt about a student from Germany. You could just feel the silence like a blanket over the whole class.

As soon as I could I sent her on an errand, and then I said, "Look, students, I want you to realize that the Germans I hate are not the ones born in these days. I hate their parents, but this has nothing to do with Gisella's generation. Children are not responsible for their parents." And I could feel the answer in their eyes.

Stephan Ross from Lodz, Poland, spent five years being shunted from one slave-labor camp to another. He escaped and was with the partisans. His parents were killed at Treblinka. The Quakers arranged his journey to America when he was seventeen. He now lives in Boston, Massachusetts, and is a psychologist, married, with two children. He works as an administrator of Community and Student Affairs at Northeastern University in Boston.

I didn't choose to come to America. I was selected by the United States Committee for Children from an orphanage in Germany. In 1941, before my family was taken away to a town near Lublin, my parents sent me to a farm. I was maybe eight or nine, but there was nothing to eat where my parents were. People were dying of hunger, and some were eating their own relatives when they died. That's how bad it was. I used to steal potatoes from the fields, stuff them into my shirt and pants and bring them back to my mother. When the farmer's wife gave me some bread and milk to eat out in the field where I was working I would save half to bring to my mother. But she didn't want to take, she would say, "Eat it, here." It's impossible to describe my feelings about all that.

Then the family was sent to Treblinka, except that I didn't know where they were, and I had five years dragging around in eleven different camps. Then I was with the partisans and they taught me to cross myself and pray in Polish and what to say if

I'm captured by the Gestapo. But the biggest problem was that the Gestapo would check for the circumcision, and if they found it you were done for. I don't want to go into all the details. It's all in a paperback, *Prisoners Of War* by Philip Hirsch. Chapter 5 is my story. He interviewed me and paid me $200. All the details are there.

Anyway, when the war was over I was freed by the Ninth Armored Division, and I ended up in an orphanage on the Chiemsee. The Friends and Quakers came to tell us about life in the United States and how we could adapt ourselves, and in 1948 I was brought to a hotel in New York.

I couldn't speak English. I couldn't read or write anything. I could just speak Polish, German, Russian, Yugoslavian, Yiddish and Ukrainian. But if I needed to write a letter to my brother who was in Germany I had to find someone to write it for me.

I was in New York for about six months and then the Jewish Family and Children's Service sent some of us to Boston. We were very mature for our age because we had suffered so much, but we were also very frightened. I had a broken back; I was beaten by the Germans with rifles and they broke my spinal column and it grew together wrong. But I was afraid to tell people I had a bad back because I was scared they'd send me back to Germany. We were very experienced in reading people's behavior, but they didn't have sensitivity to us. For example, they saw us boys clinging to each other with a kind of dependency and closeness that doesn't exist here. The professional social workers throught we were homosexuals and they brought us to a psychiatrist. He asked us, "Do you sleep with each other?" I said, "Yes, I sleep with my friend Mike and he sleeps with me." And this indicated to him that we were homosexuals.

It wasn't so at all. We loved girls and we all had girls we were very fond of, and we wanted to love and be loved. We just clung to each other because everything was so strange and we had so many problems.

I found a job in a plastic factory where I made thirteen dollars a week, and went to the Berlitz School for English lessons. And then the Jewish Family Service paid my tuition to the school in Lenox, Massachusetts. I was about eighteen and I'd never been to school before. I did all right. I was there for three years. I had a very good relationship with the other kids and I was in the student government. I also worked in the furnace room to pay for my room and board.

One Christmas some Spanish-speaking boys from Mexico took me to midnight mass and I was crying all night long: "Where is my father? Where is my mother? How come all this happened to me?" It just hit me.

Then I was drafted during the Korean War. I tried to tell them about my back and they thought I was faking. But when they saw it was really serious I got out on a medical discharge and went back to Lennox. I finished school but I had no other home. I went to Bard College for a year but I couldn't pay the tuition, and they were kind of shook up because I couldn't pay back the loan.

Next I found a job on Cape Cod and lived in a little basement room in Hyannis. I worked at a gas station and saved my money until I had enough to go to Goddard College. It was a small school and cost about two thousand a year. I also had a family in Malden I stayed with, and they let me stay even if I didn't have the ten dollars a week to pay them.

When I graduated from Goddard I was accepted in the Boston University School of Social Work. I always wanted to do social work. It was in me. I wanted to bring about a better understanding among people. While I was at Boston University I lived and slept in my car. It was an old broken-down 1939 jalopy with a rumble seat. I learned car fixing in the gas station and tried to get it to last the year. I also had a dog, a big shepherd, and he lived in the rumble seat and I lived in the front seat until I got sick with pneumonia. Then I went back to the family in Malden and they took me in.

I was very disappointed with the people in the School of Social Work. They talked about dignity and love and affection, but when it came time for them to be human beings they were fakers. I switched to the School of Education, and when I completed my master's later on, in 1967, I went to the dean to tell him I finished my task, no thanks to him. I was only able to pay for my tuition when I got my restitution money from Germany.

I was working all those years at Columbia Point, a housing development where I was the director of education, providing programs for all the age groups. I had a group of Jewish senior citizens that I sang Jewish songs to, and I helped them with the housing authority and the police. Some were dying and needed homemakers or nurses. They were the urban renewal refugees, the mommies and daddies of children who didn't want to identify themselves. I used to wonder how I would feel if my children put me in a housing project and forgot me. And with the kids I was coaching basketball and baseball and running talent shows. I never volunteered information about myself. Some saw the number on my arm and knew I came from Europe, but that was all.

I'm not a person who goes around advertising my life, but sometimes it just comes up. I was talking on delinquency and I got a question about my own experiences, and it was hard to share them. I'm not ashamed that I came from poverty. I lived in the gutter and I'm not ashamed to talk about it. I was poor but I feel proud that I came from a respected family. We were just made to live that way because of our religion.

I respect people who don't push their weight around with who they were and where they came from and what they are now. I think you should tell people who you are without putting on airs. I say just be yourself. Most people don't want to be themselves. They come through with a veneer in front of them.

I enjoyed working with all kinds of older people. The professionals tell you not to get too intimately involved with people. I tell you, you've *got* to be intimately involved if you want to do something for them. Sometimes you even have to let them know who you are.

The Hillel at Boston University used to invite me to talk to young people. I used to tell them a little bit about my life and how fortunate they are to have been born here, with homes and families, in a world where they are not persecuted. It's hard to convey such a message when there are good times and people can't imagine anything else.

I had no difficulty establishing rapport with kids, black or white. While I was going to school I worked for United Community Services and they sent me to different areas in the city as a kind of troubleshooter to find out why kids are on drugs and why they're hanging out on corners. I was in Hyde Park, Roxbury, Dorchester, Mattapan. After I got the master's in education at Boston University I supervised students and taught at Northeastern. In 1973 I completed four years of part-time study at Northeastern that earned me a Certificate of Advanced Graduate Studies.

I'm always looking for things, always have an iron on the fire; I always have something going. At the moment I'm the administrator of community and student affairs at Northeastern. I also supervise counseling services and work as a community affairs liaison. I go to meetings, learn what happens in communities on a daily basis. I find out what happens with schools, with integration. We have about two hundred and seventy people spread out throughout the city doing exactly what I'm doing.

We work with delinquents and predelinquents, to help with employment, occupational information, recreational activities. We introduce kids to what is going on outside their poor neighborhoods, and I've been able to place many kids in colleges who never would have known by themselves where to go and how to get there.

My latest effort was to get my license as a psychologist from the state of Massachusetts. When I was in college I felt like I was digging for gold when I was reading a book, that adding to my knowledge was like accumulating bags of gold. In those twelve summers that I worked in the gas station at Hyannis I would read between customers. I devoured the great Russian, American and French novels. And I still have this passion for learning new things.

I am an individual who does things spontaneously. I don't meditate. If there is a problem I sit down with my wife and we discuss it and figure out what to do. But mostly I learn and function by ear. Something happens. Action is required. I act, I make mistakes. I learn from my mistakes.

I remember when I was a frightened kid in Germany. I had tuberculosis and I knew they'd never let me come to the United States if I wasn't healthy. So at the moment I was supposed to go behind the X-ray machine I pulled over this healthy guy and they took his chest X-ray under my name. I had already been in a sanatorium to be treated, but this was Germany and I was always afraid to take the medicine. I had the feeling they wanted to kill me and it was poison, so I was determined to get out of there.

Every year on the tenth of April my old friend Mike who came with me calls me from wherever he is. He called this year from Mexico, where he works for some company. I pick up the phone and I hear, "We're here now twenty-seven years. Just don't forget it!"

Now he is married and settled and I am married and have a six-year-old daughter and a three-year-old son. My wife came from an observant Jewish family in Connecticut. She's a speech therapist at the Children's Hospital. When the children are older I will tell them about my life. I also want them to be educated to some extent in Judaism—not to be rabbis, but to know a little bit of the philosophy. I'd like them to know more than what I know, because I don't know too much. I kind of feel that they should know how to say a prayer and a little bit of what happened to Jews throughout history. I know enough to know that I can't be anything else but what I am and I will defend my position as a Jew the best I can. I would hope my children will also be able to defend themselves.

I want them to be educated people, knowing the sciences and the history of the country in which they live. We live in Jamaica Plain and have very nice people all around us. I have lots of non-Jewish friends, dear friends, good friends, true human beings and true Christians, but I see myself as a member of the Jewish community.

It's as a member of the Jewish community that I feel very strongly toward Israel. I feel that in order for me to be free here I have to have a homeland. The reason my name became a number and my people were burned was because we didn't have a country of our own. This is how I feel, even though I don't participate in any of the organizations that work for it and I've never been there.

I don't know how to say it, but my work has kept me in touch with the problems that people have in this country, and I have to say that as bad as it is, I think this is a very good country. I am absolutely positive I would never have had the chance in any other country in the world. I came here as a sick, fearful kid and found decent people who were willing to extend themselves, to be of service. And it means a lot to me to be among decent people extending themselves to kids right now.

When I see students striking and committing violence to show they disapprove of the American system I don't think they're achieving anything. If they are such dedicated people with such respect and feeling for their fellow man they should extend themselves. They should be missionaries and come down to a place like ours and give eight hours a week of service to their fellow men who don't have their good chances. I tell them to stand up and be counted, to go to a prison and show their dedication and good feeling.

It's easier to throw a monkey wrench into the machinery and break it up than fix it. It's easier to break the will of a man than to correct it. It's easier to corrupt a man than to shape him. I think my job is harder than the revolutionary's or the radical who throws out slogans. That's all I have to say. I hope the tape fosters good will. That's the most important thing.

Robert Spitz from Budapest survived Bergen-Belsen and Theresienstadt. He was fluent in seven languages and worked for the U.S. Army after liberation. He came to the United States in 1948 at the age of nineteen. After living in Columbia, South Carolina, and Kansas City, Missouri, he settled in Dallas, Texas, where he is a successful businessman and leader in the Jewish community.

In 1948 I was assigned to the United States State Department, on temporary duty, and I decided finally to come to the United States. I was then nineteen, naive, idealistic and a bit foolish. I had the choice of settling in New York, Philadelphia, Boston, Baltimore, Atlanta and San Francisco, but it was my philosophy that I should avoid the East Coast and any area heavily populated with newly arrived Jewish people or even Jews from earlier immigrations. I did not wish to find myself in a self-created ghetto. I wanted to see a part of America unaffected by foreign influences.

One of the communities which offered to accept me as their ward was Columbia, South Carolina. This was a town of seventy-two thousand people, more than half black. There were about two hundred fifty Jewish families divided into congregations. Among them were some German Jewish immigrants who came to Columbia before World War II. It was and still is a very prosperous community. They had created a society called the Hebrew Immigrants Society in order to sponsor and care for four families. Actually, two families and two single boys accepted their hospitality, and I was one of them.

I came on an old Army troop carrier, the only one of the thousand immigrant passengers who spoke English. There were Lithuanians, Latvians, Estonians, Greeks, Polish, Hungarian and

438

German Jews and I was the interpreter for them all. Every time the doctor of the ship was summoned I was pulled out of bed to go with him. After fourteen days at sea we arrived in Boston. I went through immigration and the Hebrew Aid Society people told me how to take a cab to the train. They were of the opinion that the train I boarded in Boston went directly to Columbia, South Carolina.

So I arrived at Grand Central Station in New York on May 19, a very hot Friday afternoon. Though I had been to Paris, London, Rome and Berlin I had never before seen so many people confined in one space. The train from Boston didn't go all the way to South Carolina, of course, and I had no idea of where to go or how to get there. I kept buttonholing policemen and asking how to go to Columbia, South Carolina, but no one could tell me. Finally someone tells me to get over to Penn Station. I say, "What's Penn Station?" And they say, "Take the shuttle. Change at Times Square." I knew what Times Square was but I never heard of a shuttle. And all the time I was wondering what was happening to the other nine hundred and ninety-nine passengers who got off the ship with me and didn't have any English to ask with.

To make a long story short, I found my way to Penn Station, got the right train and came to Columbia, South Carolia. I received a very warm welcome, but I had a hard time convincing them that I had made my living as an interpreter for three and a half years even though I never finished high school. They knew of an adult high school where I could complete my studies at my own pace and I enrolled immediately.

The students were GIs who left the mills and cotton fields of North and South Carolina to go to war. They took me in immediately and made me feel very comfortable. The teachers went out of their way to show their concern, and the students nominated me for the student council. I started the first of June, 1949, and got my diploma in August 1949. Then I found out I needed to study South Carolina and Confederate history before I could enroll at the University of South Carolina. I became so well-versed in the state's history that I won a competitive exam and became the historian of the South Carolina National Guard. Just before I enrolled as a freshman in the university I joined the Air National Guard. I had always wanted to fly as a jet pilot and I thought I could get the opportunity this way. Unfortunately I couldn't be a pilot trainee without being an officer, and I couldn't be an officer because I wasn't yet a citizen, but later on I did well in the National Guard. After seven years I was a captain on my way to becoming a major.

I was on the staff of the adjutant general and I saw state politics from a very interesting perspective—one I'd rather not have known. People created names for themselves by, forgive the expression, shouting "nigger" the loudest, and I can't tolerate unjust discrimination or prejudice, especially when they are directed against a group of people.

Let me be frank. It was easy to condemn everybody who was less tolerant than I was when I was not exposed to the problems in a personal way. As the years went by and I acquired positions in which people from minority groups were my responsibility, my dedication to humanity diminished with the direct contact with individuals.

Let me explain. While I was going to college I had a part-time job in a local department store. The way I got the job, you might say, was a case of reverse discrimination. The city was dying. Jobs were hard to find. But the employment manager said, "You talk funny. Where are you from?" I told him I'd just come from Europe and the whole story. And he says, "Why were you in a concentration camp?" And I say, "Because I was Jewish." So he says, "Why didn't you say so? If you're Jewish you know clothing." I didn't know why I should know clothing, but in two days I had a job in the men's work-clothes department. Then I was put in charge of all the night workers. This was an all-Negro crew and I felt very strange about being their supervisor. It was especially bad when I was sent to the police station on Monday afternoon to bail out the men who worked for me, because many were picked up on Saturday for rowdy, drunken behavior. I would bail 50 or 60 percent of my workers out for five dollars apiece and then the company would take the five dollars out of their pay at the end of the week.

I had several different educations. I got a bachelor's degree in business in three years. I learned about the resentment and distrust of the Jewish youth on campus. A Jew was a Jew. The Jewish fraternities didn't want me because I had no social status to offer. It was only when I became president of the International Students' Association and the political commentator on the campus newspaper that I attained a bit of prestige. It was easier to get along with the non-Jewish kids who saw me as a foreigner and a unique personality.

I found the girls were more fascinated with me than with the native-born fellows and the fraternities accepted me after a while, even though I was never the fraternity type. I taught Jewish history and philosophy in the adult education classes of the Reform temple. I was expected to be active in the temple because 80 percent of the members considered themselves my surrogate parents. I would get forty-two invitations for Rosh Hashanah dinner and Thanksgiving and Passover, and people would be hurt when I refused them.

When I finished college I had an assistant buyer's job waiting for me in the store where I had worked part time. Soon after I became a full-fledged buyer. I married, had two children. We were divorced after twelve years. A year later I remarried.

I left South Carolina for a great opportunity in Kansas City. I joined a small company that grew into a giant and I did very well. We had five stores when I came and two hundred and forty when I left. I was the director of advertising, operations, and merchandising, and spent eighteen out of every fifty-two weeks a year in Europe and North Africa.

But I kept my interest in education. I gave lectures and made arrangements to bring guest speakers to Temple B'nai Yehuda in Kansas City. Just last week I spoke at a junior high school in South Oak Cliff, Texas, which was one-third Chicano, one-third black and one-third white. They were really interested in my discussion of the Holocaust.

Now that Dallas is my home I'm active here in the Jewish and the larger community as well. I'm a director of the East Dallas Chamber of Commerce, the only Jew in the entire East Dallas Chamber of Commerce. And whenever we have big affairs I'm asked to serve as a chaplain and the prayer always comes from the Reform Jewish prayer book: "May the time not be distant, oh Lord." I'm also a member of the American Notions Council, a trade organization for the sewing industry. In the Jewish community I belong to the Dallas Action Committee for Soviet Jews. I'm a member of the American Jewish Committee and Temple Emanuel Dallas and I'm the chairman of the Continuous Jewish Education Program at Temple Emanuel. I also personally started the adult Jewish education program at the Jewish Community Center and gave nine lectures there in the last three months, not only on the Holocaust but also on the political and economic developments that made it possible for a nation such as Germany to start the Holocaust.

I'm convinced that the Holocaust could have been prevented if the major nations had taken a different attitude. But I think that in World War II if there was one fellow with a white hat it was the United States.

To go back to my interest in education. As a child I had no Jewish emotional background but I had a tremendous amount of knowledge pumped into me without emotional activation or motivation. We were taught to know for the sake of knowing and had the privilege of not believing as long as we knew. The option was there.

I was very anxious to give my children the same option. They never missed a year at Hebrew school. My son went to Hebrew three afternoons a week until his *Bar Mitzvah*, and my daughter did the same. They went only to Jewish summer camps and on Saturday afternoons they were enrolled at the Jewish Community Center in Kansas City. Two of my children have spent summers in Israel.

I'm asked how I would react to my children marrying non-Jews and all I can say is that I have no control over that. My former wife, the mother of my two children, came from a very devout family. Our marriage, however, was a total failure. I couldn't help but think many times that religion or religious background is not as important as people play it up to be. After all, I wouldn't have grown up to be a Jew if not for Hitler. If any of my children end up marrying non-Jews it will be only because they themselves are not Jews.

Everything depends on the individual. Life plays some very funny tricks. The three children I acquired in my second marriage are turning out to be the scholars I hoped my own children would become. My son is interested only in the business world. He makes good money and is more competent than I in business matters. My stepchildren ask questions about the European way of life, my background, and they are very interested in the Holocaust and have studied it on their own. Each of the five children who have been in contact with me have grown up differently. Some are indifferent to the subjects I bring up; I can't yet tell whether they are hostile. One or two claims to have some pride in the Jewish heritage. The others say that it is immaterial. They won't deny it, but they say their Jewish upbringing hasn't been important. What does that mean? One daughter tells me she lights candles every Friday night and makes the blessing for the Jewish kids in the sorority house; another would never consider doing such a thing. I can't find any common denominator. Each child responds differently to the activities my wife and I have undertaken.

At the present time I'm working closely with the Russian families in Dallas. I can remember the help I received from the Jewish immigrants in Columbia, South Carolina, when I arrived, and now I have the opportunity to help others assimilate and adapt to a new environment.

I guess I am like other American Jews in that I identify very much with the underprivileged. Like the majority of American Jewry I consider myself a Democrat. I feel that the greatest crime of this country is its inability to tap its human resources. I get very angry when I see beautiful human resources left undeveloped because they belong to women, to blacks, to Indians or Chicanos.

I see America as a country where the values are created by material accomplishments, and I was caught in the American mercenary race. I guess I have to admit I have no one to blame but myself, but I often have regretted the road to success which I have taken. Many times I wished I had another orientation as a child. I was, after all, born and reared with the values of the twentieth century—to go to school, get educated, find a profession, succeed, raise a family, get rid of the children . . . and retire.

I'm not religious, even though I take pride in the fact that my ancestors were Hebrews. I feel very Jewish ethnically, though I had no ethnic or religious feelings as a child before the rise of Nazism. Survivors should not be placed under one identifying umbrella. I can remember the arrival of the trains and the extraordinary variety of people coming into the camps. I was astonished to see the Sephardic Jews from the Balkans and Greece, so different from any Jews I'd ever seen. I think of all those different kinds of people when I examine the regional differences of American Jews. There is no such thing as a typical American Jew, and there is no such thing as a typical survivor. In Kansas City, where I spent thirteen years of my life, I met many former inmates of concentration camps, and many times I looked in the mirror and said to myself, "Am I like Joe or Bill or Tom?" And I found I was not like them, but sometimes they resembled each other in just a few small ways. What we share, however, is feelings about America. In spite of everything else we might say about it, it is still the country where the right of the individual is more powerful that the people who are in power. That means something to me . . . I choke up when I try to speak of it. These things mean an awful lot to me.

The Steins from Krakow, Poland, fled to the East; from Lublin to Vilna and Moscow, on the Trans-Siberian Express to Vladisvostok, by ship from Tokyo to the United States, where they were not permitted to embark. They entered Mexico illegally and waited for the opportunity to settle in New York. Their travel saga ended in 1942 when the precious visa was obtained. Dr. Stein opened a medical practice and he and his wife Rose devoted themselves to raising an observant Jewish family. Rose and Emanuel were interviewed together. Dr. Stein speaks for both of them in the following excerpt.

My sister found us in a furnished two-room apartment on 76th Street and we were told to go to the Service for New Americans. I came to ask for a loan but instead they filled out a form for fifteen dollars a week and thirty cents every other day for the child's milk and a dollar fifty a month for shoes and so on and on. I sat there with open eyes and didn't know what to do. "All I want is a temporary loan," I said but she said that was not possible and I left.

My brother-in-law heard that the State Department was looking for people for the Office of War Information, and I went to apply. I was hired to make Polish-language recordings for the BBC. I had a Ph.D. My accent was as good as any Pole's. My wife left the baby with a woman who took in little babies and went to work as a salesgirl at Helena Rubenstein.

I finished my medical studies in about six months and was able to get a license. And there I was, in the middle of New York, starting a practice with no connections whatsoever. I had a bank loan and was up to my ears in debt until the day my daughter Ruthie was born in 1947; that was the day smallpox arrived in the United States and everybody had to be vaccinated and it was the first time my office filled up with patients. The practice grew little by little. I couldn't afford a car for the first four years, but by 1952 my debts were paid off, even the payments on the cardiograph.

Our two daughters grew up very nicely. They went to public school but we were educating them so they should not be of the 50 percent that's intermarrying. That would have brought us deep unhappiness. My wife and I drove them crazy with our brainwashing. They could go to Jerusalem but not to Paris. It was Hebrew summer camp or none at all. Though we're not religious, we observed all the holidays and belonged to an Orthodox synagogue. Ceremony is very important in life. Children brought up in ceremonies will understand even the Holocaust. The home has to have a special character and of course there must also be Jewish learning and Jewish history.

The girls were not allowed to date on Friday night. The world could go to pieces but they had to be with us for Friday night dinner. They tried to rebel. There were high school dances on Friday night and the two of us were so cruel, they used to say. Parents of their friends used to tell us we are absolutely too cruel, but their children are assimilated and ours aren't.

Our older daughter went to Hebrew College before going to medical school. She went to Barnard while she was getting her degree in Hebrew teaching. Both girls went to Hebrew-speaking camps in summer. Now our oldest is a pathologist at Albert Einstein, married to a surgeon. The younger one went to the University of Chicago. Her husband teaches at the Hebrew University and they live in Jerusalem.

Our daughter was married in Jerusalem to the son of old friends of ours. A hundred eighty people came to the wedding and nobody had to be introduced. We feel very much American, but we think of Israel as our ancestral home. We have a retirement apartment in Israel which we originally bought for our daughter when she lived in Jerusalem before she was married. Our ties to Israel have always been very strong.

Personally, my wife and I have been very lucky people. Our two daughters are married and have their own children, but we lost a great deal of our family, a tremendous number of friends. The Holocaust is not something abstract for us. We are mourning like everybody else. I'm as pained by the losses from intermarriage and assimilation as I am by the losses in the Holocaust. We feel like the counterbalance in a time of assimilation. In one or two generations there will be no more Jews in America. In previous ages the natural growth of the Jews made it possible to recover from the persecutions but now the recovery is impossible.

Our grandchildren, meanwhile, are going to Hebrew day school. Our children keep semikosher homes. We see ourselves successful in our Americanization. We think that by maintaining our culture and ancestral ties we contribute to the culture of America. We are Jews in America, not American Jews. We think we are good citizens. We are not closed to other cultures, as you can see if you look at the books in our library; but we are biased in favor of our own.

Vera Steiner from Rakamaz, Hungary, came to the United States in 1949, after having spent the war years with false papers in Budapest, and settled in Hollywood, California. Memories of the German and Russian occupations still make her insecure and fearful of the future.

When we left Hungary we sold our belongings for two hundred dollars and we were so worried about the dollars because it was forbidden to have foreign money in Europe. When we arrived, I remember buying an apple with the American money I had saved so long. It's hard to describe what an experience that was.

The Hebrew Immigrant Aid Society met us at the boat. Maybe I shouldn't say it, but they told us that they wouldn't help us if our relatives came, so my aunt stayed away. It wasn't that they didn't want to take care of us, but they had only a little one-bedroom apartment and there was no place for us. This way we were put up in a hotel on Lexington Avenue for a month. My husband found a job in a week. He was a carpenter and right away earned seventy-five cents an hour. And then we found a little apartment in Coney Island, and the HIAS gave us a hundred and fifty dollars to buy furniture, so we were all set. In Germany we were sharing a room with two or three other people, so our tiny little summer bungalow was a luxury for us. We took pictures and sent them to Hungary.

My husband got a job building apartments. He joined the union. When we saved a thousand dollars we decided to go to California. We had relatives there and they were very helpful. When I came to Los Angeles I went to evening school to get my citizenship papers and then I started to work. My son was three years old and my daughter was six. I dropped them off at nursery school and they stayed from morning till evening. I was sewing all day.

And the years slipped by. My daughter graduated from Berkeley a few years ago. She worked as a substitute teacher in Oakland and then decided to go to Israel. She had been in Israel after she graduated from high school—we sent her for a summer on a *kibbutz*—and she always thought of going back, and she did. My daughter has our values, but she's fighting for independence and she's blaming me: "Do you want to tie me to your apron strings? Do you want me to be your copy?" and all that. I see that she is fighting with herself and fighting with us. But she's very sentimental and a warm-hearted girl. In the meantime, she says, "Why do I have to sacrifice? Why can't I do what makes me happy?" So she lives in Israel now five years. She writes to me very week. You should see the letters, it's like a book.

Either we go to Israel for the holidays or she comes to us. We were there the last time for Passover and my husband made the *Seder* and my son Robert came with us. All the neighbors were invited. It was very nice. You have to know that one reason for going to Israel was that she was in love with a non-Jewish boy. I found out accidentally. I picked up the extension on the telephone and she was talking with her girlfriend, and I heard her say that she would never marry him because it would kill her father. So she went to Israel instead—to be with Jews. If it was up to my husband he would be there too. He would just pick himself up and go. Maybe I'll give up one of these days and move there.

I just feel we've moved so much and started all over so many times from scratch. I'm really happy here and I have real friends. I appreciate America, the goodness, what they give us. And I am more materialistic than my husband. He's more idealistic. He's active raising money for a project in Israel. We committed ourselves to raise a quarter of a million dollars for the Haifa university. We just finished a dormitory for the Mt. Scopus campus and the library. We've been involved with this since 1948, when there was a shortage of homes and we were raising money for housing. My husband is president now for three years. I used to be vice-president but when he became active I stepped down.

We are really American Jews, however. We belong to Temple Beth-El and go to the Jewish Center on Sunday nights to hear the lectures, and my husband goes to the Hebrew classes. I reminded my husband that we decided during the war when we were hiding that we would never join any organization or put our name in any temple records. We were going to deny that we were Jewish and hide it as much as possible. Now I would have to laugh to have such an idea. It was from a time of insecurity. Now it wouldn't occur to us to deny or to be ashamed of being a Jew.

But we still feel that our security in America is just as shaky as it was for the Jews of Europe. German and Hungarian Jews felt very secure. We were such big Hungarians you have no idea; we were wearing the national dress on any national holiday and going to the plaza with the other kids. The Jews were very good Hungarians, and we were hurt too much. Now we still feel vulnerable because American Jews feel just as secure today as we did before World War II.

I can't stand it when people who came from Hungary talk Hungarian and go to the Hungarian shows and movies and they go back, even though they don't have anybody, and say the food is so good and Budapest is so gorgeous. It isn't gorgeous at all. We went back several times because my husband's father was still living. The only place we went was to the cemetery. My sisters were both killed in Budapest; a bomb hit the house where they were living. My father died there after we left. My father-in-law survived in the Budapest ghetto. My three sisters-in-law were taken to Bergen-Belsen in December. They all had typhus but they were able to come back. They remained in Hungary and finished their education. One was a school teacher. The others had government jobs. They became good communists and we have lots of arguments when we go there. We try to give them our point of view. We ask them, "How can you live here?" And they don't know how we can live in America. They hear propaganda about the Nazi party in America and think all the Nazis are here now. They don't understand America, and they have no wish to see it or understand it.

My only bad feeling about America is that my husband and I both feel we failed our children, in a lot of ways. We wanted them to be American and we wanted to give them everything we didn't have, and it's no good. They don't have the family life. Maybe we gave them too much. For example, my son is very talented. He is in calligraphy and teaches part-time. He lives in Berkeley. He quit school . . . When I think how much we wanted to go to school and we *had* to quit—it's a tremendous aggravation. We just can't understand him and he can't understand us. He started architecture but he had to take subjects in which he wasn't interested and he saw it as a waste of time. So he has a junky little apartment in Berkeley and earns just enough to exist. We bought him a car a few years ago. When he needed money he sold the car and bought a bicycle. He said he didn't want to pollute the air. He has ideals, but no sense of responsibility. He's a nice boy but he's twenty-six and not thinking of getting married. He came home on Yom Kippur and was fasting and went to temple with us. But now we haven't heard from him for three months. We sent him a check and a package for Hanukkah and he didn't even call to say Happy Hanukkah. It's unbelievable. I just don't know. . .

We are traditional people. Not kosher, but we keep holidays. My husband goes to Sabbath services every week. We have a beautiful *Seder* and a house full of guests for High Holidays. My son and daughter went to Hebrew school. My son was *Bar Mitzvah*. He knows our background. But it's like he doesn't know who he is. He used to say, "What am I? Born of Hungarian parents, born in Germany, living in America and a Jew."

We blame ourselves. We were too easy with the children. We didn't ever spank them. My husband says he should have given it to them, maybe it would be different. I think I should have sacrificed more and not sent them to the public schools. I should have sent them to Jewish school, given them more Jewish education. At the time we couldn't afford it. We had no money at all. If I could do it all over again I would have given them a different education. Berkeley had a tremendous influence on them. We're disappointed that they can't settle down. Our only wish is to see them married and with children of their own. It's the only thing we miss.

Afterword

Survivors begin and end their stories with the details of ordinary life. Those who were brought up in the Jewish tradition, with its blessings for waking, sleeping, eating and loving, were taught that life was a fragile, temporary gift from the Creator of the Universe, not to be discarded even when death was easier. To live, to have children and children's children, were the accepted goals for men and women. Survivors who grew up at a distance from the traditional teachings also often acquired a heightened sense of the preciousness of life and a mission for continuity from their experiences as witnesses of extraordinary cruelty.

In America survivors from different backgrounds repeat the same messages. Do not hate! Do not harm! Share with others less fortunate. They urge us to remember the past and learn from it. They regret that they did not teach their children their history and hope their stories will make it easier to explain what happened to them and to the millions who were lost. They share their painful memories of the dark places in recent history in the hope that they may never be so dark again.

Appendix I

Hitler's Occupation of Europe

Germany Nazis seized power, 1933
Austria Anschluss with Germany, March 12, 1938
Czechoslovakia Invaded March 13, 1939
Poland Invaded September 1, 1939 by Germany; September 17, 1939 by Russia
Denmark Invaded April 9, 1940
The Netherlands Invaded May 10, 1940
Belgium Invaded May 10, 1940
France Invaded May 17, 1940
Italy Became a partner in Germany's war, September 27, 1940
Rumania Invaded in September 1940; joined the Axis in November
Yugoslavia Invaded April 6, 1941
Greece Invaded May, 1941
Soviet Union Invaded June 22, 1941, bringing Russian-occupied Poland under German rule
Hungary Invaded March 19, 1944; joined Germany in dismemberment of Czechoslovakia, November 1938, and in its invasion of Russia, June 22, 1941

Appendix 2

Jewish Population before and after the Holocaust

	pre-1940	1945–1946
Austria	185,000	3,000
Czechoslovakia	118,000	10,000
France	350,000 (150,000 native-born; 200,000 from Eastern Europe in the 1920s and 1930s, and refugees from Hitler)	260,000
Germany	500,000	25,000
Greece	76,000	16,000
Hungary	650,000 (includes northern Transylvania and Ruthenia)	200,000
Italy	57,000 (10,000 refugees)	49,000
The Netherlands	140,000	35,000
Poland	3,300,000	50,000–70,000
Rumania	757,000	300,000

Glossary

ALIYAH BET   The Hebrew name for the "illegal" immigration of Jews to Palestine.

ASHKENAZI   A Jew from Germany or eastern Europe who observes the religious rites according to the Germanic (Ashkenazic) traditions rather than the Spanish (Sephardic) mode.

BAR MITZVAH   Literally, "son of the commandment" in Hebrew; the initiation of a Jewish male child into adulthood at the age of thirteen.

BAS MITZVAH (same as *"Bat"*)   Initiation of female children; feminine equivalent of Bar Mitzvah.

BERRIEH   A good housekeeper.

BETAR   Jabotinsky's Zionist organization.

BIMA   The podium at the front of the synagogue.

BRIS   The circumcision of a male child.

BORSHT   Beet soup.

BUND (the Jewish Socialists)   Yiddish-speaking socialist group, not religious and not Zionist.

CHALLA   The special bread for the Sabbath meal.

CHANUKAH (Hanukah)   Winter holiday commemorating the victory of the Maccabees.

CHASIDIC, CHASID, CHASIDIM   A *Chasid* is a member of a particularly pious community; *Chasidic* is the adjective, CHASIDIM the plural.

CHAZZEN   A cantor.

CHEDER   An elementary Hebrew school.

CHEVRA KADDISHA   Burial society which believes it is a good deed to help a human being out of the world with dignity.

CHOLENT   Potted meat and vegetables cooked on Friday and simmered overnight for Sabbath eating.

CHOMETZ   Food containing leaven, which is forbidden during the week of Passover.

CHUPA   Wedding canopy—a portable cloth covering attached to four poles, symbolic of the room in the home of the groom to which in ancient times the bride was escorted for consummation of the marriage.

CHUTZPA   Nerve.

CONSERVATIVE   A branch of Judaism, middle ground.

GEHENNA   Hell.

GEMARA   Section of the Talmud interpreting and discussing the law as presented in the Mishnah.

GOYIM   All people who are not Jewish.

HALACHAH   The general word for Jewish law (from *halach* = walk); the way to walk (behave).

HASHOMER   Marxist-Zionist organization for young people.

"HATIKVAH"   The Jewish National Anthem.

HIGH HOLIDAYS   The Jewish New York that begins with Rosh Hashanah and ends with Yom Kippur.

HORA   A circle dance of celebration; very popular in Israel.

JUDENRAT   A Jewish council, originally chosen by the taxpaying members of a Jewish community. In November 1939 the Germans took control of these Jewish councils and forced them to accept German orders in order to facilitate the establishment of the ghettos and, ultimately, the destruction of the Jews of Europe.

KADDISH   Mourner's prayer for a deceased close relative, usually said by the son; it is also used to refer to the one who recites the prayer.

KAPO   A supervisor in the concentration camps.

KASHRUT   The dietary laws.

KETUBA   A marriage contract.

KIBBUTZ, KIBBUTZIM (plural)   Cooperative colony or colonies in Israel, most often agricultural.

KIDDUSH   Blessing said over a cup of wine to celebrate the Sabbath or a holiday.

KOSHER   Food prepared according to the dietary laws. Meat is ritually slaughtered; pork and shellfish are forbidden; and milk and meat products are never served at the same meal or on the same plate.

KVETCHING   Complaining.

LAMED VAVNIK   One of the thirty-six "hidden saints" who were supposed to exist in every generation, unrecognized as such by their fellows. The term is from two letters of the Hebrew alphabet, *lamed* and *vav*, whose numerical values are thirty and six.

454

LANDSMANSCHAFT   An association of people from the same town or area.

LUFTGESCHAFT   Wheeling and dealing rather than producing and selling.

MALAVE-MALKE   A social gathering on Sabbath afternoons; it always includes singing.

MATZO   Unleavened bread for Passover.

MELAMED   Teacher, usually of elementary school.

MENSHEN   Human beings.

MIKVAH   Ritual bath.

MINYAN   A quorum of ten males for communal religious services.

MISHNAH   Traditional doctrines as represented and developed chiefly by the Rabbis before 200 A.D.

MITZVAH   Good deed.

MIZRACHI   A religious Zionist organization.

MOHEL   A man qualified to do circumcisions.

NUDZH   To push or to nag; also used of the person who does so.

ORTHODOX   Observant of the laws in the Halachah.

PASSOVER   The festival of freedom that celebrates the ancient exodus of the Jews from Egypt.

PESACH   Passover (see above).

PURIM   Feast of Lots in March, when the Book of Esther is read in the synagogue.

REFORM   Modernized Judaism, with prayers spoken in the language of the country rather than in Hebrew.

RECONSTRUCTIONIST   One who follows a flexible approach to Jewish tradition.

REVISIONIST   The Betar group, organized by Jabotinsky.

ROSH HASHANAH   The Jewish New Year; the beginning of the High Holidays.

SABRA   Someone born in Israel.

SEDER   The festive meal on the first two evenings of Passover; literally, "order."

SEPHARDIC   See Ashkenazi above.

SHABBAT   The Sabbath.

SHABBES   The Sabbath.

SHIKSA   A non-Jewish girl.

SHLEPPING   Dragging along.

SHMA   The most important daily prayer in Judaism.

SHOCHET   The ritual slaughterer of animals in observance of the dietary laws.

SHOMER SHABBES   Someone who observes (guards) the Sabbath.

SHUL   Synagogue.

SHTETL   A small town or village.

TALLIS, TALLEISM (plural)   Prayer shawl or shawls.

TALMUD TORAH   A Jewish elementary school.

TAMMUZ   A month in the Jewish calendar that coincides with July.

TEFILLIN   Phylacteries—leather cases containing quotations from the Old Testament—worn by Jews on the forehead and on the left arm during morning prayers.

ULPAN   A place to study Hebrew intensively.

YAD VASHAM   The Holocaust memorial in Israel.

YESHIVA   A school for advanced Jewish study.

YOM KIPPUR   The Day of Atonement—the most solemn holiday and fast.

YORTZEIT   The anniversary of a death.

YOUTH ALIYAH   An organization that brought orphaned children from Europe to Israel and took care of them in the cooperative colonies (the kibbutzim).

ZEMIROS   Songs sung after the Sabbath meal.